Music of Azerbaijan

Ethnomusicology
Multimedia

Ethnomusicology Multimedia (EM) is a collaborative publishing program, developed with funding from the Andrew W. Mellon Foundation, to identify and publish first books in ethnomusicology, accompanied by supplemental audiovisual materials online at www.ethnomultimedia.org.

A collaboration of the presses at Indiana and Temple universities, EM is an innovative, entrepreneurial, and cooperative effort to expand publishing opportunities for emerging scholars in ethnomusicology and to increase audience reach by using common resources available to the presses through support from the Andrew W. Mellon Foundation. Each press acquires and develops EM books according to its own profile and editorial criteria.

EM's most innovative features are its web-based components, which include a password-protected Annotation Management System (AMS) where authors can upload peer-reviewed audio, video, and static image content for editing and annotation and key the selections to corresponding references in their texts; a public site for viewing the web content, www.ethnomultimedia.org, with links to publishers' websites for information about the accompanying books; and the Avalon Media System, which hosts video and audio content for the website. The AMS and website were designed and built by the Institute for Digital Arts and Humanities at Indiana University. Avalon was designed and built by the libraries at Indiana University and Northwestern University with support from the Institute of Museum and Library Services. The Indiana University Libraries hosts the website, and the Indiana University Archives of Traditional Music (ATM) provides archiving and preservation services for the EM online content.

Music of Azerbaijan

FROM MUGHAM TO OPERA

Aida Huseynova

INDIANA UNIVERSITY PRESS

Bloomington and Indianapolis

This book is a publication of

INDIANA UNIVERSITY PRESS
Office of Scholarly Publishing
Herman B Wells Library 350
1320 East 10th Street
Bloomington, Indiana 47405 USA

iupress.indiana.edu

Library of Congress Cataloging-in-Publication Data

Huseynova, Aida, author.
   Music of Azerbaijan : from mugham to opera / Aida Huseynova.
   pages cm – (Ethnomusicology multimedia)
   Includes bibliographical references and index.
   ISBN 978-0-253-01937-0 (cloth : alkaline paper) – ISBN 978-0-253-
01945-5 (paperback : alkaline paper) – ISBN 978-0-253-01949-3 (ebook)
1. Music – Azerbaijan – History and criticism. 2. Folk music –
Azerbaijan – History and criticism. 3. Azerbaijanis – Music. I. Title.
II. Series: Ethnomusicology multimedia.
   ML3758.A98H87 2016
   780.947'54 – dc23

                                                              2015034849

1 2 3 4 5 21 20 19 18 17 16

To my family

CONTENTS

ETHNOMUSICOLOGY MULTIMEDIA SERIES PREFACE

GUIDE TO ONLINE MEDIA EXAMPLES

Each of the audio, video, or still image media examples listed herein is associated with specific passages in this book, and each example has been assigned a unique persistent uniform resource locator, or PURL. The PURL identifies a specific audio, video, or still image media example on the Ethnomusicology Multimedia website, www.ethnomultimedia.org. Within the text of the book, a PURL number in parentheses functions like a citation and immediately follows the text to which it refers, for example (PURL 3.1). The numbers following the word PURL relate to the chapter in which the media example is found, and the number of PURLs contained in that chapter. For example, PURL 3.1 refers to the first media example found in chapter 3; PURL 3.2 refers to the second media example found in chapter 3, and so on.

To access all media associated with this book, readers must first create a free account by going to the Ethnomusicology Multimedia Project website www.ethnomultimedia.org and clicking the sign in link. Readers will be required to read and electronically sign an end users license agreement the first time they access a media example on the website. After logging in to the site, there are two ways to access and play back audio, video, or still image media examples. In the search field enter the name of the author to be taken to a webpage with information about the book and the author as well as a playlist of all media examples associated with the book. To access a specific media example, in the search field enter the six-digit PURL identifier of the example (the six digits located at the end of the full PURL address). The reader will be taken to the web page containing that media example as well as a playlist of all the other media examples related to the book. Readers of the electronic edition of this book will simply click on the PURL address for each media example; once they have logged in to www.ethnomultimedia.org, this live link will take them directly to the media example on the Ethnomusicology Multimedia website.

LIST OF PURLS

CHAPTER 1

PURL 1.1 | Uzeyir Hajibeyli, Koroghlu's aria from the opera *Koroghlu*. Performed by Bulbul. Excerpt from the documentary *To My Dear People*. Baku Studio, 1954. Video. Courtesy: Polad Bulbuloghlu.
http://purl.dlib.indiana.edu/iudl/em/Huseynova/910342

PURL 1.2 | Nazim Aliverdibeyov, *Bayati Shiraz* for organ. Performed by Rena Ismayilova. Colon, St. Joseph Church, 2008. Audio. Courtesy: Samir Aliverdibeyov and Rena Ismayilova.
http://purl.dlib.indiana.edu/iudl/em/Huseynova/910343

PURL 1.3 | Duo "Quis Est Homo, Qui Non Fleret," from *Stabat Mater,* by Gioachino Rossini. Performed by Fidan Gasimova, Khuraman Gasimova, and the Azerbaijan State Symphony Orchestra named after Uzeyir Hajibeyli. Rauf Abdullayev, conductor. Baku, the Heydar Aliyev Palace, April 21, 2000. Video. Courtesy: Khuraman Gasimova.
http://purl.dlib.indiana.edu/iudl/em/Huseynova/910344

PURL 1.4 | Azerbaijani folk song "She Has Got a House with Tiny Rooms," arranged by Fikrat Amirov. Performed by Fidan Gasimova, Khuraman Gasimova, and the Azerbaijan State Symphony Orchestra named after Uzeyir Hajibeyli. Rauf Abdullayev, conductor. Baku, the Heydar Aliyev Palace, April 21, 2000. Video. Courtesy: Khuraman Gasimova.
http://purl.dlib.indiana.edu/iudl/em/Huseynova/910345

PURL 1.5 | Haji Khanmammadov. Concerto for the *Kemancha and Symphony Orchestra* (second movement). Performed by The Youth Music Monterrey County symphony orchestra from California. Farkhad Khudyev, conductor. Imamyar Hasanov, kemancha soloist. Sunset Center, Carmel-by-the-Sea, November 9, 2013. Video. Courtesy: Youth Music Monterey County.
http://purl.dlib.indiana.edu/iudl/em/Huseynova/910346

CHAPTER 3

PURL 3.1 | Elmira Nazirova, Sonata for Cello and Piano, movements 2, 3, and 4. Performed by Isaak Turich and Elmira Nazirova. Baku, 1954. Audio. Courtesy: Elmar Fel and Mikhail Turich.
http://purl.dlib.indiana.edu/iudl/em/Huseynova/910347

PURL 3.2 | Fikrat Amirov and Elmira Nazirova, Concerto on Arab Themes for the Piano and Symphony Orchestra, excerpt from the first movement. Performed by the Royal Philharmonic Concert Orchestra at Caspian Corridor Gala. Yalchin Adigozalov, conductor. Yegana Akhundova, soloist. London, Westminster, Central Hall, March 7, 2014. Video. Courtesy: Royal Philharmonic Concert Orchestra. http://purl.dlib.indiana.edu/iudl/em/Huseynova/910348

CHAPTER 4

PURL 4.1 | Uzeyir Hajibeyli, Chorus "Night of Separation" from the opera *Leyli and Majnun.* Performed by the International Vocal Ensemble of Indiana University. Artistic Director Katherine Domingo. Aida Huseynova, pianist. Auer Hall, April 20, 2008. Audio. Courtesy: Indiana University Jacobs School of Music. http://purl.dlib.indiana.edu/iudl/em/Huseynova/910349

PURL 4.2 | Uzeyir Hajibeyli, "Arazbari" from the opera *Leyli and Majnun.* Performed by the Azerbaijan State Chamber Orchestra named after Gara Garayev. Yashar Imanov, conductor. Audio. Source: Classical Music of Azerbaijan, 6 vols. Vol. 1: Chamber Music. Track 1. Azerbaijan International, AICD1206, 1997, compact disc. Produced jointly by Amoco and Azerbaijan International. http://azer .com/aiweb/categories/music/AudioPages/CMA/cma_contents.html. http://purl.dlib.indiana.edu/iudl/em/Huseynova/910350

PURL 4.3 | Uzeyir Hajibeyli, Overture to the opera *Koroghlu.* Performed by the Azerbaijani State Symphony Orchestra named after Uzeyir Hajibeyli. Niyazi, conductor. Baku, the Azerbaijan State Philharmonic Hall named after Muslim Magomayev, 1975. Video. Courtesy: The State Museum of Azerbaijani Musical Culture. http://purl.dlib.indiana.edu/iudl/em/Huseynova/910351

PURL 4.4 | Muslim Magomayev, Two arias of Aslanshah from the opera *Shah Ismayil.* Performed by Muslim Magomayev. Excerpt from the documentary "Muslim Magomayev Sings," produced by Azerbaijanfilm Studio, 1971. Video. Courtesy: Marina Magomayeva and Tamara Siniavskaia. http://purl.dlib.indiana.edu/iudl/em/Huseynova/910352

PURL 4.5 | Asaf Zeynalli, The romance "My Country." Performed by Bulbul. Vladimir Kozlov, piano. Baku, 1956. Audio. Courtesy: Polad Bulbuloghlu. http://purl.dlib.indiana.edu/iudl/em/Huseynova/910353

CHAPTER 5

PURL 5.1 | Gara Garayev, Pastorale from Sonata for Violin and Piano. Performed by Arif Manafli and Farhad Badalbeyli. Audio. Source: Farhad Badalbeyli, *My Piano*. 2 vols. Baku: AzEuroTel, 2000. Vol. 1, Track 20.
http://purl.dlib.indiana.edu/iudl/em/Huseynova/910354

PURL 5.2 | Fikrat Amirov, Balash's aria from the opera *Sevil*. Performed by Azer Zeynalov. Production by the Azerbaijan State Opera and Ballet Theater, 2010. Video. Courtesy: Jamil Amirov.
http://purl.dlib.indiana.edu/iudl/em/Huseynova/910355

PURL 5.3| Fikrat Amirov, *Kurd Ovshari*. Performed by the Azerbaijan State Symphony Orchestra named after Uzeyir Hajibeyli. Yalchin Adigozalov, conductor. Audio. Source: Classical Music of Azerbaijan, 6 vols. Vol. 1. Symphonic Music. Track 2. Azerbaijan International, AICD1201, 1997, compact disc. Produced jointly by Amoco and Azerbaijan International. http://azer.com/aiweb/categories/music/AudioPages/CMA/cma_contents.html.
http://purl.dlib.indiana.edu/iudl/em/Huseynova/910356

PURL 5.4 | Azerbaijani folk song "Flowers Have Blossomed, Spring Has Come," arranged by Jahangir Jahangirov. Performed by the International Vocal Ensemble of Indiana University. Artistic Director Katherine Strand. Aida Huseynova, pianist. Auer Hall, April 14, 2013. Audio. Courtesy: Indiana University Jacobs School of Music.
http://purl.dlib.indiana.edu/iudl/em/Huseynova/910357

PURL 5.5 | Gara Garayev, Waltz from the ballet *Seven Beauties*. Source: film-ballet *Seven Beauties,* Rafiga Akhundova and Magsud Mammadov, choreographers. Azerbaijanfilm Studio, 1982. Video. Courtesy: Faraj Garayev.
http://purl.dlib.indiana.edu/iudl/em/Huseynova/910358

PURL 5.6 | Arif Malikov, Adagio from the ballet *The Legend of Love*. Source: film-ballet *The Legend of Love,* Iurii Grigorovich, choreographer. Central Television of the USSR, 1969. Video. Courtesy: Arif Malikov and Iurii Grigorovich.
http://purl.dlib.indiana.edu/iudl/em/Huseynova/910359

CHAPTER 6

PURL 6.1 | Gara Garayev, Third Symphony, Performed by the Moscow Chamber Orchestra. Rudolf Barshai, conductor. Moscow, 1966. Audio. Courtesy: Faraj Garayev and Walter Barshai.
http://purl.dlib.indiana.edu/iudl/em/Huseynova/910360

PURL 6.2 | Arif Malikov, Sixth Symphony, Performed by the Azerbaijan State Symphony Orchestra named after Uzeyir Hajibeyli. Rauf Abdullayev, conductor. Baku, the Azerbaijan State Philharmonic Hall named after Muslim Magomayev. Baku, November 28, 2014. Audio. Courtesy: Arif Malikov.
http://purl.dlib.indiana.edu/iudl/em/Huseynova/910361

PURL 6.3 | Faraj Garayev, Yalli from the ballet *The Shadows of Gobustan*. Production of the Azerbaijan State Opera and Ballet Theater. Maxine Braham (United Kingdom), choreographer (based on the choreography of Rafiga Akhundova and Magsud Mammadov). The Gobustan State Reserve, May 31, 2013. Video. Courtesy: Faraj Garayev and Maxine Braham.
http://purl.dlib.indiana.edu/iudl/em/Huseynova/910362

PURL 6.4 | Khayyam Mirzazade, The choreographed version of the preludes *White and Black*. Pullumb Agalliu (Albania), choreographer. Gulnara Safarova, pianist. Baku, the Azerbaijan State Opera and Ballet Theater, June 7, 2000. Video. Courtesy: Khayyam Mirzazade.
http://purl.dlib.indiana.edu/iudl/em/Huseynova/910363

PURL 6.5 | Khayyam Mirzazade, Sonata for the Violin, *Pro e Contra*. Performed by Sarvar Ganiyev. Audio. Source: Khayyam Kh. Mirzazade, compact disk, Baku: Ministry of Culture of Azerbaijan and Gilan-CD, 2011. Track 1.
http://purl.dlib.indiana.edu/iudl/em/Huseynova/910364

PURL 6.6 | Ismayil Hajibeyov, *Sketches in the Spirit of Watteau*. Performed by Ulviyya Hajibeyova. Audio. Source: Anthology of Azerbaijani Composers, 15 Vols. Baku: Azersun, 2010. Volume1, Track 13.
http://purl.dlib.indiana.edu/iudl/em/Huseynova/910365

PURL 6.7 | Uzeyir Hajibeyli, *Jangi* for the piano. Performed by Frangiz Hajiyeva. Recorded by Aida Huseynova. Baku Music Academy, January 5, 2014. Audio.
http://purl.dlib.indiana.edu/iudl/em/Huseynova/910366

PURL 6.8 | Ismayil Hajibeyov, Rhapsody for the piano and symphony orchestra. Performed by Farhad Badalbeyli and the Azerbaijan State Symphony Orchestra of the Television and Radio. Ramiz Melikaslanov, conductor. Audio. Source: Farhad Badalbeyli, *My Piano*. 2 vols. Baku: AzEuroTel, 2000. Vol. 2. Track 3.
http://purl.dlib.indiana.edu/iudl/em/Huseynova/910367

PURL 6.9 | Agshin Alizade, *Jangi*. Performed by the Azerbaijan State Chamber Orchestra named after Gara Garayev. Yashar Imanov, conductor. Oleg Grechko, soloist. Audio. Source: Classical Music of Azerbaijan, 6 vols. Vol. 1: Chamber Music. Track 11. Azerbaijan International, AICD1206, 1997, compact disc. Pro-

duced jointly by Amoco and Azerbaijan International. http://azer.com/aiweb
/categories/music/AudioPages/CMA/cma_contents.html.
http://purl.dlib.indiana.edu/iudl/em/Huseynova/910368

PURL 6.10 | Agshin Alizade, "Two Trees Are Bent Together," From *Bayati,* for a
capella chorus. Performed by the Azerbaijan State Choral Capella of Azerbaijan. Javanshir Jafarov, conductor. Baku, 1984. Audio. Courtesy: Fuad Alizade.
http://purl.dlib.indiana.edu/iudl/em/Huseynova/910369

PURL 6.11 | Frangiz Alizade, *Music for Piano,* excerpt. Performed by Frangiz
Alizade. Audio. Source: Kronos Quartet. Mugam Sayagi. Music of Franghiz Ali-
Zadeh. Nonesuch Records Inc., 79804-2, 2005, compact disc.
http://purl.dlib.indiana.edu/iudl/em/Huseynova/910370

PURL 6.12 | Frangiz Alizade, *Mughamsayaghi,* excerpt. Performed by Kronos
Quartet. Audio. Source: Kronos Quartet. Mugam Sayagi. Music of Franghiz
Ali-Zadeh. Nonesuch Records Inc., 79804-2, 2005, compact disc.
http://purl.dlib.indiana.edu/iudl/em/Huseynova/910371

PURL 6.13 | Javanshir Guliyev, *Seven Pieces in Mugham Modes.* Performed by
Teymur Shamsiyev. Baku, 1980. Audio. Courtesy: Javanshir Guliyev.
http://purl.dlib.indiana.edu/iudl/em/Huseynova/910372

PURL 6.14 | Faraj Garayev, *Khutba, Mugham, and Sura,* excerpt. Performed by
Nieuw Ensemble (Amsterdam). Ed Spanjaard, conductor. Mohlat Muslumov,
tar soloist. Amsterdam, Paradiso Concert Hall, February 3, 1998. Audio. Courtesy: Faraj Garayev and Ed Spanjaard.
http://purl.dlib.indiana.edu/iudl/em/Huseynova/910373

CHAPTER 7

PURL 7.1 | Vasif Adigozalov, "Carnation," Arrangement for the tar and chamber
orchestra. Performed by Ramiz Guliyev and the Azerbaijan State Chamber Orchestra named after Gara Garayev. Yashar Imanov, conductor. Audio. Source:
Classical Music of Azerbaijan, 6 vols. Vol. 1: Chamber Music. Track 10. Azerbaijan International, AICD1206, 1997, compact disc. Produced jointly by Amoco and
Azerbaijan International. http://azer.com/aiweb/categories/music/AudioPages
/CMA/cma_contents.html.
http://purl.dlib.indiana.edu/iudl/em/Huseynova/910374

PURL 7.2 | Said Rustamov, "Where Are You?" Arranged by Rafig Babayev. Per-
formed by Akif Islamzade and the Orchestra of the Azerbaijani Television and
Radio. Baku, 1985. Video. Courtesy: Akif Islamzade.
http://purl.dlib.indiana.edu/iudl/em/Huseynova/910375

PURL 7.3 | Tofig Guliyev, "Your Beauty Won't Last Forever." Performed by Rashid Behbudov and the Azerbaijan State Symphony Orchestra named after Uzeyir Hajibeyli. Niyazi, conductor. Courtesy: Rashida Behbudova. Audio. Source: Aida Huseynova, *Music and Culture of Azerbaijan,* Global Voices Comprehensive (MJ & Associates, Inc., 2007), DVD.
http://purl.dlib.indiana.edu/iudl/em/Huseynova/910376

PURL 7.4 | Emin Sabitoghlu, "Tonight." Performed by Huseynagha Hadiyev and Dan Ulduzu Ensemble. Gulara Aliyeva, artistic director. Baku, 1978. Video. Courtesy: Jeyran Mahmudova.
http://purl.dlib.indiana.edu/iudl/em/Huseynova/910377

PURL 7.5 | Telman Hajiyev, "Poppies." Performed by Rashid Behbudov and the Ensemble of the Song Theater of Azerbaijan. Rafig Babayev, artistic director. Baku, 1975. Video. Courtesy: Rashida Behbudova.
http://purl.dlib.indiana.edu/iudl/em/Huseynova/910378

PURL 7.6. Muslim Magomayev, "Azerbaijan," Performed by Muslim Magomayev and the Azerbaijan State Orchestra of Popular and Symphonic Music. Baku, 1980. Video. Courtesy: Marina Magomayeva and Tamara Siniavskaia.
http://purl.dlib.indiana.edu/iudl/em/Huseynova/910379

PURL 7.7 | Chingiz Sadikhov. Improvisations. From the concert of the International Vocal Ensemble of Indiana University. Artistic Director Mary Goetze. Auer Hall, April 21, 2002. Audio. Courtesy: Indiana University Jacobs School of Music.
http://purl.dlib.indiana.edu/iudl/em/Huseynova/910380

PURL 7.8 | Azerbaijani folk song "Hey Flowersome." Performed by the International Vocal Ensemble of Indiana University. Artistic Director Mary Goetze. Chingiz Sadikhov, pianist. Auer Hall, April 21, 2002. Audio. Courtesy: Indiana University Jacobs School of Music.
http://purl.dlib.indiana.edu/iudl/em/Huseynova/910381

CHAPTER 8

PURL 8.1 | Ogtay Kazimi, "Life, You Are So Unpredictable." Video clip directed by Eldar Guliyev. Baku, 1970. Video. Courtesy: Gaya group.
http://purl.dlib.indiana.edu/iudl/em/Huseynova/910382

PURL 8.2 | Azerbaijani Folk Song "Look at Me." Performed by the ensemble Beri Bakh, Artistic Director Rauf Babayev Recorded by Mary Goetze. Video. Source: *Global Voices, Grade 5,* published by MJ & Associates. Coordinated with Spotlight on Music, Grade 5, published by McMillan McGraw Hill, Inc., 2005.
http://purl.dlib.indiana.edu/iudl/em/Huseynova/910383

PURL 8.3 | Rafig Babayev, "In the Mode Bayati Kurd," Baku, 1967. Audio. Courtesy: Fariza Babayeva.
http://purl.dlib.indiana.edu/iudl/em/Huseynova/910384

PURL 8.4 | Vagif Mustafazade, "Bayati Shiraz," Audio. Courtesy: Afag Aliyeva. Source: Vagif Mustafazade. Baku: Vagif Mustafazade Foundation, 2004, compact disc. Track 4.
http://purl.dlib.indiana.edu/iudl/em/Huseynova/910385

PURL 8.5 | Vagif Mustafazade, Improvisation on the theme by Gara Garayev from the soundtrack for the film *The Man Casts Anchor.* Baku, 1970. Audio. Courtesy: Afag Aliyeva.
http://purl.dlib.indiana.edu/iudl/em/Huseynova/910386

PURL 8.6 | Salman Gambarov, Soundtrack for the silent film *Latif,* excerpt. Salman Gambarov, pianist, Fakhraddin Dadashov, kemancha, Natig Shirinov, percussions. Baku International Jazz Festival. Baku Jazz Center, April 10, 2005. Video. Courtesy: Salman Gambarov.
http://purl.dlib.indiana.edu/iudl/em/Huseynova/910387

PURL 8.7 | Salman Gambarov, Soundtrack for the silent film *Latif,* excerpt. Salman Gambarov, pianist, Fakhraddin Dadashov, kemancha, Natig Shirinov, percussions. Baku International Jazz Festival. Baku Jazz Center, April 10, 2005. Video. Courtesy: Salman Gambarov.
http://purl.dlib.indiana.edu/iudl/em/Huseynova/910388

PURL 8.8 | Shahin Novrasli, *I Went to the Garden to Pick Up Grape.* First Buta Festival of Azerbaijani Arts. London, Southbank Centre. Queen Elizabeth Hall. November 25, 2009. Video. Courtesy: Shahin Novrasli.
http://purl.dlib.indiana.edu/iudl/em/Huseynova/910389

PURL 8.9 | Emil Afrasiyab, *Two Worlds.* Baku, the Heydar Aliyev Center. September 6, 2013. Video. Courtesy: Emil Afrasiyab.
http://purl.dlib.indiana.edu/iudl/em/Huseynova/910390

PURL 8.10 | Isfar Sarabski, *Novruz.* Baku International Jazz Festival. The Azerbaijan State Philharmonic Hall named after Muslim Magomayev, October 19, 2010. Video. Courtesy: Isfar Sarabski.
http://purl.dlib.indiana.edu/iudl/em/Huseynova/910391

CHAPTER 9

PURL 9.1 | *Mugham Bayati Shiraz.* Performed by the ensemble Garabagh Nightingales, Artistic Director Murad Rzayev. Excerpt from the documentary Gara-

bagh Nightingales. Azerbaijanfilm Studio, 1977. Video. Courtesy: Azerbaijanfilm Studio.
http://purl.dlib.indiana.edu/iudl/em/Huseynova/910392

PURL 9.2 | Murad Rustamzade performs *mugham Murza Huseyn Segahi* at the Children's Eighth Mugham Festival, excerpt. Recorded by Aida Huseynova. Baku, The Song Theater named after Rashid Behbudov, October 22, 2003. Video. Courtesy: Kainat Youth Center.
http://purl.dlib.indiana.edu/iudl/em/Huseynova/910393

PURL 9.3 | *Mugham Garabagh Shikastasi.* Arranged by Jeyhun Allahverdiyev. Performed by Nazaket Teymurova, Khari Bulbul mugham group, and the Azerbaijan State Chamber Orchestra named after Gara Garayev. Teymur Goychayev, conductor. Baku, the Heydar Aliyev Palace, December 19, 2009. Video. Courtesy: Teymur Goychayev.
http://purl.dlib.indiana.edu/iudl/em/Huseynova/910394

PURL 9.4 | Farhad Badalbeyli, *Ave Maria.* Performed by Farida Mammadova and Gulnaz Ismayilova and the Azerbaijan State Symphony Orchestra of the Television and Radio. Azad Aliyev, conductor. Baku, 2009. Video. Courtesy: Farhad Badalbeyli.
http://purl.dlib.indiana.edu/iudl/em/Huseynova/910395

PURL 9.5 | Vasif Adigozalov, "Lullaby for Shusha," Performed by Aygun Baylar and Murad Adigozalzade. The Fourth International Gabala Music Festival, July 27, 2012. Video. Courtesy: Yalchin Adigozalov.
http://purl.dlib.indiana.edu/iudl/em/Huseynova/910396

PURL 9.6 | Eldar Mansurov, "Bayatilar." Performed by Brilliant Dadashova. Azerbaijan State Television and Radio, 1989. Video. Courtesy: Eldar Mansurov.
http://purl.dlib.indiana.edu/iudl/em/Huseynova/910397

PURL 9.7 | DJ Pantelis "I Have a Dream" Composer: Eldar Mansurov. Produced and remixed by DJ Pantelis. Video, 2008. www.djpantelis.com, www.facebook.com/djpantelisofficial. Courtesy: DJ Pantelis and CEo/Sugar Factory Records.
http://purl.dlib.indiana.edu/iudl/em/Huseynova/910398

PURL 9.8 | Azerbaijani Folk Song "Fair Lady." Performed by the State Ensemble of Ancient Music Instruments. Artistic Director and soloist Munis Sharifov. Baku, the International Mugham Center, May 5, 2012. Video. Courtesy: Munis Sharifov.
http://purl.dlib.indiana.edu/iudl/em/Huseynova/910399

PURL 9.9 | Jovdat Hajiyev, *Ballade.* Performed by Murad Adigozalzade. Audio. Source: Murad Adigozalzade. *Selections of Azerbaijani Piano Music.* Baku: Az-

ercell, 2004. 2 Vols. Volume 1, Track 5.
http://purl.dlib.indiana.edu/iudl/em/Huseynova/910400

PURL 9.10 | Gara Garayev, Three Preludes. Performed by Murad Huseynov. Baku, the Azerbaijan National Art Museum, September 28, 2010. Audio. Courtesy: Murad Huseynov.
http://purl.dlib.indiana.edu/iudl/em/Huseynova/910401

CHAPTER 10

PURL 10.1 | Uzeyir Hajibeyli, *Layla and Majnun,* Chamber arrangement by the Silk Road Ensemble and Yo-Yo Ma, final episode. Recorded at the New College Theater, Harvard University. November 29, 2007. Video © Courtesy of Silkroad.
http://purl.dlib.indiana.edu/iudl/em/Huseynova/910402

PURL 10.2 | Uzeyir Hajibeyli, *Layla and Majnun,* Chamber arrangement by the Silk Road Ensemble and Yo-Yo Ma, part 2. Recorded at the New College Theater, Harvard University. November 29, 2007. Video © Courtesy of Silkroad.
http://purl.dlib.indiana.edu/iudl/em/Huseynova/910403

EPILOGUE

PURL E.1 | Said Rustamov, "Getme Getme" (Don't Leave Don't Leave), excerpt. Performed by Kronos Quartet, Alim Gasimov and Fargana Gasimova. Audio. Source: Kronos Quartet. Floodplain. Nonesuch Records Inc., 518349-2, 2009, 2014, compact disc.
http://purl.dlib.indiana.edu/iudl/em/Huseynova/910404

ACKNOWLEDGMENTS

This book in its present form is significantly different from what it was twelve years ago, when I began working on it. While it is natural for any serious research to go through many stages before taking its final shape, for me, coming from Azerbaijan and writing a book for an American press, this process has entailed many additional challenges. I knew the object of my research in all respects and envisioned the general concept of my book, but I had to develop the right methodology to complete my "American book about Azerbaijani music." As I was going through this process, I was constantly changing as a musician, scholar, and individual. This development would have been impossible without the community and the support of my friends and colleagues on both sides of the Atlantic, and regrettably it is only possible to give particular mention to some of them here.

The very idea of my studying Azerbaijani music in the light of encounters between East and West emerged in Baku, under the roof of the Baku Music Academy, my alma mater. I am deeply indebted to Elmira Nazirova, my piano professor and genuine spiritual mentor. She exposed me to the versatile repertoire of Azerbaijani music – and to her own amazingly rich life and career that developed on the crossroads of many cultures and that included encounters with the luminaries of twentieth-century music.

I would like to express very special thanks to the pianist Farhad Badalbeyli, who is the present rector of the Baku Music Academy. Without the motivation and encouragement he gave, I would not have completed this research. As a musician combining within himself many cultural energies coming from East and West, Professor Badalbeyli realized the importance of my study as a contribution to the academic world not only in the United States but also in Azerbaijan. The same was true of the musicologist Ulviyya Imanova, who was my constant source of support during this journey. At various stages of my project, I shared my ideas with Professor Imanova, and her feedback helped me either to finalize or to modify them. Particularly important was her expertise as a specialist on neoclassicism in Azerbaijani music. I am tremendously grateful to the music theorist Nigar Rahimova, who was my continual inspiration and advisor behind the scenes. Professor Rahimova was literally the first person with whom I shared all the updates, joys, and concerns of this project. I thank her for our endless discussions pertaining to each and every aspect of my research and particularly to modality, in which she is an expert.

This book would have been poorer without my encounters with Alim Gasimov, the outstanding master of Azerbaijani *mugham*, and his daughter and student, Fargana Gasimova. I was fortunate to be a part of their residencies and concerts in various parts of the globe. These gave me the precious chance to follow their creative processes from behind the scenes and to develop a new understanding of the essence of Azerbaijani music as embodied in *mugham*. I am indebted to the pianist Chingiz Sadikhov, whose mastery of piano improvisation introduced me to one of the unique and long-lasting traditions of Azerbaijani music that exists on the crossroads of cultures. I was honored to collaborate with Mr. Sadikhov on various occasions, and I have had many professional encounters with him, both in Azerbaijan and in the United States. I appreciate being able to include performances by Alim and Fargana Gasimov, as well as by Chingiz Sadikhov, all fabulous musicians who are unique in their fields.

I am grateful to Frangiz Alizade, the chair of the Union of Azerbaijani Composers, for supporting the idea of this research since its very first stages and for extending to me all possible assistance on behalf of the union. I had the honor of participating in numerous festivals and concerts in the United States that featured the music of Frangiz Alizade. These experiences facilitated my understanding of the creative and cultural energies shaping the contemporary composed music of Azerbaijan.

I would also like to express deep appreciation to the musicologist Alla Bayramova, the director of the State Museum of the Musical Culture of Azerbaijan, for giving me free access to the relevant materials preserved in the museum collection and forgranting me permission to use rare archival photos and media materials. I am indebted to the musicologist Nigar Akhundova, the adviser for Humanitarian Affairs at the Embassy of Azerbaijan to Russia, without whom I would have been unable to reach out to many outstanding Moscow-based musicians who fell within the scope of my project. I am thankful to Dr. Akhundova for sending me valuable sources related to Azerbaijani music that were published in Russia and that would have been unavailable to me otherwise.

This book was heavily informed by conversations and interviews with Azerbaijan's most distinguished musicians, including the composers Agshin Alizade, Arif Malikov, Khayyam Mirzazade, Frangiz Alizade, and Faraj Garayev; the traditional musicians Alim Gasimov and Ramiz Guliyev; the ethnomusicologist Ramiz Zokhrabov; and the jazz pianist Salman Gambarov. I thank them for sharing their valuable thoughts about their own professional experiences and on the overall state of Azerbaijani music during the last several decades. I am grateful to the composer and music theorist Parviz Guliyev for letting me refer to his transcriptions of the jazz compositions of Vagif Musta-fazade and for permission to publish the excerpt from them. The beautiful work of art on the cover of my book appears courtesy of the Azerbaijani artist Sanan Samadov; I express my deepest gratitude to him.

There is a place of incredible value that has been a home to my inspiration, courage, and professional development: the Indiana University Jacobs School of Music. I have enjoyed the rich academic and professional environment that the jsom has provided. But first and foremost, I have been surrounded by a fabulous group of people who have helped me commence and complete my project. My sincere gratitude goes to Dean Gwyn Richards for supporting my teaching and my academic and professional endeavors that led to writing this book. I am also deeply thankful to Dean Richards for granting me permission to use the recordings of my performances of Azerbaijani music with the Indiana University International Vocal Ensemble (ive); these recordings have become highly relevant in the context of this book's focus on the multicultural essence of Azerbaijani music.

My first experience working with the ive occurred in 2001, when the group was led by the choral conductor and educator Mary Goetze, the ive's founder and first artistic director. Professor Goetze has my eternal gratitude for many things in my career and life, and these go far beyond the acknowledgments section of this book. As we worked on several projects related to Central Asia, I developed an outsider's view of the music of Azerbaijan that has complemented my insider perspective. I am honored to use the recording that Professor Goe-tze made during her visit to Baku in August 2000. She was the first reader of my manuscript many years ago, and she was always standing by me and encourag-ing me to continue even when I was about to give up.

It is with immense gratitude that I acknowledge the help of the musicolo-gist and pianist Constance Cook Glen, the director of the Music in General Studies program at IU, for which I have had the honor to teach. Professor Glen truly cared about me, a newcomer from a very distant place, and she supported me in all possible ways, making me feel comfortable in my new American home. She created abundant professional and academic opportunities for me, valuing my research from its very first steps and introducing me to scholars in similar fields; this eventually led to many wonderful friendships. All these are things I will never forget.

It gives me great pleasure to acknowledge the support I received at earlier stages of this project from the scholars in the IU community: the musicologists

Jeffrey Magee and Gayle Magee who inspired me to write this book; the musicologist Malcolm Brown and Lewis Rowell, an ethnomusicologist and music theorist, who provided encouraging feedback on my proposal. All this gave me energy and incentive to continue and complete the manuscript. I would also like to thank saxophonist Thomas Walsh and violinist Dena El-Saffar, whose professional endeavors took them to Azerbaijan. They have graciously allowed me to include their insights about Azerbaijani music. I am grateful to my colleague musicologists at IU, Rika Asai and Daniel Bishop, who assisted me in proofreading my manuscript. Their help was vital, as English is not my native language. But this project never would have become a reality without Virginia Whealton. Ms. Whealton has my heartfelt gratitude for her sincere interest in the subject matter, for her meticulously reading through a number of drafts of my manuscript, and for her extremely helpful musicological suggestions and comments. In addition to the contribution of the JSOM, I express my thanks for the funding the school provided to help defray the expenses of proofreading my manuscript and preparing it for publication.

I am deeply indebted to my many colleagues and friends at IU outside of the music school who supported this study. I had many scholarly exchanges with William Fierman, a political scientist and expert on Central Asia. In his capacity as the director of the IU Inner Asian and Uralic National Resource Center, Professor Fierman made it possible for me to be a part of numerous projects, some related to Azerbaijani music, others outside that realm. He helped me comprehend Azerbaijani music and culture within the context of the larger region of Central Asia, and he gave me his valuable feedback on the historical sections of the book. Professor Fierman has my everlasting gratitude for listening, offering me advice, and supporting me throughout this project. I enjoyed participating in academic and professional endeavors with Shahyar Daneshgar, a specialist on the Persian and Azerbaijani languages and an enthusiastic promoter in the United States of music from the Middle East and Central Asia. Professor Daneshgar introduced me to many scholars and musicians from that region, for which he has my deep appreciation.

My life and work in the United States put me in touch with many musicians and institutions that have had a significant impact on this book. Collaboration with the Silk Road Project (SRP) offered more than exposure to the outstanding musicianship of Yo-Yo Ma, the artistic director, and to each and every member of the group – though that was incredible in itself. My collaboration with the SRP was of decisive importance in developing the intellectual frameworks of my research, as I was able to come to a new understanding of Azerbaijani music as a product of the historical Silk Road. I am grateful to Yo-Yo Ma, as well as to other ensemble musicians, especially Jonathan Gandelsman, Colin Jacobsen, and Kojiro Umezaki, and to the artist Henrik Soderstrom, all of whom shared their valuable comments on the Azerbaijani component of the ensemble's repertoire. Their thoughts appear in the last chapter of my book, and they enhance my discussion of Azerbaijani music as interpreted and performed outside of the country and in the contemporary world. I would like to extend my gratitude to all staff members of the SRP with whom I had encounters for their genuine support over many years. My sincere thanks go to Isabelle Hunter, SRP program director, who provided outstanding help with clearing all the materials related to the activities of the Silk Road Ensemble that I have included in my book. I am indebted to the Sound Postings/Office of Yo-Yo Ma – particularly to Jessica Harsch – for confirming my use of verbal, photo, and media resources featuring Yo-Yo Ma. I am grateful to the photographer David O'Connor for letting me publish his picture of the Silk Road Ensemble with Yo-Yo Ma.

I always treasure that special moment during the Silk Road Ensemble's residence at Harvard University in 2007 when I met Theodore Levin, an ethnomusicologist and expert on the music of Central Asia. I am indebted to Professor Levin for a true breakthrough in the development of my project. He identified strong points and weaknesses in my book proposal and gave me the confidence that I needed to follow up with this project. Throughout these years, Professor Levin always took time out from his extraordinarily busy schedule to answer my constant stream of questions promptly and comprehensively. In his capacity as senior project consultant of the Aga Khan Music Initiative, Professor Levin invited me to be a part of a number of activities sponsored by that organization. I am tremendously grateful to the Aga Khan Music Initiative for putting me in touch with many wonderful musicians, particularly with the Kronos Quartet. My thanks go to each member of this outstanding group for their mastery and inspiration as they performed pieces of Azerbaijani repertoire. My gratitude also goes to Janet Cowperthwaite, managing director, and Sidney Chen, artistic administrator, for giving me permission to use Kronos' recordings of Azerbaijani music.

I would like to express my gratitude to the ethnomusicologist Inna Naroditskaya and to the anthropologist Anna Oldfield, whose books on Azerbaijani music preceded mine and served as inspiring examples for me. Professor Naroditskaya has been very supportive at all stages of my project. We met both in Bloomington and in Chicago, where she resides, and we always found time to discuss questions related to my book project. I am thankful to Professor Naroditskaya for her valuable suggestions and comments on my manuscript that helped me improve it. We had many academic exchanges with Professor

Oldfield in the United States and during her extended stays in Baku. I have a high regard for Professor Oldfield's deep knowledge of Azerbaijani music and culture and I was delighted to receive her encouraging feedback and insightful comments on the final version of my manuscript. I am thankful to the ethnomusicologist Izaly Zemtsovsky, whom I met in Seattle and then in San Francisco. We had several scholarly exchanges, which have been immensely helpful. Dr. Zemtsovsky's insightful comments on traditional and composed Azerbaijani music and his answers to my questions have helped me develop some of my book's major concepts.

My heartfelt thanks go to Betty Blair, a Los Angeles–based journalist and folklore specialist, who is the founding editor of the *Azerbaijan International* magazine. Ms. Blair has been my heartiest supporter and an encourager extraordinaire. She helped me understand what is special about Azerbaijani music and why it is important to share it with the world. All my articles that I wrote for *Azerbaijan International* gave impetus to my further research activities. Ms. Blair has my deep gratitude for granting me permission to use media examples published by *Azerbaijan International*. I am deeply indebted to Diana Altman, Executive Director of the Karabakh Foundation, for supporting me throughout all stages of my work on this project.

My profound gratitude goes to the editors, designers, and entire staff of Indiana University Press, who have shepherded the creation of this book in all aspects. A special thank you goes to my editor, Raina Polivka, for guiding me through the process, and for her tireless and skilled efforts throughout all these years. I am grateful to IU Press board members and to my external reviewers, who helped me focus on the most valuable points of my narrative and who gave me the courage to make major changes to the content and organization of the book. Janice Frisch, editor's assistant; David Miller, the Press project manager; Nazareth Pantaloni, copyright program librarian; and Karen Hallman, copyeditor, have my sincere gratitude for their patience and understanding in putting together this book. I am immensely indebted to all professionals and friends who helped me in the process of publication: to Nicholas Cline, who prepared my musical examples; to Theresa Quill, who designed the maps; and to Parvin Babayeva, who edited all historical photos.

I would like to emphasize the critical role of the Fulbright Scholar Program. The Fulbright fellowship, which I received in 2007–2008, allowed me to complete a significant part of my research related to Azerbaijani jazz. I am honored to receive support from the Andrew W. Mellon Foundation's Ethnomusicology Media (EM) series. Through this collaborative publishing initiative, I am able to share media examples illustrating my study. My sincere thanks go to Mollie Ables, EM assistant project manager, who patiently led me through this process.

I would also like to thank all the individuals and institutions from all around the globe to whom I owe the opportunity of including musical examples, images, and media examples in my project. Many thanks to the Sikorski Music Publishing Group and G. Schirmer, Inc. for allowing me to include the excerpts from the scores they have published. My sincere gratitude goes to Nonesuch Records as well as to the recording companies and their sponsoring organizations in Azerbaijan, including the Ministry of Culture of Azerbaijan, as well as Azercell, AzEuroTel, and Azersun. I am grateful to Azerbaijanfilm Studio, the Azerbaijan State Television and Radio Company, and its Madaniyyat (Culture) subdivision for allowing me use their sources.

Last but not least, I wish to thank my family for their unconditional love and enormous support throughout, and as always my mere expression of thanks does not suffice. Khanimana, Natella, Nemat, and Emin understood how much this project meant to me, and they did not need to read or to see my writing to say that I had to continue and finish it. I dedicate this book to them – with all my love and gratitude.

NOTE ON LANGUAGE
AND TRANSLITERATION

Several important matters should be clarified for the reader. The first point concerns the original Azerbaijani names and titles that I have transliterated and translated into English. Some of them appear in Russian sources in a distorted way, having been rendered according to Russian pronunciation rules. This, subsequently, has created discrepancies in transliteration in scholarly sources, with different spellings appearing within the English-language musicological literature. For example, the name of the composer Jovdat Hajiyev (Cövdət Hacıyev) appears in various sources as Jevdet Hajiyev, Jevdet Gadjiyev, or Dzhevdet Gadzhiev. Besides, several names are spelled various ways, although for reasons unrelated to the Russian language. For example, the composer Frangiz Alizade in some English-language publications appears as Franghiz Ali-Zadeh (Alizadeh), and in German sources as Frangis Ali-Sade. The last name of the jazz musician Vagif Mustafazade is also shown as Mustafa-Zadeh in some publications. The spelling of the name of the traditional singer Alim Qasimov does not follow official transliteration rules, either (it should be Alim Gasimov). In my book, the orthography of all names is consistent throughout. I have chosen a spelling based on transliteration from the Azerbaijani language. If I am translating from a primary source that uses a different spelling, then my chosen spelling appears in brackets or parentheses.

Another concern refers to some last names that have been modified after Azerbaijan's independence in late 1991. The Russian suffix "-ov" sometimes has been replaced with "-li" to reveal the nation's Turkic origins. The name of the composer Uzeyir Hajibeyli – who was known during the Soviet era as Uzeyir Hajibeyov – is the most representative example. The reversion to the pre-Soviet spelling of his name was officially announced in Azerbaijan in 2008, and since then, respective changes have been made in all domains of Azerbaijani society and culture that contain references to Hajibeyli. Accordingly, although this composer is known in all English-language musicological sources as Hajibeyov (Hajibekov, Gadzhibekov, Gadjibekov), I think it is essential to refer to the pioneer of the composed music in the country by recognizing his original Azerbaijani name, Hajibeyli.

The third matter that needs clarification is "Azerbaijani," one of the most important terms in the present research. Several alternative versions of the English translation of this adjective exist, including "Azeri" and "Azerbaijanian" ("Azerbaidzhanian"). In the entire range of publications related to Azerbaijan, all three versions are used interchangeably, although each has its own historical, ethnographical, and lexicological justification. In my original text, I use Azerbaijani; however, the other two versions also appear throughout the book within quoted texts.

The fourth issue relates to pronunciation rules for texts in the Azerbaijani language that are used within quotations in musical examples of vocal pieces. Over its history, the Azerbaijani language has experienced three major alphabet changes. Arabic script was used for nearly a thousand years until Latin became the official script in 1929. In 1939, Cyrillic replaced Latin and remained in use until 1991, when a modified Latin was adopted as the official Azerbaijani alphabet. I have provided the transliteration table for the current Azerbaijani alphabet; this table uses the symbols of the International Phonetic Alphabet:

Table 0.1. Pronunciation of Azerbaijani alphabet

A a	[ɑ]	G g	[gʲ]	Q q	[g]	S s	[s]
B b	[b]	Ğ ğ	[ɣ]	L l	[l]	Ş ş	[ʃ]
C c	[dʒ]	H h	[h]	M m	[m]	T t	[t]
Ç ç	[tʃ]	X x	[x]	N n	[n]	U u	[u]
D d	[d]	I ı	[ɯ]	O o	[ɔ]	Ü ü	[y]
E e	[e]	İ i	[ɪ]	Ö ö	[œ]	V v	[v]
Ə ə	[æ]	J j	[ʒ]	P p	[p]	Y y	[j]
F f	[f]	K k	[k]	R r	[r]	Z z	[z]

For the transliteration of any portions of my text that are taken from Russian-language sources, I have used the Library of Congress system, although in the modified form. I have followed all the rules of this system, except for the ligatures and diacritical marks.

One final remark refers to the way of differentiating musicians who have the same last name but different first names: Agshin Alizade and Frangiz Alizade; Fikrat Amirov and Jamil Amirov; Afrasiyab Badalbeyli and Farhad

Badalbeyli; Gara Garayev and Faraj Garayev; Fidan Gasimova and Khuraman Gasimova; Tofig Guliyev and Javanshir Guliyev; Soltan Hajibeyov and Ismayil Hajibeyov; Rauf Hajiyev and Jovdat Hajiyev. To avoid any confusion throughout the text, I have added, as needed, the initial of the first name: A. Alizade or F. Alizade, G. Garayev or F. Garayev, etc. This is necessary in the sections that involve the discussion of both musicians having identical last names; I skip the initial if the section focuses on one of the musicians only.

Music of Azerbaijan

INTRODUCTION

WHAT IS AZERBAIJANI MUSIC?

January 2014: I am taking the subway across Baku, the capital city of Azerbaijan. As the train pulls into each stop along its route, a brief excerpt of music comes through the sound system. These excerpts are musical welcoming messages. Each of the city's twenty-three subway stations has its own distinct snippet of music that alerts passengers to their arrival at the station. My subway journey creates an eclectic musical experience. Some stops play *mugham*, the quintessential genre of traditional Azerbaijani music. Other stations feature pieces by Azerbaijani composers. These compositions include the chorus from the opera *Leyli and Majnun* (1908), by Uzeyir Hajibeyli (1885–1948), and the Waltz from the ballet *Seven Beauties* (1952), by Gara Garayev (1918–1982). To me as an ethnic Azerbaijani, born and raised in Baku, and indeed to most people on the train, all of this music – folk tunes, symphonic pieces, popular songs, romances, and jazz compositions – is Azerbaijani. All of the pieces I hear constitute "our national" music.

Yet the concept of "composed music," by which I mean a musical composition that is consciously constructed and written down in fixed musical notation – is itself a Western one, and the idea that Western-style composed music could form a vital part of Azerbaijan's musical heritage raises several important questions. How did composed music, Western in origin even if adopted by Azerbaijani musicians, so readily become accepted as an artistic expression of Azerbaijani national identity? Why are operas and ballets penned by Azerbaijani composers considered to be as much a part of the national soundscape as traditional *mugham* or folk song? What was the key to the successful fusion, accomplished in the composed music of Azerbaijan, of Azerbaijani traditional music idioms with principles of Western music? Such questions and others like them need not be asked in the same way about the music of a Western country,

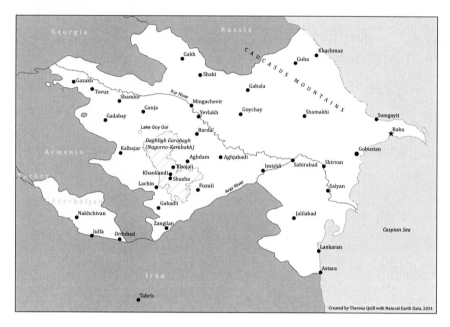

FIGURE 0.1. Map of Azerbaijan. *Prepared by Theresa Quill.*

since the concept of "composed music" originated in the West. But the situation is different with Azerbaijan, a small country in Transcaucasia that since antiquity has been at the crossroads of East and West.

For centuries, the music of the Azerbaijani people was a branch of the musical traditions of the Eastern hemisphere. The territory where the Azerbaijanis lived belonged to the Persian, Arab, Mongol, and Turkish empires, all of which were expansive and facilitated the Azerbaijani people's connections with the Middle East and Central Asia. The land on which the northern Azerbaijani people lived, a territory roughly corresponding to the modern Republic of Azerbaijan, was subjugated to the Russian Empire in the early nineteenth century, marking the beginning of a period of rapid Westernization and modernization. These two processes have become integral in building Azerbaijani national identity. Music, one of the most revered arts in Azerbaijan, became important to Azerbaijani nationalism, and appropriately Azerbaijani music has reflected Westernization and modernization in significant and powerful ways.

As accepted in most studies on nationalism, Westernization and modernization do not contradict nationalist agendas, or at least not during the first

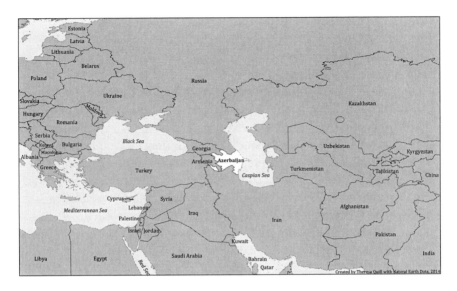

FIGURE 0.2. Map of Azerbaijan in its regional contexts. *Prepared by Theresa Quill.*

stage of the emergence of national identity. In his study of nationalism in nine-teenth-century European music, the musicologist Carl Dahlhaus mentions that "in the first half of the century the 'nationalist' was also, perhaps paradoxically, a 'cosmopolitan,' a 'citizen of the world.' . . . Most nineteenth-century composers tried to effect a compromise between cosmopolitan ideas, which had not faded altogether, and their own sense of national identity."[1] Although not directly analogous, we should acknowledge the similar position of Azerbaijani musicians. The desire to have a "national" opera or a national conservatory was central to the activities of Azerbaijani musicians at the turn of the twentieth century, the period during which this Western-style nationalism bore its first fruits in Azerbaijan.

In the early twentieth century, Azerbaijani musicians began to master the major genres of Western music, establishing a national tradition of composed music. Beginning in the 1920s, the Soviet Union, the Russian Empire's successor, continued to stimulate the development of Western music as a cultural form. During the Soviet era, Azerbaijan cultivated an "excellent school of composers," according to Dmitry Shostakovich, and Azerbaijani performers made successful appearances in prestigious Western contests such as the Vianna da Mota International Music Competition and the Maria Callas Grand Prix.[2]

A vibrant, internationally respected jazz movement developed in the 1960s. Nonetheless, Azerbaijanis carefully preserved their indigenous musical heritage, even though their traditional music was and continues to be affected by the growth of Western music.

Azerbaijan is not the only country in which a native tradition has changed in response to Western music, whether as a result of imperialism or globalization. The ethnomusicologist Bruno Nettl has described the various ways non-Western musical traditions can respond to the impact of the Western world. In this book, I invoke Nettl's descriptions of "syncretism," "Westernization," and "modernization" as he has outlined them in his works. He defines each as follows: "Syncretism results when the two musical systems in a state of confrontation have compatible central traits; westernization, when a non-Western music incorporates central, non-compatible Western traits; modernization, when it incorporates non-central but compatible Western traits."[3] All of these are key to understanding developments in Azerbaijani music since the early twentieth century, although the impacts of syncretism and Westernization have been more profound. These two processes facilitated the great revolutions in Azerbaijani music. All major innovations of native musicians in the fields of composed music, jazz, and music education have resulted from integrating central traits of native music with central traits of Western music.

My research entails precise understandings of "nation," "national," and "nationalism." The Azerbaijani *nation* can be understood either "as-people" or "as-state," according to the terminology accepted in most contemporary studies on nationalism. The nation as-people refers to a community affirming a common language, culture, ethnicity, and history. The nation as-state is defined as a group of people inhabiting the same territory and sharing citizenship of the same state. This study deals with the music of the Azerbaijani nation that currently exists *as-state*, in other words, as the Republic of Azerbaijan that was declared after the breakup of the Soviet Union in 1991.

It should be noted that some other works use Azerbaijani to refer to Azerbaijan *as-people*. This is because there is a large territory populated by ethnic Azerbaijanis in the northwestern part of Iran; this Azerbaijani population outnumbers that of the Republic of Azerbaijan by at least threefold. The historical destiny, culture, and music of Azerbaijanis in Iran have differed in many senses from those of their fellow ethnic Azerbaijanis within the Republic of Azerbaijan. After the Russo-Persian Wars of 1804–1813 and 1826–1828, Russia annexed the northern part of Azerbaijan from Iran, dividing Azerbaijan, as-people, into two groups and creating the split of culture between Northern and Southern Azerbaijanis that continues to the present. Nonetheless, since the early nineteenth century, Azerbaijanis on both sides have retained a sense of deep connection with "the other half," despite their notably different historical destinies.

Since this book focuses on the Republic of Azerbaijan, I do not undertake a comparative study of its music and that of the Iranian Azerbaijanis. Nevertheless, my historical survey does make a significant claim about the musical differences between the Azerbaijani peoples: I argue that Russian and Soviet influence in what is now the Republic of Azerbaijan had certain positive effects on the emergence and maturation of Azerbaijani national identity there. The development of a national music in the territory of the modern Republic of Azerbaijan faced many challenges and experienced numerous setbacks due to the impact of these foreign powers; however, the uniqueness of Azerbaijani traditional music has been preserved, and significant progress toward the development of Western composed music has been and continues to be made. Azerbaijanis in Iran have encountered different challenges. They live in a society in which Persian music and culture is predominant. Azerbaijanis are considered an ethnic minority, and Azerbaijani musical traditions in Iran have not greatly been affected by the Westernization that Iran experienced in the nineteenth and twentieth centuries. As a result, the major accomplishments of Iranian Azerbaijanis mostly have occurred in the realm of traditional music. The presence of "two Azerbaijani musics" has and will continue to create a unique opportunity for scholars to compare the divergent ways the same tradition develops depending on social, political, and cultural contexts.

WHY I WROTE THIS BOOK

Azerbaijan provides a quintessential case study in musical syncretism, but no English-language scholarly literature or research has discussed Azerbaijani musical syncretism in any depth. In general, scholars have been inclined to address Azerbaijani traditional music as the most "genuine" music of the Azerbaijani people, and scholars touch little upon the oeuvres of the national composers. With regard to traditional music, two recently published books offer valuable insights. The first study is *The Song from the Land of Fire: Continuity and Change in Azerbaijanian Mugham,* by Inna Naroditskaya, an Azerbaijan-born American musicologist.[4] She examines *mugham,* the central genre of Azerbaijan's traditional music, from historical, cultural, sociological, and ethnomusicological perspectives. Naroditskaya only briefly considers Azerbaijani composed music and the social and cultural forces that shaped the development of Azerbaijani music in the twentieth century and beyond. The second study, *Azerbaijani Women Poet-Minstrels: Women Ashiqs from the Eighteenth*

Century to the Present, is by the American anthropologist Anna Oldfield.[5] Old-field researches the unique Azerbaijani female bardic tradition, which she studied over the course of two years of fieldwork. Her publication deals exclusively with the traditional oral form of *ashig* art and is an example of anthropological, rather than ethnomusicological, research. Some studies of Azerbaijani composed music can be found in sources that focus on Russian and Soviet music, but these sources' "Azerbaijani" sections are far from comprehensive and accurate.[6] They have many gaps and significant factual errors, and they do not consider of the relationship between Azerbaijani composed music and traditional music. Moreover, most of them ignore the accomplishments of Azerbaijani music before the Soviet era, since they place Azerbaijan in the same category as the neighboring Central Asian countries, whose composed music traditions began under the Soviets. Having been all but absorbed into the larger stream of Russian-Soviet music by Soviet and even post-Soviet scholars, Azerbaijani composed music has remained terra incognita to Western musicologists.

This book makes the rich history of the contemporary music of Azerbaijan accessible, for the first time, to the English-speaking world. This study delineates the major social, political, cultural, and aesthetic factors that facilitated the fusion of native Azerbaijani musical traditions with the Western traditions of classical music, popular music, and jazz, and with the cultural forms associated with Western music, including concerts and conservatories. I consider, in historical perspective, the dynamic interaction between East and West in Azerbaijani music, with my main focus being on the twentieth century. As a caveat, I do not seek to imply any colonial subtext in my use of the terms *East* and *West*. I consider these terms to be categories signifying two cultural realms. My position is based on that suggested by the historian Terry Martin, who indicates that these categories are characteristic of colonialism, but he also maintains that they may yet be used in a globalized, postcolonial context to denote "cultural distinction," that is, differences in mentality, lifestyle, and social rules and values.[7] This cultural distinction, or, to use the definition accepted in sociology, East-West dichotomy, affects music as well, since the East is traditionally associated with extensive improvisation, the prevalence of oral forms, and modality, whereas the West is associated with composed music, its forms and genres, notation, and tonal or atonal rules.

My book draws upon recently released documents from the KGB (Komitet Gosudarstvennoi Bezopasnosti) and Communist Party archives, as well as upon interviews with leading Azerbaijani musicians, scholars, media workers, and leaders of institutions. This study also reflects my personal experience, since I lived in Azerbaijan during the Soviet and post-Soviet eras and witnessed their many major historical changes. I was born in the year when Leonid Brezhnev, the father of the "stagnation period," the last historical era of the Soviet Union, came to power (1964), and I graduated from high school in the year of his death (1982). Two years after Mikhail Gorbachev, the last Soviet leader, declared perestroika (1987), I defended my master's thesis, and in 1992, the year after the collapse of the Soviet Union, I completed my doctoral dissertation.

My musical studies and academic endeavors have always occurred at the crossroads of cultures. I grew up speaking Azerbaijani and Russian both with my family and at school. Since early childhood, I have enjoyed a highly diverse musical environment. Pyotr Ilych Tchaikovsky, J. S. Bach, and Louis Armstrong were a part of my life along with Azerbaijani folk songs, *mugham,* and pieces created by native composers. I studied at Azerbaijan's and Russia's best music schools, where I continually explored the issue of East-West synthesis. The role of the Russian composer Reinhold Gliere (1874–1956) in Azerbaijani music became the subject of my master's thesis, which I wrote at the Azerbaijan State Conservatory. In my doctoral dissertation, defended at the Saint Petersburg Conservatory, I explored the processes by which Azerbaijani composers mastered Western opera. I used the works of Muslim Magomayev (1885–1937), one of the pioneers of the Azerbaijani composed music tradition, as a case study. My college experience also included training as a classical pianist, and it likewise brought together East and West. Alongside the works of Azerbaijani composers, I played pieces by the French composer Claude Debussy, the Austrian composer Alban Berg, and other Westerners. Sometimes I abandoned composed music altogether, improvising on themes from Azerbaijani traditional and folk music. Improvisational exercises were not a part of my school's requirements, but we students were all "unofficially" encouraged to do them. Today I appreciate these exercises even more than I did at the time because they were a powerful way to become adept at the centuries-old tradition of improvisation in Azerbaijani music. My travels throughout the Soviet Union also expanded my multicultural awareness. Trips to Russia, Georgia, Kazakhstan, and Turkmenistan helped me understand the differences between various parts of the Soviet Union in terms of music and music education, and I gained a clearer picture of my home country in the process.

After the collapse of the Soviet Union in 1991, I experienced, firsthand, the turmoil that accompanied the transition to independence, and I did so both as a citizen of my country and as a musician and teacher. The extreme "patriotic" forces appeared on the political scene, and they drew a sharp distinction between "native" elements and "foreign" elements in Azerbaijani culture. I remember the gloomy times when we faculty members at the Azerbaijani

State Conservatory were given the recommendation to remove Mussorgsky and Beethoven from school curriculum in order to focus on national music exclusively. We never did this. By the mid-1990s, thanks to a political shift and the efforts of local intellectuals, those voices advocating a nativist return to traditional styles were muted, and Azerbaijani music continued to evolve as a syncretic East-West phenomenon.

As a result of my travels over the course of the next decade, I gained a new and broader understanding of the syncretic nature of Azerbaijani music. While conducting research and giving lectures at universities in the United States and Europe, I became involved in many international projects related to my native music. Most notably, I served as a consultant and interpreter for two groups: the Silk Road Project, directed by the world-renowned cellist Yo-Yo Ma; and the Aga Khan Music Initiative, a program of the Aga Khan Trust for Culture, which focuses on performing, teaching, and documenting music from Central Asia, South Asia, the Middle East, and North Africa. My work with the Aga Khan Music Initiative put me in touch with another group of remarkable musicians, the Kronos Quartet. Both the Silk Road Ensemble and the Kronos Quartet performed pieces of Azerbaijani repertoire, and I had the honor of being a part of their artistic laboratory and traveling with them, which shaped my perspective on Azerbaijani music outside of Azerbaijan. I witnessed my native music as a truly multicultural phenomenon.

In sum, this book draws together layers of knowledge, years of experience, and many professional endeavors. My study is the result of scholarly research and performing activities, and these have always occurred in my life at the crossroads of Azerbaijani native tradition and Western classical music. Through my experience, this book mirrors the multilayered richness of a musical culture that merges East and West. But most of all, this study is an attempt to convey love and admiration for those Azerbaijani musicians who, from antiquity down to the present, created the history of Azerbaijani national music in the face of daunting obstacles – especially in the twentieth century.

AN OIL-RICH COUNTRY ON THE CROSSROADS OF EPOCHS AND CONTINENTS

Three major factors facilitated the emergence of East-West synthesis in Azerbaijani music: geography, history, and economy. Azerbaijan has long been at the crossroads of Europe and Asia and at the intersection of various geopolitical regions, including Europe, Transcaucasia, Central Asia, and the Middle East. The shape of the Republic of Azerbaijan as portrayed on maps has often been compared to that of a bird flying from the West to the East, and this is more than poetic imagery. It symbolizes the country's historical involvement in both Eastern and Western hemispheres, as well as the mobility and the ever-changing balance of influences from the various geopolitical regions that have shaped Azerbaijani culture and continue to do so. Indeed, Azerbaijan fits within a variety of cultural and geopolitical contexts, and within each context it maintains a unique combination of characteristics that gives it a distinct identity. Azerbaijan is the only nation-state in the Middle East and in Central Asia with a Turkic-speaking population who predominantly practice Shia Islam.[8] Within Transcaucasia, Azerbaijan is both the largest country and the only Muslim nation-state in the region. Azerbaijan is also, along with Turkey, understood as "lesser Eastern/Asian" because it is located at the border of Europe and can directly communicate with it. All these cultural and geopolitical intersections are essential for understanding the multicultural identity, musical or otherwise, of Azerbaijanis.

Subjugation to Russia in the early nineteenth century was a decisive historical factor in promulgating Westernization in Azerbaijani music, as through Russia, Azerbaijani music came into direct contact with the Western world, and consequently Azerbaijani musicians mastered composed music and established performing arts and schooling in the Western format.

Another powerful influence that stimulated rapid Westernization was the economy. In the 1870s, Baku became the capital of the world oil boom. This oil boom marked the beginning of the era of capitalism in Azerbaijan. The British author James Dodds Henry wrote in the early twentieth century, "Baku is greater than any other oil city in the world. If oil is king, Baku is its throne."[9] The world's leading oil companies, as well as prestigious investors such as the Rothschild family and the Swedish Nobel brothers, who later established the Nobel Prize, started branches of their businesses in Azerbaijan. Westerners streamed into the country, creating a demand for Western music and concert life. Simultaneously, a native-born bourgeoisie emerged who invested their fortunes in the development of national music and culture. Azerbaijan's oil barons supported many projects that sought to bring the splendors of Western civilization to Azerbaijan. Businessmen brought in Russian and European architects, who designed hundreds of buildings in the Renaissance and Gothic styles, forever changing the image of Baku.[10] Among these buildings are the Azerbaijan State Philharmonic Hall, erected in 1910, and the Azerbaijan State Opera and Ballet Theater, which was constructed in 1911 and was the first opera house in the Middle East. Oil barons also provided financial aid to many talented native individuals studying in Russia and Europe.

FIGURE 0.3. The Azerbaijan State Philharmonic Hall. *Photo by Aida Huseynova.*

Urbanization, another consequence of the oil boom and of the growing influence of the West, had a decisive impact upon the destiny of the city of Baku and its role in Azerbaijani culture. The historian Audrey Alstadt-Mirhadi has noted that Baku became not just a geographical crossroads, but a site at the forefront of modernity: "For over ten centuries, it [Baku] lay on the frontier between the Christian West and the Muslim East. . . . The oil industry placed the city on the frontier of the Industrial Age, and Baku thus enjoyed the technological and cultural benefits of wealth and development."[11] The new buildings in European styles transformed the city's physical appearance, but of even greater importance was the intense demographic change that occurred as a result of substantial immigration from all neighboring countries. By the early twentieth century, Baku was no longer a purely Eastern city; it was a multicultural metropolis. Large communities of Russians, Jews, Armenians, Poles, Germans, and other ethnic groups coexisted peacefully beside native ethnic Azerbaijanis. This stimulated cultural cosmopolitanism that became typical for the cultural life of Azerbaijan's capital city ever since. Musical pluralism and eclectic variety were the main features of Baku's musical identity. Even as traditional music

FIGURE 0.4. The Azerbaijan State Opera and Ballet Theater. *Photo by Aida Huseynova.*

flourished, the city's social and cultural life featured an impressive variety of concerts and recitals of Russian and European music, productions of opera and ballet, and jazz gigs. The Russian composer Sergei Rachmaninoff, the Polish clavecinist Wanda Landowska, and the Spanish ballerina Isadora Duncan performed for Baku audiences, as did many prominent Italian opera singers and French and German instrumentalists. It is not accidental that this fast-growing city was and continues to be a center of experiments, accomplishments, and failures that contribute to the ongoing process of East-West synthesis in Azerbaijani music and culture.

The emergence of the national intelligentsia was a decisive development in Azerbaijan in the late nineteenth century, and as the historian Benedict Anderson has observed, in colonial contexts, the intelligentsia were indispensable in nationalist movements.[12] By the 1860s, Azerbaijan produced a cohort of bright intellectuals that included poets, writers, musicians, and artists, and these all sought to have their nation be highly educated, free of religious prejudices, and aware of European cultural values. Many of them spoke foreign languages and graduated from prestigious schools in Russia and Europe. Musicians were a central part of this newly formed intelligentsia. They created new musical forms and genres based on East-West synthesis, thus turning over a new page in their national music history, and in global music.

EASTERN ORIGINS OF AZERBAIJANI MUSIC AND CULTURE

My book considers the four periods in Azerbaijani history that have unfolded since the emergence of nationalism and the beginning of East-West synthesis in the early nineteenth century: the Russian Imperial era (1813–1918), the short yet significant period of the Azerbaijan Democratic Republic (ADR; 1918–1920), the Soviet era (1920–1991), and the ongoing period of independence after the collapse of the Soviet Union. Throughout these four historical eras, Azerbaijan's precise relationship to and involvement in various geopolitical regions has shifted and realigned in response to ongoing political changes, and this has affected the development of music as well.

The history of Azerbaijani music over the last two centuries cannot be understood without reference to the deeper past. Azerbaijani culture and music have been shaped by elements of Arab, Persian, and Turkic culture, beginning long before the start of my narrative. Persian influence was the earliest and has been long-lasting and powerful. Since the sixth century BCE, Azerbaijan has been a part of several Persian empires. Under Persian rule in the sixteenth century, Azerbaijanis adopted of the Shia version of Islam, although the initial conversion of Azerbaijanis to Islam occurred as a result of the Arab conquest in the seventh century. As for Turkic influence, it has played a decisive role in shaping the ethnic and linguistic characteristics of Azerbaijanis: the Azerbaijani language derives from Turkic sources, and the Azerbaijani ethnos itself is descended from Turkic tribes that migrated to the territories of modern Azerbaijan and northern Iran. These tribes came as early as the third century CE, and they significantly increased their presence in the eleventh. According to the historians Tadeusz Swietochowski and Brian Collins, it was at this juncture that the vernacular language of the Turkic tribes populating modern Azerbaijan and Iran transformed into "a dialect that evolved into a distinct Azeri-Turkish language."[13]

Arab, Persian, and Turkic elements were combined, filtered, and refined to shape the two major genres of traditional Azerbaijani music: *mugham* and *ashig* art. Although both are equally representative of the nation's cultural identity, they each reflect different facets of it. Azerbaijani *mugham* is a branch of the Arab-Persian *maqam* tradition, which is found in many cultures of the Middle East. *Mugham* derives from urban Azerbaijani culture, particularly the culture of the educated and upper classes. *Mugham* emerged as a vocal-instrumental genre, and in it, performers sing texts from classical poetry, which uses highly refined and elevated language. Mastering *mugham* requires years of extensive training, and historically the genre has been played by professionals for well-educated music lovers who are aware of its many rules and peculiarities. In comparison, the *ashig* tradition developed in rural communities, and it stems from the Turkic tradition of oral narrative that is present from China to the Balkan region. Although the *ashig* tradition is perpetuated through an intense master-apprentice relationship, the art itself is more democratic in nature than *mugham*. *Ashig* is addressed to a wider audience, uses rather simple language and musical formulas, and reflects upon the realities of everyday life. Throughout the history of Azerbaijani music, *mugham* and *ashig* art have interacted and borrowed from each other, and this has continued into the twentieth century, when both *mugham* and *ashig* music traditions entered the orbit of composed music.

The territory of the modern state of Azerbaijan geopolitically left the Eastern hemisphere in the early nineteenth century, when the northern Azerbaijanis became subjects of the Russian Empire. Exhausted by long-standing Persian domination, northern Azerbaijan immediately distanced itself from Iran after leaving its rule, as Alstadt-Mirhadi has noted.[14] In all domains of music, including *mugham,* musicians sought to put a distinct Azerbaijani national stamp on the Eastern musical traditions they had inherited.

Azerbaijan, in a continuing search for national identity, turned toward Turkey. Azerbaijan's affinities with Turkey manifested themselves strongly in literature, due to linguistic similarities between Azerbaijani and Turkish, but less obviously in music. Turkey had been exposed to elements of ancient Byzantine and Balkan music; Azerbaijan had not. Moreover, music in Turkey was historically closely tied to the country's role as the head of an imperial state. In the nineteenth century, the court of Ottoman Turkey invited composers such as Giuseppe Donizetti from Europe and promoted military music, but Azerbaijan, as a colony, did not have the reason or the status to sponsor music in that way.

During the ADR period, Azerbaijan's ties to Turkey continued to flourish and had a more direct effect on music. Ottoman Turkey had supported Azerbaijani independence, and the "Azerbaijani Turkic" ideal was at the center Azerbaijan's musical life during the short period of independence. Azerbaijani composers wrote pieces that highlighted the link between Turkish and Azerbaijani identities, and numerous educational endeavors, cultural initiatives, and concerts took place that promoted Turkish music in Azerbaijan.

Azerbaijan's ties to Iran and Turkey persisted into the Soviet era, despite the complicated relations of the Soviet Union with these latter two countries for the greater part of its history. In 1929, Azerbaijan emulated Turkey's alphabet reform by replacing the old Arabic alphabet with the Latin one, being one of the first Turkic nations to do so. But a decade later, Joseph Stalin changed the alphabet again, this time from Latin to Cyrillic, marking the end of this pro-Turkic campaign, which potentially could have affected the consolidation with Turkey of Azerbaijan and of all the Turkic nations of the Soviet Union. Throughout the following decades of Soviet rule, Azerbaijan's ties with Iran and Turkey were discouraged. Some of the most dangerous accusations Soviet citizens could face during the era of the Stalinist purges in the 1930s were charges of affinities with pan-Iranism and pan-Turkism, and those found guilty faced severe prosecution.

Prohibitions and repressive measures suppressed but did not eliminate Azerbaijan's historical and cultural links with both Iran and Turkey. Soviet Azerbaijanis cherished their ties with Azerbaijanis in Iran, with whom they shared the *mugham* tradition. This musical connection was a powerful source of authenticity that helped shield *mugham* from the destructive impact of Soviet ideology. The music of Soviet Azerbaijan likewise enhanced the musical life of Iranian Azerbaijanis, exposing them to the forms and genres of Western art music. When I first came to the United States in the early 2000s, I was amazed that Azerbaijanis, immigrants from Iran, had a high level of familiarity with the Azerbaijani composed music repertoire I grew up with. Historical events of the late 1940s stimulated the link in the field of composed music between the two parts the Azerbaijani people. In 1945, the Soviets attempted to establish an independent republic of Southern Azerbaijan, and the Azerbaijani composer Jahangir Jahangirov (1921–1992) wrote the national anthem for this new state-to-be. The Soviets' plan failed. Ethnic Azerbaijanis from Iran who had supported the Soviets' so-called democratic movement came to Baku and other cities in Azerbaijan and stayed, being unable to reunite with their families in Iran. A new motif emerged in the cultural production of Azerbaijan: the idea of separation, or of longing for a land lost. This concept, prominent in Azerbaijani literature, also became important in music.

During the Soviet era, Azerbaijani music never abandoned its connection to Turkey. One figure responsible for maintaining Azerbaijani-Turkish ties was the Turkish poet Nazim Hikmet (1902–1963), who had to flee from Turkey in 1951 and reside in Moscow because of his communist views. Azerbaijani writers and composers immediately established close professional and personal affiliations with Hikmet. Hikmet visited the city of Baku and benefitted from the Azerbaijanis' hospitality; they gave the exiled poet the opportunity to speak his native language and allowed him to be part of a community that shared similar cultural values. Likewise, for Azerbaijanis, the Turkish poet served as a bridge across the Iron Curtain to the Turkic culture from which they had been forcibly separated. The Azerbaijani composer Garayev became Hikmet's lifelong friend. He wrote several pieces inspired by Hikmet's literary works and established a "Turkish line" in Azerbaijani composed music that continues to the present day.[15] The ballet *The Legend of Love* (1961) by Arif Malikov (b. 1933), choreographed by the celebrated Russian Iurii Grigorovich, remains the best musical embodiment of Hikmet's poetry that appeared in Azerbaijani music, and it is one of the masterpieces of the Soviet sphere. The *New York Times* wrote on the day after the premiere of Malikov's ballet in Mariinsky Theater, "*The Legend of Love* is the departure of the rigid classic style of Soviet ballet. . . . The ballet recounts a fairy tale in ancient Turkish setting. But within this traditional framework, the Russian choreographer, Uri [Iurii] Grigorovich, achieved an expressionism of modernity and freedom of movement."[16] The ballet was performed in more than sixty theaters worldwide and was recognized as "a revolutionary development in the history of Soviet ballet" because of the combination of vivid dramatic music with innovative choreography.[17] With the new premiere of *The Legend of Love* performed in October 2014, this work is now back in the repertoire of the Russia's Bolshoi Theater.

At present, Azerbaijan's ties with Iran, musical and otherwise, are not as strong as they once were or could be. The current political situation in the

Islamic Republic of Iran, a relatively closed country ruled by religious dogmas, generally discourages activity in the field of music. Yet exchanges between Azerbaijan and Iran continue in the domain of traditional music, benefitting both parties. In contrast, Azerbaijan's connections with Turkey are flourishing. The political concept *"bir millat–iki dovlat"* (one nation–two states), advanced in the mid-1990s, clearly identifies the main priority of the foreign policy of the Republic of Azerbaijan: close relations, and in fact brotherhood, with Turkey. This policy recalls the period of the ADR: Azerbaijani composers create large-scale works inspired by Turkish themes and subjects, and they write pieces of popular music depicting Turkish styles. Another channel of the growing Azerbaijani-Turkish connection is the large stream of Azerbaijani musicians who received contracts in various Turkish universities and music institutions. These expatriates significantly contribute to the development of Western musical forms in that country.

MUSICAL AND CULTURAL LINKS WITH
TRANSCAUCASIA AND CENTRAL ASIA

Two more regional contexts – the Transcaucasian and the Central Asian – affected the development of Azerbaijani music during the last two hundred years, although with different levels of intensity and in different domains of music. Azerbaijan's links with Georgia and Armenia were facilitated by Russian imperialism during the nineteenth century, when all three countries were provinces of the Russian Empire. Georgia and Armenia are Christian and have distinctive musical heritages, including multivoiced choral singing, that differentiate them from Islamic Azerbaijan. Moreover, by the early twentieth century, Georgian and Armenian composers already possessed considerable experience in terms of mastering the forms and genres of Western music, and their nations' geographical proximity stimulated multiculturalism in Azerbaijani music. The Gori Seminary in Georgia, which offered classes on Western classical music, became the alma mater of the pioneers of Azerbaijani composed music, including Hajibeyli and Magomayev. Armenia and Georgia, in turn, benefited from increased exposure to forms and genres of music originating in the Islamic culture of Azerbaijan. *Mugham* was adopted in Armenia, although primarily in its instrumental form, since the Armenian language did not meet the requirements of the *aruz*, a poetic system that has its basis in Arabic, Persian, and Turkic languages and that was essential in the emergence of *mugham*. *Ashig* music, a product of Turkic tradition, was spread over Transcaucasia, and a cohort of trilingual artists performed in the Azerbaijani, Armenian, and Georgian languages. These processes of integration began well before the nineteenth century, although they intensified during the Russian Imperial era. Works of local Azerbaijani composers were regularly shared with audiences in neighboring countries, expanding the range of Azerbaijani music's popularity. Hajibeyli's operetta *The Cloth Peddler* (1913) is illustrative in this regard: this Azerbaijani piece was translated into Armenian and Georgian and performed in three languages in Tiflis, Georgia, on September 2, 1915, thus serving as a musical symbol unifying the three nations of Transcaucasia.[18]

Azerbaijan has many ethnic, linguistic, religious, and cultural commonalities with Central Asia, but the development of Western musical forms in Azerbaijan and Central Asia has followed divergent paths. The majority of Central Asia was subjugated to the Russian Empire only in the 1860s, that is, later than Azerbaijan. Unlike Azerbaijan, which was quickly industrialized because of the oil boom in the late nineteenth century, the Central Asian nations never experienced capitalism, which was a strong force in Azerbaijan. Instead, they jumped from feudalism to socialism after the Soviets took over in the twentieth century. Strong secularist tendencies distinguished Azerbaijani intellectuals from those in Central Asia. As Alstadt-Mirhadi has noted, the antireligious campaign in Azerbaijan in the early twentieth century was "no less virulent than subsequent Soviet attacks."[19] By way of comparison, Jadidism, the most prominent intellectual stream in Central Asia in the late nineteenth and early twentieth centuries, held the modernization of Islam as its central tenet. Thus, the many differences between Azerbaijan and Central Asia minimized commonalities in their cultural progress during the Russian Imperial and Soviet eras.

In contradistinction to Central Asia, Azerbaijan already possessed the forms and genres of Western composed music by the Soviet era. Uzbekistan established its first opera theater in 1939 and had its first native opera in the same year, whereas Azerbaijan had its first opera house in 1911 and its first opera in 1908. The first conservatory of music in Uzbekistan's capital, Tashkent, opened in 1936, versus 1921 in Baku. But only considering dates masks an even more important difference: Russian composers wrote the first pieces of composed music in Uzbekistan and in other parts of Central Asia that remained under the Soviets, and the first native composers in those nations often coauthored their works with Russians composers. In Azerbaijan, the native composer Hajibeyli already had established the foundations of national composed music styles in the early twentieth century, and he was surrounded and followed by a cohort of native Azerbaijani composers who have advanced and implemented all developments in Azerbaijan's national composed music ever since. Initially, the Soviets did not acknowledge Azerbaijan's unique position, and in the 1920s, the regime sent the Russian composer Gliere to Baku, with the mission of facilitating the development of composed music there. Nonetheless – and mainly due to Gliere's unsuccessful experience – the Soviets soon realized that this small Muslim nation was already able to rely on its own resources in the field of composed music and that it should be treated differently from its ethnic and cultural relatives on the other side of the Caspian Sea.

This phenomenon reflects a more general tendency, Azerbaijan's relatively low level of Russification, which distinguished it from many Central Asian nations. Several political scientists attest to Azerbaijan's strong resistance to Russification policies in various periods of the country's Soviet history. Chantal Lemercier-Quelquejay recognizes Azerbaijanis as "the least russified of all Muslim Turkic peoples of the USSR."[20] William Fierman indicates that Azerbaijan experienced significantly less Russification than Kazakhstan did. He accounts for this in three ways: through geography, noting that Azerbaijan was separated from Russia by the Caucasus Mountains; through history, as Russia's political and cultural influence in Azerbaijan was always balanced by Iran, and Azerbaijanis maintained close links with their coethnics in Iran and with Turkey; and through demography, since ethnic Azerbaijanis have continuously been the majority of the population in their republic.[21] Fierman also mentions the less aggressive character of the Soviets' Russification policy in Azerbaijan, Armenia, and Georgia: only these three republics out of the fifteen Soviet republics were able to retain reference to the titular language as the republic state language.[22] Accordingly, in terms of Russian influence, Azerbaijan was more integrated in the Transcaucasian geopolitical context than the Central Asian one, and this affected the field of music as well.

Another musical characteristic that aligned Soviet Azerbaijan more closely with Transcaucasia than with Central Asia was that Azerbaijan was oriented toward mastering Western music as a cultural form, whereas the Central Asian republics, following Soviet preferences, were more drawn to strictly European models. That is, in Central Asia, the forms of composed music that emerged in Europe in the eighteenth and nineteenth centuries, and the styles typical of these periods, such as the classical and the romantic, served as the main models to be emulated, leaving the full breadth of contemporary Western music conspicuously absent. As the ethnomusicologist Theodore Levin has observed in writing about the emergence of new musical forms in Uzbekistan, there is a difference between Europeanization and Westernization: "I use the term 'Europeanization' rather than 'Westernization' or 'Modernization' because it was specifically European models that Soviet ideologists had in mind as they planned the cultural future of Central Asia."[23] Such a program of "Europeanization" can partly be explained by the priorities of Russian composers, who claimed to be a part of European (rather than Western) music. But more pertinent is that the very definition of "the West" had a strong ideological subtext in the Soviet era because the West was associated with capitalism and referred to a part of the world toward which the Soviet Union was antagonistic. However, in Azerbaijan, the paradigm of Europeanization is not germane, since Westernization and modernization began in the late nineteenth century and continued into the Soviet era. The fast and fruitful development of jazz is the main indicator of a process of Westernization rather than Europeanization, and jazz reflects Azerbaijani music's Transcaucasian affinities, since both Armenia and Georgia had strong passion for and accomplishments in the field of jazz music. In contrast, the Central Asian republics never experienced such a vibrant and popular jazz culture during the Soviet era or afterward.

Accordingly, in its development of composed music, jazz, and Western performance forms, Azerbaijani music paralleled Transcaucasia more closely than Central Asia.[24] During the Soviet era, Transcaucasian music festivals held on a regular basis showcased the major accomplishments of Azerbaijan, Georgia, and Armenia in these respective areas, and they also strengthened Transcaucasian solidarity.[25] Distinctively, the field of traditional music became a significant cultural expression linking Azerbaijan and the Central Asian nations. Throughout the decades of Soviet rule, Azerbaijani *mugham* developed in close, regular, and profitable contact with the relative music traditions of Central Asia; that contact continues to the present day. Traditional musicians performed at festivals, and ethnomusicologists participated in conferences and symposiums held in various cities in Central Asia. Both activities drew together leading performers and scholars from throughout the Middle East and Central Asia and were followed by publications of papers and releases of recordings.[26] In Samargand, Levin first heard the *mugham* singer Alim Gasimov and invited him to participate in the Smithsonian Folklife Festival, which was held in Washington, DC, in 1988. This festival marked the beginning of the wide recognition in the West of Gasimov and of the Azerbaijani *mugham* that continues to the present.

In the sphere of traditional music, close collaboration between Azerbaijan and Central Asian nations has continued into the post-Soviet era and beyond. Azerbaijan's historically strong ties to Transcaucasia have weakened on some fronts after the collapse of the Soviet Union. Relations with Georgia have remained strong over the last two decades, but Azerbaijani cultural and musical ties with Armenia have been abruptly cut off because of a territorial conflict over the Garabagh district of Azerbaijan (this confrontation is often referred to as the Nagorno-Karabakh conflict). Hostilities began in 1988 and escalated into war with Armenia, leading to occupation of more than 20 percent of Azerbaijan's territory. The Azerbaijani *mugham* has suffered, since Garabagh has historically been one of main centers of this art.

Despite the abundance of the geopolitical factors – or rather thanks to them – Azerbaijani music has developed and preserved its unique voice in all fields, from *mugham* to opera. Because Azerbaijanis have a wealth of cultural elements from many different regions that they can draw upon and synthesize, Azerbaijanis have a natural versatility that has enabled them to adjust in the face of vast historical change.

MUGHAM: A BRIEF INTRODUCTION

This book has consistent and substantial references to *mugham,* and it would be useful to include a brief survey of this tradition. The native ethnomusicologist Sanubar Baghirova defines Azerbaijani *mugham* as a mode, a melodic type, and a genre.[27] *Mugham* is seen as a reflection of the Islamic aesthetic of a spiritual journey toward universal truth. The sojourn progresses through many stages of acquirement of knowledge. This spiritual idea affected the structure of *mugham.* In it, each new musical section features a gradual increase in pitch and in intensity of modal development. Scholars both inside and outside of Azerbaijan have thoroughly studied the modal system of *mugham,* its aesthetics, compositional and stylistic peculiarities, and performing practices.[28] There have been two foundational theoretical studies of the modal system of *mugham.* The first was undertaken by Hajibeyli from the 1910s to the 1940s. He considered the structure of the *mugham* modes to be based upon four types of tetrachords that can be combined in four different ways.[29] The second theoretical study was conducted by the native ethnomusicologist Mammad Saleh Ismayilov in the 1970s. He explained the inner integrity of the modal system of Azerbaijani music through the idea of the diminished octave.[30] According to Ismayilov, all scales, regardless of the types of tetrachords they employ and the ways in which those tetrachords are connected, contain the interval of the diminished octave, and through this interval, all modal and tonal changes, in both traditional music and in the oeuvres of the national composers, occur in the most natural and seamless way. Presented here are charts of the main Azerbaijani modes as defined by Hajibeyli and Ismayilov. Despite their differences, both paradigms are related, and they explore the modal system of *mugham* in the same stream: all scales are built upon two or three tetrachords, with the tonic never coinciding with the opening pitch. Ismayilov only suggests different interpretations of the

EXAMPLE 0.1. The modes of Azerbaijani music.

modes *humayun* and *chahargah,* and he considers *zabul* to be one of the main modes; Hajibeyli includes *zabul* in the category of the secondary modes.

But the scales themselves do not provide a complete picture of the Azerbaijani modes. These modes come to life and exist only as a sum of certain melodic patterns that are indicative of each mode. For example, the patterns typical of *rast* do not coincide with those of *shur*, despite the similarity of the scales of these respective modes. The role of the central tone, or tonic, is of extreme importance in the Azerbaijani modes. The tonic serves as a powerful center of gravity, and it constantly returns in the course of the *mugham*'s thematic development. The apex of improvisation in the *mugham* genre involves extensive representation of the tonic in the upper register. As such, the lower tonic and the upper tonic have different roles in the process of modal development. As seen from the examples, some modes show a duality of tonal centers: the so-called basic tone competes with the tonic in terms of serving as the principal tone of the scale. In addition, each section of *mugham* has its own tonal center, with a pitch that serves as a temporary tonic. As the *mugham* improvisation unfolds, these temporary tonal centers move up the scale. *Mugham* composition has a cyclic form: improvisational parts (*shoba*) alternate with song-like (*tasnif*) and dance-like (*rang*) sections. In *shoba*, the performer demonstrates his or her mastery of improvisation; *tasnif* and *rang* provide both performers and listeners with the chance to rest before going to the next stage of improvisation. *Mugham* exists in vocal, instrumental, and mixed forms. It is usually performed by a trio: a singer (*khanende*) also plays *gaval*, the frame drum, and two other instrumentalists play the *tar*, which is a long-necked lute, and the *kemancha*, which is a spike fiddle.

Hajibeyli divided Azerbaijani *mughams* into seven major groups, or families: *rast, shur, segah, chahargah, bayati-shiraz, shushtar,* and *humayun,* and he delineated the semantics of each *mugham*. According to him, *rast* creates feelings of courage and cheerfulness; *shur* is associated with a joyful and lyrical mood; *segah* is associated with love; *bayati-shiraz* conveys grief; *chahargah* is passionate and agitated; *shushtar* causes deep sorrow; *humayun* is distinguished by deep or, compared to *shushtar*, deeper sorrow.[31] But these characterizations are only generalizations; each *mugham* has more semantic nuances.

Mugham has served as a solid foundation for Azerbaijani music for centuries. It was preserved and transmitted aurally – primarily, through the centuries-old cultural form of *majlis*. *Majlis*, a public gathering of musicians, poets, and art lovers, resembled the European tradition of music salons and were similarly held in private houses. *Majlis* participants shared their mastery of performing traditional music and poetic recitations. Accordingly, the *majlis* combined creativity and education, serving as an effective means of passing down knowledge of *mugham* and other forms of traditional music from accomplished masters to younger generations. Since the twelfth century, the *majlis* tradition has existed in many Azerbaijani cities. Those in the Garabagh area, Shamakhi, and Baku, however, had a particularly high status. In the late nineteenth and early twentieth centuries, *mugham* entered the space of East-West syncretism and has remained a significant and constant source for nativism in Azerbaijani music ever since, affecting all genres of composed music and jazz, as well as music education.

INSIDE THIS BOOK

The chapters in this book consider historical, social, aesthetic, and stylistic aspects of East-West syncretism in Azerbaijani music. Chapter 1 examines Westernization and modernization in Azerbaijani music during the pre-Soviet and Soviet eras. Through entering the political orbit of Russia in the early nineteenth century, Azerbaijan became separated from the Eastern hemisphere within which it had developed for centuries, and this change helped Azerbaijanis to comprehend their own distinctive identity. As a part of the Russian Empire, Azerbaijan gained access to the treasures of Western music and methods of Western music education. All this facilitated strong integration of Western values as Azerbaijani nationalism developed in the nineteenth century, and eventually it brought about native composed music in the early twentieth century. *Leyli and Majnun* (1908), by Hajibeyli, was the first piece of composed music ever written in Azerbaijan and the first precedent of the unique genre defined as "*mugham* opera." East-West synthesis continued during the Soviet era. The national and cultural policies of the Soviets strengthened both the development of native traditions for each nation and the mastery of (or refinement of already mastered) Western forms and genres. Hajibeyli's *Koroghlu* (1937) marked the emergence of Azerbaijani national musical style and paved the path for the further explorations of Azerbaijani composers and their mastering of all major styles of Western music. Nationalism under the Soviets was complicated and dramatic because communist ideology imposed rules that distorted the free progress and exchange of ideas, and this chapter aims to show the dynamics created during the "Janus-faced" Soviet era.

Chapter 2 explores the role of three Azerbaijani composers whose careers can be understood in light of the Herderian theory of cultural nationalism. Hajibeyli, the pioneer of composed music in Azerbaijan, was a musician, writer, journalist, educator, and scholar, and in all of his professional roles, he championed the national ideal. Garayev and Fikrat Amirov (1922–1984) continued to develop the already established field of East-West synthesis, and they established the opposition of "Westernizers" and "Easternizers" essential for Azerbaijani music in the period that followed. Garayev developed a new, supranational vision of Azerbaijani music as a part of global music, and he showed Azerbaijanis their place as a part of the world community. Amirov's works revealed the more distinctively Middle Eastern heritage of Azerbaijani music.

Any exploration of the East depicted by means of the West cannot help but refer to the cultural critic Edward Said.[32] I agree with the colonial subtext of the term *orientalism* that Said first suggested in defining orientalism as a style that signified domination of West over East, and I also recognize the colonial subtext the musicologist Richard Taruskin continues to explore in his research on Russian musical orientalism.[33] For historical reasons, I support the musicologist Marina Frolova-Walker's argument that the revival of Russian nationalism in Soviet music since the 1930s led composers from the former Eastern provinces of the Russian Empire to adopt the orientalist models of Russian composers.[34] But I disagree with her vision of Russian musical orientalism as the benchmark of musical style in non-Russian republics, particularly Azerbaijan. Azerbaijani composed music was born in the early twentieth century, before the Soviet era. Despite the many deviations and adjustments caused by Soviet ideology, one can still trace a solid and unbreakable line of succession through the twentieth-century history of Azerbaijani music. Some national composers were influenced by Russian musical orientalism, since it was natural for composers in the young art music tradition to consider how established Russian composers had so powerfully depicted the East. But the true discoveries of Azerbaijani composers lay in reimagining and reinterpreting the well-known forms and genres of Western music through the lens of their native music and culture rather than through Russian orientalist clichés. For example, Russian orientalist tropes could not offer a way of creating the tonal structure of sonata form via the national mode *shur,* or of using ternary form to project the contrasts typical of *mugham* composition. And these are the true accomplishments of Azerbaijani composers that allowed and encouraged me to pursue this study. Azerbaijanis were aware of the developments of Russian music, but I am more concerned with Russian music as a model of professionalism and a source of stylistic updates rather than as one for direct compositional emulation. This opposition of "Russian oriental" versus "Azerbaijani national" aesthetic approaches and stylistic means is discussed in several sections of the book.

Chapter 3 presents two contrasting stories that show how Russian musicians became involved in the process of Azerbaijanis mastering Western styles. The first case study is of Gliere, who failed in his attempt in the 1920s to reshape Azerbaijani composed music into an oriental branch of Russian music. The second case study concerns Shostakovich, who stimulated the development of the symphony and the overall growth of professionalism in Azerbaijani music after the 1940s. Shostakovich's influence on Azerbaijan went well beyond typical "intra-Soviet" cultural and national exchange. He had close ties with Garayev, his student and lifelong friend. Shostakovich had a deep personal connection with Elmira Nazirova (1928–2014), his female student, and embedded her name in the Tenth Symphony. Having studied with Nazirova at the Baku Music Academy, I maintained a friendship with her that allowed me access to this story and to the letters sent to her by Shostakovich. Drawing upon my personal communications with Nazirova, my book will bring to light the history of her intimate friendship with Shostakovich.

Chapters 4, 5, and 6 delineate and explore the various stylistic sources of Western music that influenced Azerbaijani composers. These sources include Viennese classicism, romanticism, the Italian operatic tradition, French impressionism, Shostakovich, Prokofiev, Igor Stravinsky, the Second Viennese School, and various modern and postmodern styles. I analyze the aesthetic and stylistic fusion of these Western musical means with national Azerbaijani music idioms. The result was new compositional models – both for Azerbaijani and Western music. Pieces by leading national composers included in this analysis show the variety of forms and genres present in the panorama of Azerbaijani composed music. Chapter 7 introduces the rich and versatile song tradition of Azerbaijan. In contradistinction to those working in the other genres of composed music, Azerbaijani songwriters have not strongly emulated Western music, thus preserving traditional characteristics to the present day.

That Russia has never been the only source of influence on Azerbaijani music is also manifested by the growing popularity of American jazz in Azerbaijan across the whole of the twentieth century, including during the Soviet era, despite all prohibitions imposed by the Soviets. Jazz has become not only a significant part of the national soundscape, but also a source of impressive accomplishments in the international arena. Chapter 8 introduces the "jazz *mugham*," the predominant style of Azerbaijani jazz since the 1960s, and discusses the characteristics of "jazz *mugham*" fusion, which was founded by Vagif Mustafazade (1940–1979).

The era of Russian-Soviet political dominance and strong influence on Azerbaijan and its music is over, and even the post-Soviet era is behind us. If all the new forms of music that emerged during the centuries of Russian-Soviet rule had been artificially created due to imperial or Soviet policy, then it would be time for them to pass into oblivion. But the realities of contemporary Azerbaijani music show rather the opposite: composed music continues to develop, jazz is at center of musical life, and music schools of the Western type are at the peak of their popularity. Growing nativism and exposure to the West, without any mediating force, is the main feature of musical life in contemporary Azerbaijan. The country's historical victory at the Eurovision song contest in 2012, as well as the wide range of activities focusing on *mugham* held both inside and outside of the country, show these new tendencies. The economy has a valuable share in shaping Azerbaijani life, too, and again, because of an oil boom – a second one – that began in the mid-1990s. Chapter 9 considers new forms of East-West synthesis, as well as the problems and change in priorities that Azerbaijani music is now experiencing. Chapter 10 and the epilogue explore the paradigms of East-West synthesis that emerged out of the country and that show the continuing importance of the pieces created by the national composers before and during the Soviet era. I report on a new chamber arrangement of Azerbaijan's first opera, Hajibeyli's *Leyli and Majnun,* made by the Silk Road Ensemble under artistic direction of Yo-Yo Ma in 2007–2009. The chapter includes an interview with Yo-Yo Ma in which he shares his views of this project and of Azerbaijani music as an East-West phenomenon. The epilogue introduces the Kronos Quartet's collaboration with Azerbaijani musicians and the quartet's input on Azerbaijani musical synthesis as it is on the cusp of a fresh and exciting stage of its history.

Both the subject and object of this book – study of the composed music produced by a non-Western culture – required integrating methods and approaches pertaining to both ethnomusicology and musicology. This brings us back to the discussions that took place in the scholarly publications of the past century. In his article about the new scholarship on nineteenth-century Europe, the ethnomusicologist Philip Bohlman mentions scholarship's eventual progress toward "a new understanding of music and history both in the culture of 'the Other' – that is, the non-European world – and in Europe itself."[35] Referring primarily to the music of the Middle East, the author points out that "the discovery and investigation of non-Western music had provided fundamental evidence for the emergence of one of the axial endeavors of modern musicology: the attribution of historical process to music."[36] The composed music, jazz, and popular music of Azerbaijan are appropriate subjects for ethnomusicological study because they emerged outside of the Western world and are strongly connected to traditional music. Nonetheless, conceptually and stylistically, they are indebted to paradigms of Western music. The artistic result has a value not only as a new product of the native music system but also as a new stratum of Western music. Hence ethnomusicology and musicology become one in the present research, while I also take into account viewpoints from within the culture itself. The purpose is not only to show what Azerbaijanis borrowed from the West to create their national composed music, but also to demonstrate how their findings enhanced the panorama of Western forms and styles. My research does more than bring to light notable accomplishments of Azerbaijani musicians in the field of East-West synthesis: I do hope that my study is not just another chapter in the history of Western music, but one that calls for a reevaluation of what the history of music should be.

1 AZERBAIJANI MUSICAL NATIONALISM DURING THE PRE-SOVIET AND SOVIET ERAS

> At the intersection of new and old in the early twentieth
> century Azerbaijanian composed music was born.
>
> INNA NARODITSKAYA, *Song from the Land of Fire*

THE EMERGENCE OF MUSICAL NATIONALISM

When Geography Turns into History

A great geopolitical transformation occurred in Transcaucasia between 1813 and 1828. As a result of the Russo-Persian wars, Russia annexed Persia's (Iran's) northern territories populated by ethnic Azerbaijanis. Subjugation to Russia profoundly altered the history of the Azerbaijani people. For centuries, all Azerbaijanis had been a part of the Eastern hemisphere, had predominantly practiced Shia Islam, and had spoken vernacular Azerbaijani Turkic. Now the southern part of the Azerbaijani ethnos remained in the Persian Empire, while the northern part belonged to the Russian Empire, in which Orthodox Christianity was the prevailing religion and Russian, a Slavic tongue, the official language. Just as tectonic plates move and realign during an earthquake, so too did the geopolitical ties that shaped the development of Azerbaijani music and culture find a new balance in the face of vast historical change.

Azerbaijan remained a colonial state, but Russia imposed its distinct cultural energies on Northern Azerbaijanis' social and cultural life. For the first time in Azerbaijani history, music and culture became involved in a direct, intense, and multifaceted encounter with Western music, education, and forms of concert life. This situation provoked two responses. The first, the more natural and expected one, can conditionally be called "cosmopolitanism," which was marked by Westernization and modernization in all domains of life, including music. The second reaction was what Alstadt-Mirhadi calls "localism," which is "not merely the study of local history and language, which began soon after the Russian conquest, but pride in the local heritage."[1] Together, localism and cosmopolitanism were a powerful impetus to the rise of nationalism, and they shaped the national identity of Azerbaijanis. Political geographer Robert Kaiser argues that "state-sponsored 'Russification' during the late nineteenth century was at least partially responsible for rising national self-consciousness in the non-Russian periphery."[2] Another powerful factor that stimulated the emergence of Azerbaijani national identity was the oil boom and its many repercussions, which spurred the development of capitalism in Azerbaijan. Music, which held a high status in traditional Azerbaijani society and culture, appropriately played a central and prominent role in the rise of nationalism.

Freed from the cultural hegemony of Iran, Azerbaijani musicians sought to create their own national musical tradition by developing a musical language that could be understood as specifically "Azerbaijani." Azerbaijan's most emblematic traditional music – the quintessential genre, *mugham,* and the most popular plucked string instrument, the *tar,* – demonstrate this process. Azerbaijani *mugham* had developed for centuries as a branch of the large Middle Eastern and Central Asian *maqam* tradition, with Persian *destgah* as the Azerbaijani *mugham*'s closest relative. By the 1870s, Azerbaijani musicians had established *mugham* as an independent genre, with unique modal, melodic, and structural characteristics that distinguished it from parallel genres. *Mugham* also acquired a more specific Azerbaijani textual identity by the early twentieth century thanks to the Azerbaijani *khanende,* or *mugham* singer Jabbar Garyaghdioghlu (1861–1944). He was the first to perform *mugham* in Azerbaijani, rather than Persian, and Azerbaijani musicians ever since have followed his example.

Comparative study of the Azerbaijani *mugham* and the Persian *destgah* remains important in contemporary ethnomusicological research, and scholars even beyond Azerbaijan have traced how *mugham* developed a distinct national identity as Azerbaijani musicians synthesized characteristics from the many different musical and cultural traditions with which they engaged. Jean During, a French scholar and one of the world's leading experts on *mugham,* notes the following features distinguish the Azerbaijani *mugham* from the Persian *destgah:* "the influence of *ashig* songs," "a tendency toward extraversion, dramatization vs. introversion," and "a greater tendency to heterophony or polyphony."[3] As explained in the introduction, the *ashig* tradition was of Turkic, rather than Persian, origin, and this democratic genre addressed a wide audience. *Ashig* music's powerful presence accounts at least in part for the more extraverted nature of Azerbaijani *mugham*. Intense multicultural processes shaping the development of Azerbaijani music since the early nineteenth century stimulated musicians' realization of the polyphonic potential of *mugham*.

Modification of the *tar* in the 1870s was another sign of the growing desire for a specifically Azerbaijani national music tradition. During attests to this tendency in writing about Mirza Sadig Asadoghlu (1846–1902), known as Sadigjan, who invented the Azerbaijani *tar*, which replaced the Persian *tar* across Caucasia. According to During, the revolutionary rise of the Azerbaijani *tar* was, above all, a revelation of the ever-strengthening identity of the young Azerbaijani nation.[4] The Azerbaijani *tar* had a brighter timbre and more opportunities for virtuosic display than its Persian counterpart did, since Sadigjan increased the number of strings from five to eleven, straightened the back of the sound cavity, and changed the position in which one plays the instrument so that it is held on the chest instead of on the knees. Azerbaijani musicians soon exploited these unique qualities. Until nowadays, *mugham* and the *tar* continue to serve as the major national musical emblems of Azerbaijan; both have been included in the UNESCO (United Nations Educational, Scientific, and Cultural Organization) Representative List of the Intangible Cultural Heritage of Humanity, *mugham* in 2003, and the *tar* in 2012.

Azerbaijani traditional music developed more distinct national traits in the hands of the native musicians, but Westernization and modernization also exerted their influence on Azerbaijani music. Recording technologies expanded the audience of *mugham* far beyond Azerbaijan's borders. From 1909 to 1915, Garyaghdioghlu and his ensemble traveled to Warsaw, Riga, and Kyiv at the invitation of Sport-Record and Gramophone to record *mugham* compositions. Their popularity was indisputable: in May of 1909 alone, Garyaghdioghlu recorded twenty-five separate tracks with the Gramophone Company, and twelve of them were released by the end of the year.[5] Thus, even as Azerbaijanis were affected by Westernization, they also exported their traditional music to the West.

But a more important development occurred within a country: in the early twentieth century, for the first time in Azerbaijan's history, *mugham,* which was traditionally played and appreciated within a narrow circle of music lovers, came onto public stages. In 1901 and 1902, Baku had a series of Western-style concerts, titled Eastern Concerts, which featured Azerbaijani *mughams*. The appearance of renowned masters of native music on stage was of decisive importance, allowing the audience to become accustomed to hearing *mugham* in the setting of a large theater. Such performances were a vital precedent of the uniquely national *mugham* opera, a genre created a few years later that marked the birth of composed music in Azerbaijan.

FIGURE 1.1. Uzeyir Hajibeyli. *Courtesy of the State Museum of Azerbaijani Musical Culture.*

1908: Beginning of Azerbaijani Composed Music

An incredible musical breakthrough symbolized Azerbaijanis' growing self-identity: the twenty-three-year-old Uzeyir Hajibeyli wrote the opera *Leyli and Majnun.* The work premiered in Baku on January 25, 1908, ushering in the era of composed music in Azerbaijan that continues to the present day. The significance of Hajibeyli's work extends far beyond Azerbaijan. For centuries, oral music traditions were the only native ones in the entire Muslim East. Hajibeyli forged a new path.

Leyli and Majnun was later defined as *mugham* opera because it combined *mugham* in its traditional form with elements of Western opera. Hajibeyli replaced classical operatic arias with *mughams*, which were improvised in the course of operatic performance. Choruses and ensemble numbers, appearing between the improvised *mugham* sections, were fully notated. Even so, these choruses and ensembles were written in the style of the song-like and dance-like interludes characteristic of the traditional *mugham* form. Because of the juxtaposition of these two elements – sophisticated improvised parts and relatively simple notated episodes – *Leyli and Majnun* can be seen as one, large *mugham*, presenting on a grand scale the contrasts and aesthetic of progression found in traditional *mugham*. This is why the musicologist Elmira Abasova defines this genre as not simply *mugham* opera, but as "opera-*mugham*."[6]

Leyli and Majnun was enthusiastically received by music lovers, supporters of Hajibeyli's ideas, and Azerbaijani society in general, as shown by the remarkable story of its premiere. The performance was sold out long before the opening night, but, hoping to get in, a huge crowd came to the square in front of the theater. When the theater was completely full, Hajibeyli requested that all the windows and doors be opened so that people outside could listen to the opera. Everybody stayed for almost three hours despite the cold winter weather. As one reviewer wrote, "After *Leyli and Majnun* . . . Muslim audiences that had enjoyed all these European style theatrical productions, were not interested in the old-style performances anymore."[7] Inspired by the success of *Leyli and Majnun,* Hajibeyli wrote five more *mugham* operas in which he successively increased the presence of Western features, as for example he included more choral episodes and arias and reduced the number of *mughams*.[8]

The other pioneer of art music in Azerbaijan, Muslim Magomayev, initiated an even more radical way of westernizing *mugham* opera: his *Shah Ismayil* (1916) combines *mughams* with operatic arias, and he alternates using traditional Azerbaijani singing style and Western bel canto, which he fuses with traditional music idioms (see chapter 4). Still, no other composition could achieve the artistic level of *Leyli and Majnun,* which remains the purest embodiment of the idea of *mugham* opera and is a work of unparalleled historical significance in Azerbaijani music. Krebs acknowledges the uniqueness of *mugham* opera, describing Hajibeyli's *Leyli and Majnun* as "still the closest to a truly Azerbaidzhanian opera any composer has written."[9] Krebs problematically narrows nationalism in Azerbaijani composed music to the direct use of traditional music, whereas Azerbaijani composers throughout the twentieth century and beyond have found many subtle ways to incorporate their national heritage. Nonetheless, Krebs conveys the two essential characteristics of

Hajibeyli's work: first, its being an opera; and second, its being a product of the national music of Azerbaijan.

Some scholars do not believe that *Leyli and Majnun* is truly composed music because of the extensive presence of *mugham* within it. Frolova-Walker argues that "the results [of Hajibeyli's work] did little more than . . . highlight the incongruity of two very different musical traditions," and she denies the value of *Leyli and Majnun* as the beginning of composed music in Azerbaijan.[10] I contend that *Leyli and Majnun* is a fusion, rather than an incongruous mishmash, of two different musical traditions, and that it is a product of the composed music tradition. The very concept of this work results from individual creativity as opposed to the collective creativity typical of traditional music. The musical language of the written episodes includes harmony, orchestration, and form, drawing on the conventional means of Western composed music. And at a deeper level, Hajibeyli engages with the same intellectual issues as did modernist composers in Europe. His compositional language may be simpler than that of Schoenberg or Ravel, but Hajibeyli just innovatively creates a fusion of past and present. The combination of many chronological, cultural, aesthetic, and stylistic layers in this first Azerbaijani opera has drawn the attention of numerous contemporary musicians, most notably the Silk Road Ensemble and its artistic director, Yo-Yo Ma. In 2007, they created a new arrangement of *Leyli and Majnun* that realized the rich multicultural potential of Hajibeyli's work and made it a part of contemporary soundscapes (see chapter 10).[11]

Even if one were to argue that *mugham* opera is not composed music, composed music still began in Azerbaijan before the Soviet era. Hajibeyli composed three operettas that do not involve *mugham* and are entirely notated.[12] Among them *The Cloth Peddler* (1913) is particularly significant on several counts. The plot reflects the realities of contemporaneous Azerbaijani society, particularly drawing attention to issues of spiritual freedom and women's emancipation. The elaborate vocal style transcends the generic norms of operetta and is closer to comic opera. Some passages are reminiscent of folk melodies, but most of the musical material is entirely original. Thus, in both music and plot, *The Cloth Peddler* exemplifies a perfect balance of localism and cosmopolitanism, which might explain its enormous popularity both within and outside of Azerbaijan. This operetta has been translated into about eighty languages and performed in about two hundred theaters across the world. It was filmed four times (in 1916, 1937, 1945, and 1965). The 1937 production was made in the United States. According to American historian Alan Gevinson, the film, produced by the Marana Films, was included in the catalog of the American Film Institute as the first Armenian-language sound film ever made in the United States.[13] Azerbaijani journalist Sevinj Ahmadova reports that the name of Hajibeyli was not mentioned at all in the Marana Films production.[14] However, the film version of the operetta produced in the Soviet Union in 1945, which was widely promoted in the international arena, did attribute authorship to the Azerbaijani composer.[15]

Unlike *Leyli and Majnun, The Cloth Peddler* does not include any *mugham* and therefore does not require a cast that can perform them, which facilitates its appearance on non-Azerbaijani operatic stages. In September 2006, Hajibeyli's operetta was produced and performed by an international cast at the Viennese Cammeroper Theatre, and in September 2013, it was put on at the Dorothy Chandler Pavilion in Los Angeles. Both productions were at once modern and experimental, yet they presented the music "as is," without any changes to the original score. The *Huffington Post* wrote after the Los Angeles performance, "What makes *The Cloth Peddler* extraordinary is not only the music of Hajibeyli, which is world-class, but the fact that the operetta was among the first ever composed and performed in the Muslim world."[16] A hundred years after its creation, and despite the many further discoveries and accomplishments of Azerbaijani composers, Hajibeyli's operetta maintains its historical and artistic value, reminding audiences of the origins of composed music in Azerbaijan.

The growing number of Azerbaijani compositions in the musical theater repertory in the early twentieth century created a need for actors and singers who could convey the particularities of traditional music and perform composed music in the Western format. Finding male singers was relatively easy, and very soon a cohort of outstanding musicians had emerged as stars of early Azerbaijani operas and operettas. Finding female singers, on the other hand, was enormously difficult, if not impossible, since according to Islamic religious dogma women were prohibited not only from appearing on stage but even from sitting in the hall next to men. For this reason, with few exceptions, men performed all female parts in early Azerbaijani operas. A breakthrough occurred in 1912 when Shovkat Mammadova (1897–1981), the first female operatic singer in Azerbaijan, appeared on stage in Baku. The program of her concert included arias from Italian and Russian operas. To avoid persecution, Mammadova had to hide in the oilfields for several days afterward. During the Soviet era, she pursued a brilliant career, both as an operatic singer and teacher. Mammadova was awarded the highest artistic titles that the Soviet Union conferred, and for decades she was a prominent voice professor at the Azerbaijan State Conservatory (now the Baku Music Academy).

At the turn of the twentieth century, two decades before the Azerbaijan State Conservatory was founded, Azerbaijan saw the establishment of its first Western-style music school. In 1900, the young Russian pianist Antonina Ermo-

FIGURE 1.2. Scene from the film *The Cloth Peddler,* 1945. From right to left:
Rashid Behbudov as Asgar, Alakbar Huseynzade as Soltanbey, and
Minavvar Kalantarli as Auntie Jahan. *Courtesy of Rashida Behbudova.*

laeva opened the first private music school in Baku. This institution was reorga-
nized as a branch of the IRMO (short for *Imperatorskoe Russkoe Muzykal'noe
Obshchestvo* (Imperial Russian Music Society) on October 9, 1901.[17] The IRMO
branch marked the beginning of systematic Western music education in Azerbaijan, since the school offered music classes. The following lines from the local
newspaper *Kaspii* show awareness of Baku's new status in the musical world:
"So far, those interested in art and music have been more attracted to Tiflis
[Georgia] as the only music center in the entire Caucasus which, in addition to
everything else, had the IRMO music school. From now on, Tiflis is not the only
place in this regard; Baku is equally satisfying the needs for pursuing serious
study in music and enjoying high quality performances."[18]

Azerbaijan was the only Muslim province of the Russian Empire in which
the IRMO was active, and the Baku branch hosted a resident string quartet,

FIGURE 1.3. Shovkat Mammadova. *Courtesy of the State Museum of Azerbaijani Musical Culture.*

beginning in 1906, and a resident symphony orchestra, beginning in 1909. Ermolaeva imported skilled musicians from Moscow and St. Petersburg to teach, and in November 1916, after making revisions to its curriculum and increasing its academic requirements, the institution became the IRMO Music College. Nonetheless, the Baku music school was of limited importance to Azerbaijani nationalism. The school's faculty members all came from Russia; the only language of instruction was Russian; and the school targeted the Russians and the Russian-speaking part of the population rather than native Azerbaijanis. The first native pianist and teacher Kovkab Safaraliyeva (1907–1985) reported that the first Azerbaijanis joined the IRMO music classes only in 1908–1909. In 1912, the number of Azerbaijani students reached seven, still only 5 percent of the total enrollment.[19]

The national music of Azerbaijan made significant progress during the Russian Imperial era. Azerbaijanis discovered and began to realize Azerbaijani music's rich potential for fusion with Western forms. This process sped up dramatically after the collapse of the Russian Empire, when Azerbaijan stepped into independence.

AZERBAIJAN DEMOCRATIC REPUBLIC: THE OBSCURED PAGE OF THE NATIONAL HISTORY

The ADR (1918–1920) was the first democracy in the Muslim world, and Westernization was an important component of its nationalist agenda.[20] The ADR period was too short to experience a flowering of new trends in music and culture; however, direct exposure to the West and freedom from the colonial rule of Russia gave a strong impetus to both localism and cosmopolitanism in Azerbaijani music. The Soviets remained reticent to acknowledge this period of Azerbaijan's history, and all Soviet sources on music history provide no information about the accomplishments of Azerbaijani musicians during the time of the ADR. Recognition of Azerbaijani compositions from the ADR period came only after the Soviet Union collapsed, when the archives opened and hitherto unknown scores from the ADR period became available. Among them is the first national anthem of Azerbaijan, which the modern Republic of Azerbaijan now uses. Written by Hajibeyli and the poet Ahmad Javad (1892–1937) in 1919, the anthem embodies the essence of Azerbaijani musical nationalism. Hajibeyli bases the melody on the mode *bayati-shiraz,* and he finds affinities between that mode and the Western minor scale, harmonizing his melody with chords from it. The simple melodic and rhythmic patterns of the composition offer the same double reference: they point both to solemn marches in Western

music and to instrumental compositions in the traditional Azerbaijani repertoire. That Azerbaijan's anthem is written in minor, not in major, is unusual
and verges on denying the musical semantics of national anthems, which tend
to use the major scale or can be interpreted in that context. But Hajibeyli's
national anthem appropriately draws on the characteristics of Azerbaijani folk
music, which often has a minor-related modal basis.

Another product of Hajibeyli and Javad's creative teamwork, the song "The
Black Sea Was Waving," reveals the close links between Azerbaijani and Turkish identities that was typical of social life and music during the ADR period.
The second line of the song renders the Turkic reference explicit: "while looking
at the Turks' banner." Hajibeyli's music brings together traits of Turkish and
Azerbaijani music. Quite tellingly, the song is written in *shur,* one of the seven
modes of Azerbaijani music; this scale is also the most popular in Turkish music. The melody has a descending contour, which is highly typical of Azerbaijani and Turkish folk songs. Its opening exclamatory pattern, highlighting the
fifth of the tonic and immediately moving toward the tonic, is also representative of both traditions.

The title of one of Hajibeyli's articles published during the ADR period –
"About the Music of Azerbaijani Turks" – reveals the same Azerbaijani-Turkish
paradigm. Originally appearing in the collection of articles "Istiglal" (Independence), dedicated to the first anniversary of Azerbaijan's independence in 1919,
this article soon mysteriously disappeared from scholarly awareness. Perhaps
"mysteriously" is not an adequate explanation here; obscuring this article was
beneficial for the Soviets, since it helped them present Hajibeyli's fundamental
monograph *Principles of Azerbaijani Folk Music* (1945) as an independent project entirely sponsored and supported by the new regime. Thanks to the efforts
of the native musicologist Farah Aliyeva, historical justice has been rendered,
and she republished "About the Music of Azerbaijani Turks" in 2005. This article is comparable in terms of its size and contents to a brochure or perhaps a
small book, the format in which it was actually republished. It introduces many
of the key concepts of Hajibeyli's modal theory, which was an integral part of
his concept of East-West synthesis in Azerbaijani music. Later, he refined and
advanced these concepts.

Hajibeyli published the article after having penned six operas, three operettas, and a number of songs and therefore after having internalized the modal
theory he promulgated. Hajibeyli did not simply wish to analyze the modal
or rhythmic peculiarities of Azerbaijani music. Instead, he explored ways in
which specific traits of Azerbaijani music paralleled those of Western music,
and he clearly articulated the importance and feasibility of East-West synthe-

sis in Azerbaijani music. The long-lasting absence of Hajibeyli's article from scholarly awareness has caused misunderstandings in Western musicology about the composer's work. For instance, Frolova-Walker discusses Hajibeyli's concept of reconciliation between the Azerbaijani modal system and the Western tonal system as only referring to the composer's scholarly publications during the Soviet era. As a result, she relates Hajibeyli's concept of modal synthesis exclusively to Soviet cultural policy and to the directives given by the communists. Frolova-Walker also claims that in the late 1920s and early 1930s, Hajibeyli changed his initial priorities under pressure from the Soviet system. She writes, "Hajibeyov [Hajibeyli] soon accepted that Azerbaijani composers would have to settle for twelve-note equal temperament; the matter had already been decided by Kuliyev, the Minister of Education, and composers would have found it difficult to mount a serious challenge."[21] Neither the minister of Education nor any other Soviet authority forced Hajibeyli to make decisions about the importance of equal temperament. In his 1919 article, Hajibeyli had already presented the adoption of twelve-note equal temperament as a matter of high importance and urgency for the future development of Azerbaijani music and as a condition of accomplishing East-West synthesis. Hajibeyli writes, "While some believe that quarter tones give Eastern music an advantage over Western music, those who recognize them as unnecessary and as causing obstacles remain in a stronger position."[22] Hajibeyli makes a comparison to the historical path of Western music, which has passed the stage of unequal division of the scale. He writes, "In the past, these quarter tones existed in Western music as well. Eventually, for the sake of progress, these intervals that were barely distinguished by ear were recognized as unnecessary, and even harmful, and they were eliminated from musical practice."[23] Removing quarter tones accelerated and facilitated the development of composed music in Europe, and Hajibeyli foresaw the same outcome for his nation. This prediction is the key to understanding the true incentive of Hajibeyli's eagerness for equal temperament: he was concerned about creating new musical spaces for his native music, rather than sacrificing its authentic rules to the ideological agendas of the Soviets.

In this article, Hajibeyli discusses the applications of the major and minor scales in Western music and then argues, "We have to build up similar scales for our music; this will serve as a strong means for future progress." What follows is Hajibeyli's chart of all the main scales of Azerbaijani music, each adjusted to the idea of the twelve semitone division of the scale in Western music. He compares *rast, segah, mahur,* and *chahargah* with major, and *shur, bayati-kurd, bayati-shiraz,* and *shushtar* with minor.[24] The list of the Azerbaijani modes is slightly different from that presented in the 1945 monograph (see introduction), and Hajibeyli had not yet developed his theory of tetrachordal structure. Otherwise, this 1919 article clearly sets out the significant claims of Hajibeyli's modal theory, or rather, his theory of synthesis between national modality and the tonal system of Western music.

Through all the historical and geopolitical transformations that Azerbaijan experienced in the nineteenth and early twentieth centuries, an underlying current persisted: a growing nationalism that incorporated the goal of being a part of–or on par with–the Western world. This process helped Azerbaijan face the Soviet era with an already-formed concept of national identity.

THE JANUS-LIKE SOVIET ERA

National Music during the Epoch of "Socialist Realism"

The Soviet period in Azerbaijan's history was an era in which the national identity of Azerbaijanis continued to become more defined. As argued in most contemporary studies on nationalism and national policy in the Soviet Union, this last empire in human history provided favorable conditions for the process of developing the national identities of all peoples within it. Francine Hirsch writes about the Soviet Union as "an empire of nations," and Ronald Suni mentions that "rather than a melting pot, the Soviet Union became an incubator of new nations."[25]

Music was at the center of Soviet-inspired nationalism, since the Soviet regime considered national music to be one of the "symbolic markers of national identity."[26] In Azerbaijan, the notion of national music already encompassed the Western genres and forms that native composers had mastered in the early twentieth century. This, again, resonated with the goals of Soviet cultural and national policy, which endeavored to bring all non-Slavic nations into the fold of European civilization. Consequently, the Soviet era created a favorable environment for the further realization of nationalism in Azerbaijani music. Traditional music, composers' works, performing arts, jazz, music education–all were touched by a nationalist ideal. Certainly "socialist realism," the main aesthetic doctrine of the Soviets, implied limitations on the expression of the national ideal in music. According to this doctrine, music and art in general could be "national in form," only to the extent that this did not interfere with being "socialist in content." In the other words, only those forms of nationalism were allowed that did not contradict the ideological agenda of the Soviets. Metaphorically speaking, the Soviet system resembled the figure of Janus, simultaneously showing its two sides, one supportive, the other restrictive, as it guided the development of music throughout the vast territory of the Soviet Empire. The main challenge that Azerbaijani musicians, and all Soviet musicians, faced was that Azerbaijan's two nationalist musical sources, traditional music and composed music, were treated by the Soviets as two parts of the same Azerbaijani identity that needed to be synthesized with each other and integrated into their Soviet world. Traditional music tended to be "institutionalized," whereas Western music genres were pushed closer to folk idioms. By promoting this course, musical policy during the Soviet era aimed to reduce the authenticity of traditional music and to temper the Western component in composed music. It was a first step toward Soviet national and cultural policy's long-term goal of merging all forms of national music and culture and all national traditions into a homogenous all-union socialist culture.

Azerbaijani music developed effective methods of coping with the Soviet system, since the gains it offered substantially outweighed the losses it brought. During writes:

> How has the Republic of Azerbaijan, which has only seven million inhabitants, managed to produce so much music of high quality, so many singers and instrumentalists of high technical and musical quality – not to mention Western music, where they are also brilliant? Was this quality achieved thanks to Soviet cultural politics, or despite it? The answer deserves to be nuanced according to the different epochs and domains in which it was active. Be that as it may, by all likelihood, cultural politics – which was the same in all of the Soviet republics – did not have any effect on the passion of the Azeris for music.[27]

During's questions are far from rhetorical, and the author appears to have provided a clue to their answers in his later writings, in which he characterizes Azerbaijanis as "a nation that always had a strong ethnic and cultural identity."[28] This identity helped Azerbaijanis cope with the Janus-like Soviet system and develop new forms of musical nationalism. Another factor in the successful development of music in Soviet Azerbaijan was the convergence of Soviet and Azerbaijani values: the Soviet Union generously supported music, and music traditionally held a high place in Azerbaijani society. Music played an important role in Soviet politics, as music has in the politics of all empires, because it created an artistic façade for the regime and served as an effective vehicle for propaganda. On the other hand, historically, music and literature were considered "the art of arts" in Azerbaijan. This assessment can be attributed to the legacy of the Middle Eastern court tradition, in which poets and musicians were highly revered. On this common ground between traditional Azerbaijani society and Soviet politics, major breakthroughs in twentieth-century Azerbaijani music occurred.

Major Breakthroughs

Two works of Azerbaijani music premiered in 1937: the opera *Koroghlu* by Ha-jibeyli, and a solo piano piece, *The Statue in Tsarskoe Selo,* by Gara Garayev. These works are at opposite ends of the spectrum of composed musical genres, but that difference is not the most significant distinction between them. These compositions demonstrate the presence of a newer wave in Azerbaijani music alongside an older one. Hajibeyli's composition drew on the stylistic language of Viennese classicism, as befitted his long-held mission to create a national style using the musical languages of earlier eras of Western classical music. In contrast, Garayev's piece has a strong impressionistic flavor. The composition was among the first to display the composer's drive to advance Azerbaijani music toward the idioms of Western twentieth-century music.

In *Koroghlu,* Hajibeyli revisited and surpassed all of his previous accomplishments in the field of East-West synthesis, creating a work that had no markers of being a product of a young composed music tradition. For passages featuring soloists, he replaced *mughams* with well-developed operatic arias. *Koroghlu's* melodies demonstrate true synthesis. Instead of alternating traditional performance forms with operatic singing, Hajibeyli created an integrated melodic style that melded traditional vocal techniques with bel canto. In harmony, too, Hajibeyli pushed forward with East-West synthesis. Rather than using the simple methods of harmonization he had employed earlier in his career, Hajibeyli brought together the principles of Western tonal music and those of the national modal system. By scoring *Koroghlu* for a large symphonic orchestra, he expanded the scope of his performing forces, having used an ensemble of string and wind instruments in *Leyli and Majnun.* In his first opera, Hajibeyli had employed traditional musical instruments only during the accompaniment sections of *mugham* episodes, and these instruments stayed mute during the rest of the opera while the orchestra accompanied the fully notated episodes. In *Koroghlu,* he firmly integrated the traditional instruments into the symphonic score and used them throughout the duration of the work. Hajibeyli created a complex, multipart choral texture that combined features of Western polyphony with the contrapuntal elements typical of traditional performances. *Mugham* is rich in imitative polyphony and call-response relations among musicians, and this is what Hajibeyli elaborated on when creating the "new Azerbaijani polyphony." This, too, was an advance on the heterophony he had employed in his first opera. In comparison with *Leyli and Majnun, Koroghlu* was a new embodiment of the national idea, and the opera reflected a new stage of the evolution of Azerbaijani composed music.

Koroghlu provided a strong impetus for the new vocal style of Azerbaijani music that can be called "Azerbaijani bel canto." The tenor singer Bulbul (Murtuza Mammadov, 1897–1961), who sang the part of Koroghlu, created this fusion between operatic bel canto and the traditional Azerbaijani singing style, which has distinctive embellishments and a specific type of vibrato (PURL 1.1).[29] Perfectly aware of all of the nuances of *mugham*-style singing, Bulbul also learned the techniques of operatic vocal art through his study at the world-renowned La Scala opera house in Milan, Italy, where he went for training from 1927 to 1931. Upon his return, Bulbul accomplished this fusion and employed it in all of his performances of Azerbaijani music. His legacy continues to the present day. Without exception, each and every opera singer in Azerbaijan is now capable of singing in this mixed style that has become an attribute of performances of Azerbaijani repertoire, be it romances, popular songs, arrangements of folk songs, or operatic arias.

Within a decade after *Koroghlu,* Azerbaijani composers mastered two large-scale genres of Western composed music with which they had yet to engage: the ballet and the symphony. Afrasiyab Badalbeyli (1907–1976), the composer of the first Azerbaijani ballet, *The Maiden's Tower* (1940), approached creating nationalistic music in a manner similar to how Hajibeyli had in *Koroghlu.* Badalbeyli composed original melodies based on folk idioms, and his harmony and orchestration draw on both Viennese classicism and traditional music. The first national symphonies, on the other hand, highlighted the growing role of Garayev and his modernist aesthetic. The first three Azerbaijani symphonies premiered in 1944, and they were penned by Garayev and two young native composers of his generation, Soltan Hajibeyov (1919–1974) and Jovdat Hajiyev (1917–2000). All three composers had just returned to Azerbaijan after studying with Dmitry Shostakovich at the Moscow State Conservatory. The symphonies demonstrate a new stage of evolution in the Azerbaijani national style. All idioms of the Azerbaijani musical style were now conveyed through complex harmonies and intricate orchestral textures inspired by Shostakovich's symphonic works, as discussed further in chapter 3.

These new developments did not compromise the value of the previous accomplishments of Azerbaijani composers who had drawn on earlier styles of Western music. Even as the previously mentioned composers created modernist works, Fikrat Amirov suggested new ways of applying the idioms of Azerbaijani traditional music through the medium of rather conservative styles of Western music. In 1948, only a few years after the three Azerbaijani symphonies inspired by Shostakovich, Amirov created a new generic synthesis that echoed Hajibeyli's concept of *mugham* opera: "symphonic *mugham*." This innovative genre fusion

FIGURE 1.4. Bulbul. *Courtesy of the State Museum of Azerbaijani Musical Culture.*

used the prism of the symphony, or, to be more precise, of the symphonic suite, to create a romanticist interpretation of traditional *mugham*. Amirov's *Shur* (1948) and *Kurd Ovshari* (1948), both named after the respective eponymous *mugham*s, were performed by Charles Munch and Leopold Stokowski (who later recorded *Kurd Ovshari*).[30] Twenty-three years later, Amirov returned to this genre, writing *Gulustani Bayati Shiraz* (1971) and thus completing a trilogy of symphonic *mugham*s. Symphonic *mugham*s can be found in the oeuvres of many Azerbaijani composers of the Soviet period and so can many other exemplars of "*mugham* plus" genre fusion, including "choral *mugham*" and "organ *mugham*" (PURL 1.2). In the 1960s, Vagif Mustafazade created "jazz *mugham*" by combining the modal formulas of *mugham* with the structural and rhythmic rules of jazz. His work became a watershed in the history of Azerbaijani music (see chapter 8), as his music demonstrated major accomplishments not merely in Europeanization, but in Westernization as well.

Just as Hajibeyli's *Koroghlu* catalyzed the emergence of a new operatic style and new native cadres of singers, innovative developments in Azerbaijani composed music in the late 1930s and early 1940s prompted new trends in the performing arts. Gamar Almaszade (1915–2006) appeared in A. Badalbeyli's *The Maiden's Tower* and became the first Azerbaijani ballerina. The appearance onstage of an ethnic Azerbaijani woman who came from a rather conservative family was a major breakthrough indeed. Almaszade starred in numerous productions of the Azerbaijan State Opera and Ballet Theater and was followed by many generations of native ballet dancers. The intense "decade of symphonic music" – the 1940s – stimulated the development of national conductors and the Azerbaijani orchestral performing tradition. Many generations of Azerbaijani composers owe their masterful interpretations to the conductor Niyazi (Niyazi Taghizade-Hajibeyov, 1912–1984). Niyazi possessed a versatile musical gift, as he was a prolific composer, a transcriber of folk music, and even codirector of the jazz orchestra of Azerbaijan in the 1930s. His diverse experience contributed to his mastery as a conductor. While discussing the 1961 premiere of the ballet *The Legend of Love* by Arif Malikov, Shostakovich particularly mentioned the contribution of Niyazi: "Niyazi possesses an exceptionally clear sense of musical structure. The score has been interpreted impeccably and with real inspiration, which resulted in creating a symphonic stream of high voltage."[31] These words can apply to all of Niyazi's many interpretations, both of the scores of Western composers and of Azerbaijani symphonic, operatic, and ballet music.

The "decade of symphonic music" established a solid basis for the further development of modernist styles in Azerbaijani music, with Garayev leading the

FIGURE 1.5. Gamar Almaszade. *Courtesy of the State Museum of Azerbaijani Musical Culture.*

FIGURE 1.6. Niyazi. *Courtesy of the State Museum of Azerbaijani Musical Culture.*

avant-garde. After having assimilated Shostakovich's style and the Germanic model of neoclassicism that Shostakovich represented, Garayev proceeded to neobaroque styles and polyphonic technique.[32] Eventually, he developed an interest in Prokofiev and Stravinsky. Garayev's debt to these composers is evident in his two ballets: *Seven Beauties* (1952) and *The Path of Thunder* (1958). Both works were hailed as major successes of Soviet ballet and were included in the repertoires of the world-renowned Bolshoi Theater in Moscow and of the Kirov (later renamed the Mariinsky) Theater in Leningrad (itself later renamed St. Petersburg). In *The Path of Thunder,* Garayev sensationally expanded his creative horizons: the Azerbaijani composer turned to an African subject and to African musical traditions. The ballet's African plot allowed Garayev to explore jazz – a genre for which he had a great passion – despite its being strongly discouraged by Soviet authorities in the late 1950s. Garayev applied modal and rhythmic formulas of American jazz to idioms of African music. Metaphorically speaking, for Garayev, *The Path of Thunder* became the path to America's musical scene. Three years later, in 1961, the suite from this ballet was included in the program of the International Music Festival at the University of California, Los Angeles, and Garayev traveled to the United States as a member of the delegation of the Soviet Composers Union. Garayev's first ballet, *Seven*

Beauties, also arrived in the United States, although significantly later: its US premiere took place in October 2014 and was performed by the renowned San Diego Ballet and Grossmont Symphony Orchestra.

Garayev returned from Los Angeles with a bitter verdict: "We are behind . . . fifty years!" and he immediately began the process of updating the stylistic image of Azerbaijani music.[33] His Third Symphony (1964) and his Violin Concerto (1967), both based on twelve-tone techniques, suggested a new understanding of what Azerbaijani national music could be. From this point forward, authentic melodic contents in the tradition of *mugham* or *ashig* art, harmonies based on modal formulas, and the use of national instruments were not sufficient to convey the essence of national music; instead, Garayev referred to the fundamental qualities of traditional music, such as the tetrachordal structure of the national modes, and fused it with twelve-tone technique. This synthesis became emblematic of the modern and postmodern styles that arrived in Azerbaijani music in the 1970s and 1980s. Azerbaijani composers used traits of traditional Azerbaijani music that had commonalities with new Western styles thus expanding the space of East-West syncretism in the national music. Aleatory was fused with the improvisatory nature of *mugham;* minimalism corresponded with the principle of thematic development from a tiny modal formula as was essential in *mugham;* the prepared piano could evoke the voices of traditional instruments. Even the idea of "instrumental theater," which attracted Azerbaijani composers, resonated with the theatrical potential of the performance dynamics of the traditional *mugham* trio (see chapters 4–6).

After Garayev's Third Symphony and Violin Concerto, Azerbaijani composers were no longer trying to catch up with the West, and at the same time Azerbaijani musicians held their own in the international sphere. The pianist Farhad Badalbeyli (b. 1947) made a breakthrough for both himself and his country upon becoming a laureate at the Smetana International Piano Competition in Czechoslovakia in 1967, and a year later he won the Grand Prix at the Vianna da Mota Piano competition in Portugal. Garayev proudly reflected on the celebrated success of the twenty-one-year-old Badalbeyli thus, "Baku is not a province in the world of piano music anymore."[34] Nonetheless, at that time, Badalbeyli was never introduced as an Azerbaijani pianist; he was representing the Soviet Union and was perceived by many as a Soviet or even a Russian pianist. As Badalbeyli admitted, "I always carried a map of Azerbaijan with me and showed it to the people around, explaining to them where Azerbaijan is."[35] Badalbeyli's historic victory paved the way for the successes of many other Azerbaijani musicians, such as the two soprano singers Fidan Gasimova (b. 1947) and Khuraman Gasimova (b. 1951), who became winners at several pres-

FIGURE 1.7. From left to right: Khuraman Gasimova and Fidan Gasimova. *Courtesy of the State Museum of Azerbaijani Musical Culture.*

tigious international contests.[36] Badalbeyli and the Gasimova sisters typify the model for Azerbaijani performers in the field of Western music. Their performing style accords with the highest professional standards of the West, and their repertoire encompasses many genres, from pieces of Western music to works by the national composers (PURL 1.3 and PURL 1.4).

Through all the genres, styles, approaches, and individualities present in Azerbaijani music since the early twentieth century, one constant feature remains: the binary of Easterners and Westerners. Garayev and Amirov helped crystallize this opposition in the 1940s (see chapter 2), and successive generations of Azerbaijani musicians continued it in the fields of composed music, popular music, and jazz. The alternation between two approaches in Azerbaijani music stimulated debates and discussions, sometimes even provoking battles between the followers of the opposing streams; however, it always served as a source of creative energy and as a catalyst of further development. The East-West binary seems to be the destiny of all non-Western music traditions within the Asian sphere – suffice it to refer to the Westernizer Tchaikovsky and the Russianizer composers of the Mighty Handful in nineteenth-century Russian music. This East-West binary should not be simplified as there have been no pure Easterners or pure Westerners in Azerbaijani music, due to its complex multicultural essence. Musicians have switched from one model to another or applied both of them in the course of their career. East-West synthesis allowed energies from both sources to crisscross and intersect, creating different vectors of power and resulting in new balances within the fusion.

The Procrustean Influence of the Soviet Ideology

From the earliest to the most recent scholarship on the periodization of Soviet music, all scholars recognize 1932 as an important and pivotal year in which the new regime established a system of total control over art and culture and introduced the aesthetics of "a socialist realism." This turn was preceded by the decade that the musicologist Anna Ferenc characterized as the era of "modernism and *Proletkul't* [short for *proletarskaia kul'tura* 'proletarian culture']."[37] Azerbaijani composed music was too young to engage with modernism in the 1920s. But Azerbaijani composed music experienced – and survived – the challenge of *Proletkul't,* which declared war on the cultural heritages of all Soviet nations. *Proletkul't* sought to suppress remnants of pre-Soviet nationalism, which was deemed regressive, and instead to turn the masses toward their communist future. In Azerbaijan, this radical policy led to attacks against two musical phenomena: the *tar* and *mugham* opera. As emblems of Azerbaijani musical nationalism, the *tar* and *mugham* were proclaimed to be unnecessary – and even dangerous – relics of the past. The first generation of national composers also faced severe criticism, since their vision for the future of Azerbaijani music included the *tar* and *mugham* opera.

Instead of being celebrated as precious national accomplishments, Hajibeyli's early operas were now denigrated by *Proletkul't* critics as inferior and harmful works. As one of the reviewers wrote: "We need contemporary, cultured opera that would serve as a vehicle to educate the working masses, since existing Azerbaijani opera does not meet such criteria. . . . The content of Azerbaijani operas is absolutely unacceptable. They are permeated by ideas of pessimistic love (*Leyli and Majnun*), religious issues (*Asli and Karam*), or idealization of the kings (*Shah Abbas and Khurshud Banu*)."[38] Through denying the historical significance of Hajibelyli's compositions, the *Proletkul't* followers pursued one goal: to begin the history of Azerbaijani composed music with the Soviet era, writing into Azerbaijani music the "red ink" of Soviet ideology.

The *tar* was proclaimed to be too sophisticated an instrument, one that was unnecessary to the masses as they built a communist world. The destiny of the *tar* became a subject of a polemical exchange between two Azerbaijani poets: Suleyman Rustam (1906–1989) and Mikayil Mushvig (1908–1939). Rustam supported the ideology of *Proletkul't* in stating: "Stop *tar,* stop *tar*! You are not loved by the proletariat!" This line became a slogan of the local *Proletkul't* followers. And Mushvig wrote in response: "Sing *tar,* sing *tar*! Who can forget you!" Mushvig was arrested and sentenced to death during the era of Stalinist repressions, and his participation in this discussion about the *tar* could have been one of the acts that made the Soviets label him as an "enemy of people."

Heated arguments were not confined to intellectual circles. *Mugham* operas were excluded from the repertoire of the Azerbaijan Opera and Ballet Theater. *Tars* were publicly burned and broken, making people afraid to keep them in their homes. The ideology of *Proletkul't* had disappeared by the early 1930s, and both the *tar* and *mugham* opera returned to Azerbaijani musical life. The next decade, however, brought little hope or optimism.

In the 1930s, Stalinist repressions seized Azerbaijan and the entire Soviet Union, bringing horror and fear to all they touched. In the field of music, persecutions were not as severe as in literature or the social sciences – perhaps due to music's nonverbal nature, which made it more difficult to directly critique. Nonetheless, many musicians were executed, exiled, or sent to labor camps in Siberia. The reasons why they were targeted usually could be traced to family wealth, anti-Russian or anti-Communist activities during the pre-Soviet era, having relatives who were living abroad, befriending foreigners, or carrying out professional activities that challenged communist ideology. Although Hajibeyli was a prime target because of his having been an active supporter of the ADR and because of having a brother who was living abroad who was zealous anticommunist, he did weather the repressions, though not without great fear. Reportedly, he even slept in his day clothes, since officers arresting suspects usually came in the middle of the night (see chapter 2).

In the same decade during which the cruelly repressive Stalinist mechanism was highly active, the Soviets established a subtler – or, perhaps, merely less visible – system of guiding art and culture. The open expression of intense polemics and diverse viewpoints in the media and similar forums was gradually squelched. From then on, substantial issues related to music were discussed not in public, but instead behind closed doors in the respective departments of the organizations responsible for the control of all spheres of cultural life.[39] This system continued until the end of the Soviet era in 1991, although after Stalin's death in 1953, the social environment became more liberal, and composers received more opportunities to express their individual voices. Nonetheless, the Soviets' main goal remained the same: all musical activities would meet approved ideological agendas and fulfill the main tenet of their cultural doctrine, known as socialist realism.

The ideology of socialist realism was based on three major principles. The first was *partiinost'*, which referred to the praise of communist ideology and to the belief in a happy and prosperous future under communist guidance. The second was *narodnost'*, or the direct revelation of national roots through frequent use of folkloric sources. The third, *realism,* maintained the necessity of realistic, rather than abstract modes of expression. This infamous ideological triad affected the creativity of composers, traditional musicians, performers, musicologists, and educators, as well as that of music critics and media workers.

The Fate of Traditional Music

I would have been unable to use this subhead in any of my publications in Azerbaijan in the 1980s because officially, there was no realm of "traditional music" in Soviet music and music studies. The term was strongly disapproved of because it implied having cultural roots in the past, and the Soviets believed that nations that had a unique historical past could potentially claim a unique future, one apart from the Soviet brotherhood. Besides, *traditional* could be interpreted as "old-fashioned," and being old-fashioned was to be opposed to Soviet ideology, since traditional things could distract the masses from the struggle for "a great communist future." Under the Soviet regime, the oral musical heritage of each nation was divided into "folk music" and "professional music." In Azerbaijan, the first domain included songs and dances, and the second was represented by *mugham. Ashig* music was considered to be in between and was sometimes classified as "folk-professional." Folk music was always given priority in the hierarchy of genres, and it was presented as the main source of professional music. According to Levin, "The idea that the roots of the 'professional' *maqam* tradition are in 'folk creativity' is one of the most central and enduring ideological derivatives of both Marxist-Leninist aesthetics and Soviet Nationalities Policy."[40] Thus, the ostensibly undeniable link between *mugham* and folk music was exaggerated and served Soviet ideological agendas. Hajibeyli had to title his fundamental study on Azerbaijani modes *Principles of Azerbaijani Folk Music,* although it dealt with the entire body of traditional music. He had to do the same at the Azerbaijan State Conservatory with the class that he designed and taught that had the same name and content as his book.

Putting aside terminological issues, traditional music in the Soviet Union was the subject of intense modernization and Westernization. Ensembles of traditional instruments and folk dances operated under the Philharmonic Society and other state-supported organizations, recordings were released, and respective classes were offered under the umbrella of Western-type music schools. It is hard to deny the positive effect of all these activities in keeping the traditional music of the Azerbaijani nation alive. By way of comparison, Azerbaijanis in Iran never had such a wide range of opportunities to demonstrate and share their musical heritage. But indisputably, Westernizing and modernizing tendencies in the field of traditional music posed a threat: they came very close to eliminating native agency, tradition, and individuality. Nonetheless, the integrity of traditional music remained, and Westernization and modernization contributed to the wide promotion of traditional music within native society and beyond.

Traditional musical instruments and their modification during the Soviet era superbly illustrate how Westernizing tendencies modified traditional music but did not destroy its integrity. As a result of Soviet policy, most Azerbaijani instruments became equally tempered, making them sound closer to their Western counterparts. Equal temperament allowed music for traditional instruments to be notated and enabled traditional instruments to play in large groups or in ensembles with Western instruments. Similar developments occurred in neighboring cultures that were also experiencing the impact of modernization, although not because of communist ideology. Nettl comments on this innovation and the attitude of the pioneer of composed music in Iran, Ali Naqi Vaziri (1887–1979), mentioning that Vaziri accepted equal temperament and was ready to live with it and its consequences.[41] Hajibeyli, the father of Azerbaijani art music, did not simply accept equal temperament; as previously discussed, he considered it to be a catalyst – and indicator – of the new tendencies in Azerbaijani music. Azerbaijani musicians and audiences ever since have been willing to work with equal temperament as introduced by Westernization. The Orchestra of the Azerbaijani Folk Instruments was established by Hajibeyli in 1932, and it continues to function and be highly revered in contemporary Azerbaijan.

Equal temperament allowed the creation of pieces that combined traditional and Western instruments. Haji Khanmammadov (1918–2005) created the first concertos for the *tar* and the first concertos for the *kemancha* with symphony orchestra, and these remain in modern soundscapes. Contemporary performers and audiences have discovered this repertoire, showing that its value transcends the Soviet circumstances under which it was created. On November 9, 2013, the Youth Music Monterey County Symphony Orchestra from California, under Farkhad Khudyev (b. 1985), performed the Concerto for the *Kemancha* and Symphony Orchestra by Khanmammadov at the celebration of the orchestra's twenty-fifth anniversary. The soloist, Imamyar Hasanov

(b. 1975), a San Francisco–based *kemancha* player, represents the type of performer equally competent in both traditional and composed music that has become emblematic of Azerbaijani musicians down to the present day (PURL 1.5). Ramiz Guliyev (b. 1947), Azerbaijan's distinguished and outstandingly virtuosic *tar* player and one of the pioneers of such a dual identity, encapsulates the aesthetic of such musicians in a statement referring to the expansion of the repertoire for this instrument from *mugham* and Azerbaijani traditional music to the pieces penned by native and Western composers: "In the past, we used to play our music for ourselves. Hajibeyli changed this in the early twentieth century and further generations of Azerbaijani composers continued this path. They created large-scale concertos and other pieces involving the *tar* but not confined to the space of traditional music. I am happy that the Azerbaijani *tar* now speaks many languages."[42]

In an effort to promote the collectivism and grandiosity so central to Soviet ideology, officials sought to modify the format of *mugham* performances. Instead of using the small format of a trio (voice and drum-*tar*-*kemancha*), Soviet officials wished for *mugham* to be performed by a large group of singers and instrumentalists. In Uzbek and Tajik music, Soviet influence was stronger and resulted in singing *shashmaqom* in groups, but a similar change never took place in Azerbaijan with *mugham*, despite official encouragement. During states, "Here the traditional style of performance has never changed: a singer with percussion, a *tar* lute and a *kamanche* fiddle. . . . Neither have Azeri bards allowed themselves to be forcibly formed into orchestras. At the very most, a few come together on a stage and play one after the other."[43] Orchestras of traditional instruments often accompanied *mugham* singers, but they never replaced the traditional *mugham* trio. As for the second part of During's passage, indeed, there were duel-like performances of *mugham* singers on stage that showed each musician's individual approach to the same *mugham*, but the singers never performed together.

Notation of traditional and folk music was another sign of the "academization" of the national heritage. Notation also fulfilled the Soviets' goal of gaining control over oral forms of music, particularly those based on improvisation. Improvisation, an activity reflecting and stimulating spiritual freedom, always has frightened totalitarian regimes. But transcription of *mugham* was a challenging task and one that defied attempts at academization because it was impossible to take a notational snapshot of this improvisational music and to convey all the melodic and rhythmic patterns of *mugham*. Perhaps this is why the Azerbaijani composer Magomayev never published his transcription of *Rast*, even though he was the first to notate *mugham*, doing so beginning in 1925.

Azerbaijani musicians continued to notate *mugham,* and many of their projects received recognition for being particularly successful. Still, none of these transcribers conveyed all the peculiarities of *mugham.* But they did not claim to do so. Their collections were primarily used as reference sources for scholarly activities or as textbooks in classes on the theory of Azerbaijani folk music. Their works could also be studied outside of Azerbaijan by those who were interested in knowing more about *mugham,* but these transcriptions were never used by those who wanted to learn how to play *mugham* professionally. *Mugham* continued to be an improvisatory art, and even though these ideologically driven transcription projects dealt with *mugham,* they never destroyed its integrity. Similar transcription projects were going in Iran, where the notation of traditional music was finally accepted by the majority of local musicians as revealing "the Westernization of musical thought, within a framework of Persian musical style and genres."[44] Despite all differences between Azerbaijan and Iran, in both cases, notation was allowed to enter the orbit of traditional music, but to a limited degree, so as not to compromise its integrity.

The verbal component of *mugham* was also a subject for modernization in the Soviet context. The lyrics of *mugham* were historically based on classical literature from the twelfth through the nineteenth centuries and often contained religious motives and explicit descriptions of love – even eroticism. None of these topics were in line with Soviet ideological agendas. Thus, performers were encouraged to focus on Soviet literary sources instead of medieval ones. Musicians did, but they never stopped using classical texts. Local ethnomusicologists were similarly exhorted to "contemporize" *mugham.* The ethnomusicologist Ramiz Zokhrabov recalled, referring to his book published in Moscow on the *tasnif* tradition: "One of reviewers, the musicologist Viktor Iarustovskii, who also worked for the Central Committee of the Communist Party, recommended that I extend the chapter dedicated to the Soviet period and omit references to *tasnif*s written on classical medieval sources. I was forced to do this revision, because otherwise I would not have ever seen my research published."[45]

What also disturbed the Soviets about *mugham* was its typical motifs of sadness and melancholy. Accordingly, *mugham*s that evoked particularly sorrowful feelings, such as *Shushtar, Humayun, Rahab, Zamin Khara,* or *Kasma Shikasta,* were more or less suppressed. This policy produced an imbalanced development of the art of *mugham* in Soviet Azerbaijan. Cheerful *mugham*s were performed more frequently, and they became more elaborate in terms of intonation and structure than sad *mugham*s.

The Azerbaijani *mugham* suffered from ideological attacks, but it survived and kept its integrity throughout the Soviet era. The general concept of *mugham* was not damaged, and *mugham*'s verbal contents and overall philosophy were not distorted. In discussing what protected the Azerbaijani *mugham* from all ideological attacks, the ethnomusicologist Izaly Zemtsovsky mentions "a 'fixed' poetic text" as the main factor that made it impossible to include new ideology in the *mugham*.[46] I agree with this statement, because the poetic text of *mugham*, regardless of the epoch in which it is produced, can only be about love and separation, joy and sorrow, or life and death. The intimate atmosphere of private gatherings in which *mugham* continued to develop also helped preserve the integrity of the genre. Finally, as mentioned, the Azerbaijani *mugham*'s link with the parallel tradition in the Azerbaijani province of Iran served as a strong force in protecting this genre from the destructive tendencies of the Soviet era.

Conversely, *ashig* music was easily manipulated by the new regime, just as were parallel bardic traditions in Central Asia. *Ashig*'s combination of cheerful music and contents, as well as its rather simple lyrics connected to contemporary life, made *ashig* art an ideal tool for delivering messages of communist propaganda. Since the early 1920s, in addition to their traditional epics, *ashigs* began performing compositions dedicated to Lenin and communism. This immediately earned *ashigs* the reputation of being somewhat privileged among the traditional musicians in the country. The Soviets encouraged *ashig* performances and even established an assembly to gather *ashigs* from all regions of Azerbaijan and to "unify" their creative efforts. It would be hard to imagine a similar gathering of *mugham* performers.

All genres of music associated with religion were condemned with the understanding that they would soon pass into oblivion. Islam did not have a strong connection with music, so in Azerbaijan the range of banned religious musical activities was limited. Nonetheless, all musical traditions associated with Islam were strongly discouraged. *Azan*, the call for prayer, performed from the top of mosque five times a day, was usually prerecorded and broadcast at a very low volume. Some Islamic rituals that incorporated music, such as *shabih*, or *taziye*, were strictly prohibited. *Shabih*, the religious mystery, involved a group of men, some presenting the main characters of the drama, and others singing *marsiyya*, which are choral songs performed mostly in unison or with simple elements of heterophony. Prohibition of *shabih* was a crude invasion of the natural evolution of Azerbaijani music, since this genre had extensively influenced Azerbaijani art music traditions, particularly *mugham* opera. According to the native musicologist Saadat Seyidova, "*Shabih* undoubtedly stands among the primary sources of the national opera of the Azerbaijani Turks."[47] Indeed, the choral episodes of *shabih* served as the prototypes for the choruses in Hajibeyli's *Leyli and Majnun*.

Despite all these hardships, these and other forbidden types of music continued to exist in Soviet Azerbaijan. This is acknowledged by During, who argues that "in the domain of classical music, Azerbaijan offers the most resistance."[48] Sad *mughams* were still performed within circles of music lovers. The rituals of *shabih* continued to take place, although mostly in villages, far from public attention. *Marsiyya* was always performed when a family lost its dear ones, and there was no mosque in the country that did not have *azan*. Overall, the cultivation of Azerbaijan's traditional musical heritage during the Soviet era was not thwarted by the new developments; traditional music persisted, damaged but uncorrupted.

"Today He Is Playing Jazz, and Tomorrow He Is Going to Betray the Country"

This famous slogan of the early Soviet era reflected the attitude of the communist regime toward jazz. From its first appearance in the Soviet Union, jazz was subjected to serious ideological constraints, and they were similar to those applied to traditional music. This situation is paradoxical only at a first glance, because both jazz and traditional music in Azerbaijan were based on improvisation, a quality that has horrified totalitarian regimes. To eliminate this essential characteristic of jazz, the Soviets aimed to institutionalize and academize the genre, just as they did with traditional music. For example, the leadership of the Azerbaijan State Jazz Orchestra, created in 1939, was entrusted to Tofig Guliyev (1917–2000) and Niyazi, two academically trained composers. Several measures were taken to make Soviet jazz more predictable and less spontaneous, more entertaining and less evocative. This plan also implied the tactic of "dissolving" jazz by integrating it entirely into popular music. At many times throughout the history of jazz, jazz and popular music have been intimately connected. But in Soviet jazz, close ties between jazz and pop were triggered by ideological concerns, rather than by musical or commercial ones.

Jazz faced particularly serious ideological attacks in the late 1940s and early 1950s with the beginning of the Cold War. The saxophone was banned completely because it was regarded as the voice of the capitalist world. According to the Azerbaijani poet and jazz expert Vagif Samadoghlu, performances of Ravel's *Bolero* in Baku at the time substituted the bassoon for the solo saxophone.[49] Even the most general and benign characteristics of jazz, such as pizzicato bass playing, use of a drum set, or applying bluesy harmonic progressions, were strictly forbidden. The story of Parviz Rustambeyov (1922–1949), often called the "Soviet Benny Goodman" for his outstanding talent, is very telling in this regard. In 1946, Rustambeyov returned to Baku after two years of playing in the orchestra of the famous Polish jazz trumpeter Eddie Rosner (1910–1976).[50] He established his own orchestra and played in Baku cinemas. In January 1949, Rustambeyov was dismissed for his "anti-Soviet and pro-American activities," and in May 1949, he was arrested.[51] Rustambeyov was sentenced to fifteen years of prison; on the day of his trial, however, he died in his prison cell under highly suspicious circumstances.

In the 1960s, a liberal turn in the social and political climate created more favorable conditions for the development of jazz in Soviet Azerbaijan. Voice of America, Liberty, and BBC broadcasts became the main means of staying up-to-date with Western jazz. Despite being signal-jammed, these shows still exposed locals to current trends in jazz. Samadoghlu recalled those days, saying, "I have so many fond memories of . . . the endless hours we used to listen secretly to the short-wave radio programs of the BBC just to catch some of the jazz they broadcast. . . . Afterwards, we would try to reproduce the music that we had heard on the old piano in the apartment."[52] This was the environment in which jazz *mugham* was born.

"Censored!"

In 1977, after the performance of the Sonata for Two Performers by Faraj Garayev at the Azerbaijan State Conservatory, an anonymous letter was sent to the Central Committee of the Communist Party of the Soviet Union. The author of the letter accused the composer of "avant-gardism" and recommended that Moscow "investigate" the situation. Perhaps the author objected to the musical language of the piece, which included twelve-tone, aleatoric, and pointillist techniques. The author may also have found the quotation from Lord Byron used as the epigraph to be ideologically dangerous. As recalled by the composer, "What helped me was the intervention of Tofig Guliyev, who was the First Secretary of the Azerbaijani Union of Composers at that time. He found the 'right' ways to prevent possible severe counter-measures."[53]

This account, which F. Garayev shared with me in 2006, reminded me of another story I discovered in the 1990s when I was working with the archival materials of the composer Magomayev at the Institute of Manuscripts in Baku. I found that censoring organizations rudely interfered with his opera *Nargiz* (1935), causing the final edition to significantly differ from the work as the composer had earlier envisioned it. The manuscripts of the libretto are covered with comments by Ali Ibrahimov, the head of the Department of Literature and Art in the Central Committee of the Communist Party. Ibrahimov's major concern was to ensure the ideological correctness of the plot, rather than to preserve Magomayev's original artistic and musical concepts. For instance, the following critical remark appeared in the margin next to the love duet of Nargiz and Alyar, the protagonists: "Replace with an appeal to all the masses and develop on the revolutionary theme." The title character's act 1 aria was marked: "Develop a revolutionary spirit."[54]

Magomayev used extensive diplomacy to appease the officials and defend his initial idea. Still, the concept of *Nargiz* became distorted through the intrusion of ideological matters. When the composer began writing the libretto, he had a clear idea of how he wanted to develop the story line. It would be a "love triangle" in the spirit of old legends and folktales, in which two ill-fated young lovers – Nargiz and Alyar – are separated by the wealthy landlord Aghalar Bey. Then Magomayev was forced to add a political component: Nargiz and Alyar were identified as communists, and Aghalar Bey became a member of the Musavat Party, the ruling party during the ADR period.[55] As a result of the continuing "recommendations" on behalf of the censoring organizations, at the end of the story, Nargiz was made to shoot two antagonists, which was a bizarre turn of events for the young and innocent beauty.

Such a distortion of a main character spoils the entire narrative. The clear existence of both the old and the new interpretations of the libretto creates grating incongruities. Even the musical material itself becomes inconsistent. Some episodes are distinctly lyrical, but when the libretto includes interpolated didactic political messages, march-like material abruptly and often illogically intrudes. Yet lyricism remains dominant throughout the opera, and it embodies Magomayev's passion for romanticism, which was a brand new style for Azerbaijani music at that time. Some of the first reviewers of the opera's premiere mentioned that the music did not quite match the revolutionary plot and that the main characters were focused on love, rather than on social struggle.

Even after Magomayev died in 1937, his opera continued to suffer from revisions that altered its content and musical style. The Russian composer Reinhold Gliere was assigned to prepare a new version of the opera before its presentation at the Decade of Azerbaijani Literature and Art in Moscow in 1938. Among the many changes Gliere implemented was a new character, Jafar, a worker from Baku who arrived in the village to help the peasants. The name of this new character was an attempt to flatter Mir Jafar Baghirov, the Communist leader of Azerbaijan. Ironically, after Stalin died and Baghirov was tried and executed, having such a character in the opera prompted the removal of *Nargiz* from the Opera Theater's repertoire. The fate of Magomayev's opera is thus on many levels particularly tragic, and it remains absent from the operatic repertoire today, receiving only occasional concert performances of its arias and other lyrical episodes.

Magomayev's work deserves to be reedited and freed from the ideological clichés imposed by the Soviets. It needs to be rehabilitated and returned to the stage, just as two other works already have been: the ballet *The Maiden's Tower* by A. Badalbeyli, and the opera *Sevil* (1953) by Amirov. In 1998, the pianist F. Badalbeyli and composer Musa Mirzayev (b. 1933) carefully removed all obviously Soviet ideological interpolations from the plots and music of both works. The new versions of both *Sevil* and *The Maiden's Tower* successfully premiered and are now back on stage.

Censorship penetrated all aspects of musical and cultural life in the USSR. Concert organizations and media had to be cautious about the content of public performances. Censors frequently visited the Philharmonic Hall and other concert venues, often disguised as audience members. "They sat in the hall, listened to the program, and then disappeared without saying a word," said Zokhrabov, who worked as music editor at the Philharmonic in the 1960s. "After that, in a week or so, we got a list of remarks that had to be taken into consideration."[56]

I had my own encounter with the Soviet censorship system. In September 1985, as a student at the conservatory, I was assigned to deliver a speech at the celebration of the centennial of Hajibeyli's birth. This festivity was a splendid event that was attended by national leaders, officials of high rank from all over the Soviet Union, and guests from around the world, and it was broadcast on live television. My speech was a huge responsibility and honor for me personally, as well as for the school, since I was supposed to speak on its behalf. A week before the event, I was urged to send the text of my presentation for clearance to the Department of Ideology at the Central Committee of the Communist Party of Azerbaijan. When I got it back, I sadly noticed some substantial changes serving ideological goals. For instance, my statement "Hajibeyli designed a course on the modal system of Azerbaijani music that has been taught at our school ever since, facilitating nativism in local musical activities" was followed by the following, "By doing so, he acted as a genuine Soviet composer, considering *narodnost'* as a priority for the future generations of Azerbaijani musicians." I could not ignore these interpolations because if I had, I, the school, and the many people who supervised my involvement in this event would have been subjected to severe administrative measures.

Music Education

In 1909, when working on the production of his opera *Sheykh Senan* that had extensive choral episodes, Hajibeyli went to the Baku synagogue to procure a choir for the work's premiere, because the country had no other suitable ensemble and no tradition of choral singing.[57] Hajibeyli thus knew from experience how frustrating the discrepancy between the demands of composed music and the skills of available performers could be. In Soviet Azerbaijan, this discrepancy disappeared in less than two decades. By the mid-1930s, with the assistance of Russian musicians who taught at the conservatory in Baku, Azerbaijan had produced national cadres of soloists, choirs, and orchestras that could undertake any performance desired. Using women performers initially posed problems because of the strength of Islam in Azerbaijan, but significant progress had been made by the Decade of Azerbaijani Art and Music, held in Moscow in 1938. Native musicians performed all of the roles, including the female ones, in the Azerbaijani operas featured there.

The emergence of cohorts of Azerbaijani professional musicians would have been impossible without the systematic education instituted under the Soviets. In 1921, the Azerbaijan State Conservatory opened in Baku, and by the end of the 1930s, the country had a wide network of music colleges and public music schools. Their curricula were designed in accordance with those of the conservatories in Moscow and Leningrad which, in turn, borrowed from Germanic models.

A Westerner visiting the Azerbaijan State Conservatory at any point between 1921 and 1991 would have discovered a rather familiar academic environment. Students played pieces of Bach, Mozart, and Beethoven on the piano, violin, and French horn; discussed the music of ancient Greece and the works of Benjamin Britten; wrote polyphonic exercises in the style of Palestrina and Hindemith; played harmonic progressions and sequences; and studied sonata and rondo forms. Student recitals and symphonic, chamber, and choral concerts took place in the conservatory's Large Hall, and conferences were held on various topics ranging from Gregorian chant to Stravinsky.

At the same time, our hypothetical Western visitor would have discovered something very different from his or her experience back home: the native music of Azerbaijan was incorporated into all parts of music instruction. He or she could see a *tar* student practicing the works of Amirov with a pianist colleague or discussing issues related to *mugham* with a musicologist friend. A Western visitor could attend a concert that combined performance of a traditional *mugham* trio and Brahms's string quartets. Naroditskaya rightfully states, "The coexistence of the two different musical traditions and two systems of teaching, Western and native, under the same administrative and academic roof was a challenge."[58] I agree with this statement, but I would also add that it was a beneficial experience on both sides of exchange. Classically trained performers played the national repertoire with more knowledge of the roots of its language, and traditional musicians were able to read scores and participate in performances of works of composed music. The reflections of F. Garayev on the 1998 premiere of his work *Khutba, Mugham, and Sura* (Sermon, Mugham, and Prayer) in Amsterdam, Holland, speak to this: "The *tar* part implies [an] improvisatory *mugham* episode in the second movement, and notated music in the first and third movements. The *tar*ist Mohlat Muslumov did both with the same level of confidence, and his mastery of improvisation, along with the ability to follow the metrical and rhythmical labyrinths of the score, particularly struck the Dutch audience. When being asked about how this was ever possible, I said: 'This is the result of the "imperfect" Soviet education system that he went through during his study at the Azerbaijan State Conservatory.'"[59]

As a musicology major, I was supposed to show the same level of awareness of both the development of operatic genres in Europe and the evolution of *mugham*. Otherwise, I would not have been able to conduct any research on the operas of Azerbaijani composers, which drew on the music idioms of the West yet were rooted in the traditional music of Azerbaijan. This duality was what Hajibeyli advocated and carefully preserved in the education system as well.

At an earlier stage of the Soviet era, Hajibeyli had one major opponent: the pianist and teacher Khadija Gayibova (1893–1938), who founded the Courses of Eastern Music, often referred to as the Eastern Conservatory, in 1920. Gayibova's main goal was to minimize Western influences and preserve the purity of traditional Azerbaijani music. The core elements of her institution were traditional instruments, the history of Eastern music, and ways of arranging traditional and folk music for piano and choir. Gayibova designed the curriculum and invited well-known *tar* and *kemancha* players to teach at the school. But her project did not survive, as it contradicted the notion of integrity between native and Western music, an idea that the Soviets prized. Gayibova's institution was analogous to the School of Eastern Music, which was founded by Abdurauf Fitrat (1886–1938) in Uzbekistan in the 1920s. Tellingly, both Gayibova and Fitrat were arrested and executed in the same year. Their school projects were not officially listed among the major accusations posed against them, but these activities certainly contributed to their reputations as being persons pursuing anti-Soviet activity.

In the schools that were approved by the new regime, there was a poisonous element that spoiled the entire Soviet system of music education: communist ideological goals. The ideology distorted the contents of music history classes. Beethoven was introduced as a bold revolutionary, and Haydn as a miserable victim of a bourgeois society. We never discussed early music in the way that it deserved, always being convinced that all that occurred before Bach was not worth thorough consideration. Now I understand that the true reason for this discrimination was the religious connections of that music that were viewed as inappropriate in an atheistic state. In fact, even in the music of Bach or Handel, we never discussed religious contexts.

The school also provided minimal exposure to twentieth-century Western music. For most of Soviet history, those in charge of official aesthetics considered this music to be a reflection of Western cultural values that were unnecessary to, if not antagonistic toward, Soviet society. An extracurricular, more informal, opportunity to study new music presented itself in the same time period thanks to the activities of the Composers Club that opened at the Azerbaijan State Conservatory in the late 1970s and served as a window to the outside world. If any faculty members or students managed to get any score or recording of a Western composer, they brought it to the club session to share and discuss with their peers. The Composers Club could be compared to the entire community of Azerbaijani musicians who stayed in an imposed state of isolation from the developments of Western music and used each and every opportunity to get information from the other side of the Iron Curtain.

The puritanism of Soviet society led to the avoidance of some sensitive academic topics, such as the impact of Sigmund Freud's theory of psychoanalysis on the aesthetics of European expressionism. Thanks to our curiosity, our teachers' creativity, and our mutual access to underground literature, we were never unaware of such matters. Even beyond music, many sought to bring "real knowledge" to Soviet society, or at least to its intelligentsia, but this knowledge circulated in complex ways. I still remember the leather-bound, carefully typed-out copies of Freud's works that we treasured and read secretly, sometimes even during boring lectures on Marxist-Leninist theories. The translations of such works might not have been perfect, but this did not prevent us from completely immersing ourselves in their contents. One memorable instance in our Opera Dramaturgy class perfectly exemplified this whole process. When lecturing on Shostakovich's opera *The Nose,* our professor, Liudmila Karagicheva, mentioned that the contents of Gogol's story that Shostakovich used could not be confined just to humor, as most Soviet critical sources maintained. "If you are familiar with Freud's ideas," she said, "you should know that situations and events in human life may signify more than appears at first glance." Our minds began to work at high speed, and using our imaginations, we easily comprehended another whole side of Shostakovich's opera.[60] Both teachers and students seemed to know the rules of the game we were forced to play.

"Wise Pharmacist"

Despite all these hardships, Azerbaijan exited the "empire of nations" with major accomplishments in all domains of music. The development of a highly skilled group of national composers was the main gain of Azerbaijani music during the Soviet era. Compared to Iran and Turkey, Azerbaijan produced a significantly large number of composers in the twentieth century. There were many epigones and those who simply pleased the system, but the number of composers of high professional and artistic caliber is still quite impressive for such a small nation. Unlike in Turkey and Iran, composed music in Azerbaijan developed in strong and constant conjunction with traditional music. Any piece written by composer in Azerbaijan has always been presented and perceived as a piece of the national music. Arif Malikov recounts concerning the music of Hajibeyli: "I frequently find myself humming Gadzhibekov's [Hajibeyli's] melodies. If my memory lets me down and I have trouble at some point, then any person standing beside me, even if he has no background in music, is capable of helping me out and correcting my mistake."[61] Malikov's statement shows the status of Azerbaijani composed music as a beloved product of native music and culture rather than as a borrowed model enhanced with the national elements.

The evidence of how advanced the Azerbaijani composed school was in comparison with the rest of the Muslim East is that in the 1990s, immediately after the collapse of the Soviet Union, hundreds of Azerbaijani musicians received contracts in those countries, mostly in Turkey, which had linguistic and cultural similarities.[62] Just as Azerbaijani music had been affected by an influx of Russian musicians in the early twentieth century, so too has Turkish music now been affected by an influx of Azerbaijani musicians at the turn of the millennium.

Azerbaijanis continue learning from their Soviet past. They honor musicians who survived the attacks on their musical and cultural heritage, the purges of the nation's intellectual potential, and the doctrine of a closed society. It is easy to judge those who never raised their voices against the system. It is fairer, though, to acknowledge their courage and the compromises they made to be able to defend the cultural heritage of their nation and to develop new forms of native music. As F. Badalbeyli states, "Today, while using new opportunities, we should not lose the accomplishments of the past. We should act as a wise pharmacist who measures 'right' doses from both the past and the present to be able to create the 'right' future."[63]

2 PIONEERS OF THE NEW AZERBAIJANI MUSICAL IDENTITY

When Hajibeyov [Hajibeyli] . . . died in 1948, the seeds he had sown in laying the foundations of Azeri music and musical life had only just begun to blossom. A whole generation of composers, including Fikret [Fikrat] Amirov and Kara Karaev [Gara Garayev], would shortly make their mark not only in Azerbaidzhan, but also in the rest of the Soviet Union and abroad.

MATTHEW O'BRIEN, *Uzeyir Hajibeyov [Hajibeyli] and Music in Azerbaidzhan [Azerbaijan]*

UZEYIR HAJIBEYLI: THE FATHER OF AZERBAIJANI ART MUSIC

The Three Epochs of One Life

He has always been referred to as "Uzeyir *bey*." In traditional Azerbaijani society, a *bey* placed beside a male's first name signified a person of nobility. Hajibeyli, like all Azerbaijanis, had to Russify his family name under the Russian and then the Soviet empires. By substituting a Russian suffix, "Hajibeyli" became "Hajibeyov" or even, when Russian transliteration rules were also applied, "Gadzhibekov." Yet none of the political systems could eliminate the respectful "*bey*" added to the composer's name, although the combination of "Uzeyir *bey*" with "comrade Gadzhibekov" strikes the Azerbaijani ear as bizarre. This paradoxical juxtaposition reflects the life and career of the composer, who witnessed and became involved in the tumultuous historical changes that occurred in twentieth-century Azerbaijan.

Born in 1885, Hajibeyli lived his first thirty-three years under the Russian czar. He belonged to a cohort of Azerbaijani intellectuals and enlighteners who advanced the idea of national culture and who combatted backwardness in

Azerbaijani society. Hajibeyli spent the next two years (1918–1920) as a citizen of the independent Azerbaijan Democratic Republic. He emerged as a hearty supporter of the new government, as its declaration of spiritual freedom and cultural openness resonated with his own vision of Azerbaijani music's future as a syncretic East-West phenomenon. For the final twenty-eight years of his life, Hajibeyli lived under Soviet rule. He became a part of the Soviet musical establishment, experiencing both the positive and negative sides of holding such a status. Like all renowned Soviet composers, Hajibeyli was forced to produce musical works praising the Communist Party and to write (or probably simply to sign) articles glorifying the Soviet regime. The composer paid this price for the irreplaceable opportunity of accomplishing his larger aesthetic project, namely the synthesis of his native musical traditions with the principles of Western music. Throughout changing political situations, Hajibeyli continually pursued this overriding goal, which was an integral part of his broader nationalist concept. The composer envisioned Azerbaijan as a well-educated nation, and he believed that in all domains of life, including music, Azerbaijanis would thrive by drawing on their unique geographical, cultural, and historical position at the crossroads of East and West. From the turn of the century until the end of his life, Hajibeyli worked toward this endeavor of East-West synthesis, and during the Soviet era, he utilized all the available mechanisms communist ideology had to offer.

Naroditskaya acknowledges Hajibeyli's East-West project as a phenomenon that, although it may have resonated with Soviet political realities, actually emerged both before and regardless of them. She argues, "Respected in intellectual circles in pre-Soviet Azerbaijan, his reformist ideas were consonant with the socialist political agenda and likewise fit the nationalist stream in music of the post-Soviet period."[1] Naroditskaya's position differs from the viewpoints advocated by several Western musicologists who present Hajibeyli primarily as a product and a servant of the Soviet system. Krebs acknowledges Hajibeyli for his major accomplishments in giving Azerbaijanis their first opera, music school, choir in the Western classical tradition, and academic study of their own musical heritage, but he misinterprets the motivating forces behind Hajibeyli's work. According to Krebs, "It was . . . easy to persuade him [Hajibeyli] of the primitive level of the *mugam*-based music of his people," and he became "one of the key-stones of the Russification in his country."[2] Frolova-Walker holds a similar position to Krebs and argues that Hajibeyli refuted his national heritage and imitated Russian musical models.[3] Both Krebs's and Frolova-Walker's statements do not recognize the true motivations of Hajibeyli's work. *Mugham* remained the main source of inspiration for Hajibeyli throughout his life, and he proceeded from the use of *mugham* "as is" in his early works toward its application through the various means of composed music in his later ones. A unique hybrid genre of *mugham* opera was his first composition, and among his last opuses are two romances, "Without You" (1941) and "Beloved" (1943), on the lyrics of Nizami that the composer defined as *gazal*s, after the main poetic form used in *mugham* lyrics. And it was *mugham* and constant references to it in composed music that helped Hajibeyli and the entire body of Azerbaijani music survive the ordeal of Russification. Earlier sources of Western musicology also represent Hajibeyli as an obedient child and an apologist of the Soviet cultural agenda. For instance, Alexandria Vodarsky-Shiraeff states that Hajibeyli only became prominent as a composer in the Soviet period, and his major works worthy of mention include only the operas *Leyli and Majnun* and *Koroghlu*.[4] Putting aside the serious mistake of presenting Hajibeyli as a product of the Soviet era, this statement contains another discrepancy: *Leyli and Majnun* was Hajibeyli's first work, and it premiered in 1908, twelve years before the Soviet era in Azerbaijan. Michel Dimitri Calvocoressi also confines Hajibeyli's legacy to these two operatic works.[5] Misinterpretations of Hajibeyli's career found in the earlier Western publications on Soviet music can be accounted for by scholars' lack of access to objects for research, such as scores and manuscripts, which in turn was caused by the former status of the Soviet Union as a closed country. But access aside, another problem continues to prevent many Western musicologists and ethnomusicologists from adequate comprehension of Hajibeyli's motivations and contributions. No scholar has undertaken a thorough comparative study investigating the composer's style and the traditional music of Azerbaijan. Without such work, it is impossible to define authenticity versus Russianness in Hajibeyli's music or to grasp the intricacies of his musical style. Chapter 4 contains analyses comparing Hajibeyli's style with folk music prototypes. For now, it is important to discuss the main aesthetic foundations of his East-West project.

Important "Firsts"

Hajibeyli's musicianship derives from the national music tradition and can be defined as its reincarnation in a new aesthetic context. As Garayev wrote, "Gadzhibekov's [Hajibeyli's] music is a powerful vehicle which shook and brought to life several of the hitherto static traditions of past Azerbaijani music . . . that had remained concealed for centuries."[6] This statement identifies the deep sensibility of nativism typical of Hajibeyli's music. Such a strong connection to the Azerbaijani musical tradition resulted from many factors. Foremost among them was the environment in which Hajibeyli lived and worked. He was born in Azerbaijan's district of Garabagh, nearby the city of Shusha. This city has historically been one of the main musical centers of Azerbaijan and the cradle of one of three existing schools of *mugham*.[7] Hajibeyli deepened his knowledge of Azerbaijani musical traditions throughout his life by collecting folk melodies and researching the modal system of his native music.

Even early in his career, Hajibeyli viewed the music of his nation as a living and constantly developing phenomenon. A product of the era of Westernization and modernization in Azerbaijani society and music, he considered mastering the traditions of Western music to be an integral part of the further development of his native music. In this regard, Hajibeyli's experience can be compared to that of Mikhail Glinka (1804–1857) and Ali Naqi Vaziri (1887–1979). They were, respectively, the pioneers of composed music in Russia and Iran, the two neighboring cultures with the greatest influence on Azerbaijan in Hajibeyli's time.

Like Glinka, Hajibeyli was driven by nationalism when creating his music style. Many musicologists acknowledge that Glinka's direct and strong links with Russia's folk heritage helped him found the Russian tradition of composed music. For instance, David Brown characterizes Glinka's melodic nationalism as "effortless."[8] Most of his melodies are almost indistinguishable from Russian folk melodies in their style. Such an assessment can be applied to Hajibeyli as well. As stated by the composer Agshin Alizade, "Hajibeyli's musical world seems to be produced by, and to belong not only to him but to the entire Azerbaijani nation. It is as if, through Hajibeyli, Azerbaijanis discovered new forms of their own native music."[9] Hajibeyli's style maintains links with tradition not because he directly and purposefully emulated folk models. Instead, he suggested new interpretations of the fundamental principles of traditional Azerbaijani music. As a result, his style is based on the essential principles of his native musical heritage, applied in a highly unique, individual way. As for the ties with the Iranian Vaziri, Nettl's characterization of Vaziri as "at once a Westernizer and a champion of modernization" also applies to Hajibeyli.[10] Like Hajibeyli, Vaziri did not aim to preserve the purity of tradition; rather, he considered mastering the musical and cultural forms of the West, along with updating the stylistic panorama of his native music, to be a necessity and a condition of the Persian tradition's continuous and successful development.

Hajibeyli's progress as a composer parallels that of Glinka and Vaziri, who left their homelands to study abroad. Glinka and Vaziri went to Europe, while Hajibeyli traveled Russia to expand his knowledge of Western musical traditions and experience in them. He took music classes at the Moscow Philharmonic Society (1912–1913) and the Petersburg Conservatory (1913–1914). Due to

World War I and financial difficulties, Hajibeyli was unable to complete his studies in Russia. Nonetheless, he significantly increased his awareness of Western music under the instruction of his teachers, all well-known names in Russian music circles.[11]

Although Hajibeyli's work as a musical pioneer demonstrates similarities in aesthetics and biography to that of Glinka and Vaziri, Hajibeyli occupies a unique position in other respects. Glinka and Vaziri were the first native composers in their countries, but unlike Hajibeyli, they benefited from the musical legacy of European musicians who had worked in Iran and Russia and introduced Western forms of music to native audiences. These guest composers served as catalysts of musical synthesis and were followed by the first national composers who continued to reimagine their native music traditions within the context of Western music. The development of composed music in Turkey followed a similar course. Guest musicians from Italy and Germany established the foundations of the synthesis of Turkish native musical idioms and Western music, with the first national composers known as "the Turkish Five" coming onto the stage afterward. The trajectory of the development of composed music traditions in Transcaucasia also differs from that of Azerbaijan. The Armenian Komitas (1869–1935) and the Georgian Zakharii Paliashvili (1871–1933), the leaders of composed music in their respective countries, belonged to a cohort of native composers. Although they were the foremost members of their circles, they did not have to build their composed music traditions from the ground up. They had Armenian and Georgian colleagues living both in and outside of Transcaucasia, and these composers had already started to use the forms and genres of the West to engage their native music.

Hajibeyli's mission was different. He was truly the first composer in Azerbaijan. He did not have any predecessors, either inside or outside of Azerbaijan, who sought to synthesize Azerbaijani and Western music. Without the aid of being able to draw on any historical precedents, Hajibeyli wrote the first Azerbaijani works in a Western format. Muslim Magomayev and Zulfugar Hajibeyli (1884–1950), both Hajibeyli's contemporaries, became composers and his colleagues, but they generally followed his concept of East-West synthesis instead of offering competition or proposing alternative paths.

Hajibeyli also stood apart from the composers of the Central Asian nations. The first national composers of Uzbekistan, Tajikistan, Kazakhstan, Turkmenistan, and Kyrgyzstan emerged only during the Soviet era and only after the significant input made by Russian "missionary" composers sent by Moscow. Hajibeyli never relied on the direct assistance of Russian composers. He never wrote any opus in coauthorship with a Russian composer, as many of his Central Asian colleagues had to, and in doing so Hajibeyli set a precedent for future generations of national composers.

A high level of responsibility fell on Hajibeyli, who never had the luxury of making mistakes, so to speak, because an error on his part would have jeopardized the entire project of Azerbaijani composed music. Perhaps this is why his output is rather small, but almost every piece of it holds the status of a "first" in Azerbaijani music and culture. Most of Hajibeyli's important "firsts" have been discussed in the previous chapter: the *mugham* opera *Leyli and Majnun* that marked the birth of Azerbaijani art music, the operetta *The Cloth Peddler* that significantly accelerated the development of national opera, and finally, the opera *Koroghlu,* in which the national style of Azerbaijani composed music reached its efflorescence. Hajibeyli also wrote the first Azerbaijani anthem and the first Azerbaijani cantatas, romances, and instrumental fantasies, and in these he elaborated on different aspects of East-West synthesis. Hajibeyli's merits as the founder of Azerbaijani national ethnomusicology were directly related to his creative work. He aimed to establish a theoretical basis for his concept of synthesis, and through this theoretical endeavor, he hoped to facilitate and encourage other composers' activities in drawing together East and West. In scholarly publications from the 1910s through the 1940s, Hajibeyli thoroughly studied the modal and rhythmic rules of Azerbaijani music, and he articulated the possibility of the synthesis of those rules with the principles of Western classical music.

Alongside his accomplishments as composer and scholar, Hajibeyli powerfully contributed to the founding of music education in Azerbaijan. He aimed to create a system that would produce performers, composers, and scholars who were equally knowledgeable of and competent in their native musical heritage and Western repertoire. Hajibeyli personally auditioned thousands of Azerbaijani children in order to select talented ones and urge them to study music. My father was among them. He still remembers that day in 1937 when he met Hajibeyli:

> Uzeyir *bey* played a tune on the piano and then asked me to sing it. I did. After that, he clapped a simple rhythmic pattern that I was supposed to repeat. At the end of our meeting, Uzeyir *bey* grabbed the violin sitting on the table, and asked, "Sweetheart, do you want to play this beautiful instrument?" I got confused first, but then replied, "Yes, I do." Uzeyir *bey* turned to my parents and said, "Your son wants to study music, and I see that he is fully capable to do that. Let us give him such a chance.

The family was happy for this new opportunity and very proud of it, and my father started attending public music school where he took violin, music theory,

FIGURE 2.1. Baku Music Academy. *Photo by Aida Huseynova.*

and music literature classes. Although my father never became a professional musician, he keeps memories from that precious childhood music experience that he, like many Azerbaijanis, owed to Hajibeyli.

"Do We Need to Study European Music?"

"Do we Azerbaijani Turks need to spend time, energy, and means to study . . . European music? Yes, we do and we should, because via studying European music we comprehend the centuries-old art of music that produced a number of great masters whose works cannot remain alien to any nation that claims to be recognized as a cultured one."[12] This concept articulated by Hajibeyli, along with his call to intensify "research and artistic activities in the field of folk music" that "would finally place Eastern music in an honorable place along with Western music," has become axiomatic for many generations of music educators in Azerbaijan.[13]

As the nation's most accomplished composer, Hajibeyli became a key figure in the founding of the Azerbaijan State Conservatory in 1921. Among

Hajibeyli's principal achievements was importing the finest musicians and educators from Russia, and in the 1920s, 1930s, and 1940s, he personally invited them to come and teach at the new school. His work recruiting Russian musicians was particularly intense when he served as the vice-director and director of the conservatory from 1938 to 1948.[14] In large part due to Hajibeyli's efforts, music education in Azerbaijan made a revolutionary jump from level zero to being able, within only three or four decades, to produce world-class musicians. Hajibeyli carefully considered each potential candidate for the conservatory not only in terms of professional skills, but also with regard to his or her compatibility with the Eastern mentality, culture, and musical traditions. He maintained personal contact with Russian musicians, requesting that they accept students from Azerbaijan into their classes at the Moscow and Leningrad conservatories.

Hajibeyli worked hard to establish a strong national component within music education in Azerbaijan. He caught even the subtlest of fluctuations in the Soviets' policies toward nationalism and responded accordingly. In the early 1920s when, as a result of the inertia of the past, a certain freedom of thought was still allowed in the Soviet empire, and when the nationalistic and democratic ideas of the ADR continued to linger in the collective Azerbaijani consciousness, Hajibeyli founded the Department of Eastern Music within the Azerbaijan State Conservatory. This small citadel of nativism, which offered classes on Azerbaijani traditional instruments and *mugham,* was destroyed in 1933. The official justification was sharp and unequivocal: "We remained in a permanent shock with . . . the existence of autonomous 'Eastern department.' . . . It has been liquidated, and now the *tar* and the *kemancha* are a part of the curriculum on par with European instruments; study of these instruments will be based on the notated system only."[15] Although the *tar* and *kemancha* students indeed learned to read from and play musical scores, they never stopped playing *mugham* impromptu. The power of tradition was too strong to be stopped so abruptly.

Another of Hajibeyli's nationalist initiatives was the Turkic Music College, which he founded in 1922. This school primarily focused on traditional music, although under the auspices of a Western-style educational model. The composer provided a strong defense for his proposal by referring to the low percentage of ethnic Azerbaijani students in the Azerbaijan State Conservatory. This reality was one of the challenges of this early stage of music education in Azerbaijan. In 1922, of the 366 conservatory students, only 17 were ethnic Azerbaijanis.[16] The Turkic Music College was supposed to attract natives, and it did: in 1922, 350 of 383 first year students were ethnic Azerbaijanis.[17] Eventually, Hajibeyli, who himself directed the college, increased the weight of the Eastern element in its curriculum by adding new classes related to the theory of Eastern poetry and music, and he also founded an ensemble of traditional instruments. Hajibeyli planned to raise the status of this institution, reorganizing it as the Azerbaijan State Turkic Conservatory.[18] Unfortunately, this school finally exceeded the limit of nativism sanctioned by the Soviets, and in 1926, they ended the Turkic Music College's independent existence, merging it with the Azerbaijan State Conservatory.

In 1924, Hajibeyli designed a course that remains intact to the present day: Principles of Azerbaijani Folk Music. It was eventually included in the curricula of all music schools in Azerbaijan and has been continuously taught across the country. This class remains among my brightest school memories from the 1980s. After – or before – practicing the dominant seventh, modulation, or sequences in a harmony class, we enthusiastically played examples of modal music on the piano, identified features of Azerbaijani modes in the scores of native composers, and wrote short compositions based on those modes.

The presence of Eastern music in musical instruction increased visibly during World War II. This was natural, as during that difficult period the Soviets stimulated the individual patriotism of all nations populating their empire to help their subjects withstand the hardships of war. Hajibeyli immediately recognized the opportunities offered by this new policy. In 1943, he opened a new department called *Azerbaidzhanskoe Otdelenie* (Azerbaijani Section) that exclusively focused on studying *mugham* and traditional instruments. This initiative did not last long, and *Azerbaidzhanskoe Otdelenie* closed simultaneously with changes in the Communist Party's policy – and with Hajibeyli's death – in 1948.

Along with composition, music education was among Hajibeyli's most effective and long-lasting projects. If not for Hajibeyli, the balance between the native and Western ingredients in the music education of Azerbaijan would have been very different. He strengthened the Eastern component of the curricula, even to the point of having it penetrate conventional Western classes. In solfège class, we wrote dictations based on the national modal system, and in harmony class, we played sequences compiled from pieces of Azerbaijani music. Hajibeyli never allowed those born in his country to forget their roots.

The Unknown Hajibeyli

For decades, sources published both inside and outside the Soviet Union portrayed Hajibeyli as a loyal Soviet citizen. A new understanding of the composer's life and work began to emerge in the mid-1980s, at the time of the decline of the communist regime, when new information became available on both sides of the Soviet border. In my life, such a moment of truth occurred in Baku on October 4, 1985, when I delivered a speech at the celebration of the centennial of Hajibeyli's birth. After the event, I was approached by an elegantly dressed man whose appearance resembled that of Uzeyir *bey*. Smiling in a manner completely unusual in Soviet culture, he introduced himself in the Azerbaijani language, but with a slight accent, "My name is Timuchin Hajibeyli, I am Uzeyir *bey*'s nephew, and I came from France." I was thoroughly confused. I thought I was aware of all branches of the Hajibeyli family tree, particularly since it is one of the most respected Azerbaijani musical dynasties. But I never had heard of any overseas extension of the Hajibeylis. I began to realize that the story of Hajibeyli had its unknown, or rather its hidden, chapters.

One such hidden component of Hajibeyli's life included his activities during the period of the ADR. All sources published during the Soviet era stated that between 1918 and 1931, the composer did not write a single bar of music. This assertion is bizarre, considering that before this time, Hajibeyli had been quite prolific, creating six operas and three operettas within only seven years. After the collapse of the Soviet Union, archives released data about Hajibeyli's life during the two years of the ADR, and they made public other materials that explain the composer's apparent lack of compositional activity during the following years. Under the ADR, Hajibeyli accumulated an impressive list of anticommunist activities. He was an energetic member in the Musavat Party and collaborated with the newspaper *Azerbaijan,* the main media outlet of the ADR. His younger brother Jeyhun Hajibeyli was *Azerbaijan*'s editor-in-chief, and in 1919 and 1920, immediately before the Soviet invasion, Uzeyir even replaced Jeyhun in this capacity. Hajibeyli published numerous articles criticizing Russia's colonial policy and warning of the danger of Russian-Soviet occupation. As a musician, too, Hajibeyli advanced nationalism during the ADR era, creating the national anthem of the independent Azerbaijan. Adding to Uzeyir's pre-Soviet sins, so to speak, was the emigration of his brother Jeyhun. Jeyhun Hajibeyli did not simply leave Azerbaijan for France, rather, he became a zealous anticommunist, expressing his political views in many interviews given to radio stations and newspapers in Europe. Having such a hazardous family connection could have resulted in severe persecution.

Hajibeyli's life was in serious danger in the 1920s and early 1930s. The composer reduced his creative work to almost nothing and was mentally prepared to share the tragic fate of thousands of other victims of the Stalinist repressions. Nariman Narimanov, a high Soviet official and ethnic Azerbaijani, is credited with saving Hajibeyli's life in the 1920s.[19] According to the Azerbaijani writer Anar, Narimanov convinced Josef Stalin of the importance of having Hajibeyli alive to serve the needs of Azerbaijani music and culture.[20] What ultimately saved Hajibeyli's life in the 1930s was his music. In 1938, *Koroghlu* was performed at the Decade of Azerbaijani Literature and Art in Moscow, tremendously impressing Stalin. There is a famous anecdote regarding Stalin and Hajibeyli's meeting after the premiere: "Stalin was among those seated in the audience for that performance. Afterwards, he and some top Communist Party officials gathered around the musicians. One of them commended Hajibeyli by saying, 'You ought to write a couple more operas like that.' Suddenly Stalin's voice inserted an emphatic 'No!' There was a long pause. Nobody knew what to say. . . . Then he broke his silence. 'Don't write a couple more,' he told the composer. 'Write two couples!'"[21] Whatever the motivation of the dictator's sadistic gesture was, for Hajibeyli it signified the end of a period of permanent fear. He was never able to write "a couple more" operas, however, since years of long-lasting mental pressure caused a serious negative impact on his health. In 1948, Hajibeyli died of diabetes at the age of sixty-three.

His Versatile Contributions

Hajibeyli's contributions went well beyond musical culture. He was a talented and skilled literary figure, as seen in the self-written libretti of his three operettas. Hajibeyli was a brilliant master of polemics and defended his ideas in numerous articles and essays published in the Azerbaijani media, beginning in 1905. A public figure, Hajibeyli struggled against the social, cultural, and religious stereotypes that had taken hold of Azerbaijani society during his time. The question of female emancipation runs through many of Hajibeyli's works, including his music, particularly the operettas, and his early satires and articles published in Azerbaijani newspapers. All three operettas convey stories of women oppressed by patriarchal social rules and struggling for independence, and all end with the heroines' triumph.[22] Getting Azerbaijani women involved in musical life was also an important goal for Hajibeyli. In 1912, he was among those who pushed for the debut concert of Shovkat Mammadova, the first female operatic singer of Azerbaijani descent (see chapter 1). On behalf of the conservatory, he visited homes and patiently talked to parents, convincing them to let their daughters study music. The first generation of Azerbaijani female composers came to the profession with his blessing. Among such women was Adilya Huseynzade (1916–2005), who significantly contributed to the development of Azerbaijani romance. Many Azerbaijani composers acknowledge Huseynzade's outstanding role in their lives and careers. She taught

FIGURE 2.2. The first women composers of Azerbaijan. From left to right:
Adilya Huseynzade, Farida Guliyeva, and Shafiga Akhundova.
Courtesy of the State Museum of Azerbaijani Musical Culture.

composition at the Bulbul Music School, which remains Azerbaijan's main precollege music educational institution to the present. Shafiga Akhundova (1924–2013) was another protégée of Hajibeyli. She later wrote the opera *The Bride's Rock* (1972), which was the first opera in the Muslim East written by a female composer.

Hajibeyli was a man of dignity and honor, as evidenced by hundreds of stories told by those who knew him – stories about the enormous generosity that led him to give a part of the special food package that he got during World War II to those who were in need, including students, neighbors, and colleagues, who would never know the source; stories about the coats that he bought for young Azerbaijani students who studied at the Moscow State Conservatory and could not afford to buy warm clothes to survive the severe Russian winters. His funeral on November 24, 1948, resembled a street rally: thousands of people from all parts of Azerbaijan arrived in Baku to escort Hajibeyli to his final rest. The singer Bulbul performed Hajibeyli's romance "Without You," and these words echoed in the hearts of millions of Azerbaijanis overcome with the sorrow of their loss.

Tremendous respect of Hajibeyli and his legacy has probably been the strongest constant in twentieth-century Azerbaijani culture and social life, remaining a strong link that none of the tumultuous political changes could eliminate or even reduce. The composer's birthday, September 18, is celebrated in the country as Music Day. On that holiday, hundreds of people come to Hajibeyli's statue in front of the Baku Music Academy, which bears the composer's name. The Azerbaijan State Symphony Orchestra, also named after Hajibeyli, always opens their memorial concert with the overture to *Koroghlu*. Every year, *Leyli and Majnun* inaugurates the new season at the Azerbaijan State Opera and Ballet Theater. Movies based on Hajibeyli's operettas are annually broadcast on television during national holidays. Hajibeyli is revered as a national genius who not only created musical masterpieces, but also accomplished more than thousands of politicians did in developing Azerbaijani national identity.

IMPLICATIONS OF EAST-WEST SYNTHESIS AFTER HAJIBEYLI

1948: A Decisive Year

The year of Hajibeyli's death, 1948, posed many challenges for the young Azerbaijani art music tradition. Bereft of the powerful and guiding presence of Hajibeyli, Azerbaijani musicians had to establish a new strategy for developing their musical future. The situation was particularly hazardous, since Hajibeyli's passing coincided with the infamous Communist Party decree on formalism and with increased pressure from the Soviet regime on musicians. Would Azerbaijani composers succeed in maintaining Hajibeyli's concept, or would they instead choose to follow an easier, yet regressive path and create music that simply fulfilled the doctrine of socialist realism? Soon it became clear that Azerbaijani music was not merely enduring these difficult times, it was turning to new stimuli that would continue its growth. Gara Garayev and Fikrat Amirov, the two leading national composers in the wake of Hajibeyli, were at the fore of these developments.

These two composers were rather young to take on this responsibility: in 1948, Garayev was thirty, and Amirov was twenty-six. Both, however, had already penned several remarkable works. Garayev had written two symphonies (in 1944 and 1946) and the symphonic poem *Leyli and Majnun* (1947). Amirov had composed a Double Concerto for Violin, Piano, and Orchestra (1946), the symphony *Nizami* (1947), and the symphonic *mughams Shur* (1948) and *Kurd Ovshari* (1948).

Both Garayev and Amirov were Hajibeyli's direct disciples in many respects. They continued his course of important "firsts": Garayev is revered as one of the first authors of the Azerbaijani symphony, and Amirov wrote the first concertos and pioneered the genre of symphonic *mugham*. Every measure of their music embraces Hajibeyli's challenging ideal of East-West synthesis built on East-West syncretism. But Garayev and Amirov did not merely reapply Hajibeyli's concept, rather, they pushed it forward. For Hajibeyli, the very idea of fusing East and West was new, and he had to prove the possibility and effectiveness of such a synthesis. Garayev and Amirov entered into East-West synthesis as an already established field, and they explored new forms and new levels of fusion. These two composers offered alternative implications of East-West synthesis. Garayev heard and placed the voice of his native music in a global context. He revitalized the stylistic landscape of Azerbaijani music by drawing from Western innovations, and he distilled folk music idioms, transforming them from national markers into universal symbols. Amirov, by contrast, emphasized the Eastern roots of Azerbaijani music. He understood his native culture as a part of the larger region of the Middle East, and he chose stylistic means of composed music that helped open the national substance of Azerbaijani music to the Western world. Garayev and Amirov were often opponents, frequently involved in the polemics about the "right" way of developing Azerbaijani music. Nonetheless, their divergent approaches signified the growing maturity of Azerbaijani composed music. These composers provided an impetus for the pluralism of styles that would continue to develop within this tradition.

Westernizer Garayev and Easternizer Amirov

As Garayev stated, "Since the very beginning, the West and the East stayed side by side within me. Literally, I am the son of two mothers."[23] And here are Amirov's words, "I adore the West. But I am a proud son of the East."[24] The contrasting positions of these two composers came about because of many factors, beginning with their family backgrounds and early childhoods. Garayev was a product of Baku's cosmopolitan, urban environment. The Garayev family belonged to the city's intellectual elite. His father was a famous pediatrician, and his mother was one of the first female college graduates in Azerbaijan. Along with traditional native music, Garayev's first aural experiences included romances, waltzes, and marches, which his mother played on the piano, and the music of brass bands, often performed outdoors in Baku in the 1920s.

FIGURE 2.3. Gara Garayev and Dmitry Shostakovich. *Courtesy of the State Museum of Azerbaijani Musical Culture.*

Amirov was a native of Ganja, an ancient cultural center and the second-largest city of Azerbaijan. He was born into the family of Mashadi Jamil Amirov (1875–1928), a distinguished *khanende*, a *tar* player, and composer.[25] Young Fikrat's early musical experiences revolved around *mugham* and *ashig* music. He grew up with the sounds of his father's *tar*, and this instrument become

FIGURE 2.4. Fikrat Amirov and Bahram Mansurov, tar player.
Courtesy of Eldar Mansurov.

Amirov's lifelong favorite. Amirov never stopped playing the *tar,* even after becoming an accomplished composer. Nor did he cease meeting with traditional musicians and discussing his composition projects with them, even late in his career.

Years of study at the Azerbaijan State Conservatory increased the Western component in Garayev's and Amirov's respective musical vocabularies. Both studied composition with guest professors from Russia.[26] Unlike Amirov, Garayev felt a persistent call to strengthen his engagement with Western music, and after having finished his study at the Azerbaijan State Conservatory, he went to Moscow, where he studied composition with Dmitry Shostakovich. Contact with Shostakovich and the luminaries of Russian music, along with the intense musical and cultural life of Moscow, extended Garayev's horizons in the field of Western music.

Both Garayev and Amirov, like thousands of students at the Azerbaijan State Conservatory, took Hajibeyli's Principles of Azerbaijani Folk Music class. They listened to and transcribed *mugham,* learned it theoretical rules, and composed in national modes. As a part of the school's requirements, both composers conducted fieldwork in distant districts of Azerbaijan, where they recorded folk melodies and interviewed local musicians. For Garayev, these years invaluably deepened his knowledge of traditional music. Later he would reflect on Hajibeyli's role in his life, saying, "He struggled for my national soul."[27] No "struggle" was necessary in Amirov's case, since his soul and mind were already entirely committed to the traditional music of his country.

All these factors – family roots, education, personality, and their individual tastes and preferences – shaped each composer's musicianship and contributed to his unique embodiment of East-West synthesis. Amirov created a romanticist interpretation of the idioms of his native music. Just as Chopin offered a new poetic vision of the mazurka, Amirov rediscovered *mugham* in the context of romantic aesthetics. The monodic roots of *mugham* profoundly shaped Amirov's style. Melody is its strongest and most expressive component; it is the "soul of his music," in the words of Shostakovich, who acknowledged Amirov's "rich melodic gift."[28] The prevalence of melody is clearly seen in all his opuses, including his masterpiece, the opera *Sevil*, which is recognized as a magnum opus of the national operatic repertoire, on the level of Hajibeyli's *Koroghlu*. Amirov's harmony is fundamentally melodic in nature, too. It is predominantly derived from accumulating the pitch contents of modes, or to be more precise, from verticalizing the scales of Azerbaijani music. The composer usually avoided polyphonic textures and only allowed modest contrapuntal techniques, such as imitative elements corresponding to the call-response technique typical of *mugham* performances. In the Soviet political climate, the authenticity of Amirov's style was both a strength and a vulnerability. On one hand, it met the requirements of *narodnost'*, a major tenet of socialist realism, securing for Amirov a relatively privileged position in Soviet music circles. On the other hand, such clear roots in folk music pushed Amirov's music into the far more controversial area of the ethnofolkloric branch of Soviet music. Composers in this vein could often conceal professional incompetence and lack of creativity through an appeal to the so-called nativism that followed official doctrine. Clearly, Amirov's aesthetics and style were determined by other factors. According to the musicologist Rauf Farkhadov, "For him [Amirov], the ethnographic approach was the way to reveal proto-historical, phenomenological musical content."[29] In the other words, Amirov elaborated on the fundamental qualities of Azerbaijani music, and he found ways to contemporize them without disturbing their essence.

Garayev's credo was different. "We should not think like this: here is us, and there are world's accomplishments. We are also a part of the world."[30] These words summarize Garayev's philosophy of the new Azerbaijani music.

As discussed in chapter 1, Garayev integrated native idioms with many stylistic sources of Western music, including neoclassicism, neobaroque styles, twelve-tone techniques, and jazz. All Garayev's works, including his two ballets (*Seven Beauties* and *The Path of Thunder*), the Sonata for Violin and Piano (1960), the Piano Preludes (1951–1963), the Third Symphony, and the Violin Concerto, are integrated into twentieth-century soundscapes, yet they maintain a unique Azerbaijani identity. An innovative spirit drove Garayev's work across a broad spectrum of activities, including research and teaching. In 1970 and 1971, he gave a series of lectures on Western contemporary music at the Azerbaijan State Conservatory, and in the late 1970s, he founded a students' chamber orchestra that focused exclusively on twentieth-century repertoire. Garayev also organized the Youth Jazz Orchestra at the Azerbaijan State Conservatory and even attempted to integrate jazz into education, which was an unthinkable novelty in Soviet Azerbaijan.

At the first glance, Garayev's style was more radical, whereas Amirov's was rather conservative. But this would be too facile an assessment. Both Garayev and Amirov were innovators of the highest caliber, profoundly expanding the space of East-West synthesis. Each found his own way of combining East and West, thus setting two alternative paths for future generations of Azerbaijani composers.

Expanding Regional Context

Taken together, Garayev's and Amirov's accomplishments expanded the semantic space of Azerbaijani music to encompass non-Azerbaijani themes and subjects. Predictably enough, Amirov turned to Middle Eastern musical and literary traditions, whereas Garayev embraced a larger array of influences, including those from Europe, America, Africa, and Asia. Despite these composers' interest in non-Azerbaijani themes and subjects, neither ceased being highly national composers. As Dahlhaus mentions about Glinka, "to assert . . . that Glinka is 'authentic' when he writes pieces of a Russian character, but 'inauthentic' when the stimulus is Spanish, would be absurd (and the musical nationalists always avoided making any such claim)." And furthermore, "In music, unlike language, works of significance can be created in 'broken' Spanish or Hungarian."[31] Such an assessment applies also to Garayev and Amirov, whose works inspired by influences outside of Azerbaijan remain an authentic product of Azerbaijani music.

In Amirov's case, the language he spoke in his "Middle Eastern" works – the Concerto on Arab Themes for the Piano and Symphony Orchestra (cocomposed by Elmira Nazirova) (1957), or the ballet *A Thousand and One Nights*

(1979), based on Arabic folk tales – was not quite "broken," following Dahl-haus's metaphor. Amirov explored traditions related to his own and focused on their similarities to his native music. After touring Middle Eastern countries, Amirov said, "They are all aware of the legend of Leyli and Majnun or Nizami's poetry. They all have similar forms of oral professional music. . . . I have become astonished at the great number of melodies and rhythms barely distinguish-able from those of Azerbaijan."[32] Deeply respectful of authenticity and heritage, Amirov relied on aural experience and direct exposure to new traditions. This is why the composer so valued his travels throughout the Middle East, where he collected folk melodies and met with traditional musicians. These experiences, in turn, inspired his own compositional activity.

Garayev's philosophy was driven by the idea of universality of music. He sought philosophical depth, intense lyricism, and drama, and his creative stimulus could derive from either his native music or an "other" tradition, even a distant one. As described by the Azerbaijani writer Imran Gasimov, "He [Garayev] holds all civilization in his hands, not as simple encyclopedic data but as deeply comprehended and – in nine occasions out of ten – originally interpreted. It was as if a crystal in his mind replicated the informational ray in a completely unexpected facet."[33] The ballet *Seven Beauties* and the sym-phonic poem *Leyli and Majnun*, both based on the poetry of Nizami, stand among Garayev's masterpieces. But no less spectacular is his ballet *The Path of Thunder,* based on the novel of the South African writer Peter Abrahams; or Garayev's two "Spanish" works, one inspired by a Cervantes novel, the other by the paintings of Goya. These compositions are, respectively, the "symphonic engravings" *Don Quixote* (1960) and the dramatic symphony *Goya* (1980) (the latter work in coauthorship with Faraj Garayev). Gara Garayev's portfolio in-cludes "French," "Russian," and "American" compositions, and works inspired by many other nationalities.[34] The abundance of multinational impulses never invalidated or obscured the deep national sensuality of Garayev's music. In the composer's own words, "I write music on Spanish, Bulgarian, Vietnam-ese themes; however, I am sure it still reflects my nationality, my Azerbaijani hands . . . I don't know how it happens, I don't even think of it."[35] Indeed, every bar of Garayev's works reflects his distinct national identity, and he re-mained, according to the Russian composer Rodion Schedrin, a "deeply na-tional composer."[36]

Privileges and Torments

By the late 1940s, Garayev and Amirov had earned official recognition, and, later on, they became among the most highly respected Soviet composers.

They received the most prestigious awards possible. Both were assigned to lead Azerbaijan's major music institutions for several years. Garayev was the director of the Azerbaijan State Conservatory (1949–1953) and chair of the Union of Composers of Azerbaijan (1953–1982); Amirov held the directorship of the Azerbaijan State Opera and Ballet Theater (1956–1959). Along with the other figureheads of Soviet music, they frequently represented the USSR overseas.

There were, however, many bitter realities below the surface of the lives of Azerbaijan's two distinguished composers. This is particularly true regarding Garayev, who had a long history of confrontation with official Soviet doctrines. His first serious battle occurred in 1948, when his First and Second Symphonies were labeled as "formalistic." The young composer was reproached for ignoring the traditions of folk and classical music, for having too abstract melodic contents, and for employing cacophonic harmonic language. As Krebs rightfully mentions, "It is well to bear in mind that criticism of Karaev [Garayev] and many of his fellow students was simply another angle of attack at Shostakovich himself."[37] Yet Krebs seems to be unaware of the range of repressions that fell onto Garayev when he depicts the composer as "only momentarily sharing the 1948 clouds of suspicion with Shostakovich."[38] The reality was significantly crueler. After its premiere in Tbilisi in 1944, Garayev's First Symphony was "not recommended" to be performed again. This veto remained in effect until the time of perestroika, when Garayev's symphony received a new premiere in Baku in February 1988. I still remember the bitter taste of that belated premiere. It was sad to listen to this work and realize that the fate of the Azerbaijani symphony could have been so different had this work not been withheld from influencing the progress of our national music.

In the 1950s, as a follow-up to the antiformalistic campaign, Garayev was accused of distorting Azerbaijani modal rules in the first two notebooks of his Piano Preludes. A new wave of criticism followed in the 1960s, when the composer was attacked for exploring twelve-tone techniques. But Garayev's use of this stylistic language was not the only factor that provoked a sharp reaction: his new works were deeper and had many layers of meaning, which was never encouraged in the Soviet context. Anar wrote about Garayev of the 1960s: "His latest works, such as the Third Symphony and, particularly, the Violin Concerto, are confessions of an extremely confused soul, full of all-humanistic worries and exclusively personal night fears. . . . In his articles and interviews he . . . said what he was supposed to, and continued writing music urged by his rowdy and incorruptible talent, with bitterness, tiredness, and sometimes even mysticism."[39] Such was the typical path of any Soviet composer who chose, despite all obstacles, to express his inner self to the maximum extent. Garayev delivered his aesthetic message regardless of his stylistic priorities and political complications, but at a deep personal cost. That is why his music even in its most splendid moments always has a sense of tragedy in it. The epoch he lived in was different from Hajibeyli's, and Garayev never experienced the danger of being physically executed. But the pressure of the system had no less virulence in the 1950s, 1960s, and 1970s, and Garayev's experience permeates his music.

Their Legacy

Garayev had a tremendous impact on the development of Azerbaijani music in the second half of the twentieth century. For him, teaching was as important as writing music, and his teaching contributed to his considerable influence. Between the years of 1946 and 1982, almost all the major composers of Azerbaijan graduated from his classes.[40] There is even a term, "Garayev's schooling," which refers to the many generations of composition students who inherited his ideals: intellectualism, openness to experiments, and the highest level of professionalism. This diverse cohort of composers includes authors of symphonies and operas, masters of music for children, songwriters, devoted followers of avant-garde techniques, and composers for traditional instruments who use the more conservative means of Western music. In contrast to Garayev, Amirov never taught, despite pleas from his friends and fellow musicians that he do so. He feared that teaching would compromise his work as composer. Instead of pupils, Amirov had followers. The stream he represented was less popular among the new of generation composers who searched for "more Western," "more up-to-date," and "more sophisticated" styles and techniques. Nonetheless, Amirov retains the highest possible status in the contemporary panorama of Azerbaijani music. Late-twentieth-century avant-garde composers, even outside of Azerbaijan, highly esteem his compositions. Among such admirers is the radical Russian composer, Viktor Ekimovsky (b. 1947). He observes that "Amirov's concept comprises such a huge area that we are still searching for keys to its understanding."[41]

Garayev and Amirov defended Hajibeyli's accomplishments in a difficult period of Soviet history and suggested two alternative directions for the further development of his East-West project. They expanded the stylistic and semantic scope of Azerbaijani music in space and time, adding the voices of other cultures and exploring various ways of synthesizing national idioms with earlier and contemporary Western styles. Amirov and Garayev contextualized Azerbaijani music within both East and West, uncovering its many historical and cultural links. They furthered professionalism and wrote works meeting the highest criteria of Western music. The empire that saw the creation of Garayev's *Seven Beauties* and Third Symphony, and of Amirov's *Sevil* and symphony *Nizami,* no longer exists. Nonetheless, these works continue to be performed, discussed, and studied, showing that the legacy of Azerbaijan's two prominent composers continues to the present day.

3 THE RUSSIAN-SOVIET FACTOR

FACILITATING OR DISRUPTING SYNTHESIS?

> Scholarly discourse is so permeated with the dichotomy
> between Russia and "the West" . . . that it appears as a
> paradox that Russia should personify "the West" in its Asian
> borderlands. Yet, Russians saw themselves as resolutely
> European in Central Asia, sharing in the European civilizing
> mission to which all imperial powers pretended.
>
> ADEEB KHALID, *The Politics of Muslim Cultural
> Reform: Jadidism in Central Asia*

AREAS OF IMPACT

The role of Russia and Russian music has always been central to discussions of
East-West synthesis in Azerbaijani music. Russian and Soviet sources proudly
emphasize the positive impact of Russian music on the development of Western art music in Azerbaijan, whereas Western authors focus more on Russia's
distortive influence. Indeed, Russia exerted significant influence on the musical
traditions of all nations under its rule in the nineteenth and twentieth centuries, and Azerbaijan was no exception. But each nation responded to Russian
influence in its own way, depending on the status of its music before Russian
governance and on the cultural energies that stimulated (or discouraged) Westernization and the emergence of new musical and cultural forms. Azerbaijani
musicians, who had been involved in cultural and musical exchanges before
the Russian era, absorbed Russian influence immediately and effectively. They
did not simply emulate Russian models, they developed new forms of East-West
synthesis that have been emblematic of Azerbaijani national music ever since.
This chapter considers the main channels, tools, and areas of Russian impact
on Azerbaijani music and explores the major artistic results of this process.

Russia affected all Azerbaijani music based on Western musical and cultural forms, but Russian influence was not a deterministic process, producing cultural hegemony. Azerbaijanis responded to that influence in varying ways in different fields.

Russian musicians' most profound influence was on the performing arts and music education. Guest musicians from Russia began arriving in Azerbaijan in the early twentieth century. Their activities intensified – and were even mandated – during the Soviet era, with the goal of helping ethnic Azerbaijanis attain the necessary level of proficiency to take over the development of their native music. By the 1950s, this program had outlived its usefulness, and ethnic Azerbaijanis became recognized as the dominant force in Azerbaijani music.

Most Russian musicians working in Baku came of their own volition. The Soviets created advantageous conditions for Russian professionals working in the provinces, but Baku offered its own incentives. The city had the reputation of being a cosmopolitan center welcoming immigrants and visitors, with no anti-Semitism or any other racist behavior. Because of the economic prosperity of Azerbaijan, it never experienced extreme poverty and hunger during the early Soviet era, unlike many other parts of the USSR. A political factor also stimulated the flow of guest musicians from Russia to Azerbaijan. Historically, in pre-Soviet Russia, all political dissidents considered any stay in the Caucasus, whether for vacation or exile, as a panacea. By keeping away from traumatic events and immersing themselves in completely different environments, they found comfort for their souls and, sometimes, even saved their lives. The Soviet era did not change this practice, although from then on, intellectual refugees could be involved in a process of developing the "virgin soil" of the provincial regions. The story of Leopold Rostropovich (1892–1942), the father of the renowned cellist Slava Rostropovich (1927–2007), reflects many of the realities of Russian guest musicians' practice in Azerbaijan.

As discussed in chapter 2, Uzeyir Hajibeyli was instrumental in bringing Russian musicians to Azerbaijan. Hajibeyli's invitation to L. Rostropovich in the early 1920s was prompted by more than the latter's reputation as a brilliant musician who had studied with the legendary Pablo Casals and toured Europe in the 1910s. From 1914 to 1916, L. Rostropovich had lived in Baku. He gave recitals, taught private cello lessons, and played the organ in the Polish Catholic church. Accordingly, L. Rostropovich was familiar with Azerbaijan and Azerbaijani culture, which was a significant factor in Hajibeyli inviting him to Baku. L. Rostropovich, in turn, had his own motivation to accept Hajibeyli's invitation. Between 1920 and 1921, he spent seven months in jail for supporting anti-Communist forces in the southern regions of Russia in the late 1910s.

L. Rostropovich happily left the epicenter of the tumultuous events in Russia that had nearly cost him his life.

The cellist stayed in Baku from 1925 to 1931, and during this time, he founded the cello department at the Azerbaijan State Conservatory and mentored many native musicians. Among his students was Asaf Zeynalli (1909–1932), one of the pioneers of the Azerbaijani art music tradition. Years of study with L. Rostropovich led Zeynalli to write "Sheep" for two cellos and piano, which was the first piece of national cello repertoire. Even accomplished native composers, such as Hajibeyli and Muslim Magomayev, took cello lessons with L. Rostropovich, which led to their composing the first Azerbaijani chamber compositions. Hajibeyli wrote three quartets, and Magomayev, one. L. Rostropovich organized a string quartet in 1925 under the auspices of the Azerbaijan State Conservatory, and that ensemble performed all these works. The quartet played in public twice a month, exposing Baku audiences to a plethora of composers and musical styles, from Mozart to Schoenberg. Even after leaving Baku, L. Rostropovich nostalgically reminisced on these years and planned to return. In 1938, he wrote the orchestral suite "Free Azerbaijan" and sent it to Hajibeyli. The cover page of this score has the author's following inscription: "Dedicated to my dearly loved Azerbaijan in memory of my work in Baku. April 6, 1938."[1] World War II prevented L. Rostropovich from realizing his plans for return.

During both the pre-Soviet and Soviet eras, the presence of Russian music in Azerbaijan was not confined to visiting professors. The Azerbaijan State Philharmonic Hall and other concert venues regularly hosted performances of leading Russian musicians. Music stores sold a large assortment of Russian artists' recordings, and they did so at an affordable price. Russia was the main destination to which Azerbaijani musicians traveled for the purposes of study, training, and professional development. The general curricula of all music schools in Azerbaijan were designed in accordance with the rules created in Russia in the nineteenth century and modified during the Soviet era. For many reasons and through many channels, Russia powerfully shaped the performing arts and music education in Azerbaijan.

Azerbaijani composers preserved their national voice from potential Russification during the pre-Soviet and Soviet eras by avoiding direct reference to the artistic paradigms created by Russian musicians. During the first two decades of the twentieth century, Azerbaijani composers had already established the precedent of drawing from a diversity of musical traditions, including Italian and French opera. The musical style of the early Azerbaijani operas, such as Hajibeyli's *Leyli and Majnun* and Magomayev's *Shah* recalled Rossini and overall Italian opera rather than Glinka and the Mighty Handful. And the first

Azerbaijani operettas, particularly *The Cloth Peddler,* show more parallels with operetta in European music than with Russian vaudeville or any other similar genre from the Russian tradition. The very access of Azerbaijani musicians to these genres and forms of European music became possible due to geographic proximity and political unity with Russia and through Russian musicians, but this differs from direct emulation of Russian styles.

Azerbaijani composers saw the music of Russian composers as a source of inspiration, creative ideas, and high professionalism. As Hajibeyli was progressing on the path of building the foundations of the Azerbaijani national style, he learned from the practices of Glinka and the Mighty Handful, as they were driven by similar intentions. Fikrat Amirov, whose music has strong romanticist tendencies, admired Tchaikovsky, whose music inspired the concepts behind his operas and symphonies. The intellectualism and dramatic intensity of Gara Garayev's music reflects the strong impact of Shostakovich. Moreover, Russian composers set high artistic criteria that the composers of the young Azerbaijani tradition strove – and succeeded – to meet.

Russian music was an effective mediator in the process of Azerbaijan's absorption of Western culture and music. This was, first of all, due to Russia's mixed Eurasian identity. Taruskin describes this Eurasian quality of Russian music. He indicates that, on the one hand, Russians "have always construed their identities in a larger European context"; on the other hand, when discussing Diaghilev's ballet projects in Paris in the early twentieth century, he states, "For the French . . . Russia was East and Other."[2] The Russian mentality has always contained a significant Eastern component. It particularly strengthened due to the Mongol invasion in the thirteenth through the fifteenth centuries.[3] Along with other factors, this Eurasian sensibility stimulated the growth of orientalism in Russian composed music, which otherwise was primarily based on the principles of European music.

Russia's impact on the composed music of the nations surrounding it was powerful but not absolute, although this claim remains contested in Western musicology. Some scholars argue that the Soviets imposed oriental models of the nineteenth century on all non-Slavic republics of the Soviet Union. Therefore, all these composed music traditions are nothing more than merely branches of Russian orientalism. These viewpoints directly correspond with Edward Said's definition of orientalism as "a Western style for dominating, restructuring, and having authority over the Orient."[4] Taruskin contributed to this discussion when characterizing Borodin's *Prince Igor* and, overall, nineteenth-century Russian musical orientalism as "the racially justified endorsement of Russia's militaristic expansion to the east."[5] Building on this idea, Frolova-Walker argued that the non-Russian composers in the Soviet Union were urged "to look towards the Kuchka's [The Mighty Handful's] Orientalist manner (leavened with some more accurate local colouring)."[6] Soviet ideologists indeed chose Russian musical orientalism as the most desirable path of development for the national traditions around Russia. But the question is whether or not it was accepted the way the Russians planned – and planted – it. The answer should be carefully nuanced in accordance with the realities of each non-Slavic republic. Otherwise, we may end up discussing the projected results instead of the musical processes that actually occurred.

Did Azerbaijani composers study the works of the Russian orientalist composers to which the Soviet system pointed them? Yes, as these pieces showed a way of reembodying the musical traditions of the East and putting them into the format of Western composed music on a high professional level. Did Azerbaijani composers prioritize the ideas of the Russian composers when building their own national style? No. Azerbaijani musicians used Russian models as a mediating force that served the purpose of building their distinctive national style. The credo of Russian orientalism was to depict the East as an exotic land, and Russian composers drew out the most extravagant features from other traditions, that is those characteristics that differed most from those in their own. For Azerbaijani composers, the East was their native tradition, and they depicted its essential qualities through the forms of Western music. Azerbaijani composed music may sound exotic to outsiders, but from within the tradition, its main features have their justification.

The composer Khayyam Mirzazade (b. 1935) states, "It is a matter of fact that Azerbaijanis have mastered forms of Western music through Russian composers. So what? Russians also learned these things from the Europeans at the time. Does this ever deny the uniqueness of the Russian composed music?"[7] It is true that Azerbaijan's position toward Russia was different from that of Russia toward the West: Azerbaijan was a subject of Russian colonial policy. But in the early twentieth century, the colonial situation was mitigated by a strong nationalist movement and the energy of Westernization. In such a context, even though Russia's imposing models of Western music in Azerbaijan was indeed part of its colonial policy, this effort responded to and resonated with the processes that emerged within the culture. The final product is neither artificial nor an epigone; it is authentic in the sense that it is self-determined. Azerbaijani composed music mirrors the national identity, just as the music of Russian composers "defin[ed] Russia," borrowing Taruskin's expression. Despite many connections with Russian music, the music of Azerbaijani composers is an independent realm, with its own aesthetics and stylistic principles.

Russians failed in attempting to replace Azerbaijanis as the establishers of the Azerbaijani national style. Russians succeeded in contributing to the growth of professionalism and enlarging the stylistic and aesthetic scope of Azerbaijani composed music. The stories that follow illustrate both the Russians' successes and their failures.

REINHOLD GLIERE: SHAHSENEM INSTEAD OF SULAMIF

The Azerbaijani Story of the Russian Composer

Since 1911, the Russian composer Reinhold Gliere had dreamt of writing his first opera. He chose a plot, the biblical Song of Songs interpreted as the story of Sulamif and King Solomon, and began drafting the libretto. The composer did indeed create an opera, but the work that appeared on stage in 1934 had nothing in common with his initial plans. Instead of *Sulamif*, Gliere composed the opera *Shahsenem*, drawing from the world of Azerbaijani fairy tales and folk melodies. How could such a crucial transformation happen? Why did Gliere change his mind and turn to a distant cultural and musical tradition? And why did Azerbaijan, which already had an operatic tradition established by Hajibeyli, invite a Russian composer to write an opera using native Azerbaijani tunes? The answers to all these questions lie in the social and political realities of the early Soviet era.

In 1917, with the advent of the Russian Revolution, Gliere became a Soviet, and not merely a Russian, composer. He was involved in the program of giving "brotherly help" to the non-Slavic republics, and Azerbaijan was his first destination. The ancient legend of the beauty Shahsenem and the *ashig* Garib, a story found across Transcaucasia and Central Asia and well known in Russia, was assigned as a new and timely option for Gliere's opera project.[8]

Gliere already had come into contact with Azerbaijan and its culture by the time he began work on *Shahsenem*. In 1914, he visited Baku and conducted a concert of Russian music with the local symphony orchestra. Gliere enjoyed his trip, as seen from his letter to his wife: "Concert in Baku went well. Generally speaking, they are generous about music here in Baku."[9] While serving as a rector of the conservatory in Kyiv, Ukraine, in 1918, the composer had another encounter with Azerbaijani music. Among the conservatory's voice students was the young Shovkat Mammadova, who would later become the first Azerbaijani female opera singer (see chapters 1 and 2). Gliere asked Mammadova to acquaint him with Azerbaijani folk songs, and she did so, with genuine enthusiasm.[10] Gliere soon arranged several of these songs for voice and piano. Although Gliere did not realize it, he was sketching episodes of his future Azerbaijani opera, since he later used all of these melodies in *Shahsenem*. And little did Mammadova know that she would perform the title role in Gliere's opera and that she and the composer would become close, lifelong friends.

In 1923, Mammadova and her husband, Iakov Liubarskii, who directed a publishing house in Baku, sent Gliere a letter inviting him to compose an opera for the Azerbaijani stage. Both contemporaneous and later Soviet musicological sources construed this as proving the viability of commissioning *Shahsenem* in Baku, rather than in Moscow. But Mammadova had strong professional motivations in asking him to write an opera for her national stage. As an accomplished opera singer, Mammadova was at odds with a native culture that had not yet produced any opera of the Western type. Hajibeyli could have done so, but he remained reticent in the 1920s, as collaboration with the pre-Soviet democratic government of Azerbaijan left him with a precarious social status (see chapters 1 and 2). To have the accomplished Russian composer write an opera for Azerbaijan seemed an ideal situation for Mammadova, and this is why she enthusiastically supported this idea. *Shahsenem* became her first triumph on the operatic stage, eventually bringing her recognition across the Soviet Union. Gliere often included episodes from *Shahsenem* in concerts of his music and would invite Mammadova to perform them.

It would be naïve, however, to understand Gliere's activities in Azerbaijan as entirely initiated by Mammadova. *Shahsenem* was a political project as much as it was an artistic one. Even the list of official Azerbaijani representatives meeting Gliere upon his arrival in Baku attests to this. It was not just Mammadova who welcomed Gliere. She was accompanied by Liubarskii; Azerbaijan's renowned poet and dramatist, Jafar Jabbarli; and three government officials, who debriefed Gliere on the political part of his mission. One representative was Mustafa Guliyev, the head of the Ministry of Enlightenment, who was known as an ardent apologist for Russification in Azerbaijan and was the strongest supporter of bringing Gliere to Baku.

The opera was supposed to premiere in 1927. The lyrics were to be in Russian, but due to the difficulties of fitting a Russian text to the Azerbaijani folk tunes Gliere wanted to use, he could not meet the projected deadline and plans changed. Jabbarli was assigned to write a new libretto in the Azerbaijani language. This version of *Shahsenem* premiered in 1934 and was regarded as a success for Azerbaijani music and for Soviet music overall. After *Shahsenem*, Gliere gained a reputation as an expert on the music of Central Asia and Transcaucasia. He was assigned to edit Magomayev's opera *Nargiz* for its 1938 premiere at the music festival Decade of Azerbaijani Art and Culture in Moscow. But *Shahsenem* remained Gliere's only complete musical work written for Azerbaijan. His further "Eastern" composition projects engage with the musical traditions of Uzbekistan and the Buriat people of Russia.

"Soviet Musical Orientalism"

Shahsenem is a prime example of what can be called "Soviet musical orientalism," a strange aesthetic that combines elements of nineteenth-century Russian musical orientalism with the tenets of socialist realism, which was pursued under the pressure of Soviet national and cultural policy. In Soviet orientalism, the East was no longer a romantically distant world, as it had been in Russian nineteenth-century orientalism. Gliere was supposed to write works on behalf of the Azerbaijani, Uzbek, and Buriat people, with the intention of facilitating their musical development. By way of comparison, it was as if Rimsky-Korsakov had composed *Scheherazade* to introduce symphonic music to Arab music and culture.

To facilitate the close-to-original character of the music written by Russian composers in non-Slavic republics, the Soviet regime supported composers' residencies in the respective countries. Gliere traveled throughout Azerbaijan several times during 1923 and 1924 and again between 1931 and 1934 transcribing original folk melodies and meeting with traditional musicians. The composer selected twenty-eight folk tunes to use in *Shahsenem* as songs, dances, and instrumental episodes. To give an illusion of authenticity, he did not add a single note to the melodic lines borrowed from traditional sources. Gliere also included *mugham* improvisations in their original form and imitated the timbres of traditional Azerbaijani instruments. For instance, he used *pizzicato* violas and cellos to mimic the timbres of the *tar* and the *saz,* and he wrote drum parts in a manner that recalls the *naghara* and the *gaval,* traditional Azerbaijani drums.

All Gliere's efforts could not eliminate the huge gap between *Shahsenem* and Azerbaijani music and culture. In his opera, Gliere conveyed his impressions of Azerbaijani culture, creating a surrogate of the national style, totally apart from the East-West path established by Hajibeyli in his early operas and operettas. This discrepancy was detected already by Igor Ledogorov in the first review of the Baku premiere of *Shahsenem:* "It would be a huge mistake to assume that Gliere could create [our] national operatic style. The composer did not even seem to pose such a task for himself. Turkic [Azerbaijani] opera must be created by Turkic [Azerbaijani] composers. This is an axiom."[11] The same viewpoint is shared by the native musicologist Nailya Mekhtieva, who wrote many years later: "It would be erroneous to consider the style of *Shahsenem* as national only because its music is based on numerous Azerbaijani folk melodies. . . . It remains the creation of a Russian composer and has never been incorporated into the mainstream of Azerbaijani music."[12] *Shahsenem* never belonged to the core repertoire of Azerbaijani music and has never been recognized as an authentic Azerbaijani opera, even though it remains one of Gliere's most significant individual accomplishments and an impressive example of Russian-Soviet musical orientalism.

But why can *Shahsenem* not be considered to be an authentic product of Azerbaijani composed music, especially since Mammadova performed it frequently? The musicologist Martin Stokes identifies authenticity as "a way of saying to outsiders and insiders alike 'this is what is really significant about our music,' 'this is the music that makes us different from other people.'"[13] To convey this message, the composer is supposed to carry the ethnic identity of the culture one represents, although this has nothing to do with his or her ethnic roots. Rather, it points to the social and cultural context that shapes one as a musician and an individual. For example, the Italian-born Jean Baptisto Lulli became a composer in the context of French music and even founded the French *tragédie lyrique*. In contradistinction, Antonin Dvořák, who wrote music based on American themes and infused with an American spirit, has never been viewed as a part of the American composed music tradition. Taruskin suggests that Dvořák practiced "tourist nationalism" and believes this explains "why many Americans considered Dvořák's advice well meant but meddlesome, and resisted it."[14] Gliere's position in Azerbaijani music can be related to "tourist nationalism" in part because he did not integrate into Azerbaijani music and visited the country only sporadically. Gliere's mission, following Taruskin's classification, was more a representation of the "colonialist nationalism" that "sought justification in the claim that it could develop local resources better than the natives unaided."[15] Indeed, Gliere's principal mission was to expand the colonial rule of Russia over Azerbaijan through musical expression. Krebs insightfully states, "Although *Shakh-Senem* [Shahsenem] contains some fine music, what Gliere helped establish was not the Azerbaidzhanian school of opera, but, rather, the tradition of Great Russian cultural hegemony over the Azerbaidzhanian minority."[16] The same applies to the score of Magomayev's *Nargiz* that Gliere edited. My master's thesis focused on the comparative characteristics of the two versions of this opera: one solely by Magomayev, the other edited by Gliere.[17] These two scores of *Nargiz* resemble parallel worlds, each built on its own rules. Magomayev's version was authentic, as all components of its musical style show direct links with tradition, but it lacks advanced compositional techniques. Conversely, Gliere's revised version met the highest criteria of professionalism, yet it sounded completely alien to Azerbaijani music. The only factor that unified the two versions was their identical melodic contents, since Gliere did not change a note in the melodic part of the operatic episodes penned by Magomayev.

Gliere's *Shahsenem,* Hajibeyli's *Koroghlu,* and Magomayev's *Nargiz* (in Gliere's version) were performed at the Moscow Decade of Azerbaijani Music and Art festival in 1938, and all three were officially acclaimed as significant accomplishments of Azerbaijani music. Only *Koroghlu* maintains a place in the Azerbaijani repertoire to this day. Both *Shahsenem* and *Nargiz* have completely disappeared from the Azerbaijani stage. The failure of Gliere's project is further demonstrated by the success of a rival Azerbaijani opera: the *mugham* opera *Ashig Garib* (1916), written by Zulfugar Hajibeyli and based on the same plot as *Shahsenem.* Gliere's *Shahsenem* was supposed to defeat, metaphorically, Z. Hajibeyli's *Ashig Garib* and to discredit *mugham* opera as a relic of the past. But *Ashig Garib* remains on stage to the present day, showing the continuing vitality of *mugham* opera as a living artistic phenomenon.

Krebs insightfully states, "It is difficult to see why Azerbaidzhan needed Gliere musically. . . . there were sufficient strong musicians with European training in Baku."[18] Fortunately, Hajibeyli resumed his creative work in the mid-1930s and Azerbaijani music, having passed the ordeal of Russification, returned to the path that he had set. This concludes the role in our story for Gliere, one of the finest Russian composers, who never wrote his opera about King Solomon and Sulamif.

DMITRY SHOSTAKOVICH AND THE AZERBAIJANI LINK

People's Artist of Azerbaijan

The Azerbaijani artist Tahir Salahov painted a portrait of Shostakovich in 1974, and this portrait, the last of Shostakovich created before his death, has been recognized as one of the best visual representations of him. In 1976, the Azerbaijani composer Gara Garayev wrote a composition to be a part of a collection of thirteen musical tributes to Dmitry Shostakovich. Composers from around the world contributed to this collective venture to celebrate Shostakovich's seventieth birthday. In 1972, three years prior to his death, the Azerbaijani government awarded Shostakovich its highest artistic title, People's Artist of Azerbaijan, for outstanding activities in developing Azerbaijani musical culture.

These events comprise far more than a collection of circumstances or a typical "intra-Soviet" cultural exchange; they form a monument of respect to the twentieth-century musical genius who had a significant impact on developing a composed music tradition in Azerbaijan. Garayev stated that, "The Azerbaijani school of composers, the foundations of which was laid by Uzeir Gadzhibekov [Uzeyir Hajibeyli], rightfully considers itself a successor to Shostakovich's traditions. . . . Turn the pages of our scores. . . . Of course it would be naïve to claim that they are on the same level as the works of the great master; nevertheless, the broad principles are being handed down, allowing us to count ourselves among his heirs."[19]

Such as a strong line of succession is quite logical, since four native composers – Garayev, Jovdat Hajiyev, Soltan Hajibeyov, and Elmira Nazirova – studied with Shostakovich at the Moscow State Conservatory in the 1940s. Garayev, Hajiyev, and Hajibeyov created the first national symphonies in 1944 and, subsequently, all three became key figures at the composition department of the Azerbaijan Conservatory. The many generations of national composers that followed inherited their principles.

Shostakovich loved Baku, visiting it often. His music first arrived in the capital city in June 1934, while he was on a concert tour with the Moscow Philharmonic under Alexander Gauk. The program of this concert included the First Symphony, the suite from the ballet *The Bolt,* and the First Piano Concerto, featuring Shostakovich as soloist. The next notable occasion was in October 1942. At this critical time during World War II, German troops were about to overrun the Caucasus and the Soviet Army was preparing to destroy the Baku oil wells. It was during those impossibly difficult times that the Seventh Symphony was played at the Azerbaijan Philharmonic by a local orchestra under the native conductor Ashraf Hasanov (1909–1983). This inaugurated the Azerbaijan State Symphony Orchestra's tradition of performing Shostakovich symphonies, a tradition that is very much alive today. In March 1952, at a concert entirely devoted to his works, Shostakovich shared his recently composed Preludes and Fugues with the Baku audience. Eight months later, in November 1952, Shostakovich attended the Baku premiere of Garayev's ballet *Seven Beauties,* and in March and April 1956, Shostakovich was an honored guest at the First Assembly of the Union of Azerbaijani Composers. He attended series of concerts in the philharmonic during the Decades of Russian Art and Culture festivals held in Baku in May 1964 and October 1972. The latter event was particularly significant: the festival opened with Shostakovich's Fifteenth Symphony, marking the first performance of this work after its Moscow premiere. Shostakovich maintained regular contact with Azerbaijanis through various music forums around the Soviet Union, as well as through summer vacations spent in the Composers' Union Resort Centers.

Shostakovich showed consistent interest in the development of composed music in Azerbaijan. As mentioned before, in 1957, he wrote an article on Azerbaijani music, which he quite symptomatically titled "Excellent School of Composers." According to the Polish composer Kshishtof Meyer, in 1959, Shostakovich named Garayev "among the most outstanding masters of contemporary Soviet music."[20] Shostakovich particularly esteemed Garayev's harmonic mastery. As the Russian composer Nikolai Martynov (b. 1938) relates, Shostakovich recommended that he study the "findings of contemporary composers, particularly those of Benjamen Britten and Gara Garayev."[21] In 1964, Shostakovich confirmed the new status of his relations with Azerbaijani musicians, which signified a new status for Azerbaijani composed music: "I am not that presumptuous to use an expression 'my student' when talking about a great Soviet composer, such as Gara Garayev. However, I will always be proud of the fact that this wonderful musician, as well as another outstanding representative of the Azerbaijani symphony, Jovdat Hajiyev, studied at the Moscow Conservatory in the composition class I had been honored to teach. . . .'Students' have not only reached 'mentors' level but also, in their turn, have taught and currently teach them many things."[22]

The accomplishments of Azerbaijani composers and the maturity of their composed music tradition facilitated close professional relations with Shostakovich. There were, however, two other stories – one of friendship and one of love – binding Shostakovich to Azerbaijan, and now we turn to Shostakovich's relationships with Garayev and Nazirova.

The Story of One Friendship

"I want to see you very much. If you ever come to Moscow, please give me a call. I would like to share with you my impressions about the Assembly, music, people, and my life," Shostakovich wrote to Garayev on April 9, 1957, after the Second Assembly of the Union of Soviet Composers.[23] Similar sentiments appear in many letters from Shostakovich to his Azerbaijani colleague and friend, the last one dated May 9, 1972. More than forty letters from Shostakovich to Garayev, published in fragments and edited with commentary by Karagicheva (*MA*), mirror their friendship: close, sincere, and based on a complicated combination of personal and professional matters. Taken together, these letters show the moral support that Garayev and Shostakovich gave each other. This correspondence also contains discussions and exchanges of ideas about music and life in general and the life of Soviet composers in particular.

The two composers met in 1937, when the nineteen-year-old Garayev came to Leningrad to pursue his cherished dream of studying with Shostakovich.

Nonetheless, this did not occur until 1943, when Shostakovich became a professor at the Moscow State Conservatory after having been evacuated from the besieged Leningrad. For young Garayev, three years of study in Shostakovich's class were invaluable in developing his musical mastery and in shaping his individuality.

Shostakovich had high expectations for Garayev's future. "Given your talent, you will become a great composer," he wrote to Garayev on June 6, 1947 (*MA*, 204). The Russian master gave feedback on almost every new work penned by his Azerbaijani colleague. In his letter of August 31, 1947, Shostakovich commented on Garayev's First Quartet, which was later dedicated to him, thus, "I liked the fourth movement the best. Very good music. Very fresh, light, meanwhile with a deep thoughtfulness inside. The harmonic style is very remarkable, too. Thus, if summarizing: the Quartet is excellent" (*MA*, 204). When, in the 1960s, Garayev began exploring twelve-tone technique, Shostakovich fully supported him. Garayev's Third Symphony, the manifestation of this new style, received the following feedback from Shostakovich in his letter of May 17, 1965: "I liked your symphony very much. It is wonderful music, serious, deep, and interestingly done. I heartily congratulate you on completing such a perfect opus. Write as much wonderful music as you can" (*MA*, 206).

At the same time, Shostakovich's words of encouragement could alternate with sharp criticism. Shostakovich was critical of what he saw as Garayev's excessive focus on music for stage and cinema. "Please, stop writing ballets, music for movies, etc. This 'genre' distracts you from the main stream. . . . You would better write symphonic and chamber music," Shostakovich wrote on October 31, 1958. And in his letter from February 6, 1960, he continued humorously: "When reading this letter you might respond: don't you do the same yourself? You have written an operetta. Generally speaking, we are all sinful before the Almighty and a 'socialist realism.' However, it does not release us as friends from mentioning each other's shortcomings. . . . I don't care about the shortcomings of Tulikov, Novikov and Koval.[24] I don't even notice them – whereas your shortcomings sadden me. They are like a knife in my heart. Don't get angry, will you?" (*MA*, 205–6). In these remarks, Shostakovich rightfully pointed out Garayev's slowness to realize his creative potential in the field of instrumental music. While *Seven Beauties* and *The Path of Thunder* are among Garayev's major accomplishments, his most innovative ideas are associated with his Piano Preludes, Third Symphony, and Violin Concerto.

The most intimate part of the Shostakovich-Garayev correspondence refers to the extreme moral and emotional hardships Shostakovich experienced in the 1940s and 1950s. These resulted from the infamous Decree of 1948 in which Shostakovich was singled out as a formalist and was dismissed from his professorship at the Moscow Conservatory. His life at that time was difficult in all senses, including financially. Like most Soviet citizens, he was too cautious to openly discuss all these matters in letters. The following words from his letter of April 17, 1949, however, are penetrated by pessimism and bitter irony: "I feel exhausted, and money is getting earned with such difficulty. I dream of finding a wealthy female admirer and establishing creative relations with her, just like those between Tchaikovsky and Mrs. von Meck" (*MA*, 207). This difficult period in Shostakovich's life seemed to be never-ending. As he mentioned in his letter of March 11, 1956, "Soon I will start feeling like Rossini. It is known that this composer created his last piece at the age of forty. And then lived until his seventies without having written a single note. Weak consolation for me, though" (*MA*, 208).

On October 1, 1972, on the occasion that would prove to be Shostakovich's final visit to Baku, Garayev delivered a preconcert lecture before the performance of the Fifteenth Symphony. This speech represented the sum of Garayev's admiration for this genius of twentieth-century music, as well as of his love and devotion for a dear friend. Garayev seemed to be speaking on behalf of Azerbaijani musicians, paying tribute to the man without whom the course of Azerbaijani national music certainly would have been poorer.

Revelations

Discoveries concerning the Tenth Symphony have come to compose one of the best-documented stories to emerge within Shostakovich studies. Following Israeli musicologist Nelly Kravetz's revelations surrounding the correspondence between Shostakovich and Nazirova, a number of scholarly publications appeared in which the Tenth Symphony was viewed in light of this new biographical data: broadly speaking, the feelings of the composer for his ex-student from Azerbaijan.[25]

I was probably among the first to whom Nazirova confided this chapter of her life. She did so in August 1990, prior to her emigration to Israel. It was a difficult time immediately before the collapse of the Soviet Union, when the perceived value of music and other forms of intellectual activities had significantly decreased, and many families chose to leave the country. Nazirova's family was one of those. By that time, we were already very close. Nazirova was more than just my piano professor at the Bulbul School and the Azerbaijan State Conservatory, she was my genuine spiritual mentor. It was no accident that I devoted my first scholarly article to my favorite teacher.[26]

FIGURE 3.1. Elmira Nazirova. *Courtesy of the State Museum of Azerbaijani Musical Culture.*

Our confidential talk seemed to last an eternity. It exposed me to another, parallel world that had remained hidden beneath the surface. I had always known that Nazirova and Shostakovich had been well acquainted with each other. I had admired for many years Shostakovich's portrait containing his written dedication "To dear Elmira from Dmitry Dmitrievich." Quite symbolically, our conversation took place right next to this portrait that was hanging on the wall in Nazirova's study. She did not seem to be excited; rather, what I noticed in her eyes was an immense sense of relief as she spoke, able to reveal so much after so many years of silence.

Nazirova's preoccupation was for her precious collection of original correspondence. "We are all aware of how complicated the issue of emigration is," she said. "Passing through customs and a lot of various official channels: I really don't know what the destiny of these letters will be. That's why I request you read them now: I hope you will write about this story some time."²⁷ More than thirty years later, these letters are in the possession of the Shostakovich family. The Tenth Symphony's Azerbaijani connection has lost its sensational edge, and the real story has finally been revealed.

Shostakovich and Nazirova first met in Moscow in the autumn of 1947. Nazirova was already known in Azerbaijan as a promising young musician. In 1944, at the age of sixteen, she presented her Piano Preludes at the Decade of Music of the Transcaucasian Republics in Tbilisi, Georgia, where her talents were highly regarded by many, including Gliere, who wrote: "Among many young composers we should credit Elmira Nazirova, who performed several simple but nevertheless very expressive preludes in the concert."²⁸ Soon after this success, Nazirova moved to Moscow to study piano with Iakov Zak and composition with Shostakovich.

Nazirova spoke to me quite nostalgically about the unique atmosphere in Shostakovich's class, in which students were encouraged to delve into the inner workings of composers' creative minds. Heated discussions occurred on a wide variety of issues in literature and in art, and performances of Haydn and Beethoven symphonies took place on two pianos. Nazirova witnessed the deeply tragic period in Shostakovich's life following the infamous 1948 Decree. Many of his colleagues and friends cut off their relations with him and even crossed the street to avoid meeting him. Nazirova remembers how, during one of the concerts in the Great Hall of the Moscow Conservatory, she chose a seat somewhere near Shostakovich or, more precisely, within the vacuum around him, and how the composer asked her, surprised, "Aren't you scared?" (EN).

Nazirova denied being aware of anything different, or special, in Shostakovich's manner of relating to her at this time. "I could not even imagine anything of that kind – I was so abashed in his presence!" she explained to me. "And he never verbalized his feelings" (EN). However, certain emotions, unconsciously perhaps, had already begun to grow in Shostakovich's heart. How else can one explain the paragraph in a letter to Nazirova dating July 29, 1953, in which Shostakovich describes his excitement in noticing her among the people who came to meet him in Baku?[29] In 1948, after Nazirova's marriage to Miron Fel, she returned to Baku and resumed her studies at the Azerbaijan State Conservatory. But the intensely active musical life in the former Soviet Union soon brought her once more into contact with Shostakovich. They met during his visits to Baku. Nazirova, in turn, often went to Moscow, participating in various projects organized by the Union of Soviet Composers. In 1951, together with the famous Soviet cellist Sviatoslav Knushevitskii, she performed her Cello Sonata in the Small Hall of the Moscow State Conservatory. Through such occasions, Nazirova met again and again with her mentor, who became her own special listener, although he remained a severe and demanding critic (PURL 3.1).

Their relationship evolved at this time into one of new and ever-growing intellectual intimacy. Shostakovich made suggestions to Nazirova about her new compositions, encouraged the young composer to turn her attention to specific genres or forms, and, at the same time, shared with her his own creative ideas. Nazirova treasured the published scores of Shostakovich's Preludes and Fugues, the Seventh and Eighth Symphonies, as well as of Robert Schumann's *Frauenliebe und -leben,* all of which the composer presented to her, along with his written dedications.

On April 12, 1953, Nazirova received Shostakovich's first letter, in which he detailed misprints in the first edition of his Preludes and Fugues. This was the beginning of a correspondence that was to last for three and a half years. Every line of these precious documents contains valuable information. Shostakovich shares with Nazirova his philosophical ponderings about the irony of life and the essence of the composer's work, both in general and regarding his own experiences. But above all, these letters reflect his incredibly profound and complex feelings in which love and admiration for Nazirova were combined with the deepest respect and appreciation of her professional abilities and successes.

Sometimes Shostakovich expressed his feelings through humorous allusion. In a letter of June 21, 1953, he simply includes the musical phrase from Lensky's arioso from Tchaikovsky's *Eugene Onegin,* with its original words "I love you!" (HTS, 38). In these letters, Shostakovich also shows his interest in Nazirova's compositions in progress, asking her for details of her compositional process. Indeed, he had a strong belief in Nazirova's compositional gift. "I wish you to compose a great deal of music and become a true composer. You have all the prerequisites," he writes in his letter of January 25, 1954 (HTS, 39).

He alludes to the apparent unattainability of the deep spiritual relationship they might have had when writing on July 29, 1953, "Will our paths ever get together? Perhaps never. There are many, too many reasons for that" (HTS, 39). Nevertheless, in his letter of July 25, 1953, Shostakovich describes his feelings toward Nazirova as "the most important event" in his life at the time (HTS, 39). This comes from the same letter in which Shostakovich informs Nazirova about his work on the Tenth Symphony. From this point on, the intensity of their correspondence greatly increases. In the roughly three-month window from July 25 to October 30, Nazirova received eighteen letters from Shostakovich. The composer informed her of each and every development of his work in progress. In a letter of August 10, 1953, Shostakovich told her about his seeing or, more precisely, hearing the music of the third movement in a dream. Finally, on August 29, she received the news concerning the third movement theme depicting her name. "This is the result," Shostakovich writes in this letter: "Even if I had not arrived at this result, I would be thinking of you constantly – whether or not this fact is recorded in my worthless manuscripts" (HTS, 39).

The Heart of the Tenth Symphony

For many years, the Tenth Symphony had remained among the most unclear areas of Shostakovich studies both inside and outside of Russia. The Russian émigré journalist and musicologist Solomon Volkov, in his controversial *Testimony,* interpreted the scherzo of the symphony as a "musical portrait of Stalin."[30] Differing opinions circulated regarding the second theme of the scherzo. The Russian musicologists Lev Danilevich and Marina Sabinina emphasized its pastoral character, pointing to the use of the French horn and intervallic structures based on fourths and fifths.[31] The music theorist Leo Mazel made a prescient guess when characterizing this theme as "old memories, sincere pleas coming from the deepness of a human heart."[32] Finally, the British musicologist David Fanning came very close to the mystery of the Tenth when he wrote, "How convenient if E-A-E-D-A could be shown to be a musical signature complementing DSCH."[33]

The semantic contents of the scherzo are based on the interplay of the two musical signatures shown in musical example 3.1: DSCH (D-E♭-C-B) and ELMIRA (E-A-E-D-A), respectively portraying Shostakovich and Nazirova.

EXAMPLE 3.1. The monograms of Shostakovich and Elmira Nazirova.

These two themes are distinct in several ways. Shostakovich's cryptogram consists of narrow melodic steps – two minor seconds, ascending and descending, that are separated by a minor third. Elmira's theme, on the contrary, is based on fanfare-like articulations of a fourth and fifth separated by a major second. Shostakovich's leitmotif has a descending contour, whereas Elmira's is directed upward. Shostakovich's theme may be imagined to symbolize the essential spirit of his music – in terms of modal and intonation peculiarities, but most of all in its tragic essence. Elmira's theme is more difficult to read as a personification; we might hear it as expressing a certain emotion, rather than a character. It is an embodiment of Shostakovich's confident, calm, self-assured, embracing call to the woman that had entered his life at a difficult time and enabled him to regain his identity. Interplay between these two themes sounds like a dialogue between the composer and his muse, or more precisely, between the composer and his inner voice revealing the love that is harbored deep inside. This dialogue reflects the extreme hardships that Shostakovich endured in the late 1940s. But these tragic events also transformed themselves into a musical countermeasure leading him back to life. The Tenth Symphony embodies the realization of this process, along with its resulting culmination. After undergoing a series of metamorphoses in the third movement, the composer's musical signature is proclaimed at the final coda as a symbol of wisdom and as a vigorous will to live.

One more element to the story of the Tenth reveals the essence of Shostakovich's and Nazirova's relationship: the similarity of the E-A-E-D-A motive to the theme depicting the ominous cries of the monkey in *Das Lied von der Erde* by Gustav Mahler. In his letter of September 17, 1953, Shostakovich expresses his sincere astonishment at this connection, stating it as "interesting food for musicological research" (HTS, 40). That Shostakovich heard Nazirova's name through Mahler's musical language might reasonably be understood as a consequence of his admiration of the Austrian composer, as well as being a reflection of the much-documented similarities between their styles. Nonetheless, the most vital aspect is the semantic closeness of Mahler's and Shostakovich's themes. Both portray tragedy (death in case of the Mahler theme, and doomed love in case of Shostakovich).

The composer invited Nazirova to the Moscow premiere of the Tenth, which took place under Evgeny Mravinsky on December 17, 1953, in the Great Hall of the Conservatory. As Nazirova told me, she felt the composer's constant gaze during the entire performance. One year later, the symphony was performed in Baku under Abram Stasevich. Shortly afterward, the score of the Tenth Symphony, including its dedication to Nazirova, arrived at the Union of Azerbaijani Composers, with the composer's request to pass it on to the dedicatee. Nazirova smiled when she recalled how the leaders of this organization were perplexed by this gesture from such a nationally distinguished figure to his young colleague from Azerbaijan.

Their correspondence gradually began to diminish. In 1954, Nazirova received only five letters, and only one each year in 1955 and 1956. In his final letter sent on September 13, 1956, Shostakovich informed her about his impending marriage to Margarita Kainova. Later, through Nazirova's attendance at various music forums around the Soviet Union, she was able to meet with Shostakovich, although very infrequently. The heightened emotions of the 1950s were now confined to the distant past. Yet they remained alive as a secret, tying their two hearts together.

For Nazirova, the mid-1950s were a period of important professional accomplishments. She toured as pianist, traveling across the Soviet Union as well as in Poland, Czechoslovakia, Egypt, and Iraq. Nazirova achieved success as a composer during this period. She is credited with writing the first etudes in Azerbaijani music. Also of high importance in the development of Azerbaijani piano music were Nazirova's Concerto on Arab Themes for the Piano and Symphony Orchestra (PURL 3.2) and the Suite for Two Pianos on Alban Themes (1955) (both pieces were cocomposed with Amirov). In 1971, she became a professor at the Azerbaijan State Conservatory, and from 1972 to 1990, she held the position of chair of the Piano Department.

The musical world has long recognized figures such as Clara Schumann, Meta Abegg, George Sand, Mathilde Wesendonck, Harriet Smithson, and Emma Debussy as muses of the great composers, and these women have become an important part of composers' biographical and musical legacies. Shostakovich, however, was not able to reveal the secret of the Tenth Symphony. He was guided by an ethical desire not to disrupt the peace in their respective families. Moreover, such an ostensibly frivolous personal dedication of a major musical work would have run counter to the dogmas of socialist realism, contradicting the very image of the Soviet composer.

The story of Dmitry Shostakovich's sincere, pure, and quite desperate love remains an invaluable page of music history, enriching our knowledge of the composer's heritage. And it remains symbolized in the immortal music of the Tenth Symphony, in which the two musical signatures – "Dmitry Shostakovich" and "Elmira" – will stay beside each other forever.

His Musical Impact

The impact of Shostakovich across the entire cultural and geographical scope of the Soviet Union and beyond is undeniable. But why has Azerbaijani music been particularly situated to absorb Shostakovich's influence? What were the main features in the development of Azerbaijani music for which Shostakovich's music served as a metaphorical lens? Finally, what were the mechanisms through which Shostakovich's influence could fuse with the national music system?

Shostakovich's main input lay in stimulating the growth of professionalism in Azerbaijani music in terms of the dramaturgical, polyphonic, textural, and orchestral skills of its composers. Through the prism of Shostakovich's aesthetics and style, Azerbaijani composers made great strides in the field of twentieth-century classical music, finally considering themselves to be an integral part of contemporary soundscapes. They did not simply adopt the principles of Shostakovich's music, but rather they rediscovered them in alignment with the principles of their national music system. Through Shostakovich, Azerbaijani composers created new ideas that revealed previously hidden resources in their traditional music heritage.

A new tragic vision emerged in Azerbaijani music as a result of Shostakovich's impact. This vision focused on the ideas of struggle and resistance characterizing Western philosophies of both art and life, rather than the patience and endurance typical of their Eastern counterparts. The idea of catharsis, essential to both *mugham* and Shostakovich's music, served as a bridge in this regard. Many Azerbaijani symphonies, including those penned by Garayev, Hajiyev, and Arif Malikov, demonstrate this tragic spirit. Due to Shostakovich, Western concepts of drama became an integral part of the symphonic dramaturgy in Azerbaijani music. By the late 1930s, national composers had already made significant progress in this direction. Hajibeyli applied a thoroughly developed system of leitmotifs in his operas and operettas and created sonata form in *Koroghlu* (see chapter 4). But Hajibeyli, as well as other Azerbaijani composers at that time, had mainly appealed to the inner contrast of *mugham* composition, namely the alternation of improvisation and song-like and dance-like episodes. But *mugham* composition also contains another, rather obscured type of contrast, bearing more similarity to the developmental processes of Western sonata form. In the improvisational sections, the performer pursues a slow, yet targeted thematic development that involves the interplay of various modal patterns. Eventually, in a process of phase-like development, the variety of modal patterns begins to work toward the purpose of providing differences, rather than similarities. As a result, the initial thematic material undergoes serious transformation, but it maintains its inner integrity. This type of contrast came into natural fusion with aspects of Shostakovich's sonata form, such as derivative relations between themes in the exposition, the development's phase-like structure, and intense transformation in the recapitulation. These features are now typical for much of Azerbaijani symphonic literature.

A type of lyrical emotion characteristic of Shostakovich – intense, indirect, continuous, and intellectualized – also entered the orbit of Azerbaijani music in the late 1940s. Such themes regularly appear in the introductory or exposition sections of sonata forms, or in second movements in the opuses of Azerbaijani composers. Again, the mechanism of fusion came via *mugham,* with its lyrical flow and its strong and powerful, yet rather introverted, nature, far from any overt personification. The syncretic unity of the intense lyricism essential in both *mugham* and the music of Shostakovich involved one more component: the music of Bach, which is distinguished by the same inseparable unity of intellect and passion. The fundamental linearism of Bach and Shostakovich, often inseparable from the lyrical flow, was also mastered by Azerbaijani musicians, as it ideally corresponded to the monodic nature of *mugham.* It was linearism again that revealed and stimulated the growth of polyphonic tendencies in Azerbaijani music.

Imitative polyphony came naturally to Azerbaijani composers, since it corresponded with the imitative qualities of traditional music in which "call-response" relations between a leading melody and supporting voices, or even within a single melody, are highly significant. The first composers of Azerbaijani art music, before and regardless of Shostakovich's input, realized the compatibility of imitative polyphony with their native music system and created fugues and fugue-like episodes. Shostakovich, however, particularly inspired Azerbaijani composers to pursue complex imitative textures and forms, in both homophonic contexts and in independent polyphonic pieces such as the passacaglia, a genre that held an important role in the instrumental music of Azerbaijani composers. A through-composed variation form constructed over an unchanging musical line, the passacaglia resonated with basic principles of Azerbaijani *mugham,* such as the modification of an initial melodic model that nonetheless remains transparent through all changes (see chapter 5).

Other genres that entered Azerbaijani music due to Shostakovich's influence were the toccata and scherzo. Garayev was a pioneer in this regard, and he mastered the toccata via the music of *ashigs*, drawing inspiration from the energetic ostinato-like patterns in their instrumental parts that are traditionally performed on the *saz*. The Azerbaijani scherzo came to life through associations with cheerful folk song and dance music. Sharp rhythmic patterns and clear-cut melodic units typical in this category of Azerbaijani folk tunes become appropriate counterparts of the scherzo. In both Azerbaijani toccata and Azerbaijani scherzo, "the Shostakovich" and "the national" parts of the synthesis are integrated into an indispensable unity.

The modal features of Shostakovich's music were particularly attractive to Azerbaijani composers, whose native tradition was also modal. The links of Shostakovich's modality to the Jewish music system, which is also a part of Eastern soundscapes, facilitated this interest. A number of crossing points enabled smooth integration of the two systems, their melodic nature being the primary similarity. The musicologist Aleksandr Dolzhanskii was the first to detect the prevalence of modal melodic relationships in Shostakovich's music.[34] The modes of Azerbaijani music are likewise built on a combination of melodic patterns specific to each mode. Another point of convergence is the tetrachordal structure of the modes. The musicologist Eleonora Fedosova detected the important role of tetrachords in Shostakovich's modal system.[35] Shostakovich thus had a natural meeting point with Azerbaijani music thanks to the plagal nature and tetrachordal structure of the Azerbaijani modal system. Shostakovich's tendency toward the use of diminished modes, including those in the ambitus of the diminished fourth and the diminished octave, is also important, corresponding with the idea of the diminished octave in the Azerbaijani modal system (see introduction).[36]

A theme in Hajiyev's Sixth Symphony (1977), shown in musical example 3.2a, demonstrates this connection between the modality of Shostakovich and that of Azerbaijani music. In his work, Hajiyev incorporated the monogram D-Eb-C-B, having it appear in the context of the Azerbaijani mode *shushtar*, with Bb as the tonic, as shown in musical example 3.2b. Shostakovich's signature theme, transposed into the respective key (squared in example), fits the patterns of *shushtar* ideally, as this mode of Azerbaijani music combines two tetrachords located within a diminished fourth. The native listener not familiar with the Shostakovich's musical motive, shown in musical examples 3.1a and 3.2b, would only notice typical patterns of the mode *shushtar*.

EXAMPLE 3.2a. Jovdat Hajiyev, Sixth Symphony, Third Movement, the monogram of Shostakovich.

EXAMPLE 3.2b. B♭ *shushtar.*

This short example serves as a perfect conclusion to the story of Shostakovich, whose life and music, for many reasons, including social, political, professional, and personal ones, became closely integrated into Azerbaijani music. These connections may be seen as circular in their nature: it was the presence of Shostakovich's cryptogram that brought to life a beautiful theme in the Azerbaijani mode *shushtar,* just as Shostakovich himself was inspired by the music and musicians of Azerbaijan.

4 THE BEGINNING OF THE NATIONAL STYLE

1900–THE 1930s

It is fairly impossible to find in the history of music
any other precedent of such a smooth progression
from folklore to a composed tradition.

VIKTOR VINOGRADOV, *Uzeir Gadzhibekov*
[Uzeyir Hajibeyli] *and Azerbaijani Music*

IMPACT OF BAROQUE AND CLASSICAL STYLES

The Azerbaijani composed music tradition witnessed the same historical sequence of musical styles – baroque, classical, romantic, atonal, and so forth – as
Western music did, although at an accelerated pace, and in the context of East-
West synthesis. These Western musical styles' emergence in Azerbaijan resembled *stretta* in polyphonic music, as every new style began to evolve before the
previous one had come to full fruition. Eighteenth-century European music
served as the first stylistic model for Azerbaijani composers. Classical styles
in particular dominated the first several decades of Azerbaijani composition,
although traces of baroque styles appeared simultaneously.[1] *Mugham* opera,
created by Uzeyir Hajibeyli in the 1900s and continued by other composers,
is the Azerbaijani tradition's most significant historical parallel to baroque
music. Considering that baroque was the era that saw the invention of Western opera, Azerbaijani composers' mirroring of baroque styles and aesthetics
through their own operas was a natural and appropriate, though not a consciously planned, response. Azerbaijani *mugham* was the genre that organically
facilitated the fusion of operatic and Azerbaijani traditions, allowing native
musicians to create their first pieces of composed music.

According to Zemtsovsky, *mugham* maintains typological links with the
music of the baroque era. For this reason, he half-jokingly calls it "Mugham

Sebastian Bach."[2] Many historical, cultural, and aesthetic factors facilitated such typological links. Both *mugham* and baroque music emerged in monarchic contexts. The former developed as court music and reached its efflorescence during the eras of the Arab Caliphate and Persian empires, and the latter was a product of the age of absolutism in Europe. As befits their elite roots, both musical traditions generally are intended for small, rather intimate performance venues (contemporary performances of *mugham* and cases such as Handel's oratorios or *Music for the Royal Fireworks* aside). Religious factors create another bond. Baroque music cannot be comprehended apart from a religious context per se, since scholars have long found a source for the dramatic aesthetics of the baroque in the principles of the Catholic reformation. The musicologist Manfred Bukofzer writes about "the mystic and aggressive spirit of the counter-reformation which overwhelmed the faithful with gigantic structure, be it in architecture, painting, or music."[3] The musicologist Friedrich Blume supports this argument by writing, "The whole altered attitude of the second half of the 16th century led, in religious feeling and thinking, to what is summed up as 'Counter Reformation and Jesuitism,' and in art to the style and the formal and expressive means that are called 'Baroque'. One is not the cause of the other, but both grew from the same spiritual disposition."[4] In a similar way, *mugham* is affected by Islamic ideals, although to a lesser extent, since the role of music in Islam is significantly lower than in any branch of Christianity. The ethnomusicologist Sanubar Baghirova indicates the strong spiritual links of *mugham* with Sufi philosophy, particularly with the idea of catharsis and ascent toward supreme truth through immersing oneself into and even focusing on inner suffering.[5] Both musical traditions, however, lost their direct links with religious contexts and have served secular purposes first and foremost. *Mugham* and baroque music feature an extreme and heightened emotional state throughout a piece or a movement of a piece, and this continuous affect mostly is conveyed through an elaborate, highly ornamented, and continuously expanding melody. Other commonalities include high theatricality, even within instrumental music genres, and the idea of a dialogue between instruments. These qualities are essential for the *concerto grosso* in baroque music and for any performance of *mugham*. The prevalence of a small instrumental ensemble signifies another baroque parallel with *mugham,* which is usually performed by a trio consisting of a singer and two instrumentalists. Deeper comparison can be made between the *mugham* trio and basso continuo, a typical baroque accompaniment that includes two instruments, one keeping the bass line and another contributing to the melodic part. In the *mugham* trio, one instrumentalist maintains the bourdon tone, highlighting the pitch that is central for the given section of the composition, while the other elaborates on the melodic line performed by the singer, although these roles constantly shift. Such typological affinities between *mugham* and baroque music allowed *mugham* to appear in an operatic context and thus establish the foundations of Azerbaijani opera.

The twenty-three-year-old amateur Hajibeyli did not go about creating *mugham* opera as a conscious translation of baroque opera into an Azerbaijani context; however, the many similarities between *mugham* opera and baroque opera, beyond even those of baroque music and *mugham* more generally, point to the essential commonalities between the musical systems of East and West and to the diverse possibilities for their fusion. Like Western opera, *mugham* opera features a story told through music on stage, has several acts, is scored for singers accompanied by an orchestra, and alternates between vocal and instrumental episodes. Each *mugham* has a distinct emotion or ethos associated with it, and Azerbaijani composers carefully choose them to heighten the drama, just as baroque composers understood the dramatic power of musical figures and affects. For instance, *Segah*, which traditionally expresses romantic feelings, is often used in love episodes. The sorrowful *Shushtar* works well for the most intense moments, and the ecstatic *Erag* for celebrations and solemn final scenes.

The principle of building operatic compositions as a set of solo expressions, each conveying specific emotions such as love, grief, revenge, and so forth, signifies the main structural and dramatic similarity between *mugham* opera and opera seria. As in opera seria, in *mugham* opera, improvisation is a key element, and in both genres singers are allowed – and expected – to demonstrate their virtuosity and to contribute to the opera's text. The prominent role of monody is another commonality: the practice of monody was a prerequisite to the creation of opera in the late sixteenth century, and Azerbaijani *mugham* is a product and a genre of monody. Both opera seria and *mugham* opera feature occasional ensembles and use the orchestra in an accompanimental role.

In a similar manner, Hajibeyli's three operettas written in the 1910s have many characteristics in common with the lighter genres of eighteenth-century European opera, particularly with German singspiel, French *opéra comique,* and Italian *opera buffa.* Like these older operatic genres, Hajibeyli's operettas avoid high-flown language, have heroes who are disguised to achieve matrimonial goals, include humorous situations involving servants, and consistently have light, cheerful music. The alternation of spoken dialogue with vocal expression is an additional similarity to French and German comic opera traditions.

Viennese classicism became the dominant source of Azerbaijani composers' explorations in the early twentieth century. Several characteristics of the

Viennese classical style facilitated its integration. First, its emotionally stable, well-balanced, and prevailingly positive aesthetic ideally corresponded with the light-hearted and cheerful nature of most genres of Azerbaijani traditional and folk music, particularly the art of *ashigs*. Second, composers in the young Azerbaijani tradition could find correspondences between Viennese classicism, which favored simple, rather than complex, means, and their own national folk songs and dances. Azerbaijani composers also may have recognized Viennese classicism's affinities with *ashig* melodies, which have strict metrical organization, clear-cut phrases, and defined cadences. Third, in the Viennese tradition, homophony prevailed over polyphony. These characteristics were also attractive for composers coming from a tradition of monody.

The influence of the Turkish Janissary bands on the styles of Gluck, Haydn, Beethoven, and particularly Mozart provided Azerbaijani composers with an encouraging precedent in Viennese classicism. The musicologist Karl Signell has coined the term "temporary Turkomania" to describe this particular species of musical exoticism, which lasted from the seventeenth century to the early nineteenth. According to him, despite dying out by the start of the romantic era, Turkophilic music contributed to "some important permanent results of . . . East-West cultural exchange."[6] Viennese *alla turca* experiments did not aim to imitate the essential features of Turkish music, nor did they serve as a model for Azerbaijani composers. Still, references to this style were useful for Azerbaijani composers and audiences, perhaps allowing them to view Viennese classicism as not a completely alien tradition. As shown in numerous reviews published in the Azerbaijani local media, with the earliest dating to 1901, Mozart's symphonic and instrumental music, including his piano sonatas, quartets, and operatic overtures, were extremely popular in Baku. In particular, the final movement from his A major Sonata K331, which remains the most popular example of "Turkomania" in Western music, was a part of Baku soundscapes. Here are lines from the review published in the Baku newspaper on January 17, 1912, about an IRMO Music College student concert: "Remarkable was the performance of Saint-Saens' *Rondo Capriccioso* for the violin, Mozart's *Rondo Alla Turca* for the piano, and Beethoven's Concerto in C major."[7] As this shows, Hajibeyli, who lived in Baku and who was exposed to the city's rich musical life, was certainly familiar with the *alla turca* style in the early stage of his career, and he could have drawn inspiration from it.

Azerbaijani music has many rich examples of Viennese classicism reimagined through the Azerbaijani music system. The opening chorus "Night of Separation" from the opera *Leyli and Majnun* by Hajibeyli is a vivid example of such synthesis. The native melody used in this chorus is based on a strophic

Table 4.1. Structure of the verse from chorus "Night of Separation"

			A			
a	a	b	b	c	b	b
4	4	4	4	4	4	4

form. The melody consists of two verses (A), with the even-numbered subsections rhymed in each verse. The scheme of the structure of the verse from Hajibeyli's chorus is given in Table 4.1. The score is given in part in musical example 4.1a (PURL 4.1).

The melodic contour of the piece can be analyzed from both Eastern and Western perspectives. This melody, in the mode E *rast* (see the scale given in musical example 4.1b), is supported with harmonies from the key of E major, which offers the best compatibility between this Azerbaijani mode and Western scales. The melody of the chorus is a typical representation of the modal development of *rast*. As seen from musical example 4.1a, in accordance with traditional modal rules, the tonic E4 is highlighted at the beginning (mm. 19–22) through stepwise patterns using the closest pitches. In the meantime, these patterns, which involve the leading tone and the mediant of E major, establish a solid E major. As is typical of traditional melodies, there is a gradual expansion of the modal space above the tonic. The melody moves to A4 and B4 in subsection b (m. 27) and then to C♯5 in subsection c (m. 37), after which it descends to G♯4 (m. 38), and finally returns to the tonic (m. 39). At the same time, the melody plainly follows the golden ratio rule, known and continuously applied in Western music since the Renaissance: C♯5, the apex, is reached in m. 19 of the twenty-eight-measure-long melody.

The rhythmic patterns of the melody display the same possibility of fitting into both Eastern and Western paradigms. The combination of quarters and eighths, occasionally (and symmetrically) disturbed by a dotted figure, is highly typical of folk melodies, and it is also found in many pieces by Haydn, Mozart, and Beethoven. As is characteristic of Viennese classicism, this rather simple melody is harmonized using primary triads. But to a greater extent than is typical in Viennese classicism, this chorus makes use of plagal harmonizations, reflecting the tetrachordal structure of the Azerbaijani modes. Throughout each strophe, the subdominant of E major increases its presence, following the growing importance of A, E *rast*'s upper fourth, in the melody. As seen from the roman numerals given in musical example 4.1a, there is no subdominant in subsection a. This chord only appears in the first measure of subsection b

EXAMPLE 4.1a. Uzeyir Hajibeyli, *Leyli and Majnun,* chorus "Night of Separation" from act 1.

EXAMPLE 4.1a. (*cont.*)

EXAMPLE 4.1a. (cont.)

EXAMPLE 4.1a. (*cont.*)

EXAMPLE 4.1b. E *rast.*

(mm. 27 and 31). The subdominant recurs frequently throughout subsection c (mm. 35–37), after which the chord again decreases its presence with the reprise of subsection b (mm. 39 and 43). The second verse marks the beginning of the same cycle featuring the gradual increase of the role of the subdominant in the harmonic development. Despite the use of dominant harmonies and authentic cadences, so important to the classical style, the subdominant's waxing and waning becomes the most notable part of this harmonization, showing the continuing influence and power of native tradition.

"Night of Separation" displays one of Hajibeyli's strategies for adapting the structural and harmonic rules of Viennese classicism within the context of

Table 4.2. Structure of "Arazbari"

Intro	A	B	C	B	D	B	B	Coda
a	a b	c	c a^1 a^2 b	d	d b	b	b	
4	5 5	8	7 7 8 4	8	5 5	8	8	4
		(2 + 3 + 3)						

the Azerbaijani music system. In this chorus, he finds traits of his native music tradition that are potentially compatible with the Western system. For example, the native melody used in this chorus is based on periodic development, highlights the central role of the tonic, and has a melodic arch similar to those found in examples of Western music. These elements facilitate the smooth, almost effortless integration of this melody with the harmonic and structural rules of Viennese classicism. In other parts of *Leyli and Majnun,* Hajibeyli takes a different approach, namely, combining idioms of Viennese classicism with *mugham.* This task is more difficult since *mugham,* with its lack of any metric structure and its thematic development entirely shaped by modal rules, is a challenging counterpart for the classical style. The orchestral intermezzo for act 5, based on *mugham Arazbari,* exemplifies this fusion.

Wisely, for this intermezzo, his first experiment in combining *mugham* and Viennese classicism, Hajibeyli chose a specific type of *mugham* called *zarbi mugham* (literally: rhythmic *mugham*), in which the flow of modal development in the melody is disciplined by a strict metrical structure maintained by the drums. The composer skipped the main parts of *mugham, shoba,* borrowing only the rhythmic instrumental interludes (*rang*) that in traditional practice are performed between *shobas.* By putting together these instrumental interludes, Hajibeyli created the orchestral intermezzo. This episode is written in rondo form, a form that flourished during the classical era. Unlike in the Western rondo, however, the even-numbered segments of the form, rather than the odd-numbered ones, serve as the refrain. According to the musicologist Izabella Abezgauz, the idea of "reverse rondo" is essential for Azerbaijani traditional and folk music, in which the gradual extension of modal space and the movement to higher pitch levels must be balanced against constant return of the tonic after each new stage of modal development. This structure facilitates the role of the even-numbered segments as stabilizers, while the odd-numbered segments bring new thematic contents, thus moving the form forward.[8] The scheme of this form can be seen in table 4.2 and in musical example 4.2, illustrating in part the thematic material of the intermezzo (PURL 4.2).

The melody consists of clear-cut units, each drawn to certain tones of the scale and ending with cadences. The flow of modal development becomes a powerful force affecting the length of structural units and determining the harmonic language's characteristics. The number of measures in each unit is rather arbitrary, because the growth of the piece is led by modal logic, and what would be considered a break of symmetry in the Western system becomes natural in the perspective of Eastern tradition. Section A, shown in musical example 4.2a, is five measures long. Section B, shown in part in musical example 4.2b, retains its length of eight measures throughout the entire piece. But it is clearly divided as 2 + 3 + 3 (instead of 4 + 4, which would be expected in Western music), pointing to the decisive role of modal development in the structural division of the form. The modal contents of the intermezzo combine F♯ *segah* in the A sections with F♯ *segah* and E *shur* in the B sections. Both native modes are shown in musical examples 4.2e and 4.2f, and clearly, D major and E minor serve as their respective Western equivalents. In a similar manner, the tonal plan of this intermezzo is constantly shifting between D major, chosen as the equivalent of F♯ *segah,* and E minor, supporting E *shur,* with the modulation to E minor occurring at the end of section B. F♯ *segah* and E *shur* are very close relatives in the Azerbaijani modal system, as they are a part of the family "*rast-shur-segah.*" These three modes share the same pitches, and their tonics are located a whole step apart (see the table in the introduction), allowing for smooth transition from one to another within the traditional music system. Their Western counterparts, D major and E minor, are closely related, too, but their regular alteration within rondo form is not common in the classical style.

Section C, shown in musical example 4.2c, is already different from section A and section B: it is larger in size and strongly drawn to the upper melodic D, which is the culminating pitch of F♯ *segah*. In addition, section C contains traits of E *shur* or, to be more precise, of the part of *shur* called "Hijaz" that is centered around the fifth of its tonic, in this case B. B competes with D in terms of serving as a center of gravity within this part of *shur,* and correspondingly B minor alternates with D major, as is shown in musical example 4.2c. Within a predominantly B minor context, a D major chord appears in m. 36, and this harmony has noticeable power corresponding with that typical of a III triad in Western music. Due to its large size and tonal changes, section C obtains developmental features and can be likened to a trio section. Consequently, the form of the entire episode combines rondo characteristics with elements of ternary form. More tonal changes follow in section D. As seen from musical example 4.2d, the melody in this section is drawn to G, which is the upper fourth of D, the basic tone of F♯ *segah*. The presence of G major is rather short and is followed

EXAMPLE 4.2a. Hajibeyli, *Leyli and Majnun,* intermezzo to act 5, section A.

EXAMPLE 4.2b. Hajibeyli, *Leyli and Majnun,* intermezzo to act 5, section B.

EXAMPLE 4.2c. Hajibeyli, *Leyli and Majnun,* intermezzo to act 5, section C.

EXAMPLE 4.2d. Hajibeyli, *Leyli and Majnun,* intermezzo to act 5, section D.

EXAMPLE 4.2e. F♯ *segah.*

EXAMPLE 4.2f. E *shur.*

by a return to F♯ *segah*-D major by the end of section D (which is not a part of the example). It is symptomatic that the tonal plan of the entire intermezzo displays a prevalence of D major and G major harmonies, since plagal relations are essential in the modal system of Azerbaijani music, as discussed previously with regard to "Night of Separation." E minor, the key built on the second degree of the main Western scale used in Hajibeyli's intermezzo, is related to the subdominant family, therefore contributing to the plagal relations as well. All these examples illustrate Hajibeyli's early accomplishments in synthesizing the two musical systems. More sophisticated and more mature representatives of such a stylistic synthesis followed in the composer's later works.

"AZERBAIJANI SONATA"

Hajibeyli clearly realized the challenge of adopting one of the main accomplishments of Viennese classicism: sonata form. Perhaps this is why, before creating an "Azerbaijani sonata," he undertook a course of apprenticeship that has been a time-honored tradition for developing composers: reworking the compositions of an established master. In Hajibeyli's case, this meant transferring Western compositions into the Azerbaijani music system. In the *fantasies Chahargah* and *Shur* (both 1931), written for an orchestra of traditional instruments, Hajibeyli borrowed the contents of the first movement of Mozart's C major Sonata K V545 and rewrote them in the context of the Azerbaijani modes *chahargah* and *shur*. A comparison of the two themes from the expositions of the two parallel opuses, given in musical example 4.3, demonstrates that Hajibeyli's *Chahargah* is not simply an Azerbaijani clone of Mozart's Allegro.

Even these short examples show how Hajibeyli reconsiders Mozart's original melodic contour in accordance with the modal rules of Azerbaijani music. In both Hajibeyli's and Mozart's works, the opening patterns of their themes 1 and 2 clearly indicate the key. In m. 1 of musical example 4.3a and m. 14 of musical example 4.3d, Mozart highlights the melodic contour of the tonic and dominant triads of C major and G major (serving as the local tonic), respectively. In mm. 1–2 of musical example 4.3b and mm. 14–17 of musical example 4.3e, Hajibeyli pursues the same goal of establishing a solid tonic, but the melodic patterns he uses to reinforce the tonic are typical of C *chahargah* and G *chahargah* shown respectively in musical examples 4.3c and 4.3f. Mozart's themes have a defined harmonic structure created by both the right and the left hand. In theme 1, the right hand arpeggiates the tonic triad and has scalar flourishes using the notes of the C major scale, while the left has a light Alberti bass with simple progressions reinforcing the tonic triad. In theme 2, the right hand follows the con-

EXAMPLE 4.3a. Mozart, Sonata in C major (KV545), First Movement, theme 1, excerpt.

EXAMPLE 4.3b. Hajibeyli, Fantasie *Chahargah* for the orchestra of traditional instruments, theme 1, excerpt.

EXAMPLE 4.3c. C *chahargah*.

EXAMPLE 4.3d. Mozart, theme 2, excerpt.

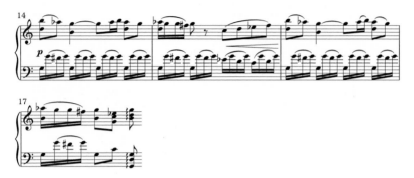

EXAMPLE 4.3e. Hajibeyli, theme 2, excerpt.

EXAMPLE 4.3f. G *chahargah.*

tours of the dominant triad, which the left hand's sixteenth notes reinforce. In contradistinction, Hajibeyli's themes do not suggest the same harmonic logic. Both themes consist of modal patterns woven into a horizontal line. This line is strongly drawn to the tonic (C in the first theme and G in the second), which fits the conventions of the introductory parts of any theme in Azerbaijani traditional music. As seen in mm. 1–4 of musical example 4.3b, in his theme 1, Hajibeyli promptly descends from the upper tonic to the lower one. This is a device frequently used in the introductory section of the *mugham Chahargah* called "Berdasht." In his theme 2, Mozart touches on G major, the local tonic, and then immediately turns toward D, the local dominant; this is seen in mm. 15 and 17 in musical example 4.3d. Hajibeyli, on the other hand, continuously highlights the new tonal center G through surrounding it with adjacent pitches throughout musical example 4.3e. Hajibeyli's compositional strategy reflects the national modal system, in which the tonic is literally made to be a central tone around which other pitches appear. The tempo change in the first theme of Hajibeyli's sonata is also noteworthy. Mozart had maintained an *allegro* tempo throughout his exposition, but Hajibeyli establishes *maestoso* at the beginning, thus separating the first four measures of the sonata from the rest of the first theme, interpreting Mozart's opening gesture as an introduction. Hajibeyli thus incorporates an essential component of *mugham:* a short yet weighty section, slow in tempo, that indicates the mode through showcasing the main tonic.

The rewriting of Mozart's sonata was simply Hajibeyli's experiment. The true emergence of the Azerbaijani sonata occurred in his opera *Koroghlu,* which includes five examples of this form. Hajibeyli's most remarkable and nuanced use of sonata form appears in the overture, which is a complete representation of sonata form with an exposition, development, and recapitulation, all framed with an extensive introduction and coda (PURL 4.3). The musical contents of the overture, shown in part in musical example 4.4, are completely derived from traditional Azerbaijani music in terms of their allusions to genres and thematic types, the method of contrast between the themes, and the modality employed.

The introduction begins with a powerful, quasi-improvisatory statement in the spirit of *mugham;* this opening material given in musical example 4.4a. The introduction continues with a second component based on energetic dance-like patterns. Theme 1 in the exposition continues this dance-like development, as shown in musical example 4.4c, after which theme 2, given in musical example 4.4e, is introduced, drawing on lyrical song-like material. All these genre types Hajibeyli employs – *mugham,* dance, song – could hypothetically be parts of a suite evoking a poetic picture of folk life; however, this is not the composer's purpose. These themes, which later become operatic leitmotivs, lose their direct attachment to their traditional generic context and are integrated into a dramatic sonata composition, conveying the general idea of the opera. Hajibeyli accomplishes this through establishing original structural models that are different from their classical prototypes but that still serve the goals of sonata form.

As described by Abezgauz, the two themes from the exposition fuse classical periodic structure with the phase-like modal development of *mugham.* She classified these specific structures as the "period based on the progressive diminishing of length" and as "embryo-periodic development."[9] In theme 1, the gradual diminishing of the length of units (the length of each unit is marked with brackets in musical example 4.4c) intensifies the melodic development. In theme 2, the short yet concentrated statement, marked in musical example 4.4e as "embryo," is followed by an extended phrase, marked as "periodic development," which creates an effect of summary or conclusion. By combining these two different structural principles within the exposition, Hajibeyli, according to Abezgauz, "establishes one of the main principles of the classical sonata, namely the resolution of the instability of the first theme and of the transitional material into the temporary stableness of the second theme."[10] In the introductory theme, the short quasi-improvisational declamatory patterns are placed in a steady metric context, creating another link to the classical style through mirroring a three-phrase period; these phrases are marked in musical example 4.4a with brackets.

Hajibeyli deftly weaves the nuances of the national modal system together with the Western concept of sonata form to create the tonal canvas of the piece. The tonal plan of this sonata-form overture features a powerful and intensely developing Eastern layer beneath a less eventful Western one, and it is that Eastern factor that contributes to the dramatic development of the form. In fact, five of the seven primary modes of Azerbaijani music – *rast, shur, segah, bayati-shiraz, and chahargah* – are incorporated into this relatively short piece.

C *shur* in the introductory theme (shown in musical example 4.4b) and D *segah* in the first theme (shown in musical example 4.4d) connect seamlessly, as they both belong to the family of relative modes "*rast-shur-segah*." In the context of Western music, the key change from C minor to B♭ major, with the Western tonalities functioning as equivalents of the aforementioned modes, is not typical for an introduction and first theme in a classical sonata; however, here it is justified by the Azerbaijani modal system. Interestingly, the third part of the family of relative modes – B♭ *rast* – is not completely missing in the overture, since it appears in the coda where it is interpreted in the context of B♭ major. Theme 2 of the exposition is marked by a modulation from D *segah* (interpreted as B♭ major) to G *bayati-shiraz* (shown in musical example 4.4f and interpreted as G minor). The modulation itself is typical of Western functional harmony, although not common for the tonal plan of the main themes in a sonata form. This is another example of a key change caused by the Azerbaijani modal system rather than by Western functional harmony. The development section is almost entirely in G minor. To Westerners, this is the same G minor that closed the exposition, but in the national modal context it signifies a change toward a new modal and key sphere, that is *chahargah* (D *chahargah* and G *chahaghah*). In other words, under the surface of G minor, there is a mode and key change from *bayati-shiraz* to *chahargah*.

These few examples show how Hajibeyli rediscovered the compositional rules of the classical era through the lens of his national music tradition, thus establishing a solid foundation for the national style of Azerbaijani music. He progressed slowly and carefully from the simple forms of synthesis that were based on similarities between Western and Azerbaijani musical systems toward those that fused qualities not directly echoing each other. Creating the Azerbaijani sonata was a major accomplishment within the first phase of creating a national style, and it gave a powerful impetus to the future development of symphonic, chamber, and solo instrumental music.

FIRST SIGNS OF ROMANTICISM

Romanticism was another highly attractive source for the composers of the young Azerbaijani tradition, especially since nationalist impulses profoundly shaped the music of the romantic era. When discussing the phenomenon of national musical style in nineteenth-century European music, Dahlhaus argues that "it is so closely fused . . . with the idea of nationalism . . . that any attempt to enforce a rigid separation of 'stylistic' and 'ideological' elements would be not only impossible but also inappropriate."[11] Early Azerbaijani composers were strongly driven by the nationalist ideal, and this explains their music's tendency toward the aesthetics and stylistic means of romanticism. Many components of romantic aesthetics, including highly nuanced emotions, reflections on the historical past, and praise of the beauty of nature, also appealed to Azerbaijani

EXAMPLE 4.4a. Hajibeyli, *Koroghlu,* overture, introductory theme.

EXAMPLE 4.4b. C *shur.*

EXAMPLE 4.4c. Hajibeyli, overture, theme 1.

EXAMPLE 4.4d. D *segah*.

EXAMPLE 4.4e. Hajibeyli, overture, theme 2.

EXAMPLE 4.4f. G *bayati-shiraz*.

sensibilities. Romantic genres such as the rhapsody, the *fantasie,* and their like allowed flexible and irregular rhythms and promoted an improvisational style, breaking the mold of the Viennese classical forms that were highly popular among the first Azerbaijani composers. Romantic composers' effusion of suite-like compositions with contrasting movements was projected onto analogous forms in traditional Azerbaijani music – most importantly, *mugham.*

Among the factors that facilitated the smooth adoption of romanticism in Azerbaijani music was the high level of sensuality typical of both romantic music and Azerbaijani *mugham.* The musicologist Andrew Bowie states, "The concept of feeling is vital to [the] Romantic aesthetic," and he further refers to the German philosopher Friedrich Schleiermacher's understanding of the term "feeling" as "immediate self-consciousness" and "free productivity."[12] This perspective corresponds with the aesthetic concept of Azerbaijani *mugham,* which is about moment-to-moment music-making and which can also be defined as a product of "immediate self-consciousness" and free creativity. Alongside profound spirituality and intellectualism, sensuality and even eroticism are essential components of *mugham* aesthetics. Among the European composers whose music has a deep sensual element, perhaps Wagner is closest in aesthetic to Azerbaijani *mugham.* The tendency to reconcile the spiritual and sexual dimensions of love, the unity of love and death, the idea of consistent melodic development overcoming metric regularity ("*Unendliche Melodie*"), the long-lasting and unresolved accumulation of harmonic and melodic tension are all essential qualities for Wagner that can be extrapolated to *mugham* as well, although they were stimulated by different cultural and musical factors and revealed themselves in different ways. For most of Soviet history, the official stance toward Wagner was negative, which might be the reason that despite all of the abovementioned parallels, *mugham* and Wagner never synthesized in the music of Azerbaijani composers.

Muslim Magomayev was the first proponent of romanticism in Azerbaijani music. This composer introduced many innovations: he wrote the first Azerbaijani compositions for symphony orchestra and the first Azerbaijani opera in a Western format, and he was the first ever conductor of a symphony orchestra in Azerbaijan. Undoubtedly, Magomayev was a follower of Hajibeyli's concept of East-West fusion. Nonetheless, intentionally or not, he was seeking his own, individual path within this general concept, and his predilection for romanticism was symptomatic of this. Magomayev's music is highly passionate and emotional, and it has an expressive appeal that is very different from the balanced and cheerful classical atmosphere of Hajibeyli's works. Both composers referred to the same sources from their traditional heritage – *mugham, ashig* art, folk songs, and dances. Yet, by applying them through different stylistic aesthetics, they arrived at divergent artistic results.

Magomayev generally followed Hajibeyli's model of *mugham* opera in terms of form when he wrote *Shah Ismayil* (1916). But unlike Hajibeyli, who used a classical Azerbaijani literary work as the basis of his operatic plot, Magomayev turned to the *ashig* story, or *dastan,* about prince Ismayil, focusing on two parts of the narrative that particularly appeal to romantic aesthetics. One section refers to Azerbaijan's historical past and conveys the loosely historical story of the struggle for power between two generations of the same dynasty in sixteenth-century Azerbaijan.[13] The other element of the operatic libretto inherited from *dastan* shows the main hero wandering in distant lands. Both motives – historical retrospective and travel in a search for happiness – are highly typical of romantic aesthetics.

Among the operatic characters presented in *Shah Ismayil,* one – Aslanshah – differed significantly from his presentation in the traditional epic narrative. In the original *dastan,* Aslanshah, the father of the main hero and the ruler of the country, is a despotic king, but in Magomayev's opera, he is turned into a tragic figure. He suffers from an internal struggle. He has both the feelings of a loving father and the ambitions of a tyrannical ruler who is afraid of his son's possible claim for power. Magomayev's Aslanshah suggests many associations, all from nineteenth-century opera: conceptually, he resembles Mussorgsky's Boris Godunov, whereas his vocal style, marked by passionate declamation, abundant use of syncopation, and diminished intervals, recalls the melodic style of the romantic and postromantic composers, such as Verdi and the Verismo composers.

Aslanshah is the first Western-type operatic hero in Azerbaijani music who is exclusively given arias, ariosos, recitatives, and other such conventional operatic pieces. Gulzar, Ismayil's beloved, also only has such standard Western pieces, although her characterization is less strong and vivid. Unlike with the opera's other characters, no original *mugham*s are present in Aslanshah's and Gulzar's parts, which breaks from the stylistic and generic norms of *mugham* opera and increases the weight of Western operatic characteristics. Such eclecticism in the presentation of characters perfectly serves the dramaturgical concept of the opera: Aslanshah's arias and low baritone timbre oppose Shah Ismayil's *mugham*s and high vocal range, which are typical of traditional music, thus strengthening the conflict between the main protagonists. Likewise, Gulzar's part, scored for soprano, opposes Arab Zangi, a woman-warrior who is given *mugham*s only and sings in a low voice, which is typical for female vocal performance in traditional music. These two characters are the only women in

FIGURE 4.1. The composer Muslim Magomayev. *Courtesy of the State Museum of Azerbaijani Musical Culture.*

Magomayev's opera. Both are in love with Ismayil, but Arab Zangi ultimately is rejected. Magomayev's use of different vocal timbres and of different styles highlights the contrast between these two heroines and their roles in the opera.

Magomayev's second opera, *Nargiz*, embraces the spirit of romanticism, although this work is above all a typical product of Soviet opera and contains many references to socialist realism. The story of two lovers who lead a revolt against the landlords and defeat them can be found in various instantiations in many Soviet operas written in the 1930s. Nevertheless, by emphasizing lyrical and romantic elements, Magomayev's opera diverges from the norms of this type of opera. He primarily wrote a love story, relegating the social cataclysms to second place. Since its premiere, Nargiz's lyrical arias have stood out as the most impressive pages of this work, whereas all heroic expressions, both solo and choral, have been forgotten.

Magomayev's predilection for programmatic orchestral music further reveals his romantic priorities. The very choice of the themes he depicted in his symphonic works is already telling. In *The Meadows of Azerbaijan* (1932), he created an evocative picture praising the beauty of his homeland, and in *Darvish* (1933), he drew on the motive of travel in search of truth. Literally, the term *darvish* signifies a member of the Sufi order, the mystical stream within Islam; Sufis often chose travel as a way of attaining high spirituality. It would not have been possible to overtly allude to such a religious theme in the Soviet Union at the time. Instead, the composer emphasized the motive of travel typical of many romantic pieces. He further evoked romanticism through his poetic interpretation of folk music idioms and through quasi-improvisational elements that resemble rhapsody-like and fantasy-like instrumental pieces of Western romanticism.

Magomayev's interest in taking the form and progression of complete, multisectional traditional *mughams* and reimagining them into suites or medleys points to the romantic priorities of his music. In *The Meadows of Azerbaijan*, Magomayev presents the whole scope of *mugham* composition, with all pertaining sections and contrasts. That the composer titled this piece as "rhapsody" is indicative, too; it even brings to mind historical parallels with the *Hungarian Rhapsodies* by Liszt, which have direct ties with the *Verbunkos* style. Magomayev explored translating multisectional *mugham* composition into romantic composition in his operas as well. The scene "Abu-Hamza and Ibn-Tahir" from the opera *Shah Ismayil* is entirely based on the melodic material of *mugham Rast* (in Magomayev's own transcription), evenly distributed between the vocal and instrumental parts. Some sections of traditional *mugham* are reimagined into aria-like episodes, while others are interpreted as recitatives. In *Nargiz*, the composer accomplished an even more difficult task.

EXAMPLE 4.5a. Muslim Magomayev, *Shah Ismayil,* Aslanshah's aria from act 1.

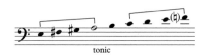

EXAMPLE 4.5b. A *bayati-shiraz.*

He merged the phase-like development of *mugham* with through-composed forms of Western music. In the arias of the two main protagonists, Nargiz (act 1) and Alyar (act 3), Magomayev keeps intact the main contour of the modal development typical of the *mughams Rast* and *Shur,* respectively. In some sections of the original *mugham* composition, he modifies the original melodic contents through incorporating the styles of the lyrical cantilena and the heroic march.

The melodic language of Magomayev reflects the romantic aesthetic and formal characteristics of his music, although the melodies he wrote do not go beyond the bounds of the national modal system. The melodic contents of Aslanshah's aria from act 1 of *Shah Ismayil,* which is given in its entirety in musical example 4.5, serve as an example (PURL 4.4).

This aria's melody does not contain a single pattern that would sound foreign in the modal space of A *bayati-shiraz,* but at the same time, this aria also displays the characteristic language of romanticism. The centrality of the tonic in mm. 9-12 and the descending sequence-like development in mm. 13-20 are typical of Azerbaijani music. The final cadence in m. 21, free of any metric structure, sounds almost like a quote from *mugham*. In a nod to Western sources, the aria's powerful opening statement begins and closes with the tonic of A minor. The composer highlights the contour of the tonic triad by placing notes belonging to it on strong beats or by assigning them long rhythmic values. For example, A appears on the downbeat in mm. 9 and 12, C is the downbeat in m. 10, and E is the longest note in m. 9. The sense of stability created at the beginning is destroyed in the second phrase, beginning in m. 13. Long stops on the last note in the first and third segments of the sequence emphasize the diminished fifth within their respective segments (B-F and G♯-D) and the diminished seventh between the beginning and the end of the sequence overall (G♯-F). Such diminished intervallic patterns naturally occur in the course of the development of any native melody, but they are never highlighted; rather, they are obscured. Magomayev reveals these patterns through rhythmic structure, and they serve as indicators of the romantic musical style. The off-beat cadence in m. 21 spans the same interval of the minor sixth from E to C that had bounded the first phrase, thus creating a melodic arch with the beginning. Accentuating the mediant to highlight the minor sixth between the dominant and the mediant of either major or minor is another meeting point for Eastern and Western practices of melodic development. This compositional strategy is typical in the Azerbaijani national music system, but it is also widely used in romantic music, particularly in the Russian tradition. In this rather short melody, through rhythmic transformation of quite traditional melodic patterns, Magomayev creates a brilliant romanticist interpretation of *bayati-shiraz*.

The melodic contents of Aslanshah's aria from act 4, given in full in musical example 4.6a, further demonstrate Magomayev's adoption of romanticism.

The melody, in E *bayati-shiraz* (shown in musical example 4.6b), has a descending contour and is shaped as "the melody descending to the tonic," which Abezgauz defines as one of the typical patterns of melodic development in Azerbaijani traditional music. Such a melody may start from any pitch, but then it displays a slow yet persistent descending movement toward the tonic.[14] This is what happens in Aslanshah's aria. Eventually, through stair-like motion and temporary stops on various scale degrees of E *bayati-shiraz*, the line descends from E4 in m. 2 toward E3 in m. 13. Magomayev simultaneously uses melodic patterns from the Western tradition. The melody is shaped as a period due to the rhythmic symmetry between the opening parts of each phrase, as can be seen in mm. 1–3 and mm. 7–9. To highlight this symmetry, the composer begins both phrases with a syncopated pattern, seen in mm. 2 and 8. The

EXAMPLE 4.6a. Magomayev, *Shah Ismayil*, Aslanshah's aria from act 4.

EXAMPLE 4.6b. E *bayati-shiraz*.

open ending of the first phrase, which concludes with the subdominant A in m. 6, also contributes to establishing the period.

Just as in Aslanshah's act 1 aria, the contours of the tonic triad of E minor are highlighted at the very beginning of the melodic development. The entirety of m. 1 accentuates B; E is the highest pitch of the piece, and it appears in m. 2; and then G is the downbeat in m. 4. Unlike the folk precedents of the "melody descending to the tonic," in which the upper tone is supposed to be thoroughly established at the beginning, here, in m. 2, E is only given briefly, a spark that quickly disappears. The triple meter of this aria is typical of many Azerbaijani folk melodies; however, in this particular context, the music seems more indicative of the waltz. This music is one of those melancholic romantic waltzes that is highly appropriate for a hero who suffers from loneliness. The waltz traits of this piece are also strengthened by a waltz pattern in the accompaniment, with the bass note occurring on the downbeat and two identical chords falling on

Table 4.3. Structure of "My Country"

Intro	A		B		Coda
F *rast*	G *shur*	E *segah*	C *shushtar*	G *shur*
F major	G minor	C major	C minor	G minor

the off-beats. At the end, in mm. 9–12, the regularity of the meter is suddenly broken by the same *rubato*-like cadence that had concluded his first aria as well. The cadence, which spans the interval of the diminished seventh (D♯-C), increases tension and brings this lyrical monologue to a dramatic close.

One final pioneer, Asaf Zeynalli, is revered as the founder of the national romance and was one of the first Azerbaijani composers to write chamber and instrumental pieces. Zeynalli was the first native composer to graduate from the Azerbaijan State Conservatory, and he was predicted by many to become the leading force of the post-Hajibeyli generation. An early death from typhus at the age of twenty-three prevented his talent from flourishing. The musicologist Rauf Farkhadov characterizes Zeynalli as the "Schubert of Azerbaijani music" due to the composer's short life, status as a pioneer, focus on song and romance, and accomplishments in the field of chamber and instrumental genres.[15] I would also add that like Schubert, Zeynalli's music combines classical and romantic impulses, and both these impulses are filtered through the lens of national folklore. Poetic interpretation of any subject, be it love for the Homeland, nature, or woman, as well as clarity of form and simplicity of harmony, further strengthen the bond between Zeynalli and Schubert. Zeynalli's romance "My Country" (1931), with the lyrics of Jafar Jabbarli, combines patriotic spirit with profound lyrical expression. The musical language of the piece, given in part in musical example 4.7, is heavily based on classical principles: the form is clearly divided, the harmony is rather modest, and the melody is based on simple hymn-like patterns. At the same time, its strong inner passion and colorful key changes are a reflection of romantic aesthetics. The modal spectrum of "My Country" combines four modes of Azerbaijani music in masterful, seamless transition from one to the next. The scheme is presented in table 4.3 and examples from each section of the piece are presented to illustrate the modality (PURL 4.5).

The piece opens with a short exclamatory phrase shown in musical example 4.7a. F *rast,* interpreted as F major and shown in musical example 4.7b is the most cheerful mode of Azerbaijani music, and it quite properly articulates the words "O my country!" Zeynalli's phrase is a combination of the five typical

Andante maestoso

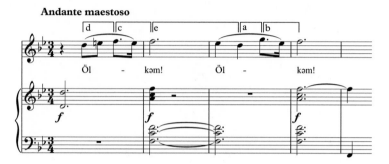

EXAMPLE 4.7a. Asaf Zeynalli, "My Country," introduction.

EXAMPLE 4.7b. F *rast*.

EXAMPLE 4.7c. Melodic cadences in the mode of *rast*. From: Hajibeyli, *Principles of Azerbaijani Folk Music* (Baku: Yazichi, 1985), 51–52.

cadential motives in the mode *rast;* these are given in musical example 4.7c and shown in context, marked with numbers, in musical example 4.7a. Section A, partly shown in musical example 4.7d, is built upon G *shur,* interpreted as G minor, which becomes the modal/tonal basis for the entire piece. In Western music practice, F major would hardly be considered to be a proper tonal base for the introductory part of a piece written in G minor, whereas in the context of the Azerbaijani modal system, the F *rast*–G *shur* combination is natural. Besides, *rast,* traditionally considered to be the core mode of the modal system, draws in features of other modes, thus serving as a perfect choice for the introduction.[16] F *rast*–F major never returns, and the opening phrase remains echoing in the listener's memory as an epigraph. Section B of the piece, given in musical example 4.7f, modulates to E *segah* shown in musical example 4.7g, which again is quite a natural development after G *shur.* C major becomes the Western equivalent of E *segah.* From the Western point of view, the G minor–C major

EXAMPLE 4.7d. Zeynalli, "My Country," section A.

EXAMPLE 4.7e. G *shur*.

combination is less characteristic, though possible because of the Lydian color added to G minor due to the characteristics of G *shur*. Section C shown in musical example 4.7h marks the change to C *shushtar* shown in musical example 4.7i. C *shushtar*–C minor signals a move from one group of relative Azerbaijani modes (*rast-shur-segah*) to another (*shushtar-humayun-zabul*), according to Ismayilov's classification.[17] The close relation of keys facilitates this change: C major and C minor are parallel keys and share the same tonic. The presence of C minor is rather deceiving here, as the melodic development is strongly drawn to G. The latter helps smooth the final return to G *shur*–G minor for a short postlude shown in musical example 4.7j.

Zeynalli's "My Country" is an example of the seamless fusion of two modal systems. Its melodic contents derive from the modes of Azerbaijani music, although in traditional music, such a short vocal piece would rarely feature four

EXAMPLE 4.7f. Zeynalli, "My Country," section B.

EXAMPLE 4.7g. E *segah* (with chromatic alterations).

EXAMPLE 4.7h. Zeynalli, "My Country," section C.

EXAMPLE 4.7i. C *shushtar.*

EXAMPLE 4.7j. Zeynalli, "My Country," postlude.

modes, especially not four modes more distantly related to each other. In Zeynalli's romance, it is the Western tonal plan based on the plagal combination G minor–C major–C minor–G minor that becomes a cementing factor.

In the first three decades of the twentieth century, Azerbaijani composers built the foundations of their distinct national style. They accomplished this through the discovery of the shared points between their traditional music on the one side and classicism and romanticism on the other. Since the 1930s, the definition "national composed music of Azerbaijan" has signified more than the existence of musical works created in Azerbaijan that use the idioms of Western composed music. Rather, this definition applies to the new national school of composers.

5 GROWING MATURITY

1940–THE EARLY 1960s

> The Union of Azerbaijani Composers is now among
> the strongest in the country [the Soviet Union], and its
> recent accomplishments are truly remarkable.
>
> DMITRY SHOSTAKOVICH, *Excellent School of Composers*

EXPLORING THE SPACE OF NEOCLASSICISM

Neoclassicism was historically the first style in Azerbaijani music that demonstrated native composers' growing synchronization with Western contemporary music. During the 1940s and 1950s, both German and French neoclassical models, associated with Hindemith and Stravinsky, respectively, entered the orbit of Azerbaijani music. At this early stage, Russian music played a mediating role in Azerbaijani composers' absorption of neoclassicism, and the styles of Shostakovich and Prokofiev were particularly influential. Eventually, native composers freed themselves from this dependence on Russia. In the 1960s, they mastered many traits of neoclassicism directly from European sources (see chapter 6). The nascent Azerbaijani composed tradition had to develop at an accelerated rate to keep in step with Western composed music, leading to the most outstanding peculiarity of Azerbaijani neoclassicism. Paradoxically, the earliest Azerbaijani neoclassical compositions did not offer the same retrospective revolution, in an aesthetic sense, that European neoclassical compositions did. Like their Western counterparts, native neoclassical composers reinterpreted the stylistic means of the deep past, even if it was not their past. But Azerbaijani composers primarily used neoclassicism to update their stylistic and generic resources and to move their national composed music out of the Viennese classical styles that had dominated their compositional landscape until the end of the 1930s. Azerbaijani musical neoclassicism thus never opposed romanticism as a "call to order," since chronologically these two styles in Azerbaijani music developed simultaneously. Nor was it a reaction to impressionism, a style which, despite having been introduced in Azerbaijan in the late 1930s, never became significant. A retrospective aesthetic in Azerbaijani neoclassicism emerged later, in the 1960s, when the growing maturity of Azerbaijani composed music allowed for and stimulated reflections on their own classical past.

Gara Garayev was a key figure in establishing the neoclassical stream in Azerbaijani music. Garayev had always valued clarity and rigidity of form. As the music theorist Leo Mazel states, "In his music, which meets the criteria of classicism by its quality and stylistic characteristics, we are able to sense his unique, 'Karaev's' [Garayev's] interpretation of the East where despite all variety of feelings, colors, and rhythms, refined intellect prevails over the flow of emotions."[1] In combination with Garayev's constant interest in innovation and modernity, the classical basis of his style stimulated his move toward neoclassicism. Garayev's First and Second symphonies marked the arrival of the German model of neoclassicism in Azerbaijani music. Abezgauz characterizes the First Symphony in B minor as a challenging neoclassical experiment in the spirit of Hindemith. This composition has abstract contents, a great amount of polyphony, and a rather unusual form in which two movements are combined with no key change.[2] The First Symphony was an experimental work, and it contained few references to the national music system, unlike the Second Symphony in C major. In this work, particularly in its fourth movement ("Passacaglia"), the composer synthesized symphonic polyphonic development with the linearism of *mugham*. Shostakovich's Eighth Symphony inspired Garayev's use of the passacaglia in this symphony; however, the Azerbaijani composer rediscovered the passacaglia through his native tradition of *mugham*.[3] The passacaglia and *mugham* share one core principle: consistent and purposeful thematic development growing out of an initial thematic cell. Both genres are characterized by a high degree of metric and rhythmic freedom. The thematic development of *mugham* is led by modal logic and does not have any metric division, and the thematicism of the passacaglia, in which improvisational qualities play an essential role, tends to overcome metric and rhythmic structure. The main theme of Garayev's "Passacaglia" uses the Azerbaijani mode *shur,* and this theme is followed by a set of six variations. The culmination occurs in the sixth variation, shown in musical example 5.1.[4] The original theme, played by brass instruments and bass, is combined with a dramatic, virtuosic, soloistic flourish in the strings. These fast, quasi-improvisational figures complement the slow and heavy rhythmic motion of the theme.

FIGURE 5.1. Jovdat Hajiyev (center) and Agshin Alizade (right). *Courtesy of the State Museum of Azerbaijani Musical Culture.*

Such dramatic, recitative-like instrumental solos are highly representative of Shostakovich's works, in which they recall pieces such as preludes that mimic improvisatory style and are typical for the baroque era. Azerbaijani composers admired this idea and borrowed it. In their interpretations, these solos were also reminiscent of the expressive instrumental elaborations on modal formulas in *mugham*. Once again, Azerbaijani musicians found typological parallels between *mugham* and baroque music, as discussed in chapter 4.

The fusion of neoclassical idioms with the modal development of *mugham* is the main characteristic of the music of Jovdat Hajiyev, the master of the Azerbaijani symphony and the most devoted follower of Shostakovich's traditions among the national composers. The first movement of Hajiyev's Fourth Symphony (1956), "Recitative and Fantasie," opens with an extensive improvisatory passage that recalls both *mugham* and Shostakovich's music. The fourth movement of the same symphony is titled "Passacaglia." Hajiyev's "Passacaglia" reflects his underlying symphonic vision by creating a heroic atmosphere and evoking theatricality, unlike Garayev's "Passacaglia." Hajiyev's heroic aesthetic parallels the symphonic concept of Beethoven, particularly as found in the *Eroica* Symphony and in the middle period compositions more generally. Like Beethoven's Ninth Symphony, Hajiyev's symphony includes quotations from

EXAMPLE 5.1. (*Facing*) Gara Garayev, Second Symphony, Fourth Movement. From: Liudmila Karagicheva, *Kara Karaev* [Gara Garayev] (Moscow: Sovetskii Kompozitor, 1960), 48–51.

other movements. These two works also share theatrical elements and the return in the final movement of themes from previous movements.

The French model of neoclassicism first appeared in Azerbaijani music in the Sonatina for the Piano (1943) by Garayev. This piece demonstrates what the composer found most attractive about French neoclassicism: the stylization of dances from the classical and baroque eras. Garayev created a more extensive experiment in French neoclassicism in the suite from act 3 of the ballet *The Path of Thunder*. This suite consists of three episodes: "Ancient Dance," combining a minuet and a sarabanda; "Dance of Sari's Friends," featuring a bourrée and a gigue; and "Sari's Gavotte." The musicologist Ulviyya Imanova characterizes these three episodes as "islands of neoclassicism" since stylistically, all of them markedly differ from this act's other music.[5] Dramaturgically, this contrast allows the neoclassical sections to create a deceptively pure atmosphere in the home of Gert, the protagonist. His racist behavior and actions cause all further tragic events. Such a contrast also adds a dose of the grotesque to the use of classical forms, tapping into another trait of neoclassicism. Prokofiev's style is the primary source of inspiration in this suite, as well as in the neoclassical "The Lullaby" from *The Path of Thunder*. Garayev retains the clarity typical of classical forms (ternary in all these cases) and uses broadly conceived melodic and harmonic diatonicism. At the same time, he incorporates some surprising elements, including sudden leaps by a seventh or even greater intervals in the melody and modulations to distant keys.

In a similar vein, the "Pavane" from the symphonic engravings *Don Quixote* (1960) shows "the facade of elegance that hides evil in people's hearts and is ready to be removed at any time," as described by Abezgauz.[6] To accomplish this goal, Garayev uses the pavane, a highly reserved and emotionally chilly sixteenth- and seventeenth-century Spanish court dance. Unlike in *The Path of Thunder*, the neoclassical episode here does not contrast with the rest of the score, and this neoclassical music seamlessly merges into the surrounding material. Throughout this composition, the composer generally avoids the exoticism or the high expressivity that is sometimes heard in pieces on Spanish subjects and which would have been antithetical to a neoclassical aesthetic. Garayev's Spain recalls his favorite painters Goya and Picasso, rather than El Greco or Velasquez.

Garayev's Azerbaijani roots can still be traced in his neoclassical works. The third movement from the Sonata for Violin and Piano, "Pastorale" (*Moderato*, G minor), is based on the siciliana, another baroque dance. This "Pastorale" has often been compared to Stravinsky's "Serenade" (*Larghetto*, C minor) from the Suite on Pergolesi's themes, which is also a stylized siciliana. Nonetheless, the

EXAMPLE 5.2. G. Garayev, Sonata for Violin and Piano, Third Movement.

compositional palette of Garayev's piece reveals the author's non-Western background, as seen in the opening theme, given in musical example 5.2 (PURL 5.1).

According to Imanova, several features of Garayev's "Pastorale" emerge from the convergence of Azerbaijani and Western musical systems. These traits include the patterns of the national modes *shushtar* and *bayati-shiraz,* which appear within the harmonic minor; the $^6_8$ signature, which indicates an organization of time common in Azerbaijani music and in baroque music; and the important role of the rhythmic motif ♪♫ that is reminiscent of the siciliana and which is one of the most representative rhythmic patterns of Azerbaijani music.[7] The abundance of sequences in Garayev's "Pastorale" recalls both baroque music and the traditional music of Azerbaijan. Indeed, Garayev masterfully chooses stylistic means that allow him to have a "dual connection" to East and West, and he organically incorporates these stylistic means into – or rather has them contribute to – the neoclassical aesthetic of this work.

Garayev's compositions of the 1940s and 1950s marked the first chapter in the development of Azerbaijani neoclassicism. The emergence of neoclassicism in Azerbaijan coincided with the acme of romanticism in Azerbaijani national music, once more calling to mind the concept of *stretta* as a metaphor for Azerbaijani music in the middle of the twentieth century.

PEAK OF ROMANTICISM

Fikrat Amirov, Garayev's permanent vis-à-vis in approaching the idea of East-West synthesis, brought "Azerbaijani romanticism" to its full efflorescence. Amirov's awe of his native land, expressed through a poetic, elevated mood and colorful stylistic means, was among the first and foremost traits of romantic aesthetics and style in his music. Scarcely any other composer in Azerbaijan dedicated as many works to glorifying his or her homeland, its landscapes, history, literature, and people. His patriotic works, such as the suite *Azerbaijan* (1950), *Azerbaijani Capriccio* (1961), and *Azerbaijani Engravings* (1976), all three for symphony orchestra, reflect Amirov's tendency toward programmatic instrumental music, itself another link with romanticism.

Amirov drew his romantic-inspired style and aesthetic from two major sources: the native composer Magomayev and the Russian composer Tchaikovsky. The idea of including a waltz in symphonic works, as Amirov did in his symphony *Nizami* for string orchestra, vividly demonstrates the intersection of the two. The symphonic waltz is emblematic of Tchaikovsky's symphonies, and Amirov certainly referred to this source. But the native composer Magomayev had developed his own interest in the waltz, having created the "Azerbaijani Waltz" in Aslanshah's second aria in the opera *Shah Ismayil* (see chapter 4). Thus, Amirov is reminiscent of both Tchaikovsky and Magomayev. This same Magomayev-Tchaikovsky connection helps explain the dramatic concept of Amirov's masterpiece, the opera *Sevil*. It is an intense story in which a woman is rejected by a man but then later rejects him herself, recalling the plot of Tchaikovsky's *Eugene Onegin* (PURL 5.2). In Amirov's case, his plot is also the story of a woman's emancipation, which appealed to the native audiences. *Sevil* furthermore allows direct analogies with Magomayev's opera *Nargiz*. The plots of both works center on a strong woman involved in social cataclysms that have a grave impact on her personal life. These two components of the plot – personal drama and social turmoil – affect the vocal writing. Operatic cantilenas and quasi-*mugham* declamatory writing appear in the more intimate scenes, while the march-like patterns of revolutionary songs characterize the social episodes. Both Magomayev and Amirov favored the personal scenes' plot and music over those of the socially directed sections. This explains why both operas, from the moment of their premieres, have been valued and appreciated as stories of love and separation, rather than as social dramas.

Parallels between Amirov and Magomayev are particularly evident in the so-called *mugham* plus genre fusion. Magomayev was the first to notate *mugham.* He was also the first to use transcribed *mugham* in its entirety, employing it in his opera *Shah Ismayil*, in a recitative scene (see chapter 4). Magomayev introduced stylistic and compositional changes to *mugham* composition, though he nonetheless retained *mugham*'s original contours. His work opened a path toward the new genre of symphonic *mugham*, which Amirov created. Far from being a simple transcription and orchestration of *mugham*, Amirov's symphonic *mugham* reimagines the dramaturgical and melodic features of *mugham* within romantic-inspired symphonic music.

Amirov's *Kurd Ovshari* is characteristic of this new genre. Some connections between Amirov's piece and traditional *mugham* are immediately apparent. These include the abundant repetitions in both the melodic and rhythmic parts, the irregularity of structure, the rich melodic melismas, and the frequent tempo and meter changes. But the aesthetic and stylistic relations between Amirov's *Kurd Ovshari* and the art of *mugham* are significantly deeper (PURL 5.3).

The piece is written in a suite-like form. It opens with a short introductory part that is followed by five sections. Each borrows the names of original *mugham*s, or of their parts. All pertain to the *shur* family, thus revealing the role of this mode as the unifying factor of the composition: introduction, "Ovshari," "Tasnif," "Shahnaz," "Kurdi," "Mani."

Except for the song-like "Tasnif," all sections are quasi-improvisational, as they are based on the material of the so-called small *mugham*s. *Mugham*s from this category are rather short and show only a part of the national mode, rather than trying to suggest its full representation. Apart from "Shahnaz," all *mugham* episodes refer to the subgenre called *zarbi-mugham*, or rhythmic *mugham*. In *zarbi-mugham*, improvisation occurs against steady rhythmic patterns maintained by drums. From the time Hajibeyli used *zarbi-mugham Arazbari* in his opera *Leyli and Majnun* (see chapter 4), this subgenre was frequently incorporated in the orbit composed music, as *zarbi-mugham* lent itself to smooth integration with Western practice. The rhythmic structure typical for this subgenre of *mugham* by default eliminates one of the challenges of East-West synthesis: the conflict between strict and regular metric and rhythmic division in Western music and their absence in *mugham*.

Potentially, the form of *mugham*, referring to its full representation called *destgah*, contains at least two features that allow its deft integration with the Western genre of the suite. The first is a phase-like modal development, which is not present in Amirov's *Kurd Ovshari*, as the composer combined several small *mugham*s and did not aim to give a full rendition of the mode *shur* in his piece. The second factor pertains to the internal contrasts of *mugham* composition, in which improvised episodes regularly alternate with sections based on steady metric patterns. In Amirov's piece, two song-like episodes – the opening of the introduction and "Tasnif" – offer a contrast from the quasi-improvisatory parts (*shoba*), but unlike in traditional practice, they do not serve as interludes between *shoba*. Instead, these song-like episodes become equal counterparts of the *mugham* episodes. This particularly is true of "Tasnif," in which Amirov gradually transforms a rather simple folk melody in triple meter into a passionate waltz that forms the lyrical center of the entire composition. Amirov's plan thus absorbs features of the Western-type suite, which consists of equally important movements, each shaped by the characteristics of different genres.

The orchestration features the same dynamic interplay of native and Western sources. The abundance of solos and the frequent juxtaposition of different groups of instruments resemble call-response relations within a traditional *mugham* trio. There are also analogues to Western genres, as for example the concerto grosso (another indirect sign of the parallels between *mugham* and baroque music), or to nineteenth-century romantic scores, such as those of Tchaikovsky and Berlioz. The same principle of featuring and juxtaposing instruments and their groups lends a theatrical air to Amirov's composition and thus draws from both Western and Azerbaijani sources. *Mugham* has rich theatrical potential, since each instrument and voice in a *mugham* ensemble is highly personified. Theatricality is also a significant part of baroque aesthetics, from the musical genres of the opera, the concerto, and the oratorio to the paintings of Caravaggio. At the same time, Berlioz and Tchaikovsky come to mind when discussing theatrical elements in the programmatic symphonic scores of romantic composers.

The orchestration of *Kurd Ovshari* reflects another essential feature of *mugham:* the leading role of the singer. The abundant expressive melodies played by the clarinet, trumpet, flute, and oboe have vocal qualities reminiscent of the voice of the *khanende* in a *mugham* ensemble. Instrumentation significantly contributes to the process of shaping form in Amirov's composition. Many instrumental solos occur at the beginnings of sections. The moments of *tutti,* on the contrary, occur at cadences at the end of sections or segments of sections, which reveals the important role of cadences in *mugham* composition.

Another sign of Amirov's close proximity to the traditional music system in this piece is that he always keeps the melodic line preeminent. Nonetheless, Amirov demonstrates creativity in reconsidering the native monodic tradition in the context of the many-layered textures of his symphonic work. He divides the melody between orchestral groups, adds imitative elements responding to the melody, and doubles the principal melody in various intervals. None of these tools aim to disturb the prevalence of the main melody, showing the continuing importance of traditional monodic roots in Amirov's style.

The same unity of Eastern and Western stylistic traits characterizes Amirov's occasional use of polyphonic elements. At the beginning of the piece, shown in musical example 5.3, the opening melody that begins in m. 5 and is performed by the clarinet dominates the section. A second theme emerges close after in the strings in m. 12 and becomes a new element of the texture, complementing the main theme. Finally, a third, ostinato-like layer in the bass that had started in m. 1 creates a background for this dialogue. This type of texture is directly inherited from the traditional performance of *zarbi-mugham* in which the vocalist performs the main melody, the accompanying ensemble (typically, strings) adds imitative and complementary elements, and the drum part maintains an ostinato-type pattern throughout. In the meantime, such a texture creates associations with the symphonic scores of the romantic composers, such as Mendelssohn, for whom melody remained an undeniable priority, whether supported by a multilayered texture that was prevalently homophonic or by modest contrapuntal elements.

Amirov's *Kurd Ovshari* offers a new rendition of traditional *mugham* in the context of Western symphonic music. Abrupt changes of textural types, instruments, rhythmic patterns, and harmonies within each section are not attributes of *mugham,* which has consistent and continuing development of its thematic contents. Increased contrasts, as well as the use of a symphony orchestra, significantly modify the quality of lyrical emotion and transform *mugham* from an intimate expression shared with a small circle of music lovers into a large-scale composition addressed to a substantial audience.

Amirov was the main proponent of romanticism in Azerbaijani music, but many other composers followed in this stream, including Jahangir Jahangirov. This composer is revered for his contributions to choral music, a field that is not highly typical in the traditional music of Azerbaijan or in the entire region of Central Asia and the Middle East. For this reason, in Azerbaijani composed music's early stages, choral genres were on the periphery of the activities of the national composers. Jahangirov changed this situation drastically with his lyrical and poetic choral pieces.

He began by creating choral arrangements of folk songs (PURL 5.4). Eventually, Jahangirov proceeded to the more challenging experiment and created a fusion genre akin to *mugham* opera and symphonic *mugham.* In the opera *Azad* (1957), Jahangirov invented the genre of choral *mugham,* which features an innovative rendition of *mugham* in a many-layered choral texture. The chorus "Chahargah" from act 1 is named after the respective *mugham* and draws

EXAMPLE 5.3. (*Facing and above*) Fikrat Amirov, *Kurd Ovshari*, opening theme.

on the patterns of *mugham Chahargah,* with C as the tonic (scale given in musical example 5.4b).

The opening theme of the chorus, shown in musical example 5.4a, combines a sequence in the soprano and alto voices ascending toward the tonic with an *ostinato* pattern in the tenor and bass voices highlighting the tonic. In

EXAMPLE 5.4a. Jahangir Jahangirov, opera *Azad*, chorus "Chahargah" from act 1.

EXAMPLE 5.4b. C *chahargah*.

fact, the composer creates a collage of two patterns that in traditional practice would have developed as a horizontal line. Nevertheless, such combinations are not completely unknown in traditional practice, as the cadence-like figuration in the low voices can be considered to be an elaborated version of the pedal point called *bam sim* (literally: "low string"). *Bam sim* in *mugham* performances highlights the central tone; meanwhile, other instruments (or a singer) perform the melody.

Romanticism significantly affected Amirov's and Jahangirov's styles, and for them it strongly and directly flowed out of their national heritage. Conversely, romantic impulses in the music of Garayev were more obscured. The plots of several of his most important works display direct links with romanticism. The symphonic poem *Leyli and Majnun* and his ballet *The Path of Thunder* dramatically depict the motive of forbidden love, and his ballet *Seven Beauties* and his symphonic suite *Don Quixote* show a hero's unfulfilled dreams and search for truth and happiness.

The Waltz from *Seven Beauties*, shown in part in musical example 5.5, is one of the most vivid examples of Garayev's romanticism. Just as in Jahangirov's

EXAMPLE 5.5. G. Garayev, *Seven Beauties,* Waltz from act 2.

chorus, the material here draws on the patterns of *C chahargah*. Unlike Jahangirov, Garayev does not preserve a quasi-*mugham* metric and rhythmic irregularity. Instead, following the generic characteristics of the waltz, the composer establishes a clearly defined triple meter. Within this rhythmic structure, he reduces the central role of C, the tonic of *chahargah*; it never occurs on a downbeat. Garayev also reduces the priority of C by preferring to use F minor as a tonal base for the melody in C *chahargah*. In doing so, he establishes a colorful duality between C and F as the "Eastern" and "Western" tonics (PURL 5.5).

Seven Beauties created a model for the continuing explorations in creating a romantic love story based on Eastern poetic sources. Arif Malikov's *The Legend of Love* (1961) followed in the line of *Seven Beauties* in terms of its musical language and dramaturgical concept. Such a succession was not accidental, since Malikov studied with Garayev and inherited many of his principles. *The Legend of Love* is based on the poem *Farhad and Shirin* by Nazim Hikmet, which shows another affinity with Garayev's work: his interest in the poetry of Hikmet, the romantic poet of Turkey (see chapters 1 and 2).

One of *The Legend of Love*'s central episodes, the Adagio of Farhad and Shirin from act 2, shown in part in musical example 5.6a, is a dramatic expression of the love seizing the main protagonists (PURL 5.6). This episode offers a compositional representation of *humayun,* one of the most tragic modes in Azerbaijani music. The role of *humayun* is profound in the score of *The Legend of Love*. In this particular episode, Malikov uses A *humayun,* which is shown

FIGURE 5.2. Jovdat Hajiyev (center) and Agshin Alizade (right). *Courtesy of the State Museum of Azerbaijani Musical Culture.*

in musical example 5.6b. Malikov's rendition of *humayun* features an enhanced scope of harmonic means, including chords of a nontertian nature, enharmonic changes, and frequent key modulations, all of which point to the weakening of tonal rules. But the key to understanding the harmonic language of the piece lies in Azerbaijani national modality. *Humayun* is the most paradoxical mode of Azerbaijani music, as *humayun* has two tonics. If translated into the Western system, the scale of A *humayun* allows for a smooth combination of A minor, F♯ minor, and A major. Malikov masterfully explores the rich potential of this national mode in the context of Western tonal and harmonic means.

The Adagio is structured as a three-phrase period, with each phrase being six measures in length (in the provided score, each phrase is marked with brackets). This three-phrase period demonstrates the main features of Hajibeyli's "embryo-period-like development" that was discussed in chapter 4.[8] Malikov's Adagio opens with a powerful statement involving the tonic and closes with descending sequence-like development. Nonetheless, Malikov puts greater weight on the "embryo" stage through creating a second phrase that is in fact the repetition of the first phrase, now in a higher tessitura. Also, the last phrase, which

EXAMPLE 5.6a. Arif Malikov, *The Legend of Love,* Adagio of Farhad and Shirin from act 2.

EXAMPLE 5.6b. A *humayun*.

shows the "periodic development" and which in Hajibeyli's paradigm is supposed to be longer than the "embryo," is of the same size as each of the preceding phrases, making the whole structure more balanced in terms of Western structural rules. Malikov's intention appears to have been to compensate for the frequency of tonal and harmonic changes through imposing a regularity of structure.

The first phrase opens with the combination of the tonic A and the pitch C♯, which are, respectively, the last note of the first tetrachord and the first note of the second tetrachord. This motive establishes A major, one of the three tonal and modal possibilities provided by A *humayun*. C♯ dominates in the melody, appearing on the downbeats of mm. 7, 9, and 11 as a dotted half note, the longest duration given to any melodic pitch. The note A also plays an important melodic role, opening the melody and returning four more times, more frequently than any other pitch. In the harmony, A exerts a strong force as well. It is constantly present in the medium layer of the texture and appears as the root, the fifth, and the third of various triads, which results in establishing the tonal zones of A major in mm. 7–8, D minor in mm. 9–10, and finally F♯ minor in mm. 11–12. The arrival of F♯ minor signifies a shift into a new modal space, driven by the second tetrachord of A *humayun*. Although a non sequitur in Western practice, the F in the harmonic voices of m. 9 is justified by its presence in the scale of A *humayun*. Malikov also employs F as an enharmonic equivalent of E♯, aiding the smooth transition from D minor to F♯ minor in mm. 10–11. The same enharmonic equivalency reveals the role of F as a facilitator of chromatic change to F♯ minor at the end of the episode in mm. 23–24.

The melodic and harmonic force of the second phrase comes from the first tetrachord of A *humayun*. The composer does not confine himself to the pitch content of this tetrachord, but he does emphasize this part of the scale more than he does others. Malikov uses the melodic material of mm. 10–11 and transposes it in mm. 14–15. The interval of this transposition is the same minor third that is essential for the structure of A *humayun*, as it defines the distance between its two tonics. In mm. 16–17, the composer presents the same motive, although he puts it in a more intense rhythmic context and develops it further, forming a culmination of the episode. In the harmonic layer, C♯ remains a central tone throughout, except during the last two measures (mm. 17–18). F♯ provides a solid foundation for the thematic development as one of the tonics, being alternated with D♯. This passage shows, once again, the importance of the minor third in the tonal and harmonic content of the episode.

In the third phrase, the first tetrachord and, by extension, A minor dominate until m. 24 in both the melody and the harmony. The melody eventually descends from E2 toward E1 through sequence-like development. The harmonic material of the third phrase is less dissonant than that of either of the two preceding phrases, and the tonic of A minor seems like it will be the final harmonic destination. But Malikov does not meet this expectation, suddenly swerving to conclude the melodic and harmonic development with the tonic of F♯ minor. Such an ending is surprising and refreshing, creating an arch with the beginning that shows, once again, the power of *humayun*. Malikov's Adagio is undoubtedly a virtuosic example of dynamic interplay between Azerbaijani modality and the Western tonal system, between the structural rules of traditional music and the formal patterns of Western periodicity.

By the early 1960s, Azerbaijani composed music had entered a new phase of its evolution. Now native composers had no limitations in terms of their proficiency, and they had enlarged the scope of genres and styles defining their native music. Azerbaijani composed music was still young, but this youth only signified its age, not its artistic maturity.

6 THE SPIRIT OF EXPERIMENTALISM

SINCE THE 1960s

> I wanted to prove that even within the rigorous
> application of all the rules of twelve-tone technique, it
> is possible to preserve the national spirit of music.
>
> GARA GARAYEV, "Tol'ko v rabote chelovek vyrazhaet
> aktivnoe otnoshenie k zhizni" (Only through work
> one can express an active attitude toward life)

THE ARRIVAL OF TWELVE-TONE TECHNIQUE

Gara Garayev's Third Symphony (1964) and Violin Concerto (1967), both based
on twelve-tone technique, marked the beginning of a new period in Azerbaijani music: the era of atonal composition. These works were recognized not
only as the first manifestations of twelve-tone technique in Azerbaijani music,
but also as among the first in the Soviet Union. The Third Symphony and Violin Concerto were met across the country with cautious enthusiasm. Nobody
could deny the high artistic value of these pieces. Nonetheless, even in the relatively liberated social and political climate of the Soviet Union in the 1960s,
dodecaphony was treated with suspicion and was perceived as a tribute to the
music of the capitalist West, according to the Soviet ideologists. Despite these
challenges, Garayev continued his efforts, and the idea of "Azerbaijani dodecaphony" powerfully resonated in his mind for years. According to Karagicheva,
Garayev studied Schoenberg's scores and translated Anton Webern's *Der Weg
zur neuen Musik* (The Path to the New Music) from German to Russian. He ex-
perimented with creating a "serial *mugham*" in the 1970s.[1] Garayev used twelve-
tone methods even in his last opus, the Twelve Fugues (1982), completed in the
year of his death.

Garayev's main goal was to find through what mechanisms Schoenberg's concepts could be integrated with native Azerbaijani music. Such a task was enormously difficult, since these two systems seemed to lack compatibility. Fikrat Amirov, Garayev's contemporary and decided opponent, argued, "There is an unsolvable conflict between the avant-garde [i.e., Schoenberg and his followers] and the traditional music systems of the East. This is because avant-garde techniques deny the core value of Eastern music: its modal organization."[2] Considering the profound role of modality as a source of melody, rhythm, form, and texture in the Azerbaijani music system, native composers pursuing the integration of twelve-tone technique with their national music faced a daunting task. Garayev's experiments can be compared to those of Béla Bartók who, according to the musicologist and linguist Malcolm Gillies, "wanted to show Schoenberg that one can use all twelve tones and still remain tonal."[3] Bartók arrived at the concept of neotonality. Garayev, who was also dealing with the modal organization of a non-Western tradition, later did the same, combining neotonality with twelve-tone methods.

Several factors facilitated the fusion of Schoenbergian twelve-tone technique with Azerbaijani music idioms. Although these traditions function differently, they have commonalities. Among them are linearism; the high value given to structural and logical rules; the importance of repeated and varied patterns in the melody, rhythm, and texture; and a thoroughly detailed and complex texture. Garayev masterfully saw the potential of these similarities and created twelve-tone series linked to the traditional modal system. The tone rows in both the Symphony and the Violin Concerto are reminiscent of the mode *shur,* and the theme used in his Twelve Fugues is related to *chahargah.* He found the key to the integration of these two musical traditions to be the centrality of the tetrachord. The Azerbaijani music theorist Nigar Rahimova offers valuable insights on the tetrachord as a structure typical in both Eastern music systems and Western ones (in the latter, extending as far back as the ancient Greeks).[4] Tetrachords are the essential building blocks of the Azerbaijani modes, and tetrachordal divisions were important to Schoenberg as well. Tetrachords can be extracted and used as bricks of thematicism in different systems, and this is what Garayev did in his respective opuses.

The prime series in the Third Symphony, shown in musical example 6.1a, demonstrates all the significant characteristics of twelve-tone technique in the Schoenbergian sense. The prime row consists of twelve tones, none of them repeated. Nevertheless, Garayev highlights F and F♯. Both are seen in the bass clef part, and their register and instrumental timbre separates them from the remaining notes of the series. Closer analysis shows the hidden reason for the

EXAMPLE 6.1a. G. Garayev, Third Symphony, First Movement, opening theme.

EXAMPLE 6.1b. F *shur* and F♯ *shur*

centrality of these two notes: they serve as the tonics of the two *shur* scales employed in this piece; these are shown in musical example 6.1b. The F *shur* and F♯ *shur* scales share five notes – D, E, E♭ (D♯), A♭ (G♯), and D♭ (C♯) – and this facilitates the combination of the two scales into a set of twelve in which every pitch of the chromatic scale is represented.

According to Abasova, Garayev's tone row consists of three segments (marked in musical example 6.1a as a, b, and c) that have a symmetrical structure and are drawn to particular tones, namely A♭ in a, D in b, and C♯ in c.[5] All three notes are among those shared by the two *shur* scales, as was just discussed. That these three notes become "centers of gravity" in each segment is not related to serial technique and is stimulated rather by the great importance of the tonic (and of temporary tonal centers) in Azerbaijani modes. Furthermore, the presence of tiny patterns has long been essential for the broader aesthetics of Azerbaijani arts and culture, being found in calligraphy, architectural design, carpet-making, and medieval miniatures, just to name a few sources. These patterns become "bricks" for thematic content and evolve through the "interplay of repetition and disruption, symmetry and asymmetry," as Naroditskaya has observed about Azerbaijani arts more generally.[6]

Ashig music is the most prevalent of the native music sources in Garayev's Third Symphony. The composer clearly emulates *ashig* music in the Scherzo, which is the second movement, and he acknowledged that it was his intention to do so. In his interview in the journal *Sovetskaia Muzyka* about the Scherzo,

EXAMPLE 6.2. G. Garayev, Third Symphony, Scherzo, opening theme.

Garayev stated that he wanted to create "not simply national music, but specifically *ashig* melody"[7] (PURL 6.1).

The Scherzo's opening theme, which serves as the refrain of this rondo-form movement, is based on the first and second sections of the tone row (each squared in musical example 6.2), but this movement's ties to *ashig* music are manifold and just as influential. Garayev uses the harpsichord, the closest Western analogue to the Azerbaijani *saz*, to strengthen the Scherzo's ties with *ashig* music. The composer evokes the ostinato-like accompaniment patterns played by *ashig*s on the *saz* through his abundant repetitions of short motives, which

EXAMPLE 6.3. Tuning of the *saz* and typical cadence in the D *shur*. From: Emina Eldarova, "Nekotorye voprosy muzykal'nogo tvorchestva ashugov" [Some questions on the musical art of ashigs], in *Azerbaidzhanskaia muzyka* [Music of Azerbaijan], ed. Jovdat Hajiyev et al. (Moscow: Gosmuzgiz, 1961), 76.

he varies with slight changes in melodic contour. This movement features one of Garayev's favorite tools: combination of symmetric and asymmetric meters, such as $\frac{4}{4}$ and $\frac{5}{4}$. This stylistic characteristic again corresponds with the nature of *ashig* performances. In *ashig* tradition, as the artist is presenting the story, he or she admits abrupt or slight changes of timing patterns as appropriate to the narration, and the instrumental accompaniment reacts to these shifts. In this theme, Garayev also draws on modal features, specifically those of *shur,* the most common mode in *ashig* music. The harmonic interval of a second (E♭-F), seen in both the harpsichord's and flute's parts throughout musical example 6.2, is, along with the fourth, a typical attribute of what is called the "*ashig* harmony." The ethnomusicologist Emina Eldarova, an expert on Azerbaijani *ashig* music, indicates that the prevalence of these intervals in *ashig* music derives from the *saz*'s tuning, which facilitates the melodic cadences of *shur*.[8] She illustrates this connection in musical example 6.3.

The orchestration of the Third Symphony also reveals the individuality of Garayev's approach to twelve-tone methods. The Azerbaijani composer avoids dividing a single theme between different timbres and, as a result, does not achieve the timbral disintegration that was typical of Webern and, at times, the other Second Viennese school composers. Furthermore, according to the composer Frangiz Alizade, Garayev "associates each theme with a certain timbre; moreover, he personifies instrumental timbres, making them facilitate the creation of certain characters or meanings in a process of development: 'fragile' oboe, 'naughty' flute, 'sad' bassoon, or 'energetic' strings."[9] This quality almost certainly derives from the monodic roots of the Azerbaijani composer's musical mind and from the high level of personification of timbre within the traditional music system, which is especially seen in the *mugham* trio.

Without significant deviation from standard Second Viennese school twelve-tone technique, Garayev created a unique "Azerbaijani" serial language by incorporating the modal characteristics, structural peculiarities, and performing practices of his native heritage. His experience marked a breakthrough in the history of Azerbaijani composed music in terms of mastering the forms and genres of new Western music. As noted by F. Alizade, who studied with Garayev in the 1960s: "Of course, we had been fascinated with Schoenberg's system. We listened to this music and analyzed and discussed it. Still, it seemed to be so distant, almost unavailable. Things changed after the Third Symphony and the Violin Concerto. The system became closer, and we realized that we could and should try it!"[10]

TWELVE-TONE APPLICATIONS AFTER GARAYEV

Garayev's works paved the way for numerous applications of twelve-tone technique in Azerbaijani music. Arif Malikov, following the success of his ballet *The Legend of Love,* which employs rather conservative stylistic means, wrote the Second Symphony (1973), which draws on twelve-tone methods. The six movements of this symphony derive from a twelve-tone row, which itself has no audible links with the national modal system. According to the musicologist Arnold Klotyn, national characteristics are revealed in the composition through "consistent monothematic development with the tendency toward the suite and variations typical of *destgah.*"[11] Malikov eventually moved to total serialism. This approach can be seen in a number of his works, such as the Sixth Symphony, titled *Contrasts* (1985) (PURL 6.2). Serialism becomes one of this composition's many techniques, which include collage, aleatory, sonorism, and montage-like dramaturgy. This last technical resource points to the impact of cinema on Azerbaijani symphonic music. *Contrasts* also shows that Azerbaijani symphonic music was participating in the broader trend of developing new paradigms in response to cinema, as was typical for symphonic music more broadly in the 1970s and 1980s.

Among Gara Garayev's followers was Faraj Garayev, his son and student, who has become a devoted disciple of the Second Viennese school, particularly of Anton Webern. F. Garayev's respect for Webern is especially apparent in his Second Sonata for the Piano (1967), his *Concerto Grosso* in memory of Anton Webern (1967), and his ballet *The Shadows of Gobustan* (1969). The last work, however, draws more on Stravinsky, particularly his *Rite of Spring.*

The Shadows of Gobustan, written by the composer at twenty-six years of age, takes its inspiration from the music, history, culture, and visual arts of Azerbaijan and conveys elements of these sources within the context of the new music of the West. This composition is a musical rendition of visual images and artifacts from Gobustan, a prehistoric archeological site to the south of Baku.

EXAMPLE 6.4. Faraj Garayev, *The Shadows of Gobustan,*
twelve-tone row.

The ballet's plot is based on the stories depicted in Gobustan's rock carvings, which feature hunting, dancing, and making fire.

The tone row in *The Shadows of Gobustan,* shown in musical example 6.4, combines two symmetrical hexachords, with the second being a retrograde of the first. The hexachords employ narrow intervallic patterns and are separated by a tritone. The row's narrow intervallic profile and abundance of half-step patterns creates the potential for any note, under certain metric and rhythmic conditions, to become a temporary tonic. In other words, any note that appears on a strong beat tends to become a "center of gravity," while adjacent notes reveal their attachment to that "central tone." Admittedly, this is a departure from Webern's practice, but it is a continuation of Garayev the elder's neotonal twelve-tone concept.

F. Garayev's approach to meter and rhythm is his main stylistic connection to Azerbaijani music and history. The ballet's plot creates the opportunity for percussion instruments and rhythm to assume central roles. Gobustan is famous for a unique artifact: the *gaval dashi,* literally "a drum stone," which produces a musical sound if hit by a smaller stone. F. Garayev's score seems to bring this ancient drum to life. The importance of percussion instruments and rhythm is particularly evident in *yalli,* the genre of Azerbaijani folk music that F. Garayev uses to mark an apex of the dramaturgical development in the final scene of the ballet. *Yalli,* a collective dance in which a group of people hold each other's hands, is depicted on the Gobustan rocks. The dance is highly typical of Azerbaijan but can be found in many other world cultures as well. According to F. Garayev, "*Yalli* derives from the ancient dance of hunters chasing the animal into the hole or onto the top of the rock. In Azerbaijan, it became known as *yalli;* in other places, say, in Africa or America, it was transformed into something different. But it is all the same dance."[12] The score of F. Garayev's *yalli,* shown in part in musical example 6.5, includes the *naghara* (marked in the score as *Naccheroni,* or *Nacch.*), a traditional drum instrument that is directed to improvise within the entire episode (PURL 6.3).

EXAMPLE 6.5. (*Facing*) F. Garayev, *The Shadows of Gobustan,* part 4,
"The Shadows of Gobustan."

EXAMPLE 6.6a. F. Garayev, *The Shadows of Gobustan,*
leitmotiv of the Hunt.

EXAMPLE 6.6b. C *shushtar.*

EXAMPLE 6.6c. C *chahargah.*

Throughout the score, the twelve-tone row is placed in various rhythmic
contexts, all representative of Azerbaijani folk music. For instance, the leitmotiv of "The Hunt," shown in musical example 6.6a, uses a segment of the tone
row and features a sharp and energetic rhythmic formula typical of Azerbaijani dance music. As a result, the first note, repeated on the strong beats and
appearing more frequently than other notes, becomes central. The prominent
pattern of a descending minor third, enharmonically equivalent to an aug-
mented second (B-Ab), creates associations with many Azerbaijani modes, including C *shushtar* and C *chahargah,* shown in musical examples 6.6b and 6.6c.

The first occurrence of the ballet's main leitmotiv, which portrays "The
People," is shown in musical example 6.7. Db is prominent here due to its position on a downbeat in mm. 40 and 43 (squared in musical example 6.7a) and
long duration. As a result, this sequence of tones contains modal features associated with the patterns of Db *bayati-shiraz.* Simultaneously, in the lower layer
of the texture, a short, repeated pattern surrounding D (squared in musical
example 6.7a) is reminiscent of the scale of *bayati-shiraz,* with D as the central
pitch. Both scales are shown in musical example 6.7b. The polyphony of two
modal layers with tonics separated by a half step is analogous with G. Garayev's
method of using *shur* in his Third Symphony.

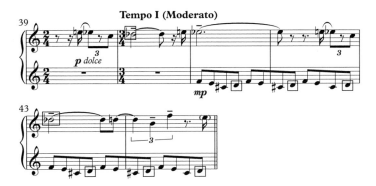

EXAMPLE 6.7a. F. Garayev, *The Shadows of Gobustan*, leitmotiv of the People, Reduction.

EXAMPLE 6.7b. D♭ *bayati-shiraz* and D *bayati-shiraz*.

All these ways in which F. Garayev weaves together twelve-tone technique and his native music system evince a highly individual "Azerbaijani" interpretation of twelve-tone serialism. The methods the composer uses to join together the two do not typify his general approach toward the application of the twelve-tone method and other means of modern Western music, which can be seen in other compositions. That approach, according to Farkhadov, is "more European than Eastern, and more cosmopolitan than national."[13] Nonetheless, the ballet *The Shadows of Gobustan* is far from an insignificant opus in the composer's portfolio; deep links with *mugham* and the music system of Azerbaijan show themselves in F. Garayev's further applications of serialism, reaching their apogee in *Khutba, Mugham and Sura* (Sermon, Mugham, and Prayer) (1997), discussed later in this chapter.[14]

F. Alizade expressed her interest in twelve-tone technique from the very first stages of her career, and she did so not only as a composer, but also as a pianist. She was one of the first in the Soviet Union who performed and actively promoted piano pieces by Schoenberg, Berg, Messiaen, Crumb, Cage, Schnittke, Gubaidulina, and Denisov. In F. Alizade's early works, such as the piano sonata *In the Memory of Berg* (1970) and the composition *In the Memory of Mahler* (1977) for violin, clarinet, and drums, she demonstrates a generically Western approach to the application of the twelve-tone system, with almost no references to her national roots. In her later opuses, such as *Dilogy* (1988), *Crossing I* (1991), *Oasis* (1998), and *Mirage* (1998), F. Alizade continued her exploration of dodecaphony, now in a manner quite similar to G. Garayev, merging twelve-tone technique with the tetrachordal structure of *mugham* modes.

BACK TO NEOCLASSICISM

The concept of neoclassicism that developed in Azerbaijani music in the late 1960s and 1970s differed from the one suggested by G. Garayev's earlier compositions (see chapter 5). In this new neoclassicism, the mediating role of Russian composers was significantly reduced and often replaced with direct references to Western sources. Several Azerbaijani composers contributed to this development. Most of them were G. Garayev's students, such as Khayyam Mirzazade, who emulated Shostakovich in his early works and later synthesized elements of Stravinsky's and Bartók's styles. By the early 1960s, Mirzazade had developed his own distinct style in which intellectuality dominates over passion. His compositions' highly reserved, rational character defies stereotypes of Eastern composers, who are traditionally associated with more emotional and open self-expression. According to the musicologist Iurii Gabai, "Eastern fanciness," that is passionate and enjoyable sound, is not typical of Mirzazade's music."[15] Mirzazade's tribute to Charles Ives (*Memory, or I Remember You, Charles Ives* for chamber orchestra [1989]) is symptomatic of the classical priorities of Mirzazade's aesthetic. The ideas of the eponymous American composer, who brought together innovation and the musical idioms of the past, corresponded with Mirzazade's own stylistic preferences.

Mirzazade has the reputation of being the guru of instrumental music in Azerbaijan. Symphonies, quartets, and sonatas are central in his oeuvre. This selection of genres itself points to the neoclassical priorities of his style, and the way that Mirzazade interprets these genres is also telling. For instance, the three movements of his Second Symphony, *Triptych* (1970), follow a "fast-slow-fast" pattern, hearkening back to Baroque instrumental music. The twelve preludes from the cycle *White and Black* (1984) were initially scored for the organ, and later Mirzazade arranged these pieces for the piano. This opus reveals a debt to the baroque organ repertory. Mirzazade alludes to baroque styles and practices in several ways: through the improvised character of most of the pieces, which was typical of baroque organ toccatas, fantasies, and preludes; by using an abundance of pedal points; and even by his notation, which employs three

FIGURE 6.1. Khayyam Mirzazade. *Courtesy of Khayyam Mirzazade.*

staves. This cycle corresponds in many ways to the famous neoclassical opus by Hindemith, *Ludus Tonalis*. Like it, Mirzazade's composition features twelve tonalities, formed around each (either white or black) piano key. The continuing popularity of *White and Black* in contemporary Azerbaijani music is indicated by the fact that this piece has been choreographed and included in the repertoire of the Azerbaijan Opera and Ballet Theater. The choreographed version of Mirzazade's cycle is an Azerbaijani response to the popularity in contemporary ballet of choreographed miniatures based on instrumental pieces (PURL 6.4).

Clarity and clear division of form is an essential feature of Mirzazade's style. His forms are well balanced, and the return of the initial thematic material is always a must. Sonata form is interpreted in a classical manner; each section and each theme is clearly distinguished. Mirzazade is also a virtuosic master of polyphony. Linearity is essential for Mirzazade's style and emerges from the interplay of many stylistic impulses, including baroque music, twentieth-century music (particularly that of Shostakovich), and the monodic tradition of

EXAMPLE 6.8. Khayyam Mirzazade, Sonata *Pro e Contra* for violin solo, opening theme.

his national music. Examples of his polyphony are abundant and striking. *Triptych* opens with a three-part canon. In *Essays-63* for symphony orchestra, one of the most impressive moments involves a two-part canon played by the violas and first violins that is based on the second theme of the sonata-allegro form. This canon occurs against ostinato-like figuration in the strings and piano that is drawn from the first theme.

Mirzazade has never favored direct reference to folk roots, although he has compositions based on the national modal system and on the structural norms of Azerbaijani folk music. The composer's greatest debt to traditional music comes from the way in which he generates form out of an initial cell. This formal technique corresponds with the main principle of *mugham* and of modal development in Azerbaijani music, even though Mirzazade's musical material may not directly be linked to Azerbaijani scales. The opening sections of Mirzazade's sonata for the violin, *Pro e Contra* (1980), demonstrate this generative method. The first theme, shown in musical example 6.8, is played on the violin's open strings. This sequence's large leaps are not typical of the Azerbaijani music system, and no modality is present in this excerpt. But the method of development recalls the opening section of *mugham* in which the initial melodic cell gradually increases in size and intensity. Every measure in this theme is longer than the previous one, and the metric division present in the score is rather arbitrary from a formal standpoint (PURL 6.5).

Unlike Mirzazade who has continually been drawn to neoclassicism, F. Garayev only had a "neoclassical decade." Although F. Garayev's Sonatina for piano (1963) contains evidence of Prokofiev's influence, F. Garayev's ballet *Kaleidoscope* (1971) and Concerto for Piano and Chamber Orchestra (1974) are directly inspired by Stravinsky's model of neoclassicism.

Azerbaijan's most devoted neoclassical composer, Ismayil Hajibeyov (1949–2006), suggested both "Western" and "Eastern" applications of the neoclassical style and aesthetic. The Western concept is depicted in Hajibeyov's Concertino (1972) and *Sketches in the Spirit of Watteau* (1972), which embrace the ideals of eighteenth-century European art and music. The Eastern concept emerged simultaneously and is represented in the Rhapsody for piano and orchestra (1975), which is based on Uzeyir Hajibeyli's *Jangi* for an orchestra of traditional instruments (1941) that the composerlater arranged for the piano. By the 1970s, Hajibeyli was already understood to be part of "the past" of the national music. This, along with Hajibeyli's status as the national "classical composer" and the founder of Azerbaijani composed music, made him a prime candidate for neoclassical resurrection.

Sketches in the Spirit of Watteau reflects Hajibeyov's experience as a composer and artist. The cycle of three piano pieces (Sonata in E, "Minuet," and "Rondoletto") is named after Jean-Antoine Watteau, an eighteenth-century French artist whose works combine aristocratic elegance with vividness of color and a clear theatrical subtext. The reference to Watteau is the key to understanding this work's stylistic palette, which draws on the forms and genres of baroque music (PURL 6.6).

In each sketch, the composer focuses and elaborates on – or rather plays with – one stylistic feature or characteristic. In Sonata in E, it is tonality. The tonic does not serve as a center of gravity throughout the piece, and in this sense, the title becomes a part of the game. Hajibeyov's music is reminiscent of the March from Prokofiev's *Love for Three Oranges*, in which the tonic of C major only appears at the very end of the piece.

In the second sketch, "Minuet," the composer plays with characteristics of genre. Hajibeyov juxtaposes the German and French branches of neoclassicism. He proceeds from the light atmosphere of an aristocratic dance in the spirit of Prokofiev's *Romeo and Juliet* or G. Garayev's *The Path of Thunder* to a heavily dramatic monologue resembling the more contemplative polyphonic opuses of Shostakovich and G. Garayev. This shift of intensity results in the ironic transformation of the elegant minuet into a tragic episode.

"Rondoletto" is the lightest and happiest piece of the cycle. The rhythm becomes the main "subject of the game" here: syncopation, shifts of rhythmic patterns, and frequent changes of time signature, combined with a relatively unaltered melodic contour, imbue the piece with a humorous flavor that contrasts with the tragic ending of the previous episode. Musical example 6.9 shows the composer's play with different rhythmic patterns for the same de-

EXAMPLE 6.9. Ismayil Hajibeyov, *Sketches in the Spirit of Watteau*, "Rondoletto."

scending figure, which moves from the dominant to the supertonic (marked with brackets).

Hajibeyov's Rhapsody for piano and orchestra (1975), based on Hajibeyli's instrumental piece *Jangi*, presents a challenging idea of "playing" with the music of the patriarch, who had always been placed on a pedestal in Azerbaijani society and culture. Hajibeyov by default held a privileged position, since he belonged to the same dynasty of musicians.[16] In addition, he reshaped Hajibeyli's music with such respect and piety that his version instantly became a part of the native soundscapes, equal in status to the original composition. All the melodic formulas of Hajibeyli's theme are recognizable, its form remains intact, and the flow of music is as vibrant and energetic as in the original source. Stylistically, the energetic rhythmic pulsation and highly developed piano part recall Prokofiev's piano concertos. Frequent rhythmic and tonal changes, in a manner often seen in neoclassicism, undermine the stability of the classical idioms originally present in Hajibeyli's piece (PURL 6.7 and PURL 6.8).

Neoclassicism has played a valuable role in the historical development of Azerbaijani music, expanding the space of East-West synthesis. G. Garayev initiated this stream and emulated the divergent models of Hindemith, Shostakovich, Stravinsky, and Prokofiev in his music. Subsequent generations applied neoclassical idioms, borrowing them directly from Western sources, without Russian mediators, but with G. Garayev's experience to draw on. For F. Garayev, neoclassicism was a passing phase, whereas for Hajibeyov, it was the dominant feature of his work. Neoclassicism affected the creative explorations of many Azerbaijani composers, including Mirzazade and Agshin Alizade. A. Alizade occupies a special place in the history of Azerbaijani music for having initiated another significant neo-style: neofolklorism.

NEOFOLKLORISM

Strictly speaking, this term may apply to the whole body of Azerbaijani composed music, as this repertoire is entirely based on the adaptation within art music forms of the nation's oral musical heritage. Nonetheless, as a signifier of a stylistic trend fusing "very old" with "very new," neofolklorism emerged in Azerbaijani music in the late 1960s and was stimulated by access to the compositions of Stravinsky, Bartók, and Orff. The neofolklorist composers of Azerbaijan reached deeper into the past than had their earlier counterparts: they retrieved layers of their oral musical heritage that had remained obscured even a generation before. The Soviet aesthetics of art and music were partly responsible for this oral music's previous neglect. As discussed in chapter 1, the Soviets discouraged the idea of any of the Soviet nations having deep historical roots that were reflected in art and music. Another reason for the earlier exclusion of certain oral music was the young age of the Azerbaijani composed tradition. Predictably enough, the first generations of Azerbaijani composers explored the upper strata of their traditional and folk heritage, leaving later composers to proceed to the deeper past. An important peculiarity of Azerbaijani neofolklorism was that the composers referred not only to pure folk music forms, but also to *mugham,* a more educated genre of traditional music. Their inclusion of *mugham* was natural, since historically it has been deeply integrated into the life of the Azerbaijani people and had developed in firm connection with genres of folk music. Like songs, dances, or *ashig* art, *mugham* has orally transmitted the Azerbaijanis' collective wisdom. Besides, *mugham* had served as the major native source for Azerbaijani composers from the outset of their work, and *mugham* could not be avoided in the experiments undertaken by the national composers. Nonetheless, the presence of *mugham* in the orbit of the neofolkloric experiments stimulated a significant change in perception: Azerbaijani composers began viewing their native tradition, *mugham* included, as being more archaic.

A. Alizade was the most devoted follower in Azerbaijani music of the neofolkloric stream. Even the titles and subjects of his works such as *Old Lullaby* (1984) for *a capella* chorus, *Ancient Games* (1990) for the piano, and *Old Khanende* (1991) for organ show the importance of reference to the past. His ballet *Babek* (1979) tells the story of the rebellion of the Azerbaijanis against the Arab Caliphate in the ninth century. The music of A. Alizade includes a large spectrum of genres and forms belonging to the traditional heritage of Azerbaijanis. *Bayati* (1969), for *a capella* chorus, is a musical rendition of Azerbaijani folk poetry. The Fourth Symphony (*Mugham*) (1984) and *Sounds of Mugham* (1991) for organ show the links of the composer's music with the eponymous main treasure of his national musical tradition. *In the Ashig Style* (1970), for string orchestra, and *Dastan* (1986), for the piano, refer to the *ashig* tradition. *Jangi* (1978), for oboe and string orchestra, revives the spirit of an ancient warriors' dance. Notably, in all these works, A. Alizade is not concerned with maintaining the integrity of the traditional and folk genres he draws on. For example, in *Jangi,* he mixes characteristics of two different genres of traditional music: an ancient warrior dance and *ashig* music (PURL 6.9).

Like the earlier examples of *jangi* written by Hajibeyli and Hajibeyov that were discussed earlier in this chapter, *Jangi* by A. Alizade is imbued with a heroic atmosphere. The energetic opening leap of a fourth, representative of the mode *rast* and seen in m. 5 of musical example 6.10a, sets the heroic mood of the piece. So does the timbre of the oboe, which is associated here with the *zurna,* a traditional woodwind instrument used during collective outdoor musical activities, including *jangi*. Nonetheless, unlike the previous examples of *jangi,* the musical material in the neofolkloric *Jangi* by A. Alizade is permeated with an archaic mood. Contributing to this are its melodic contents, which are entirely built out of short units, most of them two measures long, that are repeated with very little or no change. This characteristic is typical of the more ancient layers of Azerbaijani folk music, particularly of the old folk songs. Metric irregularity is another factor contributing to the archaic atmosphere of A. Alizade's piece. But this metric quality also reveals the deep impact of *ashig* music. Throughout the piece, the accompanimental figure in $\frac{8}{4}$ is divided as $3 + 2 + 3$, evoking the patterns of *saz* performance. The occasional stops on A in mm. 16–18 of section B, shown in musical example 6.10b, which occur due to the sustained

EXAMPLE 6.10a. Agshin Alizade, *Jangi,* section A.

EXAMPLE 6.10b. A. Alizade, *Jangi*, section B.

EXAMPLE 6.10c. G *rast.*

notes in the melody, resemble *ashig* free narration. The prevalence of seconds and fourths in the harmonic part observed in both musical examples 6.10a and 6.10b further reflects *ashig* practice.

Another piece of A. Alizade's, *Bayati,* a cycle of ten choral pieces, displays the composer's approach to folk song as a source of lyrical expression and flexible melodic patterns. In this cycle, A. Alizade uses both folkloric and modern materials. Each piece is based on *bayati,* a form of folk poetry consisting of four-line stanzas, the first, second, and fourth of which are rhymed. The third line, which is independent, conveys the core meaning of each stanza; the remaining three create a metaphoric frame. Another characteristic of *bayati* is the presence of seven syllables in each line. A. Alizade carefully follows the traditional structure of the poetic folk text in his musical setting. For example, in the episode "Two Trees Are Bent Together," the composer creates an AABA form, with identical sections A and with section B based on contrasting material. All section As shown in musical example 6.11a feature B *shur* shown in musical example 6.11b and are clearly drawn to its tonic, whereas section B,

EXAMPLE 6.11a. A. Alizade, *Bayati*, "Two Trees are Bent Together," section A.

EXAMPLE 6.11b. B *shur*.

shown in musical example 6.11c, is less related to the national modal system. Instead, it alternates between two major triads, E major in mm. 12, 14, and 16, and G♯ in mm. 11, 13, 15, and mm. 17–19, with the fourth added in each case. The contrast between the sections is also highlighted by the change of meter from $\frac{4}{4}$ to $\frac{3}{4}$ and the shift in tempo from *vivo* to *meno mosso*. All this emphasizes the importance of section B in supporting the "key line" of *bayati*. The seven-syllable-long structure of each section inherited from *bayati* stimulates irregular metric patterns and becomes the main unifying factor of the composition (PURL 6.10).

A. Alizade paved the path of neofolklorism for subsequent native composers, although each of them developed his or her own unique interpretation of this style. Among such neofolklorists is F. Alizade, who turned to neofolkloric experiments after several years of complete dedication to twelve-tone serialism, expressionism, and other styles of modern Western music. In 1979, F. Alizade wrote *Habilsayaghi* (In Habil's Style) for cello and prepared piano. This work is a tribute to the distinguished *kemancha* player Habil Aliyev (1927–2015), the master of Azerbaijani *mugham*, and appropriately bears his name. The piece employs a cello to imitate the sound of the *kemancha*, and F. Alizade fuses the

EXAMPLE 6.11c. A. Alizade, *Bayati*, "Two Trees are Bent Together,"
section B.

modal formulas of *mugham* with elements of new Western music. This synthesis has become emblematic of F. Alizade's style and has shaped her distinctive compositional voice, which draws on the newest developments in Western
music. The American composer Robert Carl has noted that F. Alizade's work
"may sound like a return to exoticism to Western ears unfamiliar with it." He
continues, "But I feel there's much more than that to this music. I am not an
expert in the source music, but Ali-Zadeh [Alizade] seems to be creating a sort
of dream of her Central Asian roots, rather as Bartok created a similar dream of
his from Central Europe."[17] F. Alizade's "dream" of *mugham* could be characterized as the reembodiment, or reincarnation, of this essential genre of Azerbaijani music through the means of the modern music of the West. F. Alizade
depicts *mugham* as a general idea and as an aesthetic phenomenon; meanwhile,
she demonstrates the deepest possible awareness of all the modal patterns and
compositional rules of this ancient genre. This paradoxical combination of the
two – general and more detailed – perspectives on *mugham* and the ability to

FIGURE 6.2. Frangiz Alizade and Habil Aliyev, kemancha player.
Courtesy of Frangiz Alizade.

achieve a new balance between these two outlooks distinguishes F. Alizade's voice in Azerbaijani music and explains the unique charm of her compositions.

F. Alizade's interest in linearism is a consistent quality of her music, illuminating its monodic roots. Linear principles even can be traced in pieces written with the use of techniques that are seemingly further away from the very idea of melody. For instance, in *Impromptus* (2004) or *In Search of . . .* (2005), both of which employ pointillism, the melody is broken and scattered over registers, yet comprehended as a single line. The embryonic growth of F. Alizade's melody corresponds with *mugham* and also is highly typical of serialism, minimalism, and other innovative techniques from the West. Likewise, the prevalence of polyphonic tendencies over harmonization in her music corresponds with contemporaneous Western developments such as the new importance placed on polytimbral combination and sonority, as well as the emergence of new polyphonic forms such as micropolyphony. At the same time, her polyphonic style also draws on the linearism of *mugham*, in which new lines emerge in the course of thematic development.

Improvisation is the key characteristic of F. Alizade's music. As the composer confesses, her pieces never coalesce into a final shape until the actual performance. "During the rehearsal process, we find a clue, a 'common denominator'; however, it is never clear what to expect during the performance."[18] Such a high valuing of spontaneous musicianship, sanctioned by the composer, is stimulated by her Eastern roots and is demonstrated in many ways: by her composing original music in *mugham* style, by her using real *mugham* as a quote, or by her relying on improvisation throughout the process of composing, rehearsing, and performing. According to Zemtsovsky, "Alizade inherits the main quality of *mugham;* its paradoxical openness. . . . Despite being a system confined within its own rules, [*mugham*] is literally open to the entire world – just as its solid (almost serial) canonic logic does not deny, but rather implies a certain freedom of performers' improvisation."[19] But once again there is also a connection beyond Azerbaijan. In newer Western styles, improvisation and indeterminacy have returned, and F. Alizade also uses respective applications of modern music, such as aleatory. In all these cases, the composer places bounds on the performer's improvisatory freedom. For example, in *Darvish* (2000), the vocal part performed by the *khanende* combines true *mugham* recitation with *Sprechstimme*.

The concept of time in the music of F. Alizade displays similar dual references to her native heritage and avant-garde Western styles. On the one hand, in the slow development of her music, the moments of meditation are inspired by the lyrical expression of Berg and Mahler. On the other hand, such meditative qualities are highly typical of *mugham* and other forms of Azerbaijani traditional music and culture, such as Sufi rituals. F. Alizade's *Darvish* is a powerful response to the Sufi idea of comprehension of truth through achieving a trance-like state. In this piece, the poetry of Nasimi, a sixteenth-century Azerbaijani poet, is a reflection of the composer's own spirituality, and this verse accumulates and conveys the many meanings and submeanings of F. Alizade's music. A similarly apt selection of text is found in F. Alizade's oratorio *Journey to Immortality* (1995/99), which uses the verses of Nazim Hikmet, the Turkish poet. The musicologist Ayanda Adilova penetratingly described the latter work as a "journey to herself," since this piece reflects the state of spiritual wandering essential to both Hikmet and F. Alizade.[20] The end of the oratorio is among the most impressive episodes of F. Alizade's music. A complex and dense choral part, which is reminiscent of Gregorian chant, is combined with the lonely voice of a muezzin performing a call for prayer.

F. Alizade's choice of instruments features the same "fine line" between the music systems of the East and the avant-garde music of the West. She often uses traditional Azerbaijani instruments in her scores. For instance, the *tutak, ganun,* and *gosha naghara* are included in *Darvish,* and the *ud* appears in *Mirage* (1998). Using traditional instruments is rather common in the modern and postmodern eras, particularly for composers coming from the non-Western world. Nonetheless, F. Alizade does not highlight the exoticism of these instruments, nor does she juxtapose them with Western instruments to create a dialogue of cultures. Instead, she obscures the border between Eastern and Western instruments by reimagining timbres from each side into the other culture. The transformation of the cello into the *kemancha* in *Habilsayaghi* and later in *Mughamsayaghi* (In the Style of *Mugham*) (1993), *Ashk Havasi* (The Melody of Love) (1998), and *Journey to Immortality* are the most representative examples. The abundance of melismas, microtonal patterns, and *glissandi* in the cello part are attributes of avant-garde music, while their application within an evidently modal context makes the cello sound like its Azerbaijani counterpart.

In F. Alizade's use of prepared piano, she admits to being inspired by John Cage, particularly by his *Sonatas and Interludes.* Unlike the American composer, who used the prepared piano for both aesthetic and practical reasons, F. Alizade had one principal aim: to emulate the *tar,* the voice of her native tradition. In *Music for the Piano* (1989/97), she calls for a prepared piano alongside an unadorned one.[21] The combination of the two piano timbres is one of the main innovations of this piece. The opposition of the two contrasting themes at the beginning of the piece has been known in Western music since Gluck's *Alceste,* although in F. Alizade's piece, this opposition is presented in a reverse order. One character sounds in a higher register and is vulnerable and submissive, and another character, solid and energetic, is placed in the lower register. These two themes seem to be irreconcilable, until the third theme comes on stage. This theme, reminding us of the Schumann's master Raro, is located in the middle part of the keyboard and aims to resolve a controversy. (PURL 6.11).

While in *Music for Piano,* F. Alizade emulates the *tar* by means of the prepared piano, in *Habilsayaghi, Impromptus,* and the first movement of *Apsheron Quintet* (2001), she evokes another instrument, the traditional drum *naghara* by hitting the case of the piano. In all three works, the composer reproduces the rhythmic pattern ♩♫ ♪♩, which Abezgauz defines as the "Azerbaijani five-syllable rhythmic formula." According to Abezgauz, this formula exemplifies the most representative qualities of rhythm in Azerbaijani folk music: the prevalence of $^6_4$ meter, the dotted opening figure, syncopation, and the hidden changeability of meter, since this pattern fits into the $^3_4$ time signature as well.[22] This rhythmic formula penetrates Azerbaijani folk music genres to such a great extent that it hardly seems special in that context, but F. Alizade abstracts this rhythmic figure and highlights its arrival every time she uses it.

F. Alizade's music has a rich visual component that evolves out of the multilayered semantics of *mugham*. *Atesh* (The Fire) (2006) and *Yanardagh* (The Burning Mountain) (2002/03) visualize burning fire, which is an image essential in the culture of Azerbaijan, given its Zoroastrian past. In *Naghillar* (Fairy Tales) (2002), in material reminiscent of *mugham,* one can sense vignettes of military battles, victories and losses, dramas, and triumphs. This is possible because F. Alizade deciphers the many layers of history and culture hidden in *mugham*. Over the course of centuries, *mugham* absorbed various impulses coming from different musical genres, including lyrical songs, historic songs, work songs, dances, and religious chants. F. Alizade extracts these hidden elements and, in addition, activates the "theatrical potential of *mugham*" that has been revealed and realized ever since Hajibeyli's *Leyli and Majnun*.[23]

Another association with *mugham* – and Hajibeyli's *Leyli and Majnun* – is clearly sensed in *Mughamsayaghi,* shown in part in musical example 6.12. This piece is another rendition of the Sufi idea of fulfillment of love through death, a concept also depicted in Hajibeyli's opera. No action or plot is present in this purely instrumental piece, which derives from *mugham,* but the cello and the violin become two characters within a drama. All events that occur in the score are no less visual than if they would have been part of a theatrical production. As seen from musical example 6.12a, the score even contains theatrical markings for the instrumentalists.[24]

The role of the cello is essential in this piece, just as in many other opuses of F. Alizade. The timbre of this instrument is associated with the expression of the composer's inner self, and the instrument becomes a means of conveying her intimate thoughts and feelings. As F. Alizade attests in the foreword to *Mughamsayaghi:* "[The] [c]ello is the composer's voice – a woman."[25] She compares the contemplative opening monologue of the cello, shown in musical example 6.12a, to a call for prayer that is trying to wake the world up. This theme returns at the end of the piece, allowing another analogy, this time with the opening chorus "Night of Separation" in Hajibeyli's *Leyli and Majnun*. Both works can be interpreted as a Greek chorus commenting on and framing the

EXAMPLE 6.12a. Frangiz Alizade, *Mugamsayaghi*, opening theme.
From: Frangis Ali-Sade, Mugam-Sayagi for String Quartet, percussion
instruments and synthesizer (tape) String Quartet No. 3 (1993).
© Musikverlag Hans Sikorski, Hamburg, for the entire world.

EXAMPLE 6.12b. C *shur.*

EXAMPLE 6.12C. F. Alizade, *Mugamsayaghi*, development. From: Frangis Ali-Sade, Mugam-Sayagi for String Quartet, percussion instruments and synthesizer (tape) String Quartet No. 3 (1993). © Musikverlag Hans Sikorski, Hamburg, for the entire world.

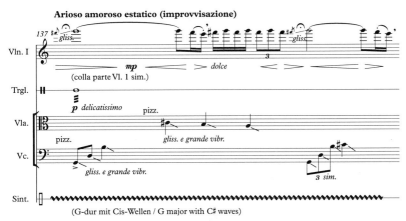

EXAMPLE 6.12d. F. Alizade, *Mugamsayaghi,* highest point. From: Frangis Ali-Sade, Mugam-Sayagi for String Quartet, percussion instruments and synthesizer (tape) String Quartet No. 3 (1993). © Musikverlag Hans Sikorski, for the entire world.

dramatic action. This association also points to the hidden theatricality in the F. Alizade's composition.

The opening section is strongly drawn to the tonic of C *shur,* shown in musical example 6.12b. The second section begins with a dramatic monologue in the first violin, and this material eventually involves the cello and transforms into a dialogue. This highly passionate phase of development results in a change of mode, establishing an ecstatic G *rast* that marks the beginning of the next section, shown in musical example 6.12c. Joy and delight are heard in the part

EXAMPLE 6.12e. F. Alizade, *Mugamsayaghi,* dance episode. From:
Frangis Ali-Sade, Mugam-Sayagi for String Quartet, percussion
instruments and synthesizer (tape) String Quartet No. 3 (1993).
© Musikverlag Hans Sikorski, Hamburg, for the entire world.

of the cello, which is joined by the violins and viola, as shown in m. 104, and
eventually, the tam-tam in m. 105. The meaning of this episode shifts from an
intimate drama to a global one.

This irresistible flow of thoughts, feelings, and desires draws to an impressive climax: the music suddenly ascends to a high range and enters a phase of
"divine play," signifying the fulfillment of the main goal – fulfillment of love
through death. As shown in musical example 6.12d, the solo of the violin in
mm. 133–137, echoed by *glissandi a grande vibr.* in the cello and viola and accompanied by triangle and synthesizer in m. 137, creates a picture of an absolute, surrealistic harmony (PURL 6.12).

Another phase of the "divine play" includes a mystical dance performed
with the accompaniment of the tambourine. The dance, shown in musical ex-

ample 6.12e, is upbeat and energetic in a manner reminiscent of a *rang,* the instrumental interlude in *mugham.* The unison strings on G, in combination with the tam-tam in the background, marks the final destination, beyond which is silence only. All participants in the drama leave the stage – and not just figuratively – except for the cello, which resumes its sorrowful, lonely monologue, just as at the beginning of the piece. The twinkling sounds of the triangle are associated with a myriad of stars, and the viola plays the same formula it did at the beginning. The reunion has occurred, though it matters not where, in this world or another. . . .

There are many other contributors to the neofolkloric stream in Azerbaijani music. Among them is Javanshir Guliyev (b. 1950), whose portfolio is not extensive but contains truly innovative pieces. In his *Seven Pieces with Interludes in Mugham Modes* (1980), Guliyev creates, within a short piece lasting only seven or eight minutes, a condensed picture of the Azerbaijani modal system. This task never could have been completed without a dose of wit, and the composer, indeed, calls his work a *humoresque.* This composition is in fact compressed mega-*mugham* in which the seven pieces are seven miniatures of mughams – *Rast, Bayati Shiraz, Segah, Shushtar, Chahargah, Humayun,* and *Shur* – that are separated by six interludes that resemble *rangs,* the interludes in *mugham* composition. The use of the prepared piano in the interludes creates associations with either the *tar* or *gaval.* The central tone – E – that serves as a unifying factor in the cycle reveals the inner integrity of the Azerbaijani modal system (PURL 6.13).

Within neofolklorism, Azerbaijani composers created their own versions of the most radical techniques of modern music, including minimalism. The Third Symphony (1983) by Rahilya Hasanova (b. 1951) became the first instantiation of "Azerbaijani minimalism." The style of Hasanova is best described as an "Eastern analogue" of minimalism that evolved out of the essential quality of *mugham,* namely the idea of short, condensed modal formulas that are repeated, varied, and combined in the course of intense development. Musicologists acknowledge the ties between American minimalism and world music. According to the British musicologist Mervyn Cooke, "minimalist composers saw in . . . ethnic musics a rhythmic and textural clarity allied to an almost hypnotic repetitiveness, and they absorbed these features into a new idiom."[26] This may serve as the key to understanding Hasanova's arrival at this close-to-minimalistic style. From *mugham,* Hasanova only borrows the idea of the essential modal formula repeated throughout, leaving aside the principle of showcasing every phase of modal development. Instead of the stair-like development of traditional *mugham,* she prefers circular, or rather spiral-like, hypnotic motion toward the main destination, which, nonetheless, often remains hidden. This is why many of her pieces have "open endings." In this regard, Hasanova's minimalistic experiments borrow from another native source: Sufi philosophy, which is formed around the idea of ascending to the Divine. Among her works that feature this concept are *Gasida* (1991), which is a symphony for organ, and *Sema* (The Sky), for instrumental ensemble (1994). Both these compositions revive the ceremonies of the Sufi order. Hasanova even named the concert of her works that took place at the Baku Music Academy in 2005 *The Night of Ascension*.

Neofolklorism was an ideal choice for a composed music tradition that was strongly drawn to a folk heritage and already equipped with many Western styles and techniques. The native component of the synthesis was never hidden in neofolkloric opuses. The postmodern tendencies that began to emerge in Azerbaijani music in the 1980s, stimulated largely by F. Garayev, followed a different path.

POSTMODERNISM

In full compliance with the aesthetics of postmodernism, F. Garayev's later works openly feature a variety of aesthetic and stylistic impulses that serve the composer's distinctive compositional concepts. As is true of much Western music since the 1950s, many of his pieces incorporate quotations. For example, Mozart's *Lacrimosa* appears in *I Bade Farewell to Mozart on the Karlov Bridge in Prague,* for the orchestra (1982); F. Garayev's suite for string quartet *In Memoriam* (1984) features themes from Berg's Violin Concerto, Chamber Concertos, and opera *Lulu;* and some reminiscences of Beethoven and Chopin are used in *Musik für die Stadt Forst* (Music for the Town of Forst) (1991), for two pianos. F. Garayev often emulates the aesthetics and stylistic tools of other composers without direct quotations. Examples include the *Concerto Grosso* (1967), which shows links with Webern's constructivism, and *A Crumb of Music for George Crumb* (1985), which the *New York Times* characterized as a "tribute to America's high priest of the sound effect."[27] The range of authors and styles integrated in F. Garayev's works is quite impressive and includes, in addition to those just mentioned, J. S. Bach, Domenico Scarlatti, Beethoven, Glinka, Grieg, Debussy, Richard Strauss, and many other composers from the Western world. F. Garayev also has employed material from the repertoire of the trio Emerson, Lake, and Palmer; incorporated a theme by Billy Taylor into a composition; and drawn on *Round about Midnight* by Thelonius Monk. Finally, the music of F. Garayev's father, Gara Garayev, and even his own music is fair game as a source

FIGURE 6.3. Faraj Garayev (standing) and the conductor
Rauf Abdullayev (sitting). *Courtesy of Faraj Garayev.*

of quotations. *Ist es genug? . . .* (Maybe Enough . . . ?), for the ensemble and tape,
written in 1993 on the occasion of the composer's fiftieth birthday and meant
to be a summary of his work until then, is built on a collage of ten of his pieces.
The work also seems to refer to the chorale *Es ist genug,* which was used by
Bach, Mendelssohn, and Berg. The musicologist Marianna Vysotskaia analyzes
the different meanings of the quotations in F. Garayev's music. Some quotations appear as the main themes, while others mark the culminating moments
of the pieces or symbolize certain emotional states. The ways of integrating the
quotations in the stylistic context of F. Garayev's works may be either seamless
or abrupt. In all cases, according to Vysotskaia, F. Garayev tends to restate the
borrowed material and to adapt it to his own stylistic parameters, rather than
to present it as a foreign element.[28]

By default, postmodernism has fewer attachments or no attachment to
national roots. National tradition could still have a place in postmodern aesthetics, but not a privileged one. For F. Garayev, postmodernism was a natural

development, since he had already gained the reputation of being a "less national" composer. Still, on a conceptual level, the music of F. Garayev is connected to his native heritage with invisible yet solid ties. The meditative essence of his music is typical of newer aesthetic streams, but it is associated with *mugham* as well. The musicologist Vladimir Barski quotes a review from the German newspaper *Tages-Anzeiger,* indicating that F. Garayev uses "*mugham* as an idea, as an emotion, as a perception of time, and, perhaps, as an abstract principle of working with melodic models."[29] Creating many versions of the same work (for instance, his *Postlude* has nine renditions, written between 1990 and 2011), all existing simultaneously, is typical in postmodernism, while at the same time these multiple versions reveal the tendency for variability within the same concept that is essential for the music of the East.

The music and personality of his father have always served as the most powerful factor linking F. Garayev to his heritage. In addition to their coauthorship of the symphony *Goya* (1980), there is another work that shows the deep spiritual connection between the two generations of the Garayev dynasty: the symphony *TRISTESSA I (Farewell Symphony),* premiered after G. Garayev's death in 1982 and was dedicated "to father, teacher, and friend."[30] The word *tristessa* is of Latin origin and means "sadness." The piece is in fact a requiem, an expression of pain and of the sorrow of an irreplaceable loss.

TRISTESSA reflects an important trend in F. Garayev's music, his interest in "instrumental theater." During the performance, the conductor leaves his stand twice to approach the piano and play G. Garayev's two Piano Preludes, in G♯ minor and A major. The first is a tragic lullaby written on the death of a young musician, a contemporary of G. Garayev, and the second is a happy piece that the composer dedicated to his wife and F. Garayev's mother.[31] There is another, third quote from G. Garayev, which is the Piano Prelude in C♯ minor. It sounds through a recording, as opposed to the live performance of the previous two pieces. The recording's sound is eventually distorted, creating a sense of death. These three quotations from G. Garayev's music become episodes of a rondo form, and for the refrain, F. Garayev wrote original material employing serialism. Symptomatically, F. Garayev uses the "reverse rondo," in which the even segments "rhyme" (see chapter 4).

The links of F. Garayev's music with native tradition include quotes from *mugham,* both recorded and live. He uses the former in the mono-opera *Journey to Love* (1978) and the latter in the piece *Khutba, Mugham, and Sura* (Sermon, Mugham, and Prayer). In both cases, these quotes function in the framework of postmodern aesthetics, but they still activate the national potential of F. Garayev's music. *Khutba, Mugham, and Sura* is based on serialism and incorporates the voice of the Azerbaijani instrument *tar* and the modal patterns of *shushtar*. In the first movement, the *tar* plays notated music, and in the second movement, this instrument improvises according to traditional practice. *Mugham Shushtar*, played by a solo *tar*, enters into the strings' chaotic world to sound as a voice of eternal truth or of the wisdom of centuries (PURL 6.14). Both movements show the importance of the modal patterns of *shushtar*. As observed by Vysotskaia, the first melodic phrase performed by the *tar*, in which the modification of the initial tone row is already present, is in fact the full representation of the scale of A *shushtar*.[32]

Postmodernism has never garnered enough followers to become a wide stream in Azerbaijani music. Neither "happenings," nor "performance art," nor "installations" have ever been tried by Azerbaijani composers, partly due to lack of exposure to these developments during the post-Soviet period. At the same time, postmodernism's depriviliging of the vivid ethnic component to which Azerbaijani music historically has been drawn may also have caused alienation. Electronic music has never received much interest from Azerbaijani composers, either, largely because of Azerbaijanis' lack of technological supplies and training in this area during the period that this trend emerged and was popular. Furthermore, the Azerbaijani music tradition's placing a high value on improvisation and spontaneous music-making is disposed against the idea of prerecorded sound and its nonnatural modification.

This discussion shows that East-West fusion in Azerbaijani composed music – in both syncretic and synthetic forms – is a multisegmented space, populated by various styles and composers' individualities. Since the 1990s, Azerbaijani music has been developing without the direct influence of the Russian factor. This new period of Azerbaijani music history, marked by regained and enhanced direct contact with the West, can be considered a "new beginning." Fresh generations of Azerbaijani composers must define a new stream of their native composed music tradition, and they must create new mechanisms of achieving the syncretic unity of East and West.

7 SONGWRITERS

> I was sleeping in a castle,
> Even shooting could not wake me up.
> But then I heard singing accompanied with the *saz*,
> And I woke up immediately!
>
> AZERBAIJANI FOLK SONG
> *Galada Yatmish Idim* (I Was Sleeping in a Castle)

GENRES, STYLES, AND TRENDS

The song tradition of Azerbaijan, as that of nearly any culture, occupies a special place in the hierarchy of musical genres, addressing a wide audience and instantly reaching people's hearts. In the twentieth century, the rich and versatile folk song tradition, with its multigenre spectrum encompassing lyrical, heroic, humorous, historical, and work songs, has been reimagined in the parallel space of composed music. This trajectory of development explains important characteristics of modern Azerbaijani song, including its direct links with traditional and folk music and the comparatively lesser role of stylistic innovations relative to other genres of Azerbaijani composed music. All songs written by Azerbaijani composers, regardless of these pieces' genre, style, topic, or time, preserve the marks of indigenous tradition. Indeed, many of these compositions have earned a status close to that of folk songs, and the country's prolific songwriters, such as Said Rustamov (1907–1983), Tofig Guliyev (1917–2000), Rauf Hajiyev (1922–1995), and Emin Sabitoghlu (1937–2000), occupy a very special niche in national culture. Even composers known to be masters of opera, the symphony, the ballet, or the oratorio, such as Uzeyir Hajibeyli, Fikrat Amirov, Niyazi, Jahangir Jahangirov, Vasif Adigozalov, and Arif Malikov, have demonstrated their alter ego through song, in which they use rather conservative compositional means. It is difficult to comprehend that the lyrical song "My Flowers" by Malikov and the poet Nabi Khazri, with its prevalence of melodic and rhythmic repetitions, abundant melodic sequential patterns, and clear delineation of the mode *bayati-shiraz,* was penned by a composer regarded as a master of the ballet and the symphony, genres in which he applied twelve-tone and aleatory techniques. Sometimes this alter ego has even competed with the composer's main explorations. Had Adigozalov only written "Carnation" (lyrics by Khurshud Banu Natavan), which dozens of Azerbaijani musicians have performed in various arrangements, it would have been reason enough for him to assume an honorable place in the history of Azerbaijani music (PURL 7.1).

Besides folk music, a large and ever-changing array of influences have shaped the field of popular song. Soviet musical influence dominated in the 1920s, 1930s, and 1940s, when the "mass song" was considered by ideologues to be an important tool to uplift the spirit of the proletariat and peasantry and to motivate them to build a communist future. All mass songs employed rather simple melodic and rhythmic patterns and had the character of heroic marches. Azerbaijan's first composers, Hajibeyli and Muslim Magomayev, have several examples of mass song in their portfolios. But this genre had a short history and was eventually replaced by what came to be known as the genre of *estrada.* The musicologist David MacFadyen defines *estrada* as a "wide-ranging term that includes pop music but also applies to modern dance, comedy, circus arts, and any other performance not on the 'big,' classical stage."[1] Nonetheless, the song component of the Soviet *estrada* was the most prominent one. Soviet-era *estrada* songs were a lighter version of Western rock and pop, and these songs characteristically had cheerful lyrics expressing patriotic, romantic, or humorous sentiments. The emphasis was on melody, and the simple and transparent instrumentation of *estrada* songs was significantly more subdued than contemporaneous Western rock's use of guitar and drums. Many of these characteristics of *estrada* can be detected in Azerbaijani song culture between 1950 and 1990, although Azerbaijani songs powerfully feature creative applications of traditional and folk music, which has kept these songs being performed and appreciated to this day.

In the 1960s, Western styles began to affect Azerbaijani popular song. National composers of that period wrote abundant lyrical and upbeat "jazzy" compositions, passionate tangos, melancholic waltzes, energetic shakes, and twists, all absorbed through the lens of the Azerbaijani modal system. Azerbaijani musicians pioneered many trends not only within their own tradition, but also within the context of Soviet music as a whole. For instance, in 1967, the composer and singer Polad Bulbuloghlu (b. 1945) wrote and performed the first Soviet song based on the formulas of shake ("Shake," with the lyrics by Onegin Gadzhikasimov). A new wave of Western influence, now with almost no ideological filtering, began during the decline of the Soviet era in the late 1980s and has been continuing ever since. Musicians were free to explore various genres of Western music, from flamenco to chanson and rock ballad. Rap music has emerged and garnered devoted followers. The emergence of rap music in Azerbaijan is particularly interesting, as it occurred in part through *meykhana,* an indigenous genre of folk music and literature that was severely discriminated against during the Soviet era. *Meykhana* came from the Baku villages and was typified by a kind of rhythmic recitative poetry that was accompanied by a simple harmonic background. *Meykhana* was fully improvised, which alone sufficed to horrify the totalitarian regime, as the free literary content of *meykhana* was open to the expression of any idea, including anti-Soviet ones. This genre happened to be an ideal match, so to speak, for rap music, as the two genres share many features. Both were created and performed by musicians who cultivated a rebellious image; both had emphasis on the verbal part rather than music; and both used slang-like street language for a poetic form that was far from elevated.

The song culture of the 1990s was truly versatile, which was natural, in consideration of its emergence in such a complex period of the nation's history. It was affected by two controversial factors – the excitement about Azerbaijan's newly gained independence and the tragedy of the military conflict around Garabagh. Both factors stimulated the growth of patriotic feelings, which immediately affected the song culture. The influence of Russian *estrada* dropped to almost nothing. Instead, Turkish music in various forms dominated the Azerbaijani popular music scene. The use of Turkish music was the result of Azerbaijan's search for its "Turkic" identity, which had been suppressed throughout the Soviet era (see chapters 1 and 9). Azerbaijani composers wrote dozens of songs celebrating the historical connections between Azerbaijan and Turkey and bridging their respective musical traditions. The popularity of Turkish pop music in Azerbaijan, linguistic similarities aside, is due in part to the fact that Turkish pop strongly prioritizes the assimilation of Western styles. According to the Turkish critic Tanil Bora, "At the very heart of [Turkish] pop music lies the urge to melt into a West-leaning universal culture."[2] At the same time, Turkish pop is distinguished by strong nationalist sympathies, which fully resonated with one of the main priorities of the Azerbaijani songwriters.

Despite their generally Turkophilic tendencies, Azerbaijanis have shown little to no interest in Turkish rock. This fact reflects a broader Azerbaijani indifference toward rock music in general. For instance, Russian rock, which despite all discriminative measures continued to exist during the Soviet era as an underground type of music, also found few followers in Azerbaijan. The native musical heritage of Azerbaijanis includes very few genres and forms expressing the ideas of social protest and struggle that are essential to much rock music. *Meykhana* is the genre that does so the most, but *meykhana* performers focus more on poetry than on music; besides, *meykhana* has been widely disseminated in only one part of Azerbaijan, the villages near of Baku. Thus, the Azerbaijani tradition did not offer significant potential for absorbing the aesthetics of rock music, and this genre has never become a part of the Azerbaijani soundscape.

One of Azerbaijan's best rock groups, Yukhu (The Dream), which was popular in the 1990s, was founded in Sumgayit, Baku's satellite city, in 1988. Because of the city's terrible environmental problems and horrifyingly concentrated industrial use of chemicals, Sumgayit was often referred to as "Soviet's Pride, Azerbaijan's Hell."[3] This city was known for its extremely diverse and rebellious population, as well as for its high poverty rate. For these reasons, Sumgayit had favorable conditions for the emergence of rock music. The musicians of Yukhu chose to leave Azerbaijan and moved to Turkey, where the group played in Istanbul restaurants until breaking up in the first decade of the twenty-first century.

THE KEY FIGURES

Azerbaijani songwriters have the same opposition of Easterners and Westerners that is found throughout the entire body of Azerbaijani composed music. Each side has suggested an original way of merging native and Western concepts. Rustamov was drawn to his native tradition probably more than any other Azerbaijani songwriter. He was a professional *tar* player, and from 1935 to 1975, he served as the artistic director and chief conductor of the Azerbaijan State Orchestra of Folk Instruments. Most of Rustamov's songs were scored for his orchestra, but these songs' enormous popularity led to their also being arranged for many other groups and soloists. Rustamov possessed an outstanding lyrical gift, which was primarily expressed through folk music idioms, though reconceived and imbued with a romantic spirit. His songs are all characterized by an intimate tone, profound lyrics, and rich melodies reminiscent of contemporary cantilena style, though they contain declamatory elements as well. All these features can be found in "Where Are You?" (1965), which uses the lyrics of Talat Ayyubov and is shown in part in musical example 7.1 (PURL 7.2).

EXAMPLE 7.1a. Said Rustamov, "Where Are You?," section A.

EXAMPLE 7.1b. Rustamov, "Where Are You?," section C.

EXAMPLE 7.1c. C♯ *shur*.

The structure of the song – ABCB – is typical of Azerbaijani folk music. Nonetheless, this song's intensity of lyrical emotion tends to blur the regularity of the structural divisions. For example, in section A, shown in musical example 7.1a, the phrase length of eight measures appears rather standard, but the opening phrase is in fact five measures long, with the remaining three measures holding G♯, the central note in this section.

This section contains many features that typify the thematic material of the whole piece. Among them is the constant use of sustained notes, all occurring on open vowels and extending over bar lines to create a sense of longing and appeal to a beloved who is far away. In musical example 7.1a, the sustained note is G♯, which is the fifth of C♯ *shur* and the dominant of C♯ minor. Even in the climactic section C, the melody rises to the upper tonic C♯, as seen from mm. 57–58 of musical example 7.1b, but then immediately slips down to the same G♯ in mm. 63–64. In both Eastern and Western theoretical paradigms, G♯ does not provide a sense of stability. The central position of G♯ contributes to building a state of unresolved longing throughout the song. The triple meter creates associations with the waltz at the beginning, although this eventually deteriorates into metric and structural irregularity. As for harmonization, the opening section is marked by simplicity and a rather archaic character. To compensate for the prevalence of the fifth in the melody, the composer avoids the harmonic use of dominant chords, displaying instead a preference for ii∅7 and III in mm. 26 and 28 of musical example 7.1a. These harmonies fall between regular appearances of the tonic in mm. 25, 27, and 29–32. The only point in the piece in which Rustamov highlights the dominant is the end of the culminating section, shown in mm. 63–64 of musical example 7.1b.

Rustamov was a typical Easternizer in the field of composed song, unlike Guliyev and Hajiyev, who had comprehensive experience in the field of Western music and who incorporated Western styles into their compositions. Both composers were key figures in the development of jazz in Azerbaijan in the 1930s, and both became prolific songwriters in the late 1950s and 1960s.

Guliyev was a versatile musician with a wide spectrum of professional interests. He was among the first native musicians to notate *mugham* and folk dances. Guliyev also had a passion for jazz and even worked as a jazz pianist in Moscow in the late 1930s. All this experience is reflected in the stylistic palette of his songs. The lyrical composition "Your Beauty Won't Last Forever" (1955), based on the poetry of Rasul Rza and shown in part in musical example 7.2, is a vivid example of Guliyev's style (PURL 7.3).

Despite significant differences between the literary content, melody, and rhythm of "Your Beauty" and those of Rustamov's "Where Are You?," both

EXAMPLE 7.2a. Tofig Guliyev, "Your Beauty Won't Last Forever," section A.

songs are based on the same ABCB form and feature the same contour of modal development. Their sections A are drawn to the fifth of the Azerbaijani mode; their culminating sections C begin from the upper tonic; and their sections B link the melody to the lower tonic through sequence-like movement. In both songs, the form and the modal development are highly typical of oral tradition. In *mugham,* the upper tonic is always the main goal toward which the material develops, and constant references to the lower tonic through this development are a must as well. Guliyev uses E *bayati-shiraz,* shown in musical example 7.2c. Section A, shown in musical example 7.2a, begins with the pitch B, although unlike Rustamov, Guliyev does not maintain the prevalence of the fifth throughout the entire section and descends from B in mm. 5–6 toward the tonic E in mm. 9–10. As seen from musical example 7.2b, section C starts on the upper tonic E in m. 25 and eventually descends to the same B in m. 32, and then section B links the melody to the lower tonic E in mm. 36 and 40. Nonetheless, Rustamov and Guliyev created completely different worlds,

EXAMPLE 7.2b. (*Facing, above*) Guliyev, "Your Beauty," sections C and B.

EXAMPLE 7.2c. (*Facing, below*) E *bayati-shiraz.*

25

Yal-qı- zam, yal - qız,   yal-qı- zam, yal - qız,

i   vi   iv

29

1.

Gəl mə-ni möh - nə - tə, o - da sa - lan və-fa - sız.

ii°7   ♭II9   I

32b

2.

sız.   Söy-lə nə- dir bu ə-da- lar, bu iş- və, bu

36

naz?_____Ge- dər, bir gün bu gö-zəl-lik sə-nə də qal-maz!

tonic

finding distinct places within a spectrum of methods of East-West synthesis. Rustamov's song represents a direct continuation of folk tradition, whereas Guliyev created a romance with elements of the tango, identifiable through the rhythmic motif ♫♪♫, which is heard throughout sections A and B, as shown in musical example 7.2a, and in mm. 33–34 and mm. 37–38 of musical example 7.2b. The composer uses colorful harmonization appropriate to the tango, including the Western harmonic device of the secondary dominant in m. 7 of musical example 7.2a.

The colorful harmonic potential comes to its fullest expression in section C, shown in mm. 25–32 of musical example 7.2b. Here the sequential development in the melody is harmonized through a progression of descending thirds: i – vi – iv – iio – bII – I. The progression involves chromatic changes (D♯ to E♭) that allow for the C minor triad (vi) in m. 26, and the progression uses the lowered version of the supertonic, which facilitates the Neapolitan (or Phrygian) II (bII) in m. 30. The latter is followed by the major tonic (E major) in mm. 31–32. Section B, which serves as the rhyming section of the form and occurs in mm. 33–40, resumes the harmonic and tonal status quo and returns the harmonic development to E minor.

Abundant melismas in the melody and embellishments in the accompaniment are attributes of Azerbaijani music. In the context of the tango, however, they also create associations with flamenco and, more generally, with the influence of Andalusian Arabic sources on Spanish music and culture. Such qualities deepen the piece's multicultural sensibility.

The Spanish features of "Your Beauty" signifies association with a musical tradition that is still at close proximity to Azerbaijan, since these lands were once integrated in the Silk Road. On the other hand, references to the New World appear in Guliyev's "Zibeyda" (1955), written on the lyrics of Anvar Alibeyli and shown in part in musical example 7.3.

"Zibeyda" is shaped and driven by the modal and rhythmic characteristics of jazz. This song is deeply influenced by Glenn Miller's orchestra, which was very popular in the Soviet Union in the 1950s. The opening section, shown in musical example 7.3a, resembles the famous "Chattanooga Choo Choo," having the same energetic instrumental background and short melodic phrases highlighting the fifth, C in this case, in mm. 8–12, and then descend to the tonic, in mm.13–14. Section B in "Zibeyda" follows "Chattanooga" by opening with a leap to the upper tonic, F5, in mm. 23–24 of musical example 7.3b. After this, however, the thematic development in the Azerbaijani song turns in a different direction than that of its American counterpart. Here Guliyev demonstrates a profound use of modality by combining F *rast* with both F major and the

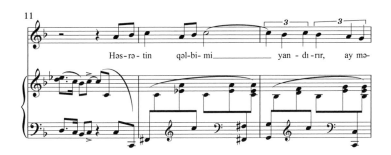

EXAMPLE 7.3a. Guliyev, "Zibeyda," section A.

EXAMPLE 7.3b. Guliyev, "Zibeyda," section B.

EXAMPLE 7.3c. F *rast*.

EXAMPLE 7.3d. F blues scale.

F blues scales, two of which are shown in musical examples 7.3c and 7.3d. The composer applies chromatic alterations within a descending sequence from the tonic to the dominant: first through two versions of E, as for instance E and E♭ m. 25 in musical example 7.3b; and second, between E♭ and D♭ in m. 29. The first switch is highly representative of F *rast,* which includes both the natural and the lowered versions of E, although in traditional practice they can never be used sequentially as a chromatic semitone, since they should be separated from each other by at least one or two adjacent notes. This is exactly how Guliyev uses these two pitches. The descending motion from F to C through E♭ and D♭ in m. 29 facilitates modulation to A♭ major and signifies a brief departure from traditional modality: A♭ and, naturally, the key based on it as tonic are foreign in the context of F *rast* but are a part of the blues scale that has F as the tonic. The chorus marks the return to *rast.* The descending sequence that shapes the melody of the chorus could easily be a part of any Azerbaijani folk song. Its jazzy spirit results from the interference of the triplets in a duple context, which adds a swung feel.

Despite being written in the same stylistic sphere as Guliyev's songs, Hajiyev's songs reflect their composer's distinctive personality. They are less intimate and more concert-like. This quality perhaps explains why they sound more convincing in their original orchestral versions and why they lose part of their charm when transcribed for the piano. Hajiyev's open, extroverted gift allowed him to write a number of patriotic songs, such as "Azerbaijan" (1966), with lyrics by Anvar Alibeyli. The verse of this work is shown in musical example 7.4. This song was part of the stream of "Soviet" patriotic songs, but it sounds specifically Azerbaijani because of the strong, unmistakably native features of the musical material.

Based on a very limited set of melodic and rhythmic patterns, Hajiyev created a rich and powerful piece that is still recognized as a musical symbol of the country. The composer highlights the typical modal formulas of G *segah,* shown in musical example 7.4b, in both the melody and the accompaniment. Syncopated rhythms appear in the melodic part in mm. 8–9 and mm. 12–13 of musical example 7.4a. These can be found in the traditional *rang*s and instrumental music of Azerbaijan, but these rhythmic patterns defy the rhythmic consistency of typical "Soviet" march-like songs. Also characteristic of the national tradition are the melismas in mm. 8–10 and m. 12, as well as the slight melodic changes within these repetitive patterns, which expand the melodic scope (compare m. 9 to m. 13).

Rustamov, Guliyev, and Hajiyev belonged to the first generation of professional Azerbaijani songwriters. They established the foundations of a new

EXAMPLE 7.4a. Rauf Hajiyev, "Azerbaijan," verse.

EXAMPLE 7.4b. G *segah.*

tradition and were followed by many composers, including Sabitoghlu, who left behind a versatile legacy. It is difficult to relate Sabitoghlu to either the Easterners or the Westerners stream, as he was dedicated to his Eastern roots and at the same time was perfectly aware of a broad spectrum of developments in Western popular music. What powerfully shaped his style was the epoch in which he came onto the Azerbaijani music scene: the 1960s, a time of increased personal freedom in Soviet society. Sabitoghlu's songs created new aesthetics in the Azerbaijani song tradition. The composer depicts the inner world of an individual, his or her complicated personality and hidden conflicts. His songs feature a broad scope of meanings. They are at once happy and tragic, humorous and contemplative.

"Tonight" (1976), with the lyrics of Zeynal Khalil shown in part in musical example 7.5, is a powerful expression of longing and the sorrow of separation.

EXAMPLE 7.5a. Emin Sabitoghlu, "Tonight," section A, beginning.

EXAMPLE 7.5b. G *shushtar.*

The song has highly metaphorical lyrics, a typical trait in Eastern poetry, and is based on distorted waltz formulas that convey the pain of separation. "Tonight" is notated in ⅜ but still has a waltz-like pulse due to the slow tempo and its clear motion, suggesting a simple triple meter. The melody has clear, regular phrasing. The syncopated patterns ♩ ♪♪♩, seen throughout the accompanimental part of musical example 7.5a, are associated with one of the many versions of the "Azerbaijani five-syllable formula" ♫♫ ♪♩ discussed in chapter 6 (PURL 7.4).

"Tonight" is an example of a convincing reconciliation of Azerbaijani modality and Western tonality. The song is notated in G minor, but the tonic function of G is merely a formality, since the melody and harmony are strongly drawn to D. Measure 17 of musical example 7.5a opens with D. The major triad above D (functioning as the dominant in the context of G minor) appears throughout this segment and closes it in m. 20. The entire song ends with the D triad as well. Here Sabitoghlu is influenced by the traditional modal characteristics of G *shushtar,* which are more centered around the lower fourth of the tonic (D) than around the tonic (G) itself, as shown in musical example 7.5b. It is difficult to imagine a more masterful and seamless fusion of the central traits of Eastern and Western tonal systems.

Children's songs have become an important subgenre within the tradition, and their authors also have contributed to the East-West project. Among such

EXAMPLE 7.6a. Gambar Huseynli, "My Little Chicks," verse.

EXAMPLE 7.6b. Huseynli, "My Little Chicks," chorus.

EXAMPLE 7.6c. F♯ *segah* with chromatic alterations.

works is "My Little Chicks" (1949), by Gambar Huseynli (1916–1961), shown in part in musical example 7.6. With lyrics written by Tofig Mutallimov, which have been translated into Russian, English, German, Japanese, Persian, Bulgarian, Polish, Serbo-Croatian, and Romanian, this song is known and loved in many countries around the world.

The melody of "My Little Chicks" has an obvious flavor of tradition, first of all, because of the clearly defined patterns of F♯ *segah* shown in musical example 7.6c, with the duality of tonal centers typical of this mode. The tonic, F♯, opens the verse shown in musical example 7.6a. The chorus, given in musical example 7.6b, is drawn to D, the basic tone of this mode. Even in the format of a children's song, Huseynli applies a main principle of *mugham* composition, the alternation of improvised and strict rhythmic parts. The verse has a quasi-improvisational quality, whereas the chorus is based on comparatively simple patterns. That is why this song may be characterized as a replica of *mugham* in an adapted, simplified version highly appropriate for children's repertoire.

PERFORMERS OR COAUTHORS?

Performers as well as composers have shaped the history of Azerbaijani popular song. Each performer has been allowed, and even expected, to go beyond the notation and to suggest his or her own interpretations of the same piece. These could entail slight changes in musical contents or even adding some improvised episodes. Although popular music traditions across the globe generally allow a greater compositional place for the performer, in Azerbaijani music such freedom was stimulated by the tradition's improvisational nature. Indicatively, most traditional singers in Azerbaijan perform composed music repertoire as well, and these musicians enhance composed songs through inserting improvisatory *mugham* episodes between the verses. This idea has become emblematic for many generations of Azerbaijani popular singers. Even those who never learn *mugham* professionally have the incentive to do so on a reduced scale in order to be able to contribute to popular song.

A highly productive partnership emerged between Guliyev and the singer Rashid Behbudov (1915–1989). As the composer confessed, "Many of 'my' songs really have the signature of both of us. . . . [T]here are some songs for which I am recognized as composer, but Rashid made so many changes that they really ought to be considered his. I'm not ashamed or embarrassed by this fact."[4] Behbudov initiated various changes, from adding melismas and tempo deviations to modifying melodic lines and adding new sections. Indeed, the alliance

FIGURE 7.1. Tofig Guliyev (at the piano) and Rashid Behbudov.
Courtesy of Rashida Behbudova.

between Guliyev and Behbudov produced many gems of the Azerbaijani song repertoire.

Behbudov's life and career remain among the brightest examples of East-West synthesis in Azerbaijani music. A lyrical tenor, he was often called the "golden voice of Azerbaijan." In any part of the Soviet Union to which my travels took me the 1980s, in any company, the people, knowing where I came from, responded with excitement: "Then you are from the land of Rashid Behbudov!" And these days, I am able to see and listen to Behbudov's recordings in all Azerbaijani homes in the United States and across the world. Behbudov's career began in opera but did not remain there. His ability to communicate to an audience and involve it in the performance, along with his talent and passion for improvisation, urged him to switch to popular song. Behbudov was a devoted champion of song until the end of his life, even founding, in 1965, the Song Theater in Baku, where he served as director until the end of his life. The roots of Behbudov's improvisation skills laid in *mugham,* the musical genre that he knew impeccably thanks to his father, Majid Behbudov (1873–1945), who was a famous *khanende* in the Garabagh part of Azerbaijan.

The genuine Azerbaijaniness of Behbudov's style and repertoire urged me to advance a project, Music and Culture of Azerbaijan, in which the history, geography, culture, and music of the Republic of Azerbaijan were expressed through ten songs from Behbudov's repertoire.[5] Each song is interpreted as a source of information about Azerbaijan. The lyrics reflect the national history and culture, and the musical content and Behbudov's performing manner show certain ways of synthesizing East and West in music. For example, the song "Poppies" by Telman Hajiyev (lyrics by Aslan Aslanov) (1972) evokes the picturesque landscapes of Ganja, a historic town (PURL 7.5). The beauty of flowers is compared to the beauty of a girl, which is a typical metaphor of Azerbaijani folk poetry. The song's musical material is based on *segah* and shows the combination of quasi-improvisational and rhythmic sections essential for *mugham.* Behbudov's short improvisation in the third verse, which is supported by the *tar,* gives a taste of *mugham,* and the arrangement's scoring for an orchestra of traditional instruments provides an exposure to the Azerbaijani instruments. Most of the songs from Behbudov's repertoire similarly serve as expressions of Azerbaijani cultural and musical identity.

Another Azerbaijani star of popular music, Muslim Magomayev (1942–2008), came to the profession with Behbudov's blessings and maintained a friendship with him. This baritone singer, the grandson of the composer Muslim Magomayev, became the idol of many generations of pop-music lovers in

FIGURE 7.2. The singer Muslim Magomayev. *Courtesy of the State Museum of Azerbaijani Musical Culture.*

the Soviet Union. Following a trajectory similar to Behbudov, Magomayev also started with opera and even studied in La Scala in 1964–1965, but then chose to follow a career in popular song. But Magomayev's performing manner and repertoire significantly differed from the Behbudov's. He was often referred to as the "Azerbaijani Frank Sinatra," and his vocal style was shaped within the sphere of Western professionalism and met its highest criteria. Magomayev's repertoire was truly versatile and included many musical traditions, among them Russian, Italian, and American music. But his voice and performing manner, regardless of the repertoire, were impregnated with specific Eastern flavor. And when Magomayev performed his native Azerbaijani music, one could clearly hear all the nuances, all the elements of the traditional singing style. Despite taking up residence in Moscow in the mid-1960s, he never lost his ties with Baku, where he was born and raised. Magomayev's song "Azerbaijan" remains a musical symbol of the country. This work sounded at his funeral in Baku in 2008, when he found his final rest (PURL 7.6).

A shared aspect of the careers of Bulbul, Behbudov, and Magomayev was that at different stages of their lives, they collaborated with the pianist Chingiz Sadikhov (b. 1929). Sadikhov, who now resides in San Francisco, is more than an accompanist in the Western sense of word. A genuine master of improvisation, he should be characterized as a collaborative pianist, always creating a dialogue with the vocalist. In addition, Sadikhov pursues a solo career, creating hundreds of compositions based on the folk tunes and composed music of his native Azerbaijan. None of his pieces are notated, and they reflect the pianist's dual background in the fields of traditional and classical music. Sadikhov's compositions are a continuation – and the culmination – of the trend of improvising *mugham* and folk music on the piano, a development that emerged within the urban culture of Baku in the late nineteenth century. From the very beginning, playing *mugham* on the piano required not so much a concern for maintaining the purity of *mugham,* but rather the ability to reimagine *mugham* through the lens of the piano and the styles of Western piano music. Sadikhov's improvisations demonstrate the influence of Liszt, Chopin, and Rachmaninoff, the composers who have always been among highlights of Sadikhov's repertoire as of classical pianist. His high virtuosity is also a result of his classical music background. But most importantly, Sadikhov's pieces show his impeccable knowledge and awe of Azerbaijani musical tradition (PURL 7.7 and PURL 7.8).

Azerbaijani popular song continues developing through contact with its own past. Local composers and performers are now far more informed of about contemporaneous Western music than were their predecessors who lived behind the Iron Curtain. Still, the most impressive accomplishments of Azerbaijani musicians are those that continue the heritage of Guliyev and Rustamov. Old songs continue to be a part of contemporary soundscapes, existing in dozens of new arrangements, many of them considerably different from the original. This continuity of tradition justifies the unique position of song in the hierarchy of genres of Azerbaijani composed music and secures it from the loss of authenticity that is all too possible in the field of popular music in our globalizing world.

8 JAZZ *MUGHAM*

> No city in the Soviet Union was more receptive to the
> fiercely rhythmic cadences of hard bop than the Turkic
> capital on the Caspian. The Azerbaijani jazz musicians
> lived a rougher and more bohemian existence than
> did the Russians, and their playing showed it.
>
> FREDERICK STARR, *Red and Hot:*
> *The Fate of Jazz in the Soviet Union*

NEW DIMENSIONS OF THE EAST-WEST PROJECT

Back in the 1990s, at the Baku Music Academy, I had a student in my Western
music history class who often stayed after the lecture to pursue conversations
on various music-related topics. Her name was Aziza. We talked about the role
of spontaneous expression in Western classical music, as well as the amount
of freedom appropriate to each musical style or individual composer's work.
Aziza always amazed me with the maturity of her thoughts and deep analyses.
It was, however, unsurprising. Aziza was considered to be one of the most talented and promising Azerbaijani classical pianists of her generation. Besides,
she already had made significant progress as a jazz pianist, gaining remarkable
success in the international arena. In 1988, at the age of eighteen, Aziza had
placed third at the Thelonious Monk International Jazz Piano Competition in
Washington, D.C. Aziza's last name was Mustafazade. She was the daughter
of Vagif Mustafazade, the pianist and composer revered as the founder of jazz
mugham, the native-born style of Azerbaijani jazz that emerged in the 1960s
through a fusion of jazz and *mugham* idioms.

Jazz mugham is defined by the musicologists Rauf Farkhadov and Fariza
Babayeva as a "fusion of the lyricism of *mugham* with the dynamics of jazz,

the synthesis of the traditional melodic and modal contents of *mugham* with the harmonic and rhythmic variety of jazz."[1] The term itself was suggested by Farkhadov in the 1980s.[2] Nonetheless, the author later came to be skeptical of the term. The main concern voiced by Farkhadov and Babayeva in their book about Rafig Babayev is that the term helps to disguise a kind of pseudo-jazz in which performers elaborate on *mugham* formulas without firm grounding in jazz technique.[3] The composer Khayyam Mirzazade is also against the term *jazz mugham*. He considers it to be tautological, comparing it to the hypothetical (and pointless) "jazz blues." According to Mirzazade, "The role of *mugham* in this fusion is limited to modality and does not have any effect on the broader paradigms of the genre. Accordingly, there is no need to indicate the *mugham* part in the definition of the genre."[4] The pianist Salman Gambarov (b. 1959) advocates a similar position, saying, "Zawinul was interested in the music of Indonesia, and McLaughlin was drawn to the music of India. Mustafazade incorporated Azerbaijani modes in jazz. But all these phenomena are nothing else than continuations of the modal jazz of Miles Davis."[5] Despite all these controversies, the term *jazz mugham* is still used in many references to Azerbaijani jazz, including those in the present book. *Mugham* not only has affected the harmonic language of Azerbaijani jazz but also has shaped its aesthetics and spiritual dimensions. The fusion of jazz with *mugham* appears in many different ways which, again, points to the large artistic span of this concept. Jazz *mugham* resonates with my inquiry into East-West synthesis, linking Azerbaijani jazz with *mugham* opera and symphonic *mugham*. Like any style or genre, jazz *mugham* may produce examples of low-quality music, but this should discredit poor musicianship rather than the concept itself or the term applied to it.

Though jazz and *mugham* arose in markedly different cultural spheres, they share many common features. Both are based on egalitarian improvisation. In jazz, this improvisation is shaped by an array of structural constraints, while in *mugham*, improvisation is controlled by modal organization. Both jazz and *mugham* are typically performed by small, combo-type ensembles in which soloists take turns displaying their virtuosity against the backdrop of the group. A great variety and a significant amount of rhythmic freedom are integral to both genres. In the Soviet era, jazz and *mugham* both experienced difficult times in Azerbaijan: jazz was denounced as the "voice of the capitalist world," while *mugham* was labeled a "relic of the past" and an exemplar of "feudal court music." Although these genres eventually entered the domain of officially recognized Soviet art and culture, they did so under conditions of strict ideological control.

What caused the smooth integration of jazz into Azerbaijani music and what allowed jazz's fusion with *mugham*? Why has jazz become a significant part of Azerbaijan's soundscape? Why, for instance, has jazz never played a significant role in the music of Iran or of countries in Central Asia, such as Uzbekistan, Tajikistan, or Turkmenistan? They also possess the *maqam* tradition, and their branches of it are as unique and highly improvisatory as Azerbaijan's. Furthermore, the Soviet part of Central Asia developed in the same sociopolitical context that Azerbaijan did.

As with all other Western genres, jazz's integration into the orbit of Azerbaijani music was stimulated by a variety of factors related to Azerbaijan's unique geographical and cultural position. Quite symptomatically, Turkey also developed a distinctive jazz tradition, similarly reflecting its geographical position at the crossroads of Europe and Asia and the country's long history of involvement with different regions and cultures. Baku, in particular, as a seaport and – since the nineteenth century – a rapidly growing multiethnic metropolitan area, was an ideal cosmopolitan environment for jazz. Quickly the city became the cradle and the main center of the genre in Azerbaijan. In Baku, a unique tradition of improvised piano performance had existed since the late nineteenth century, forming a sort of prehistory of Azerbaijani jazz *mugham*. Although these activities did not involve jazz, the very idea of piano improvisation with a strong ethnic component created a bridge, a springboard toward jazz *mugham*. This, furthermore, explains the centrality of the piano in Azerbaijani jazz. Pianists outnumber any other jazz instrumentalists, and the most impressive accomplishments of Azerbaijani jazz, including the emergence of jazz *mugham,* are closely tied to the piano. The following discussion aims to introduce the main stylistic impulses that facilitated the jazz *mugham* fusion, and this discussion also traces the history of Azerbaijani jazz through examining its most remarkable figures and their contributions.

THE PIONEERS OF AZERBAIJANI JAZZ

Jazz arrived in Baku not long after it emerged in America. Since the beginning of the first oil boom in the early twentieth century, guest artists frequently played jazz in the city's cafes and restaurants. Jazz did not disappear from Baku's musical scene even after the Soviet invasion in 1920. The persistence of jazz speaks to a broader trend in the first decade of the Soviet era. During that time, music, arts, and literature by and large continued to follow their previous paths, since the new regime was too busy struggling with internal and external enemies, poverty, and epidemics to turn its attention to cultural policy. Jazz performers from overseas continued to visit Azerbaijan in the 1920s. The Chat Sauvage Theater opened in Baku in 1922, and its shows featured live jazz music. Several jazz orchestras formed in Azerbaijan's capital city. Some, such as the Caspian Marine, were linked to the military, and others played at movie theaters. Thus, by the 1930s, jazz had already secured a niche in Baku's urban culture, although the genre still was mostly performed by foreigners. A significant breakthrough occurred between the years of 1936 and 1941, "when jazz was being Sovietised," according to Richard Stites, a historian of Russian culture.[6] In 1939, the Azerbaijan State Jazz Orchestra was founded under the artistic direction of the composers Tofig Guliyev and Niyazi. Both musicians, particularly Guliyev, were well familiar with jazz. He had worked as a jazz pianist in Moscow, where he played in the jazz orchestra led by Alexander Tsfasman. The first Azerbaijani national jazz orchestra included three trumpets, three trombones, five saxophones, a piano, a guitar, and percussion, and its repertoire combined jazz standards with jazz works from the national repertoire.

The Azerbaijan State Jazz Orchestra was one of those Soviet jazz groups that might be profitably compared to the early big bands in the United States, although the term *big band* was never applied in the Soviet Union. The importance of composed-out arrangements in the big band style, as well as big band's focus on light dance tunes, fit well with the Soviet aesthetics of jazz. Nevertheless, the role of improvised solos in Soviet jazz orchestras began to increase. In Azerbaijan, this process involved the growth of native components – namely, *mugham* – in jazz. The entrance of *mugham* into the orbit of jazz seemed inevitable, especially since Guliyev and Niyazi were known for their passion and deep knowledge of this traditional genre. Guliyev was among the first successful transcribers of traditional and folk music, and Niyazi wrote a symphonic *mugham, Rast,* in 1948. In one well-known anecdote, in the middle of a jazz performance of the Azerbaijan State Jazz Orchestra, Guliyev asked the saxophonist to play a solo in the mode *chahargah*. That remarkable solo was the "moment of truth" and the first face-to-face meeting of *mugham* and jazz. World War II interrupted the development of Azerbaijani jazz. In 1941, after the Soviet Union entered the war, the Azerbaijan State Jazz Orchestra was reconfigured as a military orchestra, and its repertory shifted to patriotic songs and military marches.[7]

BEGINNINGS OF JAZZ *MUGHAM*

Baku in the 1960s was overtaken with a spirit of jazz. There were no jazz clubs at that time, as the Soviets were still suspicious of them, but jazz was ubiquitously played in cafes and restaurants. The restaurant Druzhba, located on the top of the highest hill in Baku, had a reputation for being the best place in town to hear live jazz. It was in this jazz-friendly atmosphere that one of the most innovative musicians of Azerbaijan, the pianist and composer Vagif Mustafazade (1940–1979), came onto the scene, serving as a major impetus to the development of jazz *mugham*. Around the same time, the pianist and composer Rafig Babayev (1936–1994) also began to explore ways of merging *mugham* with jazz, coming up with his own vision of this fusion.

A chain of coincidences links the lives and careers of Mustafazade and Babayev. Both went through extensive periods of training as classical pianists at college and then at the Azerbaijan State Conservatory. This was typical for jazz musicians in the Soviet Union, as was learning jazz through radio broadcasts, recordings, and film soundtracks. At the beginning of their careers, both musicians were passionate about Bill Evans, Oscar Peterson, and other bebop and postbebop pianists. They established their own groups in the late 1950s. Babayev had a jazz quartet, and Mustafazade had a trio. Both musicians' careers encompassed popular music along with jazz. As is true of many jazz musicians, for Babayev and Mustafazade, collaboration with popular music groups and institutions offered financial security, yet it also meant that they had to sacrifice a huge amount of energy and time that could otherwise have been spent on jazz projects. Between 1965 and 1969, Mustafazade worked with Orera, a popular music group in Georgia, and in 1971, he founded the Baku-based ensemble Sevil, which existed for six years. Babayev, conversely, was seriously involved in popular music. Between 1963 and 1983, he worked with Rashid Behbudov, Azerbaijan's renowned pop singer, and with the Song Theater that Behbudov founded. In 1961, Babayev established a male quartet, Gaya, which enjoyed enormous success that went far beyond Azerbaijan and even the Soviet Union. These four handsome, elegant, charismatic, and cheerful young men were often called the "Soviet Beatles," although the group's repertoire and performing manner were more informed by jazz-pop quartets such as The Hi-Lo's and The Four Freshmen. Gaya projected jazz, rock, and pop music idioms through the prism of a native musical style. As a result, the group's distinct manner of singing went far beyond the guidelines that the Soviets set for popular music and jazz. Gaya has survived into the twenty-first century, albeit with several membership changes. In 2011, they celebrated their fiftieth anniversary (PURL 8.1 and PURL 8.2).

Both Mustafazade and Babayev lived and worked outside of Azerbaijan for extensive periods of time, which allowed these musicians to expand their stylistic and aesthetic horizons. Between 1965 and 1969, Mustafazade worked

FIGURE 8.1. Vagif Mustafazade. *Courtesy of the State Museum of Azerbaijani Musical Culture.*

FIGURE 8.2. Rafig Babayev. *Courtesy of the State Museum of Azerbaijani Musical Culture.*

in Tbilisi, Georgia. During his sojourn abroad, he began to collaborate with Tamaz Kurashvili (b. 1947), a Georgian bass player who would eventually become his long-term collaborator. Jazz critic Virgil Mihaiu characterized the duo Mustafazade-Kurashvili as "one of the notable feats of piano/bass since 1965," admitting that, "seldom [have] I heard a more significant transposal of a people's spiritual/musical resources into jazz."[8] Babayev left Baku for Moscow, where from 1960 to 1962 he worked as a pianist in one of the jazz orchestras. Both Babayev and Mustafazade participated in the Tallinn Jazz Festival in 1966 and 1967. According to Starr, the event's location in the capital city of Estonia, "in proximity to the more advanced jazz worlds of Poland and Scandinavia," allowed for "a festival in the fullest sense."[9] Mustafazade won first prize at both events, and Babayev's composition "In the Mode Bayati Kurd" was singled out by Willis Conover, an American jazz critic and host of *Jazz Time* on Voice of America, as one of the highlights of the 1967 festival (PURL 8.3).

Conover, however, was particularly impressed by Mustafazade's performances and is quoted as saying, "Vagif Mustafazade is an extraordinary pianist. It is impossible to identify his equal. He is the most lyrical pianist I have ever heard."[10] When Mustafazade died, Conover dedicated a one-hour program entirely to him and to Azerbaijani jazz.

Both Mustafazade and Babayev recorded with Melodiya, the only recording label in the Soviet Union. From Mustafazade's return to Azerbaijan in 1969 up until his death in 1979, he released nine albums with Melodiya, which was more than any other Soviet jazz musician during that decade.[11] As for Babayev, after having collaborated with Melodiya, in 1988 he opened his own studio where he made many recordings, all of which were included on the posthumous album *Farewell*, released in 2000.

The tours of Mustafazade and Babayev included both the Soviet Union and Western countries, although going to the latter was rather problematic in the Soviet context. Mustafazade visited Poland, Germany, Czechoslovakia, and Yugoslavia. His largest international success occurred in 1979, when Mustafazade won the highest award at the International Competition for Jazz Themes in Monaco. Babayev had the opportunity to perform Azerbaijani jazz overseas, often, though not exclusively, through the activities of the Song Theater. In 1976, Babayev's group Jangi received an invitation to work on the ocean liner *Odessa,* traveling from Montreal to New Orleans and Mexico. Along with other groups from around the globe, Jangi performed jazz, including pieces from the American and Azerbaijani repertoires. The tour was such a success that their contract was extended from two to eight months. Babayev's second – and last – visit to the United States occurred in 1992, after the collapse of the Soviet

Union. Together with the composer and arranger Siyavush Karimi (b. 1954), he performed several gigs in San Francisco. Sadly, both pioneers of jazz *mugham* suffered untimely deaths: Mustafazade of a heart attack on a concert stage in Tashkent, Uzbekistan, in 1979, and Babayev in a terrorist incident in the Baku subway in 1994.

Although there are numerous similarities between the lives and careers of these two musicians, the differences are also important. These musicians envisioned jazz *mugham* in different ways, thus continuing the dynamic between Easternizers and Westernizers that has been present in Azerbaijani music since its integration with Western musical styles. For Mustafazade, *mugham* was the first and most basic component of the fusion. His stance stemmed from the environment that shaped his musicianship. Mustafazade's mother, Zivar Aliyeva, was one of the first female pianists in Azerbaijan, and she was known not only for her experience with the classical Western repertoire, but also for her brilliant improvisatory skills in *mugham*. Accordingly, *mugham* was an early part of Mustafazade's existence and his first means of artistic self-expression. The deep and profound knowledge of jazz that he obtained later allowed him to find ways for the modal and rhythmic formulas of *mugham* to serve a jazz language. In the musician and jazz journalist William Minor's penetrating appraisal, "listening closely to Vagif Mustafa-Zadeh (Mustafazade) . . . I heard less Oscar Peterson and more a man with a unique background following his own cultural imperatives."[12] Indeed, *mugham* was the aesthetic basis and determinative element of Mustafazade's musical language. He was drawn to the continuous modal development of *mugham,* to its intense and indiscrete character. Mustafazade's jazz had strong links with monodic tradition, since his jazz language was based on the prevalence of a melodic line. His preference for small ensembles – trios or duos – also reflected a predilection for monodic self-expression and even created reminiscences with the format of a *mugham* trio.

Babayev, conversely, did not possess an innate, intuitive knowledge of *mugham*. Instead, Babayev studied *mugham* and grasped its rules and nuances at the same time as he went through a parallel process of learning jazz. As a result, *mugham* was never dominant in his style. Besides, Babayev was more interested in extracting discrete components of *mugham*, such as "*mugham* recitation," which he incorporated into a polyphonic texture.[13] Unlike Mustafazade, Babayev preferred playing with a large group of musicians. This aspect of his musicianship reached its apogee in 1983, when he was made artistic director of the Azerbaijan State Estrada and Symphony Orchestra, and he worked in this capacity until 1991.

Babayev's approach is evident in his composition "In the Mode Bayati Kurd" (1967), in which jazz and *mugham* form different layers of a polyphonic texture (PURL 8.3). The same concept characterizes "Besieged by Mugham" (1985), which Babayev performed with his group Portrait and the popular singer Akif Islamzade, who is also known for his mastery of *mugham*. "Besieged by Mugham" consists of three parts, each featuring a particular *mugham: Rast, Shur,* or *Segah.* The singer was given a carte blanche to improvise these *mugham*s, while the group adds an instrumental background combining *mugham* and jazz in a complex multilayered texture. Mustafazade's "Bayati Shiraz" also includes original *mugham* performed by the *mugham* singer Hajibaba Huseynov, who is supported by a rich instrumental accompaniment that includes extensive interludes. In this case, however, the spirit and modality of *mugham* penetrate all levels of this composition. It is as if *mugham* has been simultaneously conveyed in two forms – in its traditional manner and through the lens of jazz (PURL 8.4).

Through the music of Mustafazade and Babayev, Azerbaijani jazz considerably broadened its range of influences in the late 1960s and 1970s. According to the American saxophonist Tom Walsh who visited Azerbaijan in 2001, "This is a period in Azerbaijani jazz that paralleled American jazz because jazz musicians were juxtaposing different styles. For example, Miles Davis incorporated elements of popular music by using electric instruments and funk bass lines and drum grooves."[14] Both Mustafazade and Babayev started with bebop and then proceeded to embrace postbop and modal jazz styles. Writing of Mustafazade, Walsh describes "rock groove stemming from the sixties 'soul jazz' tradition, modal chord progressions with solo lines that alternate between funky blues ideas, modal slideslipping, bebop clichés." And by the end of his life, "Mustafazade had assimilated the contemporary jazz language of Chick Corea and used it to unify the disparate elements of his style, blending them into a powerful compelling voice."[15] Farkhadov and Babayeva mention the styles mastered by Babayev as ranging "from early jazz and swing to bop and cool, and from avant-garde to jazz-rock and fusion."[16] John Lewis and the Modern Jazz Quartet, in whose music counterpoint and polyphony play an essential role, also served as a source of inspiration for Babayev.

Unlike Mustafazade, Babayev was drawn to the idea of jazz rock fusion, which was inseparable from and stimulated by his active work in the field of popular music. His explorations of fusion were influenced by Miles Davis, Joe Zawinul and Weather Report, Chick Corea, and the Mahavishnu Orchestra. The Song Theater was the main arena for these experiments. Another site was the jazz group Asclepius (1967–1971) that Babayev founded at the Azerbaijan

State Medical University, and this was the first musical group in the country to use electric instruments.

In the late 1970s, Babayev and Mustafazade were planning to make a record together. Although the album never materialized, we likely have this planned collaboration to thank for Babayev's composition "The Light of Memory," a posthumous tribute to Mustafazade. Babayev performed it at the festival in Mustafazade's memory held in Baku in 1983.

In musical example 8.1 is the theme from "Bayati Shiraz," a piece representative of jazz *mugham* fusion as it was envisioned by Mustafazade. It exists somewhere between the two historically linked traditions of Azerbaijani music: piano improvisation and jazz improvisation.

The composition "Bayati Shiraz" had a particular attraction for Mustafazade. In fact, it gave impetus to the very idea of jazz *mugham* fusion. While performing the piece "Seventy Six" at the International Festival Jazz-69 in Baku, Mustafazade, as he would later describe it, "unexpectedly modulated to *bayati-shiraz,* played the last chord, and all of a sudden realized what had just happened. That was it. Mine. Truly mine."[17]

The thematic contents of the piece seem to be deeply influenced by the tradition of improvising *mugham* on the piano. The melody has a clear vocal quality and predominates over the other components. The melismas in the melody are rooted in *mugham;* they do not simply decorate the melody but are an integral part of it. The harmony is rather simple and is based on the progression i-VI-i-iv-V-i-V/V-iv-V-I. The impact of classical music is also profound. The opening figurations in the accompaniment and filigree patterns in the melody recall the piano scores of Rachmaninoff and Chopin. This was not accidental: Mustafazade went through a high-quality schooling as a classical pianist. At the Azerbaijan State Conservatory, he studied with Georgii Sharoev, a piano professor invited from Saint Petersburg who also mentored Gara Garayev and Elmira Nazirova. Mustafazade's interest for classical music revealed itself in many forms: he composed the Concerto for the Piano and Orchestra (1976) and he often used the themes from the works of Azerbaijani composers in his improvisations (PURL 8.5).

The melody from "Bayati Shiraz" encompasses both E minor and E *bayati shiraz,* opening with the fifth above the tonic in mm. 3–4, and then, through step-like motion, descending to the tonic in mm. 7–8. As discussed before, this particular pattern and, overall, the descending contour of the melodic development is highly typical of many pieces of Azerbaijani traditional music and has been naturally incorporated into composed music as well (see for example, the songs "Where Are You?" by Rustamov or "Zibeyda" by Guliyev discussed in

EXAMPLE 8.1a. Vagif Musafazade, "Bayati Shiraz", excerpt.
Transcribed by Parviz Guliyev.

EXAMPLE 8.1b. E *bayati-shiraz*.

chapter 7). The accompaniment contains both the natural and altered (sharped) versions of C, a representative quality of E *bayati-shiraz*. Following the example of the modal system, Mustafazade never uses both versions of the same pitch as a chromatic semitone combination. In the meantime, when used in a mode centered on a tonic E, C♯ implies the Dorian mode, which is common for jazz. In combination with the A♯ that appears in m. 9, C♯ signifies the secondary dominant, which is applied in m. 9. In this composition, the secondary dominant serves as a colorful harmonic device and evokes the harmonic language of romanticism.

The rhymed endings of both phrases linking the melody to the tonic seen in mm. 6–8 and mm. 11–13 are highly typical of Azerbaijani traditional and composed music. The irregularity of metric and structural division, as well as the frequent shifts from $\frac{6}{4}$ to $\frac{8}{4}$ and $\frac{7}{4}$, further signify the piece's deep links with *mugham*. Despite such a heavy presence of traditional Azerbaijani idioms, this music is still possible to identify as jazz. According to Walsh, "Different elements can be present that allow identifying a piece as jazz; it might be the instrumentation, the performance practice, the tone color, or how the musicians articulate; it might be who the musicians are. I don't know much about Azerbaijani music, but if I were at a jazz concert and heard such a piece, I would not be surprised by its being there."[18] Almost all of these criteria are present in this piece. Mustafazade carefully integrated *mugham* into the orbit of jazz while maintaining the traditional genre's uniqueness. Mustafazade was capable of playing true American jazz. Many of his recordings dating from the same time period demonstrate his impeccable mastery of playing jazz standards. But here he was led by *mugham,* which provided the model for improvisation and served as the source of the modal contents and rhythm.

A NEW STAGE

In the 1980s, the explorations of Azerbaijani jazz musicians were rooted in two stylistic sources: current American jazz and jazz *mugham,* a regional form of fusion. Among the local influences, naturally, Mustafazade and Babayev were the major sources. Among American influences, Chick Corea and Herbie Hancock were both central, with their respective followers forming two different camps. This situation differed greatly from that of the preceding decades, during which local jazz musicians were influenced by American jazz as a whole, without concern for particular factions within jazz. Another new trend in the Azerbaijani jazz of the 1980s was the advent of classically trained composers. Salman Gambarov and Jamil Amirov (b. 1957), two graduates of the composition class at the Azerbaijan State Conservatory, chose jazz as the main focus of their creative work. Their careers present the same dilemma of Westernizers and Easternizers that has already been discussed. Gambarov's style brings together ingredients rooted in American jazz, the traditional music of Azerbaijan, and the modern music of the West. In addition to composition, Gambarov majored in musicology, which also affected his style. "Before jazz, I went through writing sonatas, variations, quartets, and symphonies. I studied music history, from Palestrina to the late twentieth century. I didn't even realize at that point how important all these experiences would be in my 'next life' in jazz" (SG). A significant part of Gambarov's "next life in jazz" is related to the group Bakustic Jazz that he founded in 1996. The name of the group combines three definitions, "Baku," "acoustic," and "jazz." This combination reflects the concept of the group; they play acoustic jazz only, and their repertoire is highly versatile, just as the culture of the city of its origins. The group reflects Gambarov's own priorities juxtaposing jazz, contemporary music of the West, and national music idioms. Gambarov's impeccable sense of drama, mastery of form, and rich harmonic palette allow him to combine the influences of Miles Davis, Herbie Hancock, and Keith Jarrett with the harmonies of modern music.

The album *East or West?* (2005) reflects Gambarov's vision of Azerbaijani jazz. The title's question mark is rhetorical: "I consider the music included in the disc to be a product of both East and West, and these two sources are fused so firmly that it is impossible to answer the question posed in the title. Or, rather, everybody should find his/her own answer. I think of the city of Baku when imagining the East-West space" (SG). But this question has a second layer of meaning that points to the universal features common to music from both worlds, regardless their fusion. Gambarov explains it thus, "When Keith Jarrett plays a concert that consists of two parts, each forty minutes long, without division into separate pieces, you follow him just as a snake follows a flute, until you realize that you are in a completely different place. This is exactly what happens in *mugham* when it develops from the beginning to the culminating section. Where is the East and where is the West here, and what is the difference?" (SG).

Gambarov's "My Funny Zibeyda" is based on the theme of "Zibeyda" by Guliyev, a song that was also used by Mustafazade in his jazz composition. The title apparently refers to the song and jazz standard "My Funny Valentine" by Richard Rogers and Lorenz Hart. Both pieces open with an ascending sequence of three pitches, but this is the only obvious similarity between them. Gambarov characteristically chose a melody that does not have obvious references to the national modal system. In chapter 7, "Zibeyda" was compared to "Chattanooga Choo Choo." The modal formulas of *rast* are so masterfully integrated with the blues scale that this melody, chameleon-like, sounds Western and Eastern at the same time. Compared with both Guliyev's original composition, or with Mustafazade's version, Gambarov's complete reharmonization uses a richer vocabulary, and it combines the influences of Hancock and Corea, as well as composed music of the modern era.

One of Gambarov's original projects was the composition of a new soundtrack for the silent film *Latif* (1930, director Mikayil Mikayilov). The film itself was produced during the years of the Stalinist terror, and the plot is about the effect of this epoch on the life of the title character, Latif, a little boy who is forced to flee from his native village to the city. Gambarov's soundtrack was premiered in Baku in June 2001 at the international music festival The New Music from the Past Century. Six suites accompany the six parts of this movie, and their musical contents mix together many ingredients, including jazz, the Soviet song tradition of the 1920s and 1930s, the contemporary music of the West, and the traditional music of Azerbaijan.[19]

The first suite opens with *mugham Rast* played on the *kemancha* and is followed by a cheerful dance in a folk style. The piano part is predominantly modal, with occasional chord progressions and no swing, which was uniquely characteristic of Keith Jarrett. The use of traditional instruments and traditional music idioms significantly contributes to the meanings and stylistic scope of Gambarov's project. They create a musical portrait of Latif as a village boy. To illustrate Latif's departure from the village, Gambarov shifts from traditional idioms to avant-garde techniques. He explains it thus: "*Shur* or *segah* would hardly be appropriate to depict a train approaching the station, and this is such an important moment since it is about Latif's decision to change his life. That's why I decided to use aleatory here. *Kemancha* plays random patterns. And it works really well" (SG). As such, traditional instruments are more than signifiers of tradition here; they are integrated into the complex, multilayered aesthetic stylistic palette of the work (PURL 8.6).

The *Latif* score incorporates several quotations. One is the expressive melody borrowed from the romance "My Country" by the Azerbaijani composer Zeynalli, which was discussed in chapter 4. It is followed by the theme that is not an exact quotation but resembles the pieces from the Russian-Soviet urban folklore that were known as "abandoned children's songs." Eventually, Gambarov masterfully combines these two themes into one creating a symbol of the Motherland, suffering but still alive. Short reminiscences with the song "Burn Bonfires," a hymn of the Soviet Pioneers (the communist youth group) complete the image of the country and its people under the Soviets (PURL 8.7). All these themes speak to the local audience and, to an extent, to a post-Soviet audience at large, although young generations would not necessarily recognize the Pioneers' song. Gambarov's *Latif* is held in high esteem in the contemporary musical life of Azerbaijan as the only contemporary soundtrack for the old silent movie.

The career of the pianist and composer J. Amirov has encompassed jazz-rock fusion, drawing on a vivid national spirit, experiments with electronic instruments, and the influence of popular music. Taken together, these characteristics argue for J. Amirov being a direct successor of Babayev. But Mustafazade's influence is of no less importance, as J. Amirov possesses an intuitive knowledge of *mugham* and incorporates it in his jazz compositions. Such a bright ethnic component in J. Amirov's music emerged thanks to another powerful impetus: the music of his father, the composer Fikrat Amirov, who was discussed in chapters 2 and 5. The roots of J. Amirov's style, like those of his father, are in the history and folklore of his nation. He created the group called Gobustan, named after a historical site near Baku (see chapter 6), and many of his compositions, such as "Jangi," "Jidir" (The Races), and "Tongal" (The Bonfire), are associated with ancient Azerbaijani rituals and traditions. Azerbaijani composer, Jovdat Hajiyev, who was a master of the Azerbaijani symphony and who was J. Amirov's composition professor at the Azerbaijan State Conservatory, was another influential figure in his life. Years of study with Hajiyev equipped J. Amirov with great formal skill and a clear sense of musical dramaturgy. J. Amirov's explorations are closely tied to the development of composed music traditions. For instance, he wrote "Jangi" in the same time period as Agshin Alizade wrote his piece of the same name, which was discussed in chapter 6. Both composers masterfully create the atmosphere of a war dance and reproduce the voice of the *zurna,* the loud woodwind instrument used in traditional *jangi.* For this purpose, Alizade uses the oboe, the closest Western counterpart of the *zurna,* while J. Amirov evokes the *zurna*'s timbre by using a synthesizer.

The pianist, composer, and singer Aziza (b. 1969), whom I mentioned at the beginning of this chapter, is a devoted proponent of jazz *mugham.* "Jazziza," as Mustafazade jokingly called his daughter, has widely introduced jazz *mugham* in the international arena. Her ten albums released since 1991, including those with prestigious recording labels such as Sony Jazz and Columbia Records, show her father's continuing legacy, as do her collaborations with jazz luminaries such as Al Di Meola, Stanley Clarke, Bill Evans, and Omar Hakim. Aziza's style, however, is far from being a replica of Mustafazade's. Her knowledge of *mugham* is more practiced than intuitive, and unlike her father, she does not focus on the modal and structural aspects of *mugham*. For Aziza, *mugham* is more of a philosophy and a way of thinking: "It's much more than just music. It's religious. It's poetry. It's life."[20] Rather than treating it as indigenous practice, Aziza's compositions meditate on *mugham*'s many historical, cultural, and musical connections. For example, the piece "Shamans," from the album of the same name (2002), begins with a solo in the mode *shur*. This passage is very traditional and even resembles the beginning of the overture of the opera *Koroghlu* by Uzeyir Hajibeyli, analyzed in chapter 4. Eventually, references to *mugham* become increasingly abstract, as the music obtains a meditative quality associated with magic rituals performed by ancient shamans.

Aziza has a deep and profound knowledge of American and international developments in jazz. Bill Evans, Thelonious Monk, and Charlie Parker represent her main influences. Aziza can masterfully perform any jazz standard, and one of her performances – of "Beautiful Love" – is vividly described by Minor: "Her rendition included calculated 'negroid' slurs, a smooth scat with wide range and lovely high notes, then a fleet and feisty mostly single-note solo with fine attendant voicings underneath, building to block chords, back to the words and a poignant Lady Day ending."[21] All these sources fuse naturally and seamlessly.

Aziza is drawn to classical music in a more profound way than her father was. The music of romanticism is a major influence, and some of Aziza's compositions, such as "Dance of Fire," from the album of the same name (1995), or "Butterflies," from *Jazziza* (1997), resemble the large-format, quasi-fantasy concert pieces of the romantic composers, especially Chopin. Some of her other compositions contain direct references to classical-era sources. For example, "Mozart's Jazz Ballade" from the *Contrasts II* (2007) is a jazzy version of the Countess's aria "Porgi, amor, qualche ristoro" from *The Marriage of Figaro*. And there is yet another intriguing category of Aziza's stylized "classical" (in the general sense of art music) pieces. These elaborate on the parallels between *mugham* and baroque music, commonalities that have deeply affected twentieth-century Azerbaijani composed music. This category of Aziza's compositions includes "Bachuana," from *Contrasts* (2006), and "Bachmania," from *Contrasts II*. These energetic toccata-like pieces use the modal formulas of contemporary jazz. Another composition from the same series is called "Bach-Zadeh" (a humorous combination of the name of German composer and the ending of her own last name), from *Shamans* (2002). In this piece, Aziza performs both piano and vocal parts, and stylistically, it draws upon the instrumental and vocal styles of the baroque era. These styles are fused with scat singing and permeated by the modal patterns of Azerbaijani music.

Aziza's vocals encompass similarly diverse inspirations. She uses three distinct singing techniques, drawn from opera, *mugham,* and scat singing, respectively. Aziza's mixture of scat with traditional *mugham* singing, which she has applied to many compositions, such as "Inspiration" from *Inspirations – Colors and Reflections* (2000), is among Aziza's most impressive accomplishments. This piece is vocalized based on the modal patterns of *chahargah,* a mode admitted by many to be the most difficult to combine with jazz idioms. The use of the meaningless syllables and syncopated rhythmic patterns shows the influence of jazz, whereas the song's modality, embellishments, and microtonal patterns are related to *mugham.* The middle section unfetters these *mugham* roots, as it is entirely based on vocalizing within a prevalently modal space.

New names have appeared on the map of Azerbaijani jazz in the 1990s and in the new millennium. These musicians continue to rework the old dilemma of fusing Eastern and Western elements. The compositions of the saxophonist Rain Sultanov (b. 1965), according to Walsh, "exhibit the influence of Miles Davis' work with Marcus Miller, as well as that of Weather Report and hip hop, with occasional traces of *mugham.*"[22] The style of Shahin Novrasli (b. 1977) is shaped by modern jazz and free jazz and is highly polyphonic (PURL 8.8). Emil Afrasiyab (b. 1982) and Isfar Sarabsky (b. 1989) continue the tradition of Mustafazade in making *mugham* the primary source of their musical language and largely monodic style (PURL 8.9 and PURL 8.10).

There have always been musicians on the Azerbaijani jazz scene who did not identify themselves within East-West fusion and performed jazz in an uninflected American style. Among them is the pianist Vagif Sadikhov (b. 1946). Since 1963, Sadikhov has been residing in Moscow, where he has had the opportunity to perform with many luminaries of American jazz, including Gerry Mulligan, Milt Hinton, and Ben Riley, among others. Sadikhov's refined style is deeply influenced by bebop and postbop styles. Nevertheless, even he could not leave his cultural space entirely out of the picture. Walsh shared following story about his visit to Baku in 2001: "Vagif Sadikhov told me, 'I don't know what "jazz *mugham*" is! I cannot define it!' Yet, when he sat down to demonstrate his tune, 'Nostalgia,' its Central Asian flavor was immediately apparent. After he began playing, Sadikhov looked up, smiled and said, 'Oriental jazz!'"[23]

Upon his return to the States, Walsh included this short piece in his album *New Life*.[24]

The characteristics of Azerbaijani traditions even affect the way local jazz musicians perform jazz standards. Walsh described his experience of playing Hancock's "Maiden Voyage" with Gambarov in Baku. This vignette helps draw to a close our explorations of the still-developing history Azerbaijani jazz: "Even though it was in a traditional jazz form, and all the chords were recognizable, it had a quality that was very different from what I've played before, and it definitely placed me in a different mindset."[25] These words correspond with those of Minor, who mentioned about his meeting with Aziza: "I realized that this jazz . . . was vitally connected with larger culture, a wider source, plus a great deal of continuity. Jazz music seemed related to both folk and high arts to a degree unthinkable in the United States."[26] And when any jazz musician from Azerbaijan, whether a singer or instrumentalist, begins warming-up, the very first pattern without doubt involves the ancient formulas of *mugham*.

9 LEAVING THE POST-SOVIET ERA BEHIND

> Following Independence, each of the former [Soviet]
> republics . . . has had to reassess the conception of national
> identity that evolved during seventy years of Communist
> rule and articulate the principles under which it is presently
> striving to move forward as a national culture.
>
> THEODORE LEVIN, *The Hundred Thousands Fools of God:*
> *Musical Travels in Central Asia (and Queens, New York)*

1991: THE NEW BEGINNING

The breakup of the Soviet Union in 1991 remains among the most dramatic – and traumatic – historical events of the twentieth century. The agony of the dying regime lasted for several years, and it occurred amid political turmoil, economic collapse, and bloody ethnic and regional conflicts. Accordingly, at the end of the twentieth century, Azerbaijanis went through another round of vast social and political changes. It was, perhaps, the most remarkable transformation in the nation's entire history, as the country stepped into independence with no option of reverting to being a colonial state.

Paradoxically, the new period of East-West synthesis in Azerbaijani music that continues to the present is being shaped by an economic situation similar to that of the early twentieth century. A second oil boom, which started in the mid-1990s, has increased Western economic and cultural presence in Azerbaijan, and, correspondingly, has stimulated Westernization in all domains of life. Another consequence of the oil boom is that it has provided financial support for arts and music projects. Through the activity of various nongovernmental organizations, the oil money supports large-scale music festivals, competitions, and educational activities representing either aural or composed traditions and involving both local musicians and foreign guests. Foremost among such patron organizations is the Heydar Aliyev Foundation, led by Azerbaijan's First Lady, Mehriban Aliyeva. Many significant breakthroughs in the musical life of Azerbaijan in the twenty-first century became possible due to the sponsorship of this organization. Other similarities to the early twentieth century include significant changes in the architectural appeal and cultural infrastructure of Baku. As before, the best architects from the Western world have been invited to design new buildings in Azerbaijan's capital city. The world-renowned Iraqi-British architect Zaha Hadid designed the Heydar Aliyev Center, a multipurpose building that opened in 2012 and serves as a concert venue. Among the new concert venues that appeared recently are the two erected on the coast of the Caspian Sea: the grand Crystal Hall and the International Mugham Center, which is built in a shape inspired by the traditional instrument *tar*.

In his article about post-Soviet Uzbekistan, Levin suggests a four-fold model to explain contemporary Uzbek music. The two major trends are "nativism" and "Europeanization." These are, in turn, stimulated by one of two sources (for a total of four possibilities): "from above," that is, on behalf of the government, or "from below," that is, from within the culture.[1] This model can apply to Azerbaijan as well, with the only difference being that historically, Azerbaijan has experienced Westernization more than Europeanization (see introduction and chapter 1). The nativism evolving from below has been proactive in Azerbaijan during last two decades, which is natural for the young nation-as-state. *Mugham* and other genres of traditional music have been placed in the center of cultural life. Azerbaijani composers have recomprehended and rediscovered the genres and forms that previously had been suppressed for ideological reasons (see chapter 1). As for Westernization from below, it is less strong than nativism either from above or from below, which is hardly surprising in a non-Western culture. Nonetheless, this by no means points to a decline of Western musical forms in Azerbaijan. At present, Azerbaijani music mirrors the state policy of the Republic of Azerbaijan, which aims to bring all accomplishments of Western civilization into Azerbaijan while maintaining traditional cultural values. The government strongly supports all projects related to the promotion of Western musical forms in Azerbaijan. President Ilham Aliyev personally meets with the luminaries of Western music, such as the cellist Yo-Yo Ma and the jazz musician Herbie Hancock, when they visit and perform in Azerbaijan. The president and First Lady are frequent guests at Western classical music concerts. Interest in Western music is generated from below, too. Native composers continue to explore the genres and forms of Western music. It is true that the older generation of national composers tends to use rather conventional means of Western composed music that were mastered during the Soviet era. But the new generations of Azerbaijani composers strive to be on the same page with their Western colleagues. Jazz is now in its full zenith in Azerbaijan, and every year, new names appear in this field of the national music. Young classical and jazz musicians study abroad, participate in international competitions and festivals, and collaborate with colleagues worldwide.

Support for the development and promotion of both native and Western music forms given from above generally resonates with the processes emerging from below. Large-scale international music festivals of various kinds are held in Azerbaijan on a regular basis, and they also set the tone for the current dynamics of East-West synthesis in the country. These festivals may be sponsored by different organizations, but all occur under state patronage.

The international festival and symposium Space of Mugham is the only one in Azerbaijan that showcases Azerbaijani *mugham* in the context of the *maqam* tradition of the Middle East and Central Asia. Space of Mugham is a large-scale event, unlike the Silk Road Festival that occurs in the small city of Shaki, located on the historic Silk Road. This festival demonstrates the ancient Silk Road roots of Azerbaijani music and culture through bringing together music and musicians from the vast region touched by the old trade route. Neither Space of Mugham nor the Silk Road Festival confine their activities to the forms of traditional music, reinforcing that traditional music expressions are not isolated from the culture and forms of Western music in our globalizing world – or in twenty-first century Azerbaijan.

The contemporary music of the West, including composers' works, performing arts, and jazz, is central to the country's four major musical events: the Baku International Jazz Festival, the Rostropovich International Music Festival, the Gabala International Music Festival, and the Gara Garayev International Contemporary Music Festival. Every year, Baku becomes home to the international jazz festival, which includes the leading artists of the Western world, such as Al Jarreau, Chick Corea, and Joe Zawinul. The Rostropovich festival and the Gabala festival are likewise high-budget projects, and they bring the luminaries of Western classical music to Azerbaijan. Thanks to these events, Azerbaijanis have the precious chance to listen to Zubin Metha and the Israeli Symphony Orchestra, the United Kingdom's Royal Philharmonic Orchestra, the Verdi Chorus, the Milan Orchestra, and others. Both festivals are less than a decade old.

Distinctively, the Gara Garayev festival, which also focuses on contemporary Western music, is much older. The Gara Garayev festival started in 1986 to reflect Garayev's vision of Azerbaijani music as an integral and equal part of the Western composed music tradition. This festival emerged during the decline of the Soviet regime, and at that time, Garayev's festival symbolized Azerbaijan's growing spiritual freedom and its rejection of old ideological clichés in the field of music. Now the Gara Garayev festival enjoys new opportunities provided by direct exposure to Western music. The closing ceremony of the 2013 festival featured the Symphony by Luciano Berio, which is among the most rarely performed pieces of recent orchestral repertoire. Its performance by the Azerbaijan State Symphony Orchestra, led by Rauf Abdullayev (b.1937), in collaboration with the Questa Musica ensemble (Russia) and the Austrian pianist Kaori Nishii, was the first in the entire zone of the post-Soviet countries and in Eastern Europe. This is representative of the continuously high status of Western music in Azerbaijan, both at this festival and beyond. Like all Azerbaijani festivals focused on Western music, the program of the Gara Garayev Festival always includes pieces of Azerbaijani repertoire. The participation of local soloists, ensembles, and orchestras is another must. The 2013 edition of the Garayev festival featured works by Azerbaijani composers from three generations: Gara Garayev, Khayyam Mirzazade and Faraj Garayev, and Elmir Mirzayev. Accordingly, Eastern and Western elements are firmly represented within these prevalently Western events. There is one more festival in the panorama of Azerbaijani contemporary musical life that is also named after a native composer and that directly focuses on the idea of East-West dialogue: the Uzeyir Hajibeyli International Music Festival. Dedicated to the father of art music in Azerbaijan who advanced the idea of East-West synthesis in the national music and culture, this festival usually takes place in September on the occasion of the composer's birthday, and the event brings together musicians from Azerbaijan and beyond.

All these festivals demonstrate the new trend toward the decentralization of musical life in Azerbaijan. Two of the festivals take place in Gabala and Shaki, small picturesque towns in the northern part of Azerbaijan, and these events represent the category of summer music festivals. Holding festivals there marks a significant difference from the Soviet past, during which all major schools, orchestras, and events were concentrated in the largest city – in most cases, the capital – of the republic. The Soviets did so to control culture through centralization. These days, Baku is no longer the only option for hosting large-scale music events. In addition, Gabala is the location of the Beltmann Gilan Piano factory, which opened in 2010. Beltmann Gilan is the first such factory in Azerbaijan and in the entire region of Central Asia and the Caucasus. The factory produces between twelve hundred and fifteen hundred pianos each year, and these are used in both music institutions and private homes.

ROSTROPOVICH: BRIDGING THE PAST AND THE FUTURE

It is not accidental that one of the major music festivals held in Azerbaijan is named after the renowned cellist and conductor Slava Rostropovich. The story of this festival – as well as of Slava himself – helps illumine many historical and regional aspects of contemporary Azerbaijani music history. Few people world-wide knew before 1997 that maestro Rostropovich was born in Baku and spent his early childhood there. That was because his father, Leopold Rostropovich, taught at the Azerbaijan State Conservatory and established the tradition of professional cello performance in the country (see chapter 3). In 1997, the president of Azerbaijan, Heydar Aliyev, invited Slava Rostropovich and his wife, the opera singer Galina Vishnevskaia (1926–2012), to celebrate his seventieth birthday in Baku. It was the beginning of Rostropovich's regular visits to Azerbaijan over the next nine years.[2] The French newspaper *Le Monde* wrote in 1997: "For nearly a week, the cheerful mischief maker was driven around Baku at a crazy pace in an old limousine, windows covered with drawn black curtains. Even traffic police stood frozen at attention. The mysterious guest monopolized the headlines of national newspapers and enabled Azerbaijanis to forget about the 'downsides' and the unhappiness of their young republic, even if it were – but for a moment."[3]

Le Monde's reference to the "downsides" of the young republic is of particular significance when it comes to music. Rostropovich – born in Baku, formed as a musician in Soviet Russia, and forced to immigrate to the West – exemplified a powerful synthesis of various impulses that shaped his musicianship and personality.[4] He provided a model that the musical culture of the newly independent Azerbaijan needed to be reminded of at this new stage of its history. While in Baku, Rostropovich pursued many activities, including concerts and master classes. They all showcased a variety of national and stylistic sources. The program of the concerts included Brahms, Dvořák, Tchaikovsky, Shostakovich, Bernstein, and pieces by the Azerbaijani composers Hajibeyli, G. Garayev, and Frangiz Alizade. Rostropovich's master classes at the Baku Music Academy featured the same diversity. I still treasure a little notebook that I took with me to Rostropovich's master classes and in which I put down his remarks as well as anecdotes that he shared with the audience. Rostropovich talked about his encounters with Shostakovich and Prokofiev, with Britten and Bernstein. This renowned cellist talked of his meetings with Hajibeyli and referred to his friendship with G. Garayev and other Azerbaijani musicians. Rostropovich also recalled the stories of his Azerbaijani students whom he mentored while teaching at the Moscow State Conservatory. Through all these

FIGURE 9.1. Farhad Badalbeyli and Slava Rostropovich.
Courtesy of the State Museum of Azerbaijani Musical Culture.

stories, Rostropovich was conveying the dynamics of Western, Russian, and native factors essential for Azerbaijani music at that point. He talked about the hardships that the Soviets imposed on him, and he concluded that now it is the time to forgive the past and look forward into the future. What made Rostropovich's message more profound was that it was entirely linked to his personal experience. After his first concert in Baku in 1997, Rostropovich confessed:

> When I played Bach's *Sarabande* today, I felt my father's spirit somewhere very close, and I played as if I was continuing his sound which has been continuously resonating in my memory. My father, who died at the age of fifty-two, had never been happier in any other place than he had in Baku. He often told me this. In a letter written right before the war, he asked Uzeir Gadzhibekov [Uzeyir Hajibeyli] to organize our family's return to Baku. Unfortunately, the war began, and my father's request had to be postponed for fifty-six years. Now I have come here myself.[5]

Azerbaijan is now paying tribute to the memory of both generations of the Rostropovich family. One of the largest public music schools in Baku now proudly carries the name of Leopold and Slava Rostropovich. The small apartment where they lived in downtown Baku has been converted into the Home Museum of Leopold and Slava Rostropovich, and the street was named after them. Hundreds of rare artifacts are on display in this museum, reviving the family's unique story and showing the continuing importance of the Rostropovichs in the contemporary history of Azerbaijani music.

MUGHAM: THE MAIN MUSICAL SYMBOL OF AZERBAIJAN

In 2003, UNESCO (United Nations Educational, Scientific, and Cultural Organization) recognized Azerbaijani *mugham* as a Masterpiece of the Oral and Intangible Heritage of Humanity. Today, Azerbaijani *mugham* performers appear on the most prestigious Western stages, such as New York City's Carnegie Hall and London's Barbican. Indeed, *mugham* has become the main symbol of Azerbaijani music and culture both inside and outside the country. *Mugham* is a musical tradition that shows the distinctiveness of Azerbaijani music, and this genre reflects the power and ongoing significance of traditional music in Azerbaijan. At the same time, *mugham* exemplifies Azerbaijani music's links with the vast regions of the Middle East and Central Asia. This genre also demonstrates Azerbaijan's openness toward Western music, since the path of the national composed music began with "*mugham* opera" and proceeded to other exemplars of "*mugham* plus" fusion. *Mugham* has survived despite many historical ordeals, including the pressure of Soviet ideology, thus displaying the integrity of the nation and its strong will for a bright future.

During the last two decades, *mugham* has been performed, broadcasted, studied, and recorded by musicians of different ages, professional backgrounds, and artistic caliber, from six-year-old children to internationally recognized masters. Numerous festivals and competitions of *mugham* have been held nationwide, sponsored by various governmental and nongovernmental organizations. Among them are children's *mugham* festivals, and these deserve special mention, since they represent a unique venue for *mugham* culture in contemporary Azerbaijan. The practice of children's *mugham* festivals began during the late Soviet period, although it was not frequent at that time. I remember a group of boys ranging from eight to twelve years of age called Garabagh Nightingales who become known to practically every Azerbaijani in the 1970s and 1980s. Their interpretation of the *mugham Bayati Shiraz* with patriotic verses and a video clip showing picturesque landscapes of Garabagh is among the strongest music representations of Azerbaijan (PURL 9.1). Nonetheless, children's *mugham* performances were rather rare in those days, possibly because the Soviets tried to reduce opportunities for performing *mugham* at such a young age, in hopes of discouraging future *mugham* performances. Today, by contrast, many children are involved in performing *mugham*. The popularity of this genre with the young is evidence of the powerful energies from below, that is, from within the culture, and the strong emphasis within society to keep this ancient art alive (PURL 9.2).

The conflict around Garabagh (most often known as the Nagorno-Kara-bakh conflict) stimulated a vast increase of the role of *mugham* as a symbol of Azerbaijan's territorial integrity and statehood as a whole. As a result of the war, about one million refugees had to flee the occupied parts of Azerbaijan; those regions account for about 20 percent of the country's territory. Because most refugees were from Garabagh, all genres of Azerbaijani traditional music that are representative of that region are now facing serious challenges due to the loss of their native artistic environment, or *muhit,* which has shaped their development for centuries. Oldfield mentions the negative impact of the war on Azerbaijani *ashig* music: "Aşiqs from now-occupied Qarabağ *mühit* were . . . forced from their homes in 1992–1993, and have dispersed into refugee settle-ments in various areas of Azerbaijan. . . . There is a looming possibility that the unique features of the Göyçə and Qarabağ *mühit* could be lost within a genera-tion."[6] In addition to Garabagh, Oldfield also mentions the area around Lake Goycha, called "Sevan" in Armenian. This territory used to be densely popu-lated by ethnic Azerbaijanis and, historically, the art of *ashigs* was widespread there. Azerbaijanis were forced to leave the Goycha area, and this caused harm to the natural development of this regional branch of the Azerbaijani *ashig* tra-dition. *Mugham* has suffered even more than the *ashig* art because Garabagh, and particularly the city of Shusha, has historically been considered to be one of the centers of Azerbaijani *mugham*. Even while living far from their roots, Garabagh singers strive to preserve the original musical and poetic content of their repertoire.

The indigenous *mugham* heritage of Garabagh is now the focus of many musical and research activities, as is often the case when music speaks symboli-cally on behalf of the nation about a difficult moment in its history. In 2005, the Heydar Aliyev Foundation released a collection of twenty-four compact discs featuring performances, including rare archival recordings, of the most prominent *mugham* singers from Garabagh. *Mugham*s that are specific to the Garabagh area, such as *Garabagh Shikastasi,* are now being performed more frequently in Azerbaijan (PURL 9.3). Rare video and audio recordings of the masters of *mugham* from Garabagh are broadcast regularly, and their songs are now performed in various arrangements.

Since 2009, Azerbaijan has hosted one of the indisputably largest international festivals of traditional music, called Space of Mugham. Each of the three festivals held in 2009, 2011, and 2013 has a distinct concept. That of the first festival involved both the traditional form of *mugham* and its Western applications. The concert program included symphonic and operatic pieces based on *mugham,* and the festival equally featured traditional compositions. The second and third festivals represented traditional *mugham* only, with the third one exclusively focusing on the instrumental forms of *mugham.* The concerts of the last two festivals combined Azerbaijani *mugham* with its counterparts, including Uzbek *shashmaqom,* Iranian *destgah,* Iraqi *maqam,* Indian *raga,* and Turkish *uzun hava.* I had the honor of presenting a paper at the symposium held within the 2011 festival. I found it highly rewarding to participate in the discussions that involved world-renowned experts on the *maqam* tradition, including Jean During (France) and Jurgen Elsner (Germany). Before traveling to Baku, I met with the Iraqi-American violinist Dena El Saffar, who is based in Bloomington, Indiana, and who participated in the 2009 festival with her Iraqi Maqam group, which is called Safaafir. She vividly described a competition sponsored by the festival. Each participant was supposed to pick one of two Azerbaijani *mugham*s, either *Garabagh Shikastasi* or *Bayati Shiraz.* The musician or musicians would then present their chosen *mugham* in a new, original interpretation that showcased the distinctive features and integrity of their regional musical tradition (e.g., Uzbek *shashmaqom,* Iranian *destgah*). The Salaam group chose *Garabagh Shikastasi.* According to El Saffar, "We changed the beat from the regular duple to the irregular $\frac{10}{8}$ which is typical for Iraqi music and is divided as 3 + 2 + 2 + 3. We also changed the tonic back a quarter tone and replaced the original words with . . . [an] Iraqi poem." El Saffar summarized her impressions from the festival thus, "I walked away with the feeling that music in Azerbaijan is greatly supported by a government that has very high standards for its development. And I know that many musicians who came to Baku from different countries truly enjoyed such a great occasion to play and share their music."[7] Indeed, *mugham* is more than a form and a genre of music in Azerbaijan these days. As a musical expression of the national identity of Azerbaijanis, it is an object of governmental care, which now facilitates new opportunities for the genre's development and promotion in the international arena.

COMPOSED MUSIC: TO BE CONTINUED

The very first response among Azerbaijani composers to the breakup of the Soviet Union was probably the same as in any other Soviet republic: shock caused by the collapse of the strong system of governmental support for all music activities. The shock was also provoked by a "shift of identity": Azerbaijani composers had to cope with the fact that they were not representing the musical culture of the vast Soviet empire; they were now citizens of a small country with an unstable economy and an unsettled political situation involving a territorial and military conflict. As a result, the early 1990s were marked by a low productivity among native composers. But their creativity never stopped completely. The following figures are quite telling: in 2007, the Eighth Assembly of the Union of Composers of Azerbaijan presented 102 works written by eighty composers between the years 1990 and 2007.

Several new trends manifested themselves instantly. First, composers started exploring previously obscured layers of their cultural heritage, such as archaic forms of folklore and religious subjects (some such works were discussed in chapter 6). Native composers did not confine their explorations to Islamic roots, showing the interfaith tolerance of Azerbaijani culture. Farhad Badalbeyli wrote the romance *Ave Maria* in which the first verse is based on a canonic Catholic text and the second is written in the Azerbaijani language. The melodic material for both is identical, symbolizing the unity of religions and cultures on earth (PURL 9.4).

Azer Dadashov (b. 1946), who wrote a cycle of five arias-prayers, demonstrates a similar concept. These arias include two pieces based on the canonic texts of *Alleluia* and *Ave Maria* and have three pieces based on Azerbaijani texts written by the composer himself. The cycle was performed during the visit of the Roma Pope John Paul II in Baku in May 2002. Dadashov interpreted the religious subjects and religious texts in an all-humanistic way, although it is clear that they are penned by an Azerbaijani composer. I have my own story of encounter with this repertoire. In May 2011, I suggested that one of the five arias, titled "Thank You," be performed in Bloomington, Indiana, in the framework of the project Abraham's Children: A Prayer for Peace. I had the honor of being a part of this endeavor in the capacity of the pianist and arranger. Abraham's Children was initiated by the Turkish tenor Omer Turkmenoglu and aimed to show the unity and integrity of all religions on earth. Dadashov's "Thank You" was the only piece of spiritual repertoire representing the composed music tradition of the Muslim world.

Patriotic subjects also have increased their presence in the post-1990 works of Azerbaijani composers. Glorifying Azerbaijan, its nature, its history, and its people is not a new trend, as such pieces appeared in abundance during the Soviet era. But the tragic events around Garabagh strengthened patriotic sentiments and added new nuances to the depiction of patriotic topics. Azerbaijani

composers have penned numerous works inspired by and associated with Garabagh. Some of them present the topic in an allegorical way. For example, the
opera *Longing* (2008) by Frangiz Alizade, with a libretto by Nargiz Pashayeva,
depicts a struggle between good and evil that may be read as a protest against
any war. Together with the poet Ramiz Duyghun, the composer Vasif Adigozalov, whose family roots are in Garabagh, created the song "Lullaby for Shusha"
(1992) immediately after Armenian military forces occupied Shusha. This is
a tragic, lamenting lullaby in the mode *shur*. Love and tenderness are mixed
with pain and sadness, and the border between dream and death is obscured
(PURL 9.5).

Adigozalov also composed two heroic works related to Garabagh: the oratorio *Garabagh Shikastasi* (1989), which is a choral rendition of the original
mugham, and the opera *Natavan* (2002), dedicated to Khurshud Banu Natavan
(1832–1897), a poetess and a female ruler of Garabagh in the nineteenth century.
In addition to Adigozalov's opera, Natavan is depicted in the lyrical ballet *Journey to the Caucasus* (2005) by Agshin Alizade, which describes Natavan's real
historical meeting with the French writer Alexandre Dumas in 1858.[8]

In the early 1990s, in the chaotic transitional period, some Azerbaijani
composers left the country – some for Turkey, others for Russia, Germany, and
the United States. In the first years of the new millennium, my Western colleagues often referred to the departure of the leading Azerbaijani composers
from their home country as a sign of unfavorable conditions and an unpromis-
ing future for Azerbaijani composed music. I could hardly deny this. Nonetheless, in less than a decade, the situation changed radically. Some of the national
composers living abroad have established a flexible work schedule, allowing
them to come and visit Azerbaijan on a regular basis. Among them is Faraj
Garayev, who lives in Moscow and teaches at the Moscow State Conservatory,
yet maintains professional and personal ties with Azerbaijan and its musicians.
Quite symbolically, in November 2009, F. Garayev's Violin Concerto premiered
in Switzerland, and two years later, the work was presented in Baku. This composition has immediately been recognized as among the highest recent accomplishments of Azerbaijani music.

Other composers returned to Azerbaijan and settled there. For example,
F. Alizade came to Azerbaijan after fifteen years of work in Turkey and Germany (1992–2007), and she accepted the position of the chair of the Union of
Azerbaijani Composers. Return to Azerbaijan did not interrupt the intense collaboration with the Western musicians that she had established while residing
abroad. In May 2011, the Houston Grand Opera premiered F. Alizade's opera
Your Name Means "Sea." The opera was a commission of the "Song of Houston:

East + West" project. The opera focuses on the story of two young people: Denise, an American female painter, and Seymur, a male singer from Azerbaijan. The opera's title refers to the female protagonist: Azerbaijanis have a similar name, Deniz, which literally means "sea." In F. Alizade's instrumentation, the combination of a Western string quartet and flute with the instruments of a *mugham* trio creates a powerful dialogue of cultures.

Azerbaijani composed music has passed the Rubicon that separated the Soviet and post-Soviet periods from the new stage in its history. New generations of Azerbaijani composers have come into the arena, and their main accomplishments date to the post-Soviet era. Elmir Mirzayev (b. 1970) was probably the first composer to chart this new path. A student of F. Garayev and devoted follower of postmodernism, he penned numerous works performed at and commissioned by prestigious international festivals around the globe. I witnessed the success of his composition *Fayum Portraits* (2004) at the festival Icebreaker III: The Caucasus, which took place in Seattle in 2006. Aliya Mammadova (b. 1973) wrote String Quartet, which earned her the laureateship at the First International Jurgenson Competition of Young Composers in Moscow in 2001. Firudin Allahverdi (b. 1980) composed the chamber piece *Paradoxes,* which was selected as the best from among nearly five hundred compositions at the International Contest l'Art in Switzerland in 2008. Turkar Gasimzade (b. 1988) won First Prize at the 2010 International Contest in Melbourne, Australia, for his piano composition *Vu Cumpra.* Ayaz Gambarli (b. 1984) wrote *Methode de Sens* (The Method of Sensuality) for nine performers, which won the ALEA III International Composition Prize in Boston in 2011. Gambarli's piece was one of six selected in the semifinals from among 208 submissions. This array of facts helps clarify another question that I have been asked and had difficulty answering more than a decade ago – a question about the very existence of younger generations of Azerbaijani composers. Today those generations are a reality. And the impressive accomplishments of young composers point to the new state of Azerbaijani composed music, a tradition that has survived many historical ordeals and continues into the twenty-first century.

JAZZ AND POPULAR MUSIC

Azerbaijani jazz is now experiencing perhaps its greatest period to date. The Azerbaijani national tradition, in which improvisation is so fundamental, is developing in ever-increasing contact with the West, creating an ideal situation in which jazz can flourish. The country's current music scene is very jazz-oriented. Azerbaijani jazz musicians participate at prestigious international events, as proved by the victorious presence of Shahin Novrasli and Isfar Sarabski at the celebrated Jazz Festival in Montreux, Switzerland in 2007 and 2009, respectively. Aziza, the daughter of Vagif Mustafazade, the father of "jazz *mugham*," visited Azerbaijan in 2007 after a long absence. She has made several appearances since then, including her March 2010 performance in Baku at the extravagant celebration of her father's seventieth birthday.

Popular music is also in the spotlight these days, although for different reasons. Immediately after the collapse of the Soviet Union, popular music was caught up in a growing culture of commercialization. In this environment, a number of composers and performers emerged in the country, many of them with poor professional skills and questionable artistic taste. Songs were written and performed with rather shallow lyrics and unschooled arrangements. This problem was common throughout post-Soviet pop music and was the result of what MacFadyen indicated to be "untutored upbringing."[9] The situation began to improve in the middle of the first decade of the twenty-first century. Today popular music in Azerbaijan is eclectic and highly variable in quality, but in general composers, performers, directors, and producers work to meet the world-accepted standards of the show business.

The two stories that follow are very different, yet they show the competitiveness of Azerbaijani popular music in the global scene. The first tale is about a popular song written by a national composer. This song traveled around the world, being contextualized within various diverse and distinct musical traditions. The second story is about Azerbaijan's victory at the Eurovision song contest in 2011. That victory demonstrated the ability of Azerbaijani music to become integrated into the scope of European popular music.

"BAYATI": A WORLDWIDE JOURNEY

The song "Bayati" by Eldar Mansurov (b. 1952), with lyrics by Vahid Aziz, premiered on the Azerbaijan state TV channel on May 1, 1989. Quickly the song gained enormous popularity in its cover version by the singer Brilliant Dadashova (PURL 9.6). Despite the song's national popularity, nobody realized at that point that "Bayati" would soon make a journey around the globe, receiving dozens of new renditions that revealed its previously hidden artistic potential.

In 1991, Mansurov's song had its first performance outside of Azerbaijan thanks to the group Ashkhabad, from Turkmenistan. Subsequently, Ashkhabad's instrumental arrangement of Mansurov's song drew the attention of the record label Real World, founded by the pop star Peter Gabriel, and was included in two albums, *The City of Love* and *A Week or Two in the Real World*.[10]

Later, this version of the Azerbaijani song became part of the soundtrack for *Promises,* a 2001 documentary about the Israeli-Palestinian conflict. *Promises* won an Emmy award in 2001 and was successfully screened at festivals worldwide.

Germany became the next destination on the Azerbaijani song's journey. In 1998, the German brass band Grinsteins Mischpoche (now renamed as Bakhshish brass band) presented a new version of "Bayati," which they later included in their album *On Air.*[11] In this arrangement, the song was transformed into the style of the group's Balkan-Klezmer repertoire. Mansurov's song eventually began to appear under different titles and even with new lyrics. For example, in a Russian version performed by the singer Reno in 1992, with new lyrics by Nikolay Denisov, the song was renamed "Hello!" It was still a lyrical song, but the text had no reference to the original Azerbaijani poetic source.

A similar transformation occurred in the version that Sezen Aksu, the queen of Turkish pop, performed in 1996. Again, Mansurov's song appeared with new lyrics and under a new title, "Cruel." This version of the song appeared in Aksu's album *Dush Bahcheleri* (Dream Gardens).[12] The Azerbaijani song also inspired other Turkish pop musicians, including the singer Levent Yuksel and the rock-group Chalar Saat, who presented their own versions of "Bayati" in 1996 and 2006. Mansurov's piece traveled to Greece, where it appeared on the singer Keti Garbi's 2003 album *Emmones Idees* (Obsessive Ideas) under the title "Only You."[13] In 2004, "Bayati" moved to Brazil – the song's most distant destination both in terms of geography and style – with an avant-garde jazz rendition by the Orquestra Popular de Câmara and the singer Monica Salmaso.[14] Finally, "Bayati" has become a part of disco culture across the Mediterranean: techno remixes have been produced by Huseyin Karadayi and DJ Funky C from Turkey (*Miracles,* 2006) and by DJ Pantelis from Greece (*I Have a Dream,* 2008). DJ Pantelis's remix includes a sound clip from Dr. Martin Luther King Jr.'s speech in which he articulated those famous words (PURL 9.7).

As a result of this worldwide journey, Mansurov's "Bayati" now exists in more than twenty versions. It is hard to imagine a more Azerbaijani song. Its text is based on the form of folk poetry called *bayati,* discussed in chapter 6, and its rather simple melody draws on the typical patterns of the Azerbaijani mode *shur.* This is unsurprising, for Mansurov, a prolific songwriter and the son of the outstanding master of *mugham,* the *tar* performer Bahram Mansurov (1911–1985), has always been extremely dedicated to the Azerbaijani musical tradition in his songs. In the meantime, the journey of Mansurov's song points toward the many hidden layers of cultural and musical influences on Azerbaijani music that came to light in the new arrangements created in different parts of the globe. The Turkish adaptations showcased the Turkic component of the musical style of Azerbaijani song. This style was present in the arrangement in which Mansurov imitated the timbre of the Turkish *saz,* an instrument that is slightly different from its Azerbaijani counterpart both in construction and in timbre. The Turkic qualities, consequently, facilitated the Greek and German (in fact, Balkan-Klezmer) versions of the song, since Turkic music serves as a bridge to other Mediterranean musical traditions. The smoothness of the Russian version was stimulated by the long-standing integration of Azerbaijani popular music into the context of Soviet *estrada.* Finally, the Brazilian version fused the modal and improvisational nature of the song with parallel features in jazz.

Quite unexpectedly and due to its complicated story, "Bayati" became an indicator of the multicultural essence of Azerbaijani music. The fate of "Bayati" also brought to light the problem of limited copyright protection for Azerbaijani musicians and poets in the 1990s and in the first decade of the new millennium. Neither Mansurov nor Aziz were necessarily credited as authors in the new releases of this song, and they could not even claim their rights. Changes in titles and lyrics also occurred without their knowledge or permission. The situation has improved in the 2010s, when rules and regulations were drafted and adopted in Azerbaijan to protect intellectual property.

WINNING EUROVISION

In 2011, Azerbaijan became the winner of the annual Eurovision Song Contest, which Bohlman characterizes as "the single largest popular-song competition on an international level," recognized as "a sort of Olympics of popular song."[15] Azerbaijan first participated in the competition in 2008, and the country's fourth annual appearance secured its victory: the duo of Ell and Nikki (Eldar Gasimov and Nigar Jamal), with the song "Running Scared," was acknowledged as the winner from among forty-three participants.

The *New York Times* called it a "surprise victory" from a country "technically located in Asia."[16] Azerbaijan's alignment with European culture through this contest was, however, in the spirit of Eurovision, as the contest "has always pushed at the international boundaries of Europe, attracting Eastern European [and] ... Mediterranean nations ... and making gestures toward racial and ethnic inclusivity."[17] Azerbaijan happened to be the first nation-state from Transcaucasia to win this competition.

This historical victory was the result of hard work, carefully selected repertoire, and shrewd presentation strategy. The choice of repertoire entailed a dilemma: the song representing Azerbaijan could be either prominently Eastern or Western. Judging from the history of the contest, the latter identification has always been more successful, since it is a means to assert the idea of European unity. Besides, most of the winning entries featured the same, fairly generic European popular music style. Nonetheless, Azerbaijan tried both choices. In 2008, the duo of Elnur and Samir (Elnur Huseynov and Samir Javadzade) performed the song "Day by Day" by the native composer Govhar Hasanzade and lyricist Zahra Badalbeyli. It was written in a rock music style with a short quasi-*mugham* cadence at the end. Azerbaijan placed eighth in 2008, which was quite a success for their first appearance.

However, the country's ambitions were higher, and for the 2009 contest, a different Eastern strategy was chosen. The song "Always," written by well-known Swedish songwriter of Iranian and Azerbaijani decent, Arash and performed by him and Azerbaijani singer Aysel Teymurzade, had a strong ethnic component in it (Arash even held the *tar* and pretended to play it at the end). Despite winning third place – a coveted honor – Azerbaijan returned to the Western strategy in 2010, with the song itself being composed by European songwriters. Safura performed "Drip Drop," written by the Swedish team of Anders Bagge and Stefan Orn, with lyrics by Sandra Bjurman. This was a typical Eurovision song, and Safura placed fifth.

The 2011 performance was the summary of all previous experiences. "Running Scared," presented by Ell and Nikki, was written by the same Swedish team of authors, who used the style of old-fashioned European pop music ballads. Stylistically, this song has no Eastern references, recalling the 2010 performance, and the duo format corresponded with that of the 2008 and 2009 performances. The presentation was also "spiced" with nontraditional gender roles, combining a young, tender, and romantic male with a strong and savvy female (in real life, a mother-of-two). In sum, Azerbaijan's victory, in addition to resulting from professional performance, excellent ensemble skills, and impressive stage image, was also achieved through careful study of Eurovision's cultural priorities.

Azerbaijan's smooth integration into Eurovision and, within a short period of time, the country's achieving the contest's top award, has left its mark in the East-West dynamic of Azerbaijani music and culture. It shows that Azerbaijan is neither a stranger nor a provincial on the European pop scene. There is no doubt that "Running Scared" is more of an "export product" than a reflection of the national style of Azerbaijani music. It is, nonetheless, evident that as an example of contemporary pop music, the song is an organic part of the Azerbaijani soundscape. Ell and Nikki also demonstrated how easily Azerbaijanis combine the popular music of the West with their national music roots. At the press conference in Dusseldorf, Germany, that took place after their victory, they zestfully performed a famous Azerbaijani folk song.

NEW TRENDS IN EDUCATION

The era of independence has transformed music education in Azerbaijan. The curricula of the major music schools have switched from the Russian-Soviet model toward the so-called Bologna system that aims to ensure comparability with the standards and quality of higher education qualifications throughout Europe and, overall, the Western world. Westernization has become a stronger force at the country's leading music school – the Baku Music Academy. Undergraduate and graduate programs have replaced the five-year degrees established during the Soviet era. Russian music has taken its proper place in the context of the history of Western music, and classes related to jazz are included in the curriculum. True knowledge of Western music finally has been welcomed, a change that has occurred due to many factors, including strengthened international exchange. According to Farhad Badalbeyli, rector of the academy since 1991, "The Academy has acquired many more vehicles to 'export' and 'import' music. Our students and teachers finally had an opportunity to discuss freely, for instance, the ways of interpretation of Ravel or Debussy with French colleagues, in contrast to earlier times when we thought that only [the] Soviet school was doing things right."[18] The list of guest professors who have given recitals, master classes, and lectures at the Music Academy since 1991 is quite impressive and comparable to the number and the reputation of the occasions on which Azerbaijani students and faculty members have traveled abroad. The Eastern half of the synthesis also has increased its presence in music instruction. The historical and theoretical classes related to Azerbaijani music have earned the status of being one of the fundamental elements in the curriculum. Research on the historical past of Azerbaijani music, including the role of religion, neglected genres, and forgotten musical instruments, is now central to the activities of native scholars.

In 1991, the Laboratory on Reconstruction and Development of Azerbaijan's Ancient Musical Instruments, led by the ethnomusicologist Majnun Karimov, opened at the Baku Music Academy. Despite being small and modestly equipped, this laboratory soon demonstrated both its theoretical and practical importance to Azerbaijani musical culture. On the basis of his research, later published as a book, Karimov restored many previously forgotten instruments, such as the *chang*, a harp-like plucked stringed instrument; the *chegane*, a bowed string; and the *barbat,* a pear-shaped lute.[19] As the journalist Jean Patterson has rightfully indicated, "He has literally pieced together a portion of Azerbaijani musical history by recreating some of these ancient instruments."[20] Karimov later formed the State Ensemble of Ancient Music Instruments whose performances, now under the guidance of the virtuoso *kemancha* player Munis Sharifov, are an important part of the country's musical life (PURL 9.8).

In response to the growing interest in Eastern music, a new institution, the Azerbaijan National Conservatory, was established in 2000. The curriculum of this school focuses on traditional music, although it includes classes on Western music theory and history. The composer Siyavush Karimi, the rector of the newly created institution, envisions it as a resurrection of Hajibeyli's idea of a school focusing on the national music, which he had wanted in the 1920s.[21] Nowadays, the Music Academy and the National Conservatory are responsible for providing a new balance between Western and Eastern components in the field of education.

The present-day status of Azerbaijani music is constantly changing. The main concern of the early 1990s – that of reshaping Azerbaijani music in a prevalently nationalistic way – is no longer an important part of the cultural agenda. The national ingredient of Azerbaijani music flourishes and grows under the most favorable conditions. The Western component has had multiple stimuli for its development as well. An example from Azerbaijan's current music scene showcases these dynamics. The country's two highly accomplished classical pianists (and my former students in the music history class at the Baku Music Academy), Murad Adigozalzade (b. 1973) and Murad Huseynov (b. 1973), both graduated from the Baku Music Academy and later continued their studies in Russia and France, respectively (PURL 9.9 and PURL 9.10). In the first decade of the new millennium, they were assigned the headship of Baku's two central concert venues: Adigozalzade became the director of the Azerbaijan State Philharmonic Hall, and Huseynov of the International Mugham Center. It is very telling that these classical pianists, whose studies and careers started in Azerbaijan in the 1990s, are still equally competent in the fields of Western classical music and traditional Azerbaijani music, just as were many generations of national musicians preceding them. And this affects the repertoire policy of the institutions they are now leading. The Philharmonic Hall may host a concert of traditional music, while the Mugham Center may serve as a venue for jazz gigs.

I am far from having created a rosy picture of the contemporary state of music in Azerbaijan. The present reality poses numerous challenges for native musicians. Music schools are dealing with various problems related to the radical changes in curricula, and these require time and effort to be resolved. Non-sufficient technological support and the lack of textbooks in the Azerbaijani language are serious problems as well. But Azerbaijani musicians – both native and Western classical – continue their path. Composers write new works. Parents bring their children to Baku from the remote villages to study *mugham* with the masters of this genre and to participate in festivals and competitions. And the number of children studying Western classical music in public music schools is extremely high. Music is an object of particular governmental care, and preserving the variety of cultural forms is a priority. The newly opened state-supported TV channel Madaniyyat (Culture) broadcasts concerts of various genres of music, including traditional *mugham* and *ashig* art, classical music from the West and Azerbaijan, and jazz. All these are evidence that the tree planted by Hajibeyli more than a hundred years ago is still alive, growing, and thriving.

10 *"MUGHAM* OPERA" OF THE SILK ROAD

If something in the country is so fantastic, and people are
proud of it, then it becomes a part of the world. I think this
is what happened to Hajibeyli's *Leyli and Majnun.*

YO-YO MA, interview with the author

"WE HAVE ALL BECOME MAJNUN FOR *LAYLA AND MAJNUN!*"

This book opened with a discussion of *Leyli and Majnun,* the *"mugham* opera" created by Uzeyir Hajibeyli in 1908 that marked the beginning of the composed music tradition in Azerbaijan. Symbolically, the last chapter of this book is also about this opera, now reimagined in the twenty-first century, thousands of miles away from Azerbaijan, and integrated into contemporary soundscapes. Under the artistic direction of the world-renowned cellist Yo-Yo Ma, in 2007, the Silk Road Ensemble created a new chamber version of Hajibeyli's opera. This arrangement was titled *Layla and Majnun,* following the pronunciation of the heroine's name in Arabic culture, in which this ancient legend had originated. From 2007 to 2009, *Layla and Majnun* was a highlight of the Silk Road Ensemble's repertoire and was introduced to audiences in North America, Europe, and Asia.[1] According to Yo-Yo Ma, "This is a project in which we all had a deep personal and emotional investment. It occupies a very large place in what the ensemble has done. I am so amazed and pleased every time I hear and participate in it."[2] As Colin Jacobsen, an ensemble member, humorously said, punning on the meaning of the hero's name, "We have all become Majnun [crazy] for *Layla and Majnun!*"[3] As a participant in this project, I experienced this unique atmosphere and deep involvement that permeated every development session. Several factors – the inspiring presence of *mugham* and the master *mugham* performer, Alim Gasimov; the beauty of Hajibeyli's music; and the deepness of Fuzuli's poetry – contributed to shaping this intense artistic milieu. But the main reason for this undertaking's success was the aesthetic and stylistic concept of Hajibeyli's opera, which resonates with the philosophy of the Silk Road Project. Yo-Yo Ma launched the Silk Road Project in 1998 to reflect his vision of music as a global phenomenon in which various forms, genres, and styles are strongly tied together across history and cultures. The very term *Silk Road* is used as a metaphor for ongoing cross-cultural exchange between the Western and non-Western worlds. The musical works that the Silk Road Ensemble has commissioned and performed represent a variety of styles and create a picture of an integrated, yet diverse world. Hajibeyli's opera provided many possibilities for undertaking such musical and cultural synthesis. This is why, when Gasimov advanced the idea of creating a new arrangement of Hajibeyli's work, the Silk Road Project members met the proposal with great interest. Yo-Yo Ma explains the rationale for including Azerbaijani compositions in the Silk Road Ensemble's repertoire thus: "Everything we are exploring is in fact the incredible combination of many different things to make something unique and spectacular. Hajibeyli wrote this at such a remarkably young age, and it is so wonderful that Alim Qasimov [Gasimov] suggested that we try to make sense of this in our time and see what can happen" (YYM).

Gasimov has been a part of the Silk Road Ensemble's projects since 2000, first through the composition *Darvish* by Frangiz Alizade, in which Gasimov performed an extensive *mugham* solo.[4] He was intimately familiar with Hajibeyli's opera, as he had been involved in its productions in Baku in the 1980s. Gasimov regularly performed the role of Majnun with the Azerbaijan State Opera and Ballet Theater, although he was never satisfied with this experience. As the singer explained, these productions focused on and exaggerated just one side of Majnun, that is, the madness leading to his death. Meanwhile, the story's complex, multilayered meaning related to Sufi philosophy was ignored. Such an interpretation was expected, since the Soviet aesthetic ideologues would barely sanction any religious ideas being directly expressed in a work of art. Gasimov suffered under such a distortion of the true meaning of the story. "Sometimes I even stayed in the theater, and after everybody left, sang my part onstage in an empty hall the way I envisioned it," he admitted.[5] For his Silk Road work, Gasimov selected the portions of Hajibeyli's score that focus on Majnun's solo and duo scenes with Leyli, the main heroine, who was performed by Gasimov's daughter and student, Fargana Gasimova. The Silk Road Ensemble members Jonathan Gandelsman and Colin Jacobsen, both violinists, created a score based on this selection, and in August 2007, the group met at the Academie

FIGURE 10.1. The Silk Road Ensemble with Yo-Yo Ma. *Photo © David O'Connor.*

Musicale de Villecroze, France, for the first development session. The decisive stage of project, however, took place during the Silk Road Ensemble's residency at Harvard University in November 2007. That week in Harvard focused on the story of Layla and Majnun and its cultural role in Eastern literature and visual arts. It crystallized the group's priorities and clarified their remaining questions regarding the new arrangement of Hajibeyli's opera. According to Yo-Yo Ma, "For the Ensemble and for me personally, that may have been the moment when we became captivated by the work and by the idea" (YYM). All further meetings and performances enhanced and modified but never significantly changed the concept of the new *Layla and Majnun.*

WHY HAJIBEYLI'S OPERA?

Despite its seeming naivety, the concept of Hajibeyli's *Leyli and Majnun* draws on a vast array of Eastern and Western traditions and contains many coded messages of universal applicability, which facilitated the opera's being so naturally reshaped into a new entity. In this work, Hajibeyli combined two cultural treasures of Central Asia and the Middle East – namely, the story of Layla and

Majnun and the genre of *mugham* – and integrated these two sources within an operatic format, thus creating a link with the Western world. The story of the two ill-fated young lovers has long been widely spread among the Turks, Arabs, Persians, Indians, Pakistanis, and Afghans. Known in many poetic renditions, this story has also affected visual arts, literature, cinema, and music. Musical embodiments of Layla and Majnun appear in a variety of genres and national traditions, showing the story's continuing popularity.[6] Hajibeyli's opera – chronologically the first musical interpretation of the ancient legend in composed music – was based on *mugham,* a phenomenon shared, like the story itself, by many regional traditions. As such, this opera had rich multicultural possibilities, which Hajibeyli only partly realized. The Silk Road Ensemble revealed this potential to its fullest extent and expanded it further to the East and to the West. They rearranged the existing chronological, cultural, musical, and aesthetic layers of the opera's concept and added new ones, thus making an old composition part of the modern – and global – soundscape.

Nevertheless, this new version continues to resonate with the Azerbaijani musical tradition. The ensemble's careful and respectful approach to Hajibeyli's original was ensured by the fact that each feature of the new arrangement was confirmed with Gasimov. As Yo-Yo Ma explains it, "Obviously, we were outsiders. That's why we needed Alim's guidance and his approbation, as it led us to what would be acceptable within his tradition. If we went too far, he would guide us back onto the path; his direction gave us the confidence and courage to continue" (YYM). Indeed, Gasimov was an ideal mediator in this process. He is an outstanding master of *mugham,* possessing an in-depth knowledge of this tradition. At the same time, Gasimov is a musician known for his innovative approach toward tradition and is open to experimenting with it. His expertise contributed to creating a stylistically and aesthetically consistent work. Gasimov adjusted his own (and other Azerbaijani musicians') input in accordance with the new aesthetic and stylistic context. Meanwhile, he ensured that the Silk Road Ensemble's ideas resonated with the paradigms of Hajibeyli's opera and Azerbaijani music as a whole.

FROM THE OPERA TO A CHAMBER PIECE

In the interpretation of the Silk Road Ensemble, the story of Layla and Majnun is presented in a condensed version: the three-and-a-half-hour-long opera has been squeezed into a forty-five-minute chamber piece. The five acts are rearranged into six parts. These changes have resulted in a reordering and even an omission of many operatic episodes. The following chart visualizes the major

FIGURE 10.2. Alim Gasimov. *Photo by Aida Huseynova.*

compositional changes that occurred in the process of turning the opera into its chamber arrangement.

The most significant modifications are concentrated in the closing part of the opera. These alterations ultimately highlight the story's time-honored messages. The tale of Layla and Majnun has a strong Sufi component, according to which the love between a man and woman is a reflection of love for God. The death resulting from separation from the beloved is a supreme fulfillment, as it takes the individual into the divine. The Silk Road Ensemble acquired this understanding of the story thanks to Dr. Ali Asani, Harvard Professor of the Practice of Indo-Muslim Languages and Culture. In his lecture "*Layla and Majnun: A Classic Arabian Romeo and Juliet*," presented during the ensemble's Harvard residency, Dr. Asani elaborated on these hidden meanings of the tale.

Table 10.1. Comparative chart of the dramaturgical composition of the Hajibeyli's opera and its new arrangement created by the Silk Road Ensemble

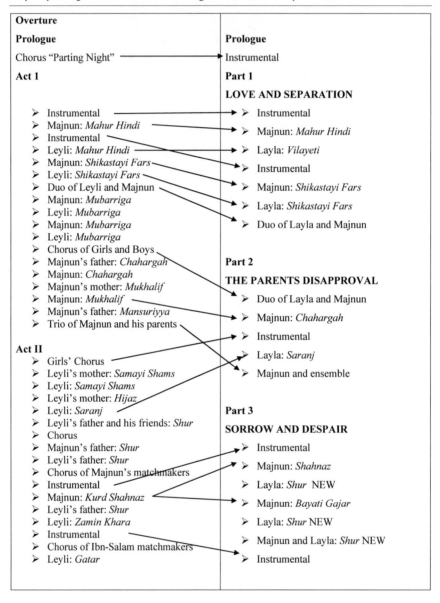

Overture	
Prologue	Prologue
Chorus "Parting Night" ──────────→	Instrumental
Act 1	**Part 1**
	LOVE AND SEPARATION
➤ Instrumental ──────────→	➤ Instrumental
➤ Majnun: *Mahur Hindi*	➤ Majnun: *Mahur Hindi*
➤ Instrumental	➤ Layla: *Vilayeti*
➤ Leyli: *Mahur Hindi*	➤ Instrumental
➤ Majnun: *Shikastayi Fars*	➤ Majnun: *Shikastayi Fars*
➤ Leyli: *Shikastayi Fars*	➤ Layla: *Shikastayi Fars*
➤ Duo of Leyli and Majnun	➤ Duo of Layla and Majnun
➤ Majnun: *Mubarriga*	
➤ Leyli: *Mubarriga*	
➤ Majnun: *Mubarriga*	
➤ Leyli: *Mubarriga*	
➤ Chorus of Girls and Boys	**Part 2**
➤ Majnun's father: *Chahargah*	**THE PARENTS DISAPPROVAL**
➤ Majnun: *Chahargah*	➤ Duo of Layla and Majnun
➤ Majnun's mother: *Mukhalif*	➤ Majnun: *Chahargah*
➤ Majnun: *Mukhalif*	➤ Instrumental
➤ Majnun's father: *Mansuriyya*	➤ Layla: *Saranj*
➤ Trio of Majnun and his parents	➤ Majnun and ensemble
Act II	
➤ Girls' Chorus	
➤ Leyli's mother: *Samayi Shams*	
➤ Leyli: *Samayi Shams*	
➤ Leyli's mother: *Hijaz*	**Part 3**
➤ Leyli: *Saranj*	**SORROW AND DESPAIR**
➤ Leyli's father and his friends: *Shur*	
➤ Chorus	➤ Instrumental
➤ Majnun's father: *Shur*	➤ Majnun: *Shahnaz*
➤ Leyli's father: *Shur*	➤ Layla: *Shur* NEW
➤ Chorus of Majnun's matchmakers	➤ Majnun: *Bayati Gajar*
➤ Instrumental	➤ Layla: *Shur* NEW
➤ Majnun: *Kurd Shahnaz*	➤ Majnun and Layla: *Shur* NEW
➤ Leyli's father: *Shur*	➤ Instrumental
➤ Leyli: *Zamin Khara*	
➤ Instrumental	
➤ Chorus of Ibn-Salam matchmakers	
➤ Leyli: *Gatar*	

If a line on the column on the left doesn't have an arrow point to the right, the respective episode from the opera is omitted in the new version.

Table 10.1. (*cont.*) Comparative chart of the dramaturgical composition of the Hajibeyli's opera and its new arrangement created by the Silk Road Ensemble

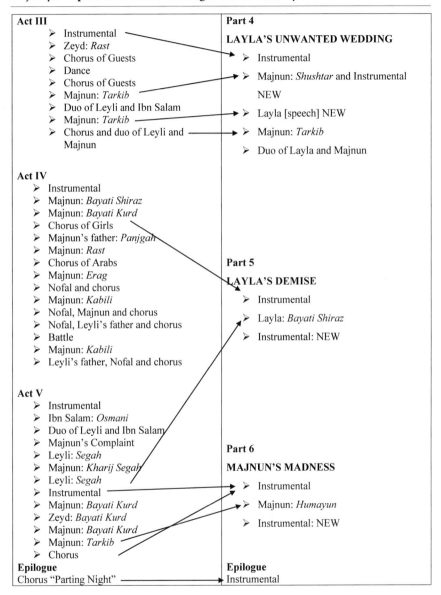

Act III	Part 4
➤ Instrumental	**LAYLA'S UNWANTED WEDDING**
➤ Zeyd: *Rast*	
➤ Chorus of Guests	➤ Instrumental
➤ Dance	
➤ Chorus of Guests	➤ Majnun: *Shushtar* and Instrumental
➤ Majnun: *Tarkib*	NEW
➤ Duo of Leyli and Ibn Salam	
➤ Majnun: *Tarkib*	➤ Layla [speech] NEW
➤ Chorus and duo of Leyli and Majnun	➤ Majnun: *Tarkib*
	➤ Duo of Layla and Majnun

Act IV
- ➤ Instrumental
- ➤ Majnun: *Bayati Shiraz*
- ➤ Majnun: *Bayati Kurd*
- ➤ Chorus of Girls
- ➤ Majnun's father: *Panjgah*
- ➤ Majnun: *Rast*
- ➤ Chorus of Arabs
- ➤ Majnun: *Erag*
- ➤ Nofal and chorus
- ➤ Majnun: *Kabili*
- ➤ Nofal, Majnun and chorus
- ➤ Nofal, Leyli's father and chorus
- ➤ Battle
- ➤ Majnun: *Kabili*
- ➤ Leyli's father, Nofal and chorus

Part 5

LAYLA'S DEMISE
- ➤ Instrumental
- ➤ Layla: *Bayati Shiraz*
- ➤ Instrumental: NEW

Act V
- ➤ Instrumental
- ➤ Ibn Salam: *Osmani*
- ➤ Duo of Leyli and Ibn Salam
- ➤ Majnun's Complaint
- ➤ Leyli: *Segah*
- ➤ Majnun: *Kharij Segah*
- ➤ Leyli: *Segah*
- ➤ Instrumental
- ➤ Majnun: *Bayati Kurd*
- ➤ Zeyd: *Bayati Kurd*
- ➤ Majnun: *Bayati Kurd*
- ➤ Majnun: *Tarkib*
- ➤ Chorus

Part 6

MAJNUN'S MADNESS
- ➤ Instrumental
- ➤ Majnun: *Humayun*
- ➤ Instrumental: NEW

Epilogue
Chorus "Parting Night"

Epilogue
Instrumental

Yo-Yo Ma acknowledged Dr. Asani's input, saying: "He made a huge change in the way we were thinking of the story. Before hearing him talk about it, we were viewing the death of Layla and Majnun as a tragedy, and we were associating it with sadness. Professor Asani explained to us that their death is a glorious moment because it becomes an expression of the transcendent love" (YYM).

This new vision has shaped the musical dramaturgy and, overall, the musical contents of the new arrangement of the ancient story. In Hajibeyli's opera, the idea of separation and death as a supreme fulfillment was conveyed through the chorus "Night of Separation," which opens and concludes the work. This episode, which was analyzed in chapter 4, can be compared to a Greek chorus because it comments on events before they occur in the narrative. Reconstituting the chorus as Yo-Yo Ma's cello solo, both at the beginning and at the end of the piece, is one of the new arrangement's most insightful interpretations: the lonely melody of cello sounds as a voice of eternity.

Before the final "Night of Separation," a new episode has been added to accentuate this magnificent moment of unification of Layla and Majnun: the solo of the *shakuhachi,* a Japanese end-blown flute. Kojiro Umezaki plays this instrument, characterizing his solo as "a musical equivalent for rising above oneself." He continues, "Where both Layla and Majnun go, is a place of fulfillment. It was important to achieve it musically and to have some kind of an uplifting closure."[7] Gasimov instantly approved of the idea of adding the solo of the *shakuhachi* in the new version of Hajibeyli's opera. This decision again indicated the deep connection among the Silk Road cultures. The *shakuhachi,* which is a ritualistic instrument in Zen Buddhist practices, has many relatives along the Silk Road. One such relative is the *ney,* an instrument common to Sufi rituals in Azerbaijan and elsewhere. Accordingly, the use of the *shakuhachi* was highly appropriate and responded to the Sufi meanings of the story and Hajibeyli's opera. In its improvised nature, this solo also parallels the *mugham* tradition. According to Umezaki, "I am converting from the introspective state of mind to the outward. At a strictly musical level, I go moment by moment. You are supposed to lose yourself, and you cannot do that if you are planning ahead. I think that *mugham* is about moment-to-moment decision-making, too."[8] This penetrating statement speaks of the philosophy of the Silk Road Project in general: musical expressions coming from different parts of the world reflect universal means of creativity and carry culturally transcendent messages (PURL 10.1).

The idea to include this solo affected the choice of *mughams* used at the end of the arrangement. In Hajibeyli's opera, the heroine died with the glorious *Segah,* and the hero with the tragic *Tarkib.* The composer's choice thus adequately depicted the glory of fulfilled love and the pain of physical death. In the new version, Gasimov decided to use the melancholic *Bayati Shiraz* for Layla's final expression and to employ *Humayun*, the most sorrowful *mugham*, for the end of Majnun's part. Both *mughams* convey the sadness of physical death, while the *shakuhachi* solo expresses the overarching meaning of the story: the glory of spiritual triumph and reunion through death. As such, in the new arrangement, the end of the story is split into two: vocal lines and poetry convey the sadness of physical death, while nonverbal musical expression sounds as a voice of the divine and clarifies the meaning of this story. The first is directly related to Azerbaijani music and literature, while the second comes from a different musical and cultural source. But they merge naturally, thus highlighting the all-humanistic meaning of the tale of Layla and Majnun – and of the new arrangement of an old opera.

THE STORY OF THE TWO

One of the major challenges of the new arrangement was that it featured only two protagonists, leaving out the other operatic characters. In both folk tradition and Hajibeyli's opera, Layla and Majnun is indeed the story of two lovers, and this was one of Gasimov's major points when he advanced the idea of the new version of Hajibeyli's opera. The singer's aim was to distill and magnify all psychological nuances of the forbidden love between man and woman and of the process of this love's eventual transformation from the earthly sphere to the divine.

One of the possible inspirations for Gasimov's project was the resonance between the characters' relationship and his own and his daughter Gasimova's musicianship. The idea of divine love is essential for *mugham* performance in general and for Gasimov's style in particular. Symptomatically, the singer compares the rehearsals with his ensemble to a gathering of *darvish*es and admits these rehearsals' achieving "a feeling of ecstasy that leads to some kind of meditation."[9] In our conversation, Gasimov confirmed his deep inner connection with Majnun. "Majnun as a personality has his earthy and divine sides, and through his love, he proceeds from one to another. In a way, all musicians follow Majnun's journey. Very few of them achieve this last stage, though. I hope to get to Majnun's destination someday" (AG).

As for Gasimova, her artistry combines strong substance with fragility and tenderness; these are qualities of an ideal Layla. And spiritual and professional ties with her father and teacher result in a harmonious presentation of the main characters. In Gasimova's interpretation, Layla is the reason or, rather, the medium that helps Majnun rise to the divine. Her heroine never falls into a trance-like state like Gasimov's Majnun does. Only death takes Layla to the transcendental world where she meets her beloved.

Several mechanisms of the new arrangement compensate for the absence of the other characters of the story and the lack of action onstage. One such beneficial adjustment was the extended role of the instrumental parts. Each timbre is highly individualized, and members of the ensemble become characters, voices of the outer world responding to the drama of the two humans. "They do not simply play their instruments; I feel as if they are talking to us," Gasimov admits (AG). This was natural, as most of the instrumental episodes in the new score were created from the choral and ensemble episodes of the original opera. For instance, in the Duo of Majnun and Layla in part 2, the melodic phrase that in the original opera conveys the words of Majnun's parents ("Let's go home, son!") was in the new arrangement performed by the ensemble with no vocal part. As Jacobsen put it, "We are the words here" (CJ). And the meaning was delivered with such a convincing power that Gasimov's verbal response to the instrumental part ("Father, Mother, my love is driving me mad!") sounded absolutely natural. A similar situation arises in the instrumental piece that opens part 5. Here the voices of Layla's friends talking to her mother ("Don't let Layla go to school anymore!") are reconsidered as instrumental solos, eventually merging in a *tutti* reflecting the high emotional level of this conversation (PURL 10.2).

In general, the scores written or arranged for the Silk Road Ensemble have always prioritized and valued timbre. This distinctive characteristic has been fostered by the format of the ensemble as a small group of bright and highly accomplished musicians. The presence of Eastern instruments rarely heard in the West is another stimulus to highlight the musicians' individual voices. And creating opportunities to hear Yo-Yo Ma's playing is always a consideration.

Two new instrumental episodes, composed by Jacobsen, were added to the score to increase the story's drama. Jacobsen explains: "We wanted to have some input into making the story of Layla and Majnun ours, without disturbing the spirit of what Alim wants, or what people who know Hajibeyli's opera want" (CJ). This goal was fully achieved in the new arrangement.

The first of these new compositions accompanies Majnun's sudden appearance at Layla's forced wedding. It has a sorrowful and anxious character, contrasting with the happy music that typically characterizes a wedding scene. Initially, Jacobsen wanted this episode to be an instrumental interlude, but Gasimov instantly suggested using it as an instrumental background for his dramatic solo in *mugham Shushtar*. As Jacobsen mentioned, "I didn't imagine singing on top of it, but Alim immediately heard something" (CJ). Clearly, Gasimov thought of the Azerbaijani *zarbi mugham,* a rhythmic *mugham* in which a singer performs over an instrumental part characterized by stable metric patterns. Jacobsen's piece involves the typical melodic patterns of *shur,* which are repeated and developed against a steady rhythmic context. The combination with Gasimov's *Shushtar* thus creates a polyphonic texture of two different layers. In contrast to *zarbi mugham,* however, the layers represent different modes (*shur-shushtar*), which would have been impossible within Azerbaijani tradition. It is interesting to hear the singer instinctively try to overcome the stylistic distance between his part and the instrumental background, resulting in an improvisation more metrically organized than he would have had within standard *zarbi mugham.*

The second new episode appears in the scene of Layla's death. Following the heroine's final monologue, slow, sorrowful music closes out the work, lamenting Layla's passing. Without a dramatic context, the piece sounds like an interlude. Gasimov described this section as "the Western expression of sorrow that sounds next to its Eastern counterpart, *mugham Bayati Shiraz,* and becomes a beautiful addition to it" (AG). Again, Jacobsen's addition contributes to the firmer integration of old and new components in the score.

CREATING A NEW BALANCE

The new arrangement of Hajibeyli's opera has created a new balance between Western and Eastern traits in the work. During the process of creating the work, the idea of improvisation and the freedom of musical expression essential for *mugham* and Hajibeyli's opera were practiced through many combinations of *mugham* with notated material. Eventually, this freedom was translated into the written musical numbers. Gandelsman commented on the work process: "We were approaching things a little bit more literally at the beginning, and as we progressed, the notes on a page became much less literal. They are still there, but the idea is to leave as much freedom for everyone in the ensemble to change anything in order to get into the world of *mugham* and the world of the music that is happening."[10] This desire served the main goal of the new version, to eliminate the borders between *mugham*s and composed parts, to find their "seamless connection, the interstitial moments," as Yo-Yo Ma puts it (YYM). In Hajibeyli's opera, these two components are kept mostly separate: the symphony orchestra plays all episodes of composed music and stays silent during the *mugham*s. In *mugham* episodes, only the *tar* and *kemancha* accompany singers. In the new version, however, the role of the ensemble – with *tar* and *kemancha* included – is crucial throughout the entire piece, and both the improvised and written parts of the composition are firmly integrated. Such a consistency has been achieved through efforts on both sides: the Silk Road Ensemble and Gasimov's group.

Azerbaijani musicians – Ali Asgar Mammadov, a *tar* player, and Rauf Isla-mov, a *kemancha* player – introduced the Silk Road Ensemble to some essential aspects of *mugham* performance and demonstrated the traditional methods of instrumental responses to a singer. The arrangers, in their turn, extracted the main *mugham* scales used in the operatic score, notating them for the ensemble members' reference. At this stage of the project, the ensemble added only a very modest accompaniment in the *mugham* sections. Gradually, new forms of ensemble participation emerged, resulting in a more substantial instrumental part characterized by plentiful melodic and rhythmic ostinatos. According to Gandelsman, "That was another extreme: we created a lot of drama in our part, and that took away from what *mugham* performers were doing" (JG). In the final version, the ensemble's participation resembles traditional practice: instrumentalists respond to the singers but never compete with them or over-shadow their parts.

The choice of stylistic means in the new arrangement was perhaps the most challenging task, as it was important to maintain the work's consistency. Hajibeyli's original harmonization was the first ever instance of verticalizing the modal rules of Azerbaijani music. The result was too simple, if not illogi-cal, from a Western point of view, although each and every harmonic device used in Hajibeyli's score had its justification in the Azerbaijani modal system. The prevalence of open chords built on fifths and fourths corresponded with the tetrachordal structure of the Azerbaijani modes, and the slow harmonic rhythm with the frequent use of tonic reflected the modal development of *mu-gham,* in which melody is strongly drawn to the tonal center. The arrangers enhanced Hajibeyli's harmonization with more advanced means but without disturbing its original spirit. Gandelsman notes, "That was a thin line. We went more into harmonizing things, and it sounded too Western. Then we decided to cut back and really enjoy that a section can be modal, without a lot of harmonic movement. We realized that we could do just a few touches, and that would be enough" (JG).

In the framework of the Silk Road Ensemble's interpretation of Layla and Majnun, Gasimov altered the selection of *mughams,* resulting in a different ar-ray of *mughams* than found in Hajibeyli's score. Most of these changes, how-ever, did not contradict Hajibeyli's concept. For instance, in Majnun's solos in part 2, Gasimov used *Chahargah,* a close relative of Hajibeyli's *Mukhalif,* and, likewise, in part 4, Gasimov used *Shushtar*, related to the original *Tarkib*. Gasimov also added some new *mugham* parts as well, but even these were still related to Hajibeyli's vision. Layla's new monologues in part 3 refer to the mode *shur* that dominates in the respective part of the original opera. More drastic changes increased the composition's sense of drama and served to condense the work. For instance, at the beginning of Hajibeyli's opera, both Layla and Majnun performed the *mugham Mahur Hindi*. In the new version, the heroine performs *Vilayeti*, which is more dramatic than *Mahur Hindi* is. In part 3, instead of the intense, yet reserved *Kurd Shahnaz*, Majnun performs the bright and ecstatic *Bayati-Gajar*. Another strategy was to use only some segments of *mugham*s, rather than their complete versions. According to Gasimov, "At the beginning of our work, we felt that something separated us from the group and cooled down the whole atmosphere. We gave it some consideration and decided to introduce only parts of *mugham*s, those that are more 'zesty.' And things changed immediately!" (AG). Short but intense *mugham* sections contributed to creating a dynamic and stylistically consistent work.

Layla and Majnun is a constantly changing and developing project. Every performance is unique, and it is impossible to take a snapshot of this work. Yo-Yo Ma called this a "part of the thrill" and described the project as "perhaps the finest example of group intelligence at work."[11] As the *Washington Post* wrote about a performance of the Silk Road Ensemble in North Bethesda in 2009, "*Layla and Majnun* was the apex of the program. Classical musicmaking rarely achieves this combination of spontaneity and superb craftsmanship."[12] Indeed, *Layla and Majnun* is a product of collective creativity, both behind and on stage.

"I AM A SERVANT OF THIS STORY"

The idea of including visual elements in the performance emerged at an early stage of the project. During the performance at Harvard University, in addition to a translation of the text, medieval miniatures coming from Arabic, Persian, and Azerbaijani sources were projected. These colorful images, each a masterpiece in its own right, illustrated the storyline. But this was admitted to be distracting from the music and, in a way, it put the piece back in time, which was not the purpose of the new arrangement. The solution was found in 2008, when Henrik Soderstrom, who had graduated that same year from the Rhode Island School of Design, won the national contest carried out by the Silk Road Project to create the new designs for *Layla and Majnun*. Soderstrom's design was used for the ensemble's North American tour in 2009. The images were created with the ideal of "serving" the story and were one of the keys to the project's success: "I am happy to make myself a servant of such a tradition's story, furthering its beautiful complexity," said Soderstrom.[13] Impressed by the "subtlety" of the musicians' movements and gestures that supplement the "rich textures" in the music, Soderstrom decided not to distract from this by adding unnecessary elements to the stage.

Another central principle for Soderstrom was the paradoxical combination of "many influences such as figurative forms, linguistic characters, architecture, garment shapes, and symbolic colors related to different aspects of the story's amazingly rich history" (HS). Illustrated manuscripts of the story dating to the medieval era served as the main source of inspiration. Soderstrom was fascinated by the idea that in the medieval albums, "many of these illustrations are framed by a calligraphic border which both highlights certain colors and forms in the image and adds a formal reverence to the content" (HS). He treated the musicians as the illustration, framing them with a moving border made of both visual imagery and the English translation of the libretto. Tapestries of projection screens, illuminated with images and words, were hung at both sides of the stage (one side corresponded to Layla, and the other to Majnun) and above the musicians. The series of images reflecting the characters' evolution throughout the story also bore the hidden influence of Middle Eastern manuscripts, as some of these images were derived from Arabic script. This concept connected the visual and musical content of the piece: the use of Arabic characters in Middle Eastern calligraphy is often paralleled to the intricate patterns of *mugham*.

Color symbolism is also a site of the paradoxical crossings of cultures. Each of the six parts of the story is dominated by certain color, and each color thus has several layers of associations. For instance, yellow, which is prevalent in part 1, "Love and Separation," makes one think of both sunshine and the colors of autumn. This interpretation is common in many world cultures. Accordingly, yellow perfectly conveys the key points of the plot, such as the joy of love and the bitterness of separation. Blue, in combination with white, appears throughout the entire piece and is associated with the sky and the infinity of love. But when the blue color scheme changes to deep blue in part 3, "Sorrow and Despair," it resembles clouds or night, and it signifies sorrow. At the same time, this creates associations with the blues, an expression of sorrow in American culture. The symbolism of red, the color widely used in part 4, "Layla's Unwanted Wedding," is quite intriguing. According to Soderstrom, this color played two sometimes contrasting roles: "In learning about Azeri traditions, specifically those related to marriage, I came to associate the color red most strongly with a red sash sometimes worn by a bride, which usually symbolizes newness, fertility, and purity. My own associations with the color . . . ring with something like violence. I tried to play these two contradictory elements . . . in tension with one another."

Francesca Lohmann, also a graduate of the Rhode Island School of Design, worked in collaboration with Soderstrom to develop the calligraphy part of the project. This component also featured a unique combination of epochs, cultures, and styles. Lohmann eliminated the chronological and stylistic gap between her original font and medieval sources, using a font reminiscent of medieval Arabic calligraphy but nevertheless unmistakably modern. This contributes to the concept of the entire performance, which is about telling a universal story that is set in no particular time or place.

The Silk Road Ensemble's *Layla and Majnun* can be considered to be an entry into a long tradition of concert suites and compilations from operatic and ballet works. Yet this new rendition of Hajibeyli's opera is distinct, as it was created a hundred years after the original work and on a far different musical and cultural ground. Moreover, this composition is a result of collective effort and is imbued with the spirit of improvisation. Hajibeyli was aware of the large cultural span of his project, in terms of its musical and literary contents; however, according to the social and cultural expectations of early twentieth-century Azerbaijan and his own professional experience – or rather, its absence, as this opera was literally Hajibeyli's first work – the composer limited the cultural, aesthetic, and stylistic scope of the opera to the context of his native culture. The Silk Road Ensemble has expanded the cultural span of Azerbaijani opera into the vast space of the Middle East and Central Asia. In addition, they have increased the Western element in Hajibeyli's score and created a work of global East-West significance. The new arrangement of an old opera is a respectful transformation of the original, now shaped by creative energies coming from many different cultural, stylistic, and temporal sources.

EPILOGUE

I had just finished writing this book when the Aga Khan Music Initiative (AKMI) invited me to participate in the residency program of the Kronos Quartet and the Alim Gasimov Ensemble at the University of California at Berkeley and Stanford University in February 2012. My book would not be complete were I not, even briefly, to reflect on this remarkable experience.

AKMI was created by His Highness the Aga Khan in 2000, and since then it has carried out many valuable projects aiming to preserve, document, and develop the musical heritages of the various regions of Eurasia and Africa and to promote them worldwide.[1] In addition to working in Central Asia (including Afghanistan), AKMI currently supports projects in Mali, Egypt, and Pakistan and works with musicians from Syria, Lebanon, India, and Azerbaijan. Support for new approaches to tradition is among the AKMI's long-term goals, and collaboration with the Azerbaijani *mugham* singer Alim Gasimov and the United States' Kronos Quartet ideally furthered this project. As mentioned in chapter 10, Gasimov has already secured his place in Azerbaijani music history as being, simultaneously, a tradition-bearer and an innovator. The Kronos Quartet, called "probably the most famous 'new music' group in the world," is known for its innovative approach to repertoire and its work with many global musicians.[2] The residency program in Berkeley and Stanford was the second time that I had enjoyed the privilege of being involved in the collaboration of Gasimov with outstanding musicians of the Western world. Unlike the earlier occasion – with Yo-Yo Ma's Silk Road Ensemble that presented the new arrangement of the Azerbaijani opera *Layla and Majnun* – here I was not a part of the creative process from start to finish. Still, I had the unique opportunity to follow the details of interpretation through rehearsals and discussions with the musicians.

David Harrington, the first violinist, founder, and current artistic director of the Kronos Quartet, was exposed to Gasimov in the 1990s and was infatuated with his voice and creative energy. Before starting its collaboration with

Gasimov, Kronos performed and recorded the music of an Azerbaijani composer, Frangiz Alizade.[3] Nonetheless, it was not until 2008 that the first musical meeting of Kronos and the Gasimov Ensemble occurred. Since then, they have been playing together at some of the world's most prestigious venues, and this music has also appeared on two recordings: Kronos' 2009 album *Floodplain* and the 2010 album *Rainbow*, which was a joint project of the AKMI and Smithsonian Folkways.[4]

As with the Silk Road Ensemble's work on *Layla and Majnun*, Gasimov was in the center of the creative collaboration with Kronos. He carefully guided his Western colleagues through the labyrinth of *mugham* and *mugham*-inspired music. Gasimov selected the pieces, recorded them, and sent them to Kronos. The arrangement created by Jacob Garchik became a base, a starting point that was later modified according to traditional improvisation. According to Levin, the main challenge of the rehearsal process was "to create a seamless interface between the note-reading Kronos players and the Qasimov [Gasimov] Ensemble, whose performances typically feature an ever-shifting blend of memorized and extemporized musical gestures."[5] With a high level of respect toward the original text and the musical tradition of Azerbaijan, Kronos and the Gasimov Ensemble created syncretic works combining several layers: the original score; improvisation, as the essential quality of Azerbaijani music; and Western stylistic sources. The Western sources used draw from the lexicon of contemporary music, but only insofar as these materials correspond with non-Western traditions. Levin indicates the impact of "the brooding modal melodies of Bartók" and "the motoric ostinato patterns of Philip Glass" in the Azerbaijani compositions performed by Kronos and the Gasimov Ensemble.[6] The repertoire for the 2012 residencies and for the earlier collaborations between Gasimov and Kronos is based on the versatile composed song tradition of Azerbaijan. As discussed in chapter 7, songs written by Azerbaijani composers overtly preserve a taste of tradition. Melodic and harmonic parts are modal, and rhythm is based on the patterns typical of traditional and folk music. Performers may take liberty and demonstrate their mastery of *mugham* improvisation between verses or elsewhere in the song. Gasimov masterfully elaborates on all these features, adding his solos in *mugham* style and varying melodic patterns, without disturbing the original text. Kronos's instrumental sections become part of this process of recreating the old song: some of them follow the call-response format typical of *mugham*, while others are rather extensive, adding new stylistic layers to the musical contents. As a result of these changes, each song transforms from a short and rather simple musical genre into a dramatic monologue, creating many associations within the Azerbaijani tradition and beyond. In "Don't

Leave, Don't Leave" by Said Rustamov, the repetition of the main phrase, used as the song title, mesmerizes, and the entire piece obtains a ritual-like character (PURL E.1).

Within this new concept, Gasimov maneuvers in the vast cultural space of the Middle East and Central Asia. For instance, in "My Spirited Horse" by Jahangir Jahangirov, singers and instrumentalists create a joyful image of the horse ride by incorporating sound effects (unusual in the traditional music of Azerbaijan) emulating snickering horses. This creates a bridge with the tradition of the instrumental music of the nomadic peoples of Central Asia, which has theatrical elements and a deep connection with nature.

The idea of dialogue is essential for this collaboration. Alim Gasimov and Fargana Gasimova are the two most important figures of this project. They are placed in the center of the stage and display various forms of interaction, from singing in unison to creating contrapuntal combinations. But then there is an instrumental octet combining an Eastern and a Western instrumental quartet, one representing the native Azerbaijani tradition (which includes *tar, kemancha, balaban,* and *naghara*), and the other one in a conventional Western string quartet format. Despite the highest possible level of integration, both groups maintain their own solidity and integrity. As a result, the dialogue between the Eastern and Western sides becomes vital for the concept of the group. Despite speaking different languages, they communicate and merge in a harmonious unity. Indeed, the collaboration of the Kronos Quartet and the Gasimov Ensemble provides a vivid illustration of how two different musical traditions enhance and complement each other's spiritual and aesthetic space while maintaining their own distinct and unique features.

My book is over, although I realize that I was able to convey only some of the examples of East-West fusion that have occurred in the music of Azerbaijan since the early twentieth century. Azerbaijani musicians continue to explore this space, creating a rapprochement between improvisation and notation, Eastern and Western timbres, modality and tonal (or atonal) systems, and the performing styles of two different musical cultures. The collaboration with Western musicians has become proactive in the twenty-first century. Through such cooperative work, Azerbaijani musicians rediscover the openness of their music tradition toward the outside world. This fascinating movement bridges centuries, cultures, and continents, bearing witness to the significance and ongoing impact of East-West synthesis in Azerbaijani music – synthesis that has entered the second century of its history.

GLOSSARY

Aruz. A poetic system used in Arabic, Persian, and Turkic classical poetry. *Aruz* is based on particular combinations of long and short syllables, and it determines many musical characteristics of *mugham.*

Ashig. A wandering musician and poet who is a master of narrating stories, singing, playing *saz,* dancing, and theatrical performance.

Azan. A call to prayer in Islam performed from the minaret of the mosque five times a day.

Balaban. A tube-like double-reed instrument with nine holes; frequently used in an ensemble with *daf, saz,* and other *balaban*s.

Bayati. A form of folk poetry consisting of four seven-syllable-long lines. The first, second, and fourth lines are rhymed, and the third, which features a significant phrase that is the key to the poem, is independent.

Darvish. A member of the Sufi order; a seeker of eternal truth.

Dastan. An epic genre performed by *ashigs* that has heroic or love themes.

Ganun. A zither with a narrow trapezoidal soundboard that is played on the lap. The strings are plucked with two tortoise-shell picks, one in each hand, or with the fingernails.

Gasida. A strophic song based on the texts from the Quran or other Islamic literary sources.

Gaval. A round-shaped frame drum with jingles that is played with the palms and fingers. Most frequently used by *khanende* to provide rhythmic background for the vocal part of *mugham.*

Gazal. A genre and a form of Eastern poetry used in *mugham.* Consists of several (usually seven) couplets (*beyt*s). A refrain appears at the end of the first lines of the first couplet and at the end of the second line in each following couplet: AA BA CA DA . . .

Jangi. One of the most ancient dances of the Azerbaijanis. It has a heroic nature and historically accompanied military expeditions.

Kemancha. A spike fiddle with a small, spherical body and nine strings passing down a long, unfretted neck. The instrument is held upright and played with a flexible bow.

Khanende. A singer of *mugham*.

Majlis. A gathering of poets and musicians sharing their mastery of performing *mugham*. The *majlis* is a form of schooling in *mugham* art.

Marsiyya. A lament-like vocal piece performed at funeral services and memorial services in Islamic cultures.

Meykhana. A form of traditional performance that has an improvisational nature and that involves reciting poetry against a modest musical accompaniment. *Meykhana* is especially associated with the city of Baku and nearby villages and usually is undertaken by at least two performers, who have a verbal duel.

Mugham. (1) A mode of the Azerbaijani music system. Such a mode has characteristic melodic patterns and specific tonal centers. (2) A genre of Azerbaijani music based on a *mugham* mode and featuring improvisation within specific melodic, tonal, rhythmic, and formal models; it consists of *shoba*s alternating with *tasnif*s and *rangs*.

Naghara. A drum with a membrane that is stretched by means of ropes that cross on the underside of the head. It is usually played with hands or two sticks. More frequently, in Azerbaijani music, a pair of naghara is used, thus being called gosha naghara (paired naghara).

Novruz. A celebration of the New Year; originally practiced in Zoroastrianism and coincides with the day of the vernal equinox (usually March 19, 20, or 21). Novruz (Nauruz, Navruz) is highly popular in Iran, Afghanistan, Azerbaijan, and many parts of Central Asia.

Rang. An instrumental interlude performed in the course of a *mugham* composition and serving as a transition from one *shoba* to another.

Sema. A Sufi ritual that involves whirling darvishes who fall into a trance-like state through endless circular motion.

Saz. A fretted lute with a pear-shaped body that has eight to ten strings over a long neck and is characteristically used in *ashig* performances.

Shabih (also *taziye*). A religious mystery play performed during the month of Maharram in the Islamic calendar. It relates the story of the grandson of the Prophet Muhammad, Imam Huseyn, who was killed in 680 CE on the battlefield near Karbala, on the bank of the river Euphrates.

Shikasta. An improvised genre of traditional music pertaining to both *ashig* music and *zarbi mugham*.

Shoba. A section of *mugham* composition showcasing a particular stage of modal development.

Sufism. A philosophical and religious stream of Islam that emerged in the eighth century and propagated the idea of mystic love and ascending to the Divine through a process of spiritual improvement and through certain rituals.

Sura. A chapter of the Quran, the holy book of Islam.

Tar. A fretted, long-necked lute with a double-pear-shaped body; integral part of *mugham* performances.

Tasnif. A song-like section of *mugham* composition that is, like *rang*, performed between *shoba* sections.

Tutak. A whistle flute woodwind instrument that has a tube-like body with eight holes.

Ud. A short-necked, fretless lute with a pear-shaped body and eight to eleven strings.

Zarb. A single-headed goblet drum positioned diagonally on the knees and played by the fingers and palms.

Zarbi mugham. A subgenre of *mugham* in which the flow of improvisation occurs against steady rhythmic pulsation.

Zurna. An instrument consisting of a wooden tube with eight holes and a small reed that has a very loud sound. It is an Eastern predecessor of the oboe.

NOTES

Introduction

1. Carl Dahlhaus, *Between Romanticism and Modernism: Four Studies in the Music of the Later Nineteenth Century* (Berkeley: University of California Press, 1980), 82–83.

2. Dmitry Shostakovich, "Otlichnaia kompozitorskaia shkola" [Excellent school of composers], *Druzhba Narodov*, no. 11 (1957): 242.

3. Bruno Nettl, "Some Aspects of the History of World Music in the Twentieth Century: Questions, Problems, Concepts," *Ethnomusicology* 22 (1978): 134.

4. Inna Naroditskaya, *Song from the Land of Fire: Continuity and Change in Azerbaijanian Mugham* (New York: Routledge, 2003).

5. Anna Oldfield, *Azerbaijani Women Poet-Minstrels/Women Ashiqs from the Eighteenth Century to the Present* (Lewison, NY: Edwin Mellen Press, 2008).

6. With different levels of comprehensiveness, references to Azerbaijani musicians and their works can be found in the scholarly publications of James Bakst, Michel Dimitri Calvocoressi, Martin Cooper, Marina Frolova-Walker, Allan Ho and Dmitry Feofanov, Stanley Krebs, Richard Leonard, Rena Moisenko, Boris Schwartz, Frederick Starr, and Alexandria Vodarsky-Shiraeff.

7. Terry Martin, *The Affirmative Action Empire: Nations and Nationalism in the Soviet Union, 1923–1939* (Ithaca: Cornell University Press, 2001), 125.

8. The majority of the population in Turkic speaking countries, which include Turkey, Uzbekistan, Kazakhstan, Kyrgyzstan, and Turkmenistan, adhere to the Sunni branch of Islam. Populations practicing Shia, such as those of Iran and Tajikistan, speak the Persian language.

9. James Dodds Henry, *Baku: An Eventful History* (London: Archibald Constable, 1905), 5.

10. Betty Blair et al., "Architecture of the Oil Baron Period," *Azerbaijan International*, Winter 1998, 29–41.

11. Audrey L. Alstadt-Mirhadi, "Baku: Transformation of a Muslim Town," in *The City in Late Imperial Russia,* ed. Michael Hamm (Bloomington: Indiana University Press, 1986), 312.

12. Benedict Anderson, *Imagined Communities: Reflections on the Origin and Spread of Nationalism* (London: Verso, 2006), 116.

13. Tadeusz Swietochowski and Brian Collins, *Historical Dictionary of Azerbaijan* (Lanham, MD: The Scarecrow Press, 1999), 3.

14. Alstadt-Mirhadi, "Baku," 297.

15. Among Garayev's most notable works inspired by Hikmet are incidental music for productions of Hikmet's plays *Stranger* (1956) and the soundtrack for the film *The Two from the Same Quarter* (1956).

16. Seymour Topping, "Leningrad Ballet in Premiere; Announces Tour of U.S. in Fall," *New York Times*, March 23, 1961.

17. Igor Stupnikov, "The Legend of Love," in *International Dictionary of Ballet*, ed. Martha Bremser and Lorrain Nicholas (Detroit: St. James, 1993), 1: 841.

18. Kamil Shahverdi, "'Arshinnye' uspekhi '. . . mal alan'a" [The impressive successes of 'The Cloth Peddler'] *Azerbaijan-IRS*, no. 4 (2002): 36.

19. Alstadt-Mirhadi, "Baku," 296.

20. Chantal Lemercier-Quelquejay, "Islam and Identity in Azerbaijan," *Central Asian Survey* 3, no. 2 (1984): 44.

21. William Fierman, "Language Vitality and Paths to Revival: Contrasting Cases of Azerbaijani and Kazakh," *International Journal of the Sociology of Language*, no. 198 (July 2009): 78–81.

22. Ibid, 87.

23. Theodore Levin, "The Reterritorialization of the Culture in the New Central Asian States: A Report from Uzbekistan," *Yearbook for Traditional Music* 25 (1993): 52.

24. The musicologist Stanley Krebs, in his fundamental study of Soviet music, aligns Azerbaijani composers with their colleagues from Transcaucasia, rather than with those from Central Asia. Three chapters are dedicated to Azerbaijani composers (Hajibeyli, G. Garayev, and F. Amirov), three to Georgian composers (Dmitrii Arakishvili, Andrei Balanchivadze, and Otar Taktakishvili), and one to an Armenian composer (Aram Khachaturyan). Krebs does not devote any chapter exclusively to a single composer from Central Asia. Krebs, *Soviet Composers and the Development of Soviet Music* (New York: W. W. Norton, 1970).

25. This series of events was held on a regular basis from the 1940s until the mid-1980s. In 1944, the first Decade of the Music of the Transcaucasian Republics took place in Tbilisi, Georgia. Transcaucasian Spring, a festival of composed music, started in 1957, and the Transcaucasian Competition of Performers began in 1961. Transcaucasian jazz festivals were regularly held beginning in the late 1960s.

26. Of particular significance were the international festivals and symposiums held in Dushanbe (Tajikistan), Samargand and Tashkent (Uzbekistan), and Almati (Kazakhstan) in the 1970s and 1980s.

27. Sanubar Baghirova, *Azerbaidzhanskii mugam. Stat'i. Issledovaniia. Doklady* [Azerbaijani mugham. Articles. Research papers. Presentations] (Baku: Elm, 2007), 224–25.

28. Azerbaijani *mugham* has been central to the investigations of Gulnaz Abdullazade, Suraya Aghayeva, Elkhan Babayev, Sanubar Baghirova, Faik Chelebiev, Jean During, Tamila Dzhani-Zade, Mammad Saleh Ismayilov, Khanlar Malikov, Jamilya Hasanova, Fatah Khalig-zade, Shahla Mahmudova, Rena Mammadova, Inna Naroditskaya, Zemfira Safarova, Aydin Ziyadli, Ramiz Zokhrabov, and many others.

29. Uzeyir Hajibeyov [Hajibeyli], *Principles of Azerbaijani Folk Music* (Baku: Yazichi, 1985).

30. Mammad Saleh Ismayilov, "Azerbaijan khalg megamlarinin gohumlug munasibetleri hagginda" [About the relative relationship among Azerbaijani folk modes] *Uchenye Zapiski Azerbaidzhanskoi Gosudarstvennoi Konservatorii* [Research Papers of

the Azerbaijan State Conservatory], no. 9 (1972): 5–43; Ismayilov, *Strukturnye osoben-nosti ladov azerbaidzhanskoi narodnoi muzyki* [Structural particularities of the modes of Azerbaijani folk music] (Baku: Azerbaijan State Conservatory, 1981).

31. Hajibeyov, *Principles,* 16.

32. Edward Said, *Orientalism* (New York: Vintage Books, 1994).

33. Richard Taruskin, "Entoiling the Falconet: Russian Musical Orientalism in Context," *Cambridge Opera Journal* 4, no. 3 (Nov. 1992): 253–80.

34. Marina Frolova-Walker, *Russian Music and Nationalism from Glinka to Stalin* (New Haven: Yale University Press, 2007).

35. Philip Bohlman, "The European Discovery of Music in the Islamic World and the 'Non-Western' in 19th-Century Music History," *Journal of Musicology* 5 (1987): 148.

36. Ibid., 163.

1. Azerbaijani Musical Nationalism during the Pre-Soviet and Soviet Eras

1. Alstadt-Mirhadi, "Baku," 298.

2. Robert J. Kaiser, *The Geography of Nationalism in Russia and the USSR* (Princeton: Princeton University Press, 1994), 9.

3. During, "The Place of the Azerbaijani Mugham in its Caucasian and Iranian Environment," in *Proceedings of the Second International Musicological Symposium 'Space of Mugham' (15–17 March 2011)* (Baku: Sharg-Garb, 2011), 71–72.

4. During, "Power, Authority and Music in the Cultures of Inner Asia," *Ethnomusicology Forum* 14 (2005): 162.

5. William Prentice, "Sharga Gramofon galir" [The Gramophone goes East], *Musigi Dunyasi,* no. 3–4 (2000): 197.

6. Elmira Abasova, *Uzeir Gadzhibekov. Put' zhizni i tvorchestva* [Uzeyir Hajibeyli: His life and music] (Baku: Elm, 1985), 178.

7. A. Yusifov, "Teatr i muzyka" [Theater and music], *Baku,* March 31, 1913, quoted in Farah Aliyeva, ed., *XX asr Azerbaijan musigi madaniyyati tarikhinin gaynaghlari* [Sources on twentieth-century Azerbaijani music], Vol. 2, *1905–1918* (Baku: Nurlan, 2005), 135.

8. Hajibeyli's five *mugham* operas that he wrote after *Leyli and Majnun* are *Sheykh Senan* (1909), *Rustam and Sohrab* (1910), *Shah Abbas and Khurshud Banu* (1911), *Asli and Karam* (1912), and *Harun and Leyla* (1915).

9. Krebs, *Soviet Composers,* 134.

10. Frolova-Walker, *Russian Music,* 321.

11. Among other contemporary arrangements of Hajibeyli's opera, there is the version that was performed by the international cast at the Thirteenth San Francisco World Music Festival on November 10, 2012. Azerbaijani *mugham* singers performed main roles, and they were accompanied by the orchestra, which included musicians from Azerbaijan, China, South Korea, India, and the United States.

12. Hajibeyli's three operettas are *Husband and Wife* (1910), *If Not This One, Then That One* (1911), and *The Cloth Peddler* (1913).

13. Alan Gevinson, *Within Our Gates: Ethnicity in American Feature Films, 1911–1960* (Berkeley: University of California Press, 1997), 54.

14. Sevinj Ahmadova, *Arshin Mal Alan pokoriaet Los-Andzheles* [The Cloth Peddler conquers Los-Angeles], accessed February 23, 2015, http://www.net-fax.org/index.php?article=news_851.

15. Rashida Behbudova, the daughter of Rashid Behbudov who starred in the 1945 production of *The Cloth Peddler,* shared her family memoirs in her interview to the *Trud* newspaper. According to her, Hajibeyli learned about the Marana Films production from the Azerbaijani musicians who visited Iran in 1943 and watched this film there. That the Soviet Union was not a member of the world convention on copyright placed Hajibeyli in a precarious situation. Hajibeyli notified Stalin, and the Soviet leader immediately assigned the Azerbaijan Film studio to produce another film based on Hajibeyli's operetta and then widely promote it in the international arena. This was how the movie *The Cloth Peddler* came onto the stage in 1945, after which Marana Films recognized Hajibeyli's authorship. Maya Mamedova, "Arshin Mal Alan, ili kak Stalin prikazal Gollivud perepliunut'" [The Cloth Peddler, or how Stalin ordered to outdo Hollywood], *Trud,* April 27, 2003.

16. Hoyt Hilsman, "An Azerbaijani Operetta at the Dorothy Chandler," *Huffington Post,* September 9, 2013, accessed February 23, 2015, http://www.huffingtonpost.com/hoyt-hilsman/an-azerbaijani-operatta-a_b_3894592.html.

17. The Imperial Russian Music Society (IRMO) was founded in 1859 in Petersburg by the composer, pianist, and conductor Anton Rubinstein under the patronage of the Russian imperial family. The society's mission was one of enlightenment, and it conducted concerts, competitions, and festivals in many regions of the Russian Empire. Russia's two major schools of music – the Moscow and Petersburg conservatories – were created under the umbrella of the IRMO. In a short period of time, twenty-seven branches were established throughout the Russian Empire.

18. "IRMO," *Kaspii* October 26, 1901, quoted in Farah Aliyeva, *XX asr Azerbaijan musigi madaniyyati,* Vol. 1, *1901–1905,* 42.

19. Kovkab Safaraliyeva, "Muzykal'noe obrazovanie v Azerbaidzhane" [Music education in Azerbaijan], in *Azerbaidzhanskaia muzyka* [Music of Azerbaijan], ed. Jovdat Hajiyev et al. (Moscow: Gosmuzgiz, 1961), 278.

20. To understand the priorities of the ADR, suffice to refer to the one notable fact: the state granted women voting rights in 1918, two years before the United States did the same.

21. Frolova-Walker, *Russian Nationalism,* 333.

22. Hajibeyli, *Azerbaijan turklarinin musigisi hagginda* [About the music of Azerbaijani Turks] (Baki: Adiloglu, 2005), 23.

23. Ibid., 23–24.

24. Ibid., 24–25.

25. Ronald Suni, *Revenge of the Past: Nationalism, Revolution and the Collapse of the Soviet Union* (Stanford, CA: Stanford University Press, 1993), 87; Francine Hirsch, "Toward an Empire of Nations: Border-Making and the Formation of Soviet National Identities," *Russian Review* 59 (2000): 204.

26. Martin, *The Affirmative Action Empire,* 13.

27. During, "Recording Reviews: Two Essays on Recordings of Music from Azerbaijan," *Ethnomusicology* 44 (2000): 537.

28. During, "Power, Authority, and Music," 158.

29. The word *bulbul* means nightingale, and the singer got this nickname because of the unique beauty and richness of his voice.

30. *Scriabin – The Poem of Ecstasy; Amirov – Azerbaijan Mugam,* performed by the Houston Symphony Orchestra, directed by Leopold Stokowski, Everest Records BooE-B1QRHO, 2013, compact disc.

31. Dmitry Shostakovich, "Neskol'ko slov o balete" [A few words about the ballet], *Za Sovetskoe Iskusstvo,* April 4, 1961.

32. Passacaglia and Three-Theme Fugue for symphony orchestra (1941), the Second Symphony (1946), the Sonata for Violin and Piano (1960), and Piano Prelude No.22 (1963), and in particular Garayev's last opus, Twelve Fugues for Piano (1981), make powerful use of a refined polyphonic technique.

33. Quoted in Liudmila Karagicheva, *Kara Karaev. Lichnost'. Suzhdeniia ob iskusstve* [Gara Garayev. His personality. Thoughts about art] (Moscow: Kompozitor, 1994), 277.

34. Kara Karayev [Gara Garayev], "Prazdnik muzykal'noi kul'tury" [The celebration of musical culture], *Bakinskii Rabochii,* October 8, 1968.

35. Farhad Badalbeyli, interview with the author, May 11, 2011.

36. Fidan Gasimova became a laureate of the Viotti International Music Competition in Vercelli, Italy (1977), and Khuraman Gasimova was honored with the highest awards at the Maria Callas Grand Prix in Athens, Greece (1981) and the International Tchaikovsky Competition in Moscow, Russia (1982).

37. Anna Ferenc, "Music in the Socialist State," in *Soviet Music and Society under Lenin and Stalin,* ed. Neil Edmunds (London: Routledge Curzon, 2004), 8.

38. Gasan Sabri, "O tiurkskoi opere v Azerbaidzhane" [About Turkic opera in Azerbaijan], *Na Rubezhe Vostoka* 3 (1929): 68. Quoted in Zemfira Safarova, *Muzykal'no-esteticheskie vzgliady Uzeira Gadzhibekova* [Musical and aesthetical views of Uzeyir Hajibeyli] (Moscow: Sovetskii Kompozitor, 1973), 99.

39. Among controlling organizations were the Central Committee of the Communist Party, the Ministry of Culture, the Union of Composers, the Committee of the State Security, and the Main Department on the Literature and Art Affairs.

40. Theodore Levin, "Making Marxist-Leninist Music in Uzbekistan," in *Music and Marx: Ideas, Practice, Politics,* ed. Regula Burkchardt-Qureshi (New York: Routledge, 2002), 197.

41. Nettl, ed., "Persian Classical Music in Tehran: The Processes of Change," in *Eight Urban Musical Cultures: Tradition and Change* (Chicago: University of Illinois Press, 1978), 163.

42. Ramiz Guliyev, interview with the author, May 27, 2011.

43. During, "Power, Authority, and Music," 155.

44. Nettl, "Persian Classical Music," 157.

45. Ramiz Zokhrabov, interview with the author, May 12, 2010. Zokhrabov refers to his book *Azerbaidzhanskie tesnify* [Azerbaijani tasnifs] (Moscow: Sovetskii kompozitor, 1983).

46. Izaly Zemtsovsky, "On Reading Three Responses," in *Proceedings of the Conference "Folklore and Traditional Music in the Soviet Union and Eastern Europe," UCLA, May 16, 1994,* ed. James Porter (Los Angeles: UCLA Ethnomusicology Publications, 1997), 42.

47. Saadat Seyidova, "Uzeyir Hajibeyov va dini musigi" [Uzeyir Hajibeyli and religious music] *Musigi Dunyasi,* no. 3–4/5 (2000): 140.

48. During, "Power, Authority, and Music," 155.

49. Vagif Samadoghlu, "The Emergence of Jazz in Azerbaijan," in *Azerbaijan International,* Winter 1997, 72.

50. Eddie Rosner, born into a Polish-Jewish family in Berlin, garnered acclaim for his brilliant trumpet playing. After the invasion of Poland by the Nazis, he fled to the Soviet Union where he became the head of the Soviet Jazz Orchestra. After the war, as a result

of the anti-Jew campaign, Rosner fell into disfavor and was sent to prison with a ten-year sentence. Rosner was released in 1953 after Stalin died. He returned to his native Berlin and died there in 1976.

51. Sultanov, Rain, ed., *Jazz in Azerbaijan: Anthology* (Baku, 2004), 113.

52. Samadoghlu, "The Emergence of Jazz," 73.

53. Faraj Garayev, interview with the author, October 24, 2006.

54. Aida Guseinova [Aida Huseynova], *Muslim Magomaev. Opernoe tvorchestvo: Opyt muzykal'no-tekstologicheskogo analiza* [Muslim Magomayev. Operas: Musicological and textological study] (Baku: Azerbaijan Gadini, 1997), 36.

55. The Musavat Party was founded in Baku in 1911. It was forbidden in the Soviet Union, although it continued its activity in exile and was resurrected in Azerbaijan in 1989.

56. Zokhrabov, interview.

57. Betty Blair and Fuad Akhundov, *About Uzeyir Hajibeyov – A Conversation with Ramazan Khalilov,* accessed February 23, 2015, http://www.hajibeyov.com/bio/bio_life/khalilov_ramazan/khalilov_ramazan_eng/khalilov_ramazan.html.

58. Naroditskaya, *Song from the Land of Fire,* 117–18.

59. F. Garayev, interview.

60. The full story is told in Aida Huseynova, "Relating Shostakovich," DSCH *Journal,* no. 18 (2003): 39–40.

61. Arif Melikov [Malikov], "Bessmertie" [Eternity], in *Slovo ob Uzeire Gadzhibekove* [A word about Uzeyir Hajibeyli], ed. Akhmed Isazade (Baku: Elm, 1985), 130.

62. Among the most common destinations for Azerbaijani musicians during the post-Soviet era were Turkey, Iran, Iraq, Syria, Kuwait, Qatar, and Egypt.

63. F. Badalbeyli, interview.

2. Pioneers of the New Azerbaijani Musical Identity

1. Naroditskaya, *Song from the Land of Fire,* 99.

2. Krebs, *Soviet Composers,* 133–36.

3. Frolova-Walker, *Russian Music,* 332–37.

4. Alexandria Vodarsky-Shiraeff, *Russian Composers and Musicians* (New York: Greenwood Press, 1940), 46.

5. Michel Dimitri Calvocoressi, *A Survey of Russian Music* (Harmondsworth: Penguin Books, 1944), 122–23.

6. Karaev [Garayev], "Ob Uzeire Gadzhibekove" [About Uzeyir Hajibeyli], in *Kara Karaev. Stat'i. Pis'ma. Vyskazyvaniia* [Gara Garayev. Articles. Letters. Observations], ed. by Liudmila Karagicheva (Moscow: Sovetskii Kompozitor, 1978), 12.

7. As old Azerbaijani proverbs say, "If you cannot sing *mugham,* then you are not from Shusha" or "Even babies in Shusha cry in *mugham* style."

8. David Brown, *Mikhail Glinka: A Biographical and Critical Study* (London: Oxford University Press, 1974), 115.

9. Agshin Alizade, interview with the author, May 18, 2012.

10. Nettl, *The Western Impact on World Music* (New York: Schirmer Books, 1985), 112.

11. In Moscow, Hajibeyli studied solfege with Nikolai Ladukhin and harmony with Nikolai Sokolovskii, both students of Sergei Taneev, and in Saint Petersburg, he learned music theory from Vasilii Kalafati, who studied under Nikolai Rimsky-Korsakov.

12. Gadzhibekov [Hajibeyli], "Muzykal'no-prosvetitel'nye zadachi v Azerbaidzhane" [The tasks of music education in Azerbaijan], *Iskusstvo*, no. 1 (1921): 10.

13. Gadzhibekov [Hajibeyli], *O muzykal'nom iskusstve Azerbaidzhana* [About the musical art of Azerbaijan] (Baku: Azerneshr, 1966), 26.

14. Up until the beginning of 1960, the head of the conservatory was referred to as the "director," but since then, this office holder has been called the "rector."

15. *Azerbaijan arkhivi: Azerbaijan Dovlat Konservatoriyasinin tarikhindan (1920–1957)* [The archives of Azerbaijan: From the history of the Azerbaijan State Conservatory (1920–1957)], no. 2–3 (1985): 91.

16. Safaraliyeva, "Muzykal'noe obrazovanie," 281.

17. Abasova et al., eds. *Azerbaidzhanskaia Gosudarstvennaia Konservatoriia imeni Uzeira Gadzhibekova* [The Azerbaijan State Conservatory named after Uzeyir Hajibeyli] (Baku: Azerneshr, 1972), 34.

18. *Azerbaijan arkhivi*, 29.

19. Nariman Narimanov (1870–1925) was a writer and physician who, from 1922 to 1925, served as the Head of the Central Executive Committee of the Soviet Union.

20. Anar [pseud.], "Dahi bastakarimiz" [Our great composer], in *Uzeyir Hajibeyov Ensiklopediyasi* [The Uzeyir Hajibeyli Encyclopedia] (Baku: Azerbaijan Nashriyyati, 1996), 15.

21. Betty Blair, "Hajibeyov's Opera 'Koroghlu' (Son of a Blind Man)," in *Azerbaijan International*, Autumn 2001, 59.

22. In *If Not This One, Then That One,* a young girl joins her beloved and defeats the old merchant who wants to marry her. In *Husband and Wife,* a smart heroine outwits her husband, thwarting his plans to get a second wife. In *The Cloth Peddler,* against existing social rules, the protagonists marry each other without the consent of their families.

23. Karaev [Garayev], "Liubov' k trem Kavkazam" [Love for the three Caucasuses], interview with Ramil Khakimov, *Vecherniaia Ufa,* November 23, 1972.

24. Svetlana Mirzoeva, "Gorzhus' tem, chto ia syn Vostoka" [I am a proud son of the East], *Bakinskii Rabochii,* September 4, 1991.

25. Mashadi Jamil Amirov is credited with establishing the first music school in Ganja in 1923 and with writing several works, such as the *mugham* opera *Seyfal Mulk* (1915) and the operetta *Honored Girl* (1923), both staged in Azerbaijan as well as in Iran and Turkey.

26. Garayev studied composition with Leopold Rudolf, and Amirov studied with Boris Zeidman. Garayev also studied piano with Georgii Sharoev.

27. Lev Grigor'ev and Iakov Platek, "Besedy s masterami: Kara Karaev" [Conversations with masters: Gara Garayev], *Muzykal'naia Zhizn',* no. 6 (1974): 15.

28. Shostakovich, "Otlichnaia kompozitorskaia shkola."

29. Rauf Farkhadov, "Fikret Amirov vo vremeni i prostranstve" [Fikrat Amirov in time and space], in *Shargi,* no. 2 (2002): 69.

30. Karaev [Garayev], "Liubov' k trem Kavkazam."

31. Dahlhaus, *Between Romanticism and Modernism,* 100.

32. Viktor Vinogradov, *Mir muzyki Fikreta* [The world of Fikrat's music] (Baku: Yazichi, 1983), 100.

33. Imran Kasumov [Imran Gasimov], "Brigantina Kara Karaeva" [The brigantine of Gara Garayev], in *Kara Karaev. Stat'i. Pis'ma. Vyskazivaniia,* 101.

34. Among Garayev's "French" works are the mono-opera *Tenderness* (1973), based on a novel by Henri Barbusse, and the musical *Furious Gasconian* (1974), after Edmon Rostan. Russian sources inspired him to write the romances "On the Hills of Georgia" and "I Loved You," both 1949, on the verses of Alexander Pushkin. *Three Nocturnes* (1958) for bass and jazz orchestra, on the lyrics of Langston Hughes, exemplify "American" pages of Garayev's legacy.

35. Viktor Bukhanov, "Iskusstvo obiazyvaet: rasskazyvaet Kara Karaev" [The art obliges: Gara Garayev talks], in *Molodezh' Azerbaidzhana*, December 18, 1963.

36. Shchedrin, "Nazidatel'nyi tvorcheskii put'" [Edifying creative path], in *Kara Karaev. Stat'i. Pis'ma. Vyskazivaniia*, 87.

37. Krebs, *Soviet Composers*, 312.

38. Ibid., 307.

39. Anar, "Svet Karaeva" [The Light of Garayev], *Muzykal'naia Akademiia*, no. 1 (2002): 177.

40. Among them are the most distinguished composers of Azerbaijan (in alphabetical order) – Vasif Adigozalov, Frangiz Alizade, Aydin Azimov, Adil Babirov, Tofig Bakikhanov, Polad Bulbuloghlu, Azer Dadashov, Elnara Dadashova, Faraj Garayev, Mammad Guliyev, Ismayil Hajibeyov. Rauf Hajiyev, Rahilya Hasanova, Sevda Ibrahimova, Afag Jafarova, Haji Khanmammadov, Arif Malikov, Khayyam Mirzazade, Musa Mirzayev, and Ogtay Zulfugarov – as well as Vladimir Shainskii, a famous Russian songwriter, now residing in the United States, who also graduated from Garayev's composition class.

41. Farkhadov, "Fikret Amirov," 69–70.

3. The Russian-Soviet Factor

1. This manuscript is now on display at the Home Museum of Leopold and Slava Rostropovich in Baku.

2. Taruskin, *Defining Russia Musically: Historical and Hermeneutical Essays* (Princeton: Princeton University Press, 1997), xv, 182.

3. The concept of Russia as a Eurasian entity was advanced by the Russian ethnographer and linguist Nikolai Trubetskoi in the early twentieth century.

4. Said, *Orientalism*, 3.

5. Taruskin, "Entoiling the Falconet," 255.

6. Frolova-Walker, *Russian Music*, xiii.

7. Khayyam Mirzazade, interview with the author, May 11, 2011.

8. In Russia, the legend of Shahsenem and Ashig Garib became popular thanks to Mikhail Lermontov's poem "Ashig Garib." This story had many attractions for Soviet musical aesthetics. In 1939, the Russian composer Boris Asaf'ev wrote the ballet *Ashig Garib*, and in 1944, the Russian composer Adrian Shaposhnikov, who worked in Turkmenistan, wrote another "missionary" opera, *Shahsenem and Garip*, in coauthorship with the local musician Dangatar Ovezov.

9. Reinhold Gliere, Letter from 29 June 1914, in *Reingol'd Moritsevich Glier. Stat'i. Vospominaniia. Materialy* [Reinhold Moritsevich Gliere. Articles. Memoirs. Materials], ed. Valerian Bogdanov-Berezovsky (Moscow: Muzyka, 1965), 1: 376–77.

10. Shovkat Mamedova [Mammadova], "Slovo o moem druge i uchitele" [A word about my friend and teacher], in *Reingol'd Moritsevich Glier. Stat'i. Vospominaniia. Materialy* [Reinhold Moritsevich Gliere. Articles. Memoirs. Materials], ed. Valerian Bogdanov-Berezovsky (Moscow: Muzyka, 1966), 2: 247.

11. Igor Ledogorov, "'Shahsenem' Gliera" [Gliere's *Shahsenem*], *Bakinskii Rabochii,* December 17, 1927.

12. Nailya Mekhtieva, "Opera R.M. Gliera 'Shahsenem': istoriia sozdaniia i nekotorye voprosy stilia" [Opera "Shahsenem" by R. M. Gliere: the history of its creation and some aspects of the style], *Uchenye zapiski Azerbaidzhanskoi Gosudarstvennoi Konservatorii* [Research papers of the Azerbaijan State Conservatory], no. 3 (1966): 39.

13. Martin Stokes, ed. *Ethnicity, Identity and Music: The Musical Construction of Place.* (Oxford: Berg, 1994), 7.

14. Taruskin, "Nationalism," in *The New Grove Dictionary of Music and Musicians,* edited by Stanley Sadie. (London: Macmillan, 2001), 17: 700.

15. Ibid., 700.

16. Krebs, *Soviet Composers,* 74.

17. Aida Guseinova [Huseynova], "K voprosu sravnitel'noi kharakteristiki avtografa i redaktsii Gliera opery Muslima Magomaeva *Nargiz*" [On the question of the comparative analysis of the original version and Gliere's version of the opera 'Nargiz' by Muslim Magomaev] (master's thesis, Azerbaijan State Conservatory, 1987).

18. Krebs, *Soviet Composers,* 73.

19. Kara Karaev [Gara Garayev], "O D.D. Shostakoviche" [About D. D. Shostakovich], in *Kara Karaev. Stat'i. Pis'ma. Vyskazivaniia,* 17.

20. Kshishtof Meyer, "Moi vstrechi s Karaevym" [My meetings with Garayev], in *Kara Karaev: Stat'i. Pis'ma. Vyskazivaniia,* 90.

21. Nikolai Martynov, "Pis'ma Shostakovicha. Stranitsy iz zapisnoi knizhki" [Letters of Shostakovich. Pages from a notebook], in *D.D. Shostakovich. Sbornik statei k 90-letiiu so dnia rozhdeniia* [D. D. Shostakovich. A collection of articles on the 90th anniversary of his birth], ed. Liudmila Kovnatskaia (St. Petersburg: Kompozitor, 1996), 282.

22. Dmitry Shostakovich, "Rady vzletu azerbaidzhanskoi muzyki" [Happy to witness the flourishing of Azerbaijani music], *Bakinskii Rabochii,* May 7, 1964.

23. Liudmila Karagicheva, "Pishite kak mozhno bol'she prekrasnoi muzyki" [Write as much wonderful music as you can], *Muzykal'naia Akademiia,* no. 4 (1997): 203 (hereafter cited in text as MA).

24. Serafim Tulikov, Anatolii Novikov, and Marian Koval were officially appraised Russian Soviet composers.

25. The new interpretation of the Tenth Symphony is suggested in the scholarly works of Nelly Kravets, Elizabeth Wilson, Kshishtof Meyer, Laurel Fay, and Ian Mac-Donald.

26. Saida Beibutova and Aida Guseinova [Huseynova], "Elmira Mirza Riza gizi Nazirova," in *Vydaiushchiesia deiateli fortepiannoi kul'tury Azerbaidzhana* [Prominent representatives of the piano culture of Azerbaijan], ed. Tarlan Seidov (Baku: Ishig, 1988).

27. Elmira Nazirova, interview with the author, August 5, 1990 (hereafter cited in text as EN).

28. Reinhold Gliere, "Muzyka azerbaidzhanskikh kompozitorov" [Music of Azerbaijani composers], *Bakinskii Rabochii,* December 29, 1944.

29. Aida Huseynova, "The Heart of the Tenth Symphony," *DSCH Journal,* no. 17 (2002): 39 (hereafter cited in text as HTS).

30. Solomon Volkov, ed. *Testimony: The Memoirs of Dmitry Shostakovich* (New York: Limelight Editions, 1984), 141.

31. Lev Danilevich, *D.D. Shostakovich* (Moscow: Sovetskii Kompozitor, 1958), 134; Marina Sabinina, *Shostakovich-simfonist: Dramaturgiia, estetika, stil'* [Shostakovich as symphonic composer: Dramaturgy, aesthetics, style] (Moscow: Muzyka, 1976), 302.

32. Leo Mazel, *Simfonii Dmitriia Shostakovicha. Putevoditel'* [Symphonies of Dmitry Shostakovich. A Guide] (Moscow: Sovetskii Kompozitor, 1960), 123.

33. David Fanning, *The Breath of the Symphonist: Shostakovich's Tenth* (London: Royal Musical Association, 1988), 52.

34. Aleksandr Dolzhanskii, "Iz nabliudenii nad stilem Shostakovicha" [From the observations over Shostakovich's style], *Sovetskaia Muzyka*, no. 10 (1959): 95–102.

35. Eleonora Fedosova, *Diatonicheskie lady v tvorchestve D. Shostakovicha* [Diatonic modes in the music by Shostakovich] (Moscow: Sovetskii Kompozitor, 1980), 78–79.

36. Dolzhanskii, "Iz nabliudenii," 33.

4. The Beginning of the National Style

1. *A History of Western Music* considers the eighteenth century "as a period in its own right," as "elements of what would become the Classical style were already present at the start of the century, and the echoes of the Baroque were still heard at the end." J. Peter Burkholder, Donald Jay Grout, and Claude V. Palisca, *A History of Western Music*, 8th ed. (New York: Norton, 2010), 412.

2. Izaly Zemtsovsky, Liner notes for *Faik Chelebi, Tar: The Classical Muğam of Azerbaijan in Solo Instrumental Performance*. Silk Road House, SRH 003, 2013, compact disc.

3. Manfred F. Bukofzer, *Music in the Baroque Era: From Monteverdi to Bach* (New York: W. W. Norton, 1947), 25.

4. Friedrich Blume, *Renaissance and Baroque Music: A Comprehensive Survey* (New York: W. W. Norton, 1967), 94.

5. Baghirova, *Azerbaidzhanskii mugam*, 80–81.

6. Karl Signell, "Mozart and the Mehter," *Turkish Music Quarterly* 1, no. 1 (1988): 9.

7. Anon., "Uchenicheskii kontsert" [Students' concert], *Baku*, January 17, 1912, quoted in Aliyeva, ed., *Azerbaijan musigi madaniyyati*, vol. 2, 11.

8. Izabella Abezgauz, *Opera "Keroglu" Uzeira Gadzhibekova: o khudozhestvennykh otkrytiiakh kompozitora* [The opera "Koroghlu" by Uzeyir Hajibeyli: About the composer's artistic discoveries] (Moscow: Sovetskii Kompozitor, 1987), 72.

9. Ibid., 90, 78.

10. Ibid., 155.

11. Dahlhaus, *Between Romanticism and Modernism*, 88.

12. Andrew Bowie, "Music and the Rise of Aesthetics," in *The Cambridge History of Nineteenth-Century Music*, ed. Jim Samson (Cambridge: Cambridge University Press, 2002), 37, 46.

13. According to the musicologist Gamar Ismayilova, Magomayev referred to the version of the *dastan* about Shah Ismayil that demonstrates the closest proximity to real historical events, that is, the struggle for power between two representatives of the same ruling dynasty in the Safavid state in the sixteenth century. Gamar Ismayilova, *Muslim Magomayev* (Baku: Azerneshr, 1986), 74.

14. Abezgauz, *Opera "Keroglu,"* 30.

15. Farkhadov, "Takaia korotkaia zhizn'" [Such a short life], *Kultura*, accessed February 23, 2015, http://www.kultura.az/articles.php?item_id=20110622044803652&sec_id=16.

16. Among musicians, *mugham Rast* is often referred to as the "mother of all *mughams*."
17. Ismayilov, "Azerbaijan khalg megamlarinin gohumlug munasibetleri hagginda."

5. Growing Maturity

1. Leo Mazel, "Vospominaniia i blagodarnost'" [Memoirs and gratitude], in *Kara Karaev: Stat'i. Pis'ma. Vyskazyvaniia*, 83.
2. Abezgauz, "'V'etnam' i 'Don Kikhot'" ["Vietnam" and "Don Quixote"]. In *Gara Garayev. Ocherklar* [Gara Garayev. Essays], ed. Gulnaz Abdullazade et al. (Baku: Chinar Chap, 2003), 31.
3. Besides the Second symphony, passacaglias can also be found in Garayev's other works, such as his Sonata for Violin and Piano (1960) and Piano Prelude No. 22 (1963).
4. The score of Garayev's Second Symphony has never been published, and this example comes from the monograph on Garayev penned by Karagicheva (Karagicheva, *Kara Karaev*, 48–51). Karagicheva had full and unlimited access to the Garayev's archive.
5. Ulviyya Imanova, "Starinnye tantseval'nye zhanry i zhanry, blizkie k tantseval'nym, v muzyke Kara Karaeva" [Ancient dance and dance-like genres in the music of Gara Garayev]. In *Gara Garayev. Ocherklar* [Gara Garayev. Essays], ed. Gulnaz Abdullazade et al. (Baku: Chinar-Chap, 2003), 58.
6. Abezgauz, "'V'etnam' i 'Don Kikhot'," 46.
7. Imanova, "Starinnye tantseval'nye zhanry," 69.
8. Abezgauz, *Opera Keroglu*, 78.

6. The Spirit of Experimentalism

1. Karagicheva, *Kara Karaev. Lichnost'. Suzhdeniia ob iskusstve*, 96.
2. Vinogradov, *Mir muzyki Fikreta*, 51.
3. Malcolm Gillies, ed. *Bartók Remembered* (London: Faber, 1990), 185.
4. Nigar Rahimova, "K probleme vostochnoi funktsional'noi teorii lada (na primere arabskikh, persidskikh makamov i azerbaidzhanskikh mugamov)" [On the problem of Eastern functional modal theory (examples of Arab, Persian maqams and Azerbaijani mughams)], in *Izvestiia Akademii Nauk Azerbaidzhanskoi SSR* [The News of the Academy of Sciences of Azerbaijan SSR], no. 1 (1987): 92–98; Rahimova, "K probleme azerbaidzhanskoi ladovoi funktsional'nosti" [On the problem of functionality in Azerbaijani modes], in *Proceedings of the Inter-Republican Research Conference "The National Music Culture: Problems and Perspectives"* (Tbilisi: Tbilisi State Conservatory, 1988), 42–44.
5. Abasova, "K voprosu natsional'nogo svoeobraziia tematizma Kara Karaeva" [On the question of the national specifics of the thematism of Gara Garayev], in *Kara Karaev. Stat'i. Pis'ma. Vyskazyvaniia*, 325.
6. Naroditskaya, "Azerbaijani Mugham and Carpet: Cross-Cultural Mapping," *Ethnomusicology Forum* 14 (2005), 25.
7. Karaev [Garayev], "Tolko v rabote chelovek vyrazhaet aktivnoe otnoshenie k zhizni" [Only through work one can express his active attitude toward life], by Liana Genina, *Sovetskaia Muzyka*, no. 2 (1978): 38.
8. Emina Eldarova, "Nekotorye voprosy muzykal'nogo tvorchestva ashugov" [Some questions on the musical art of ashigs], in *Azerbaidzhanskaia muzyka* [Music of Azerbaijan], ed. Jovdat Hajiyev et al. (Moscow: Gosmuzgiz, 1961), 76.

9. Frangiz Alizade, "Ot 'Leili i Medzhnun" k Tret'ei simfonii" [From "Leyli and Majnun" to the Third symphony], in *Gara Garayev. Ocherklar,* 107.

10. Frangiz Alizade, interview with the author, June 15, 2010.

11. Arnold Klotyn, "Voskhishchenie i razmyshleniia" [Admiration and considerations] *Sovetskaia Muzyka* no.11 (1975): 36.

12. F. Garayev, interview.

13. Rauf Farkhadov and Vladimir Tarnopolskii, "Napriazhenie Faradzha Karaeva/ Besedy o tvorchestve Faradzha Karaeva" [The tension of Faraj Garayev: Conversation about Faraj Garayev's works], in *Muzykal'naia Zhizn',* no. 1 (2006): 39.

14. F. Garayev used twelve-tone harmony in . . . *alla Nostalgia* (1989) and *Musik für die Stadt Forst* (1991), and serialism in *A Crumb of Music for George Crumb* (1985).

15. Iurii Gabai, "Monolog prodolzhaetsia" [The monologue continues] *Sovetskaia Muzyka* no. 10 (1986): 30.

16. Ismayil Hajibeyov represented the third generation of the Hajibeyli musical dynasty. He was the son of the composer Soltan Hajibeyov, who was Hajibeyli's nephew.

17. Robert Carl, Review of *Ali-Zadeh. Oasis. Apsheron Quintet. Music for the Piano. Mugam Sayaghi* by Kronos String Qartet (*Nonesuch 79804-2*) *Fanfare* 28, May/June 2005, 77.

18. F. Alizade, interview.

19. Aida Guseinova [Huseynova], "Frangiz Alizade: Sliianie mirov" [Frangiz Alizade: Merging worlds], in *Frangiz Alizade: Triumfal'nye peresecheniia Vostoka i Zapada* [Frangiz Alizade: Triumphal crossings of the East and the West], ed. Khadidzha Ordukhanova (Baku: Sharg-Garb, 2009), 39.

20. Ayanda Adilova, *Puteshestvie k sebe: mir poeticheskikh substantsii Nazima Khikmeta v muzyke Frangiz Alizade* [Journey to herself: The substance of Nazim Hikmet's poetry as depicted in the music by Frangiz Alizade] (Baku: Adiloglu, 2003).

21. When performing this piece, F. Alizade achieves the effect of a prepared piano by putting a beaded necklace over the middle strings inside the instrument.

22. Abezgauz, *Opera "Keroglu,"* 54–55.

23. Karagicheva, "Mugamnaia opera Azerbaidzhana" [The mugham opera of Azerbaijan] in *Sovetskaia muzyka,* no. 12 (1988): 89.

24. The rich theatrical potential of *Mughamsayaghi* was visualized during its performance by the Tang Quartet at the Festival of Arts in Singapore in 2007; as the music progressed, pictures of elegantly veiled yet comprehensible sexual contents were projected on a screen.

25. Frangis Ali-Sade [Frangiz Alizade], Introduction to *"Mugam-Sajahy"* (n.p.: Edition Sikorski, 1993), 3.

26. Mervyn Cooke, "The East in the West": Evocations of the Gamelan in Western Music," in *The Exotic in Western Music,* ed. Jonathan Bellman (Boston: Northeastern University Press, 1998), 278.

27. Bernard Holland, "Four Unknown Works, Four Different Styles," *New York Times,* September 27, 1994.

28. Marianna Vysotskaia, *Mezhdu logikoi i paradoksom: kompozitor Faradzh Karaev* [Between the logic and paradox: composer Faraj Garayev] (Moscow: Moscow State Conservatory, 2012), 53–60.

29. Vladimir Barski, "Faradzh Karaev: 'Genug' or 'not Genug'," in *"Ex-Oriente . . . -II": Nine Composers from the Former USSR,* ed. by Valeriia Tsenova (Berlin: Verlag Emst Kuhn, 2003), 176.

30. *TRISTESSA II* is scored for two orchestras: symphony and chamber, and *TRIS-TESSA I* is for chamber orchestra.

31. Both dedications are "unofficial" and have been revealed by Dadashzade. Zumrud Dadashzade, *Simfoniyanin fezasi. 1970–80ci illar Azerbaijan simfoniyasi: esas temayuller* [The space of symphony. Azerbaijani symphony in the 1970and 1980s: Major trends] (Baku: Elm, 1999), 131–32.

32. Vysotskaia, *Mezhdu logikoi i paradoksom,* 177.

7. Songwriters

1. David MacFadyen, *Estrada?! Grand Narratives and the Philosophy of the Russian Popular Song since Perestroika* (Montreal: McGill-Queen's University Press, 2002), 3.

2. Martin Stokes, "Turkish Rock and Pop Music," in *Garland Encyclopedia of World Music. Vol. 6: The Middle East,* ed. Virginia Danielson (New York: Routledge, 2001), 247.

3. Arif Islamzade, "Soviet's Pride, Azerbaijan's Hell," *Azerbaijan International,* Autumn 1994, 26.

4. Tofig Guliyev, "Songs That Never Die," *Azerbaijan International,* Winter 1995, 75.

5. Aida Huseynova, *Music and Culture of Azerbaijan,* Global Voices Comprehensive, MJ & Associates, Inc., 2007, DVD.

8. Jazz *Mugham*

1. Rauf Farkhadov and Fariza Babayeva, *Rafik Babaev: Ot temy k improvizu* [Rafig Babayev: From theme to improvisation] (Baku: Letterpress, 2010), 63.

2. Farkhadov, *Vagif Mustafazade* (Baku: Ishig, 1986).

3. Farkhadov and Babayeva, *Rafik Babaev,* 64–65.

4. Mirzazade, interview.

5. Salman Gambarov, interview with author, June 15, 2008 (hereafter cited in text as SG).

6. Richard Stites, "Russian Popular Music to 1953," in *Soviet Music and Society under Lenin and Stalin,* ed. Neil Edmunds (London: Routledge Curzon, 2004), 27.

7. Big bands, however, remained popular throughout many decades of Azerbaijani jazz's history. There was the Jazz Orchestra under the Azerbaijan State Philharmonic that was led by the composer Rauf Hajiyev from 1955 to 1964. Another big band–style group – the Azerbaijan Estrada Orchestra of the Television and Radio – was founded in the 1960s, and the group was led by the saxophone player Tofig Ahmadov (1924–1981) for almost four decades.

8. Virgil Mihaiu, "A 1984 Panorama of Soviet Jazz," in *Russian Jazz: New Identity,* ed. Leo Feigin (New York: Quarter Book Limited, 1985), 161.

9. Starr, *Red and Hot: The Fate of Jazz in the Soviet Union. 1917–1991* (New York: Limelight Editions, 1994), 283, 285.

10. Farkhadov, *Vagif Mustafazade,* 22.

11. Mihaiu, "Soviet Jazz," 161.

12. Willian Minor, *Unzipped Souls: A Jazz Journey through the Soviet Union* (Philadelphia: Temple University Press, 1995), 8.

13. Farkhadov and Babayeva, *Rafik Babaev,* 179.

14. Tom Walsh, interview with author, November 20, 2011. In May 2001, Tom Walsh, professor of Jazz and Saxophone Studies at the Indiana University Jacobs School of

Music, spent eighteen days in Baku, Azerbaijan, interviewing local jazz musicians, performing with them, and giving master classes and workshops.

15. Walsh, "Jazz Mugham," unpublished manuscript, 2001, 3, Microsoft Word file.

16. Farkhadov and Babayeva, *Rafik Babaev*, 61.

17. Farkhadov, *Vagif Mustafazade*, 36.

18. Walsh, interview.

19. At the festival, the composition was performed by Gambarov (piano), Fakhraddin Dadashov (*kemancha*), and Eldar Gafarov (*naghara*). On other occasions, the *naghara* part was also played by Natig Shirinov.

20. Blair, "All Eyes on Aziza: Catching Up with Azerbaijan's Famous Jazz Artist," *Azerbaijan International*, Spring 2002, 27.

21. Minor, *Unzipped Souls*, 84.

22. Walsh, "Jazz Mugham," 6.

23. Ibid.

24. Tom Walsh, *New Life*, RIAX, 2002, compact disc.

25. Walsh, interview.

26. Minor, *Unzipped Souls*, 161.

9. Leaving the Post-Soviet Era Behind

1. Levin, "The Reterritorialization," 52.

2. The dates of Rostropovich's visits to Baku are as follows: April 28–May 3, 1997; June 7–17, 1998; November 21–27, 1999; October 7–9, 2000; February 27–March 4, 2002; January 25–28, 2004; September 16–19, 2004; March 6-8, 2005; February 20-26, 2006.

3. Annick Cojean, "Rostro le flamboyant revient a Bakou" [Flamboyant Rostropovich returns to Baku], trans. Alan Mercer, *Le Monde*, May 7, 1997.

4. Rostropovich was deprived of his Soviet citizenship and forced to leave the country in 1974 because of the support he showed his friend, the dissident Russian writer Alexander Solzhenitsyn.

5. Editorial, *Bakinskii Rabochii*, 1997. Leopold's letter to Hajibeyli is now on display at the Hajibeyli Home Museum in Baku.

6. Oldfield, *Azerbaijani Women Poet-Minstrels*, 42. Oldfield refers to the following source: Human Rights Watch, 1995, viii.

7. Dena El-Saffar, interview with the author, April 27, 2010.

8. Natavan had an encyclopedic knowledge of history and literature, spoke several European languages, and was known as an accomplished chess player. When the French writer Alexandre Dumas visited Garabagh in 1858, he was impressed by her vibrancy and brilliance, which strongly contradicted European stereotypes of Muslim woman. To commemorate their meeting, Dumas presented Natavan with a chess set, now on exhibit at the Museum of Azerbaijani Literature in Baku.

9. MacFadyen, *Estrada*, 64.

10. *City of Love*, Ashkhabad group, Real World B000000HOS, 1993, compact disc; *A Week or Two in the Real World*, with Van Morrison, The Holmes Brothers, Carole Rowley, Simon Emmerson, Raw Stylus, Mari Boine, Ashkhabad, and Toto La Momposina Y Sus Tambores, Real World B000000HP9 1995, compact disc.

11. Grinsteins Mischpoche, *On Air* (c) & (P), All You Can Eat Music AYCEP 003, 2000, compact disc.

12. Sezen Aksu, *Düş Bahçeleri,* sn Müzik B002AUOHDO, 1996, compact disc.

13. Keti Garbi, *Emmones Idees,* Sony Music/Columbia B000A2GLF6, 2003, compact disc.

14. *Orquestra Popular de Camara,* Adventure Music B00022XEIQ, 2004, compact disc.

15. Philip Bohlman, *World Music: A Very Short Introduction* (Oxford: Oxford University Press, 2002), 89.

16. Jack Ewing, "Singers from Azerbaijan Win Eurovision Contest," *New York Times,* May 16, 2011.

17. Bohlman, *World Music,* 89–90.

18. Badalbeyli, "Vek nyneshnii i vek minuvshii" [The present and past century], by Leyla Abdullayeva and Farah Aliyeva, *Muzykal'naia Akademiia,* no. 1 (2002): 230.

19. Majnun Karimov, *Azerbaijan musigi aletleri* [Musical instruments of Azerbaijan] (Baku: Yeni Nasil, 2003).

20. Jean Patterson, "Piecing Together History, String by String: The Reconstruction of Azerbaijan's Medieval Instruments," *Azerbaijan International,* Winter 1997, 28.

21. Siyavush Karimi, "A Place for Mugham: Azerbaijani Music Is Focus for New Conservatory," *Azerbaijan International,* Winter 2001, 60.

10. *"Mugham* Opera" of the Silk Road

1. In June 2009, the Silk Road Ensemble performed *Layla and Majnun* in New York on the occasion of the fiftieth anniversary of the Lincoln Center and included the arrangement in the program of its North American tour in March 2009. The world premiere occurred in Doha, Qatar, in November 2008, where *Layla and Majnun* was performed at the opening ceremony of the Museum of Islamic Arts. Excerpts from the work were introduced at the United Nations General Assembly Hall on the occasion of the United Nation's Day celebration on October 24, 2008.

2. Yo-Yo Ma, interview with the author, March 19, 2009 (hereafter cited in the text as YYM).

3. Colin Jacobsen, interview with the author, March 10, 2009 (hereafter cited in the text as CJ).

4. By 2007, the Silk Road Ensemble performed several works by Azerbaijani composers. In addition to *Darvish,* their repertoire included *Mughamsayaghi* [In the style of Mugham] (1993) and *Habilsayaghi* [In Habil's style] (1979) by F. Alizade; *Caravan* (2000) by Javanshir Guliyev; "Song of a Blind Arab" (1950) by Fikrat Amirov; and "Shikasta"from the opera Koroghlu (1937) by Hajibeyli.

5. Alim Gasimov, interview with the author, March 16, 2009 (hereafter cited in text as AG).

6. Among the musical depictions of this tragic love story are the symphonic poem *Leyli and Majnun* (1947) by Azerbaijani Gara Garayev; and two more operas, *The Song of Majnun* (1992) by Chinese-American Bright Sheng and *Leyli and Majnun* (1999) by Israeli Perez Eliyahu. The charm of this story even affected the world of Western rock music; in 1970, Eric Clapton wrote the song *Layla* that was included on the record in the album *Layla and Other Assorted Love Songs,* Derek and the Dominos B000000ISR, 1970, LP.

7. Kojiro Umezaki, interview with the author, March 17, 2009.

8. Ibid.

9. Levin, Liner notes for *Music of Central Asia Vol. 6: Alim and Fargana Qasimov: Spiritual Music of Azerbaijan,* Washington, D.C.: Smithsonian Folkways Recordings SFW40525, 2007, DVD.

10. Jonathan Gandelsman, interview with the author, March 10, 2009 (hereafter cited in the text as JG).

11. Toumani, "For the Love of Layla," *New York Times,* March 1, 2009.

12. Rebecca J. Ritzel, "Silk Road Ensemble Enlivens Ancient Opera," *Washington Post,* March 14, 2009.

13. Henrik Soderstrom, e-mail message to the author, July 8, 2010 (hereafter cited in text as HS).

Epilogue

1. Aga Khan is an honorific title that has been bestowed on the Imam (spiritual leader) of the Shia Imami Ismaili Muslims since 1818. The Ismailis constitute a large Shia community in the Islamic world and are now scattered in more than twenty countries in Asia, Europe, the Americas, and Africa. The present leader of this community, the Aga Khan IV (b. 1936), succeeded his grandfather in 1957. The title His Highness was granted to the Aga Khan by Her Majesty the Queen of Great Britain in 1957.

2. James McCalla, *Twentieth-Century Chamber Music* (New York: Routledge, 2003), 59.

3. *Mugam Sayagi: Music of Franghiz Ali-Zadeh*, Nonesuch B000611PMG, 2005, compact disc.

4. Kronos Quartet, *Floodplain*, Nonesuch Records B001XJBDNA, 2009, compact disc; *Rainbow: Music of Central Asia. Vol. 8*, Kronos Quartet with Alim and Fargana Qasimov and Homayun Sakhi, Smithsonian Folkways SFW40527, 2010, compact disc.

5. Levin, Liner notes to *Rainbow*, 16–17.

6. Ibid., 28.

BIBLIOGRAPHY

Abasova, Elmira. "K voprosu natsional'nogo svoeobraziia tematizma Kara Karaeva" [On the question of the national qualities of the thematism of Gara Garayev]. In *Kara Karaev. Stat'i. Pis'ma. Vyskazyvaniia*, 314–41.

———. *Opera "Keroglu" Uzeira Gadzhibekova* [The opera "Koroghlu" by Uzeir Haji-beyli]. Baku: Azmuzgiz, 1966.

———. *Opery i muzykal'nye komedii Uzeira Gadzhibekova* [Operas and musical comedies by Uzeyir Hajibeyli]. Baku: Izdatel'stvo Akademii nauk Azerbaidzhanskoi SSR, 1961.

———. *Uzeir Gadzhibekov. Put' zhizni i tvorchestva* [Uzeyir Hajibeyli: His life and music]. Baku: Elm, 1985.

Abasova, Elmira, Daniil Danilov, Liudmila Karagicheva, and Kovkab Safaraliyeva, eds. *Azerbaidzhanskaia Gosudarstvennaia Konservatoriia imeni Uzeira Gadzhibekova* [The Azerbaijan State Conservatory named after Uzeyir Hajibeyli]. Baku: Azerneshr, 1972.

Abdullayeva, Seadet. *Azerbayjan folklorunda chalghi aletleri* [Musical instruments in Azerbaijani folklore]. Baku: Adiloghlu, 2007.

Abdullazade, Fatma, ed. *Mstislav Rostropovich: Articles and Materials*. Baku: Presidential Publication, 1997.

Abdullazade, Gulnaz. *Filosofskaia sushchnost' azerbaidzhanskikh mugamov* [The philosophy of Azerbaijani mughams]. Baku: Yazichi, 1983.

Abezgauz, Izabella. *Opera "Keroglu" Uzeira Gadzhibekova: o khudozhestvennykh otkrytiiakh kompozitora* [The opera "Koroghlu" by Uzeyir Hajibeyli: About the composer's artistic innovations]. Moscow: Sovetskii Kompozitor, 1987.

———. "Stanovlenie khudozhnika" [Formation of the artist]. *Sovetskaia Muzyka*, no. 3 (1967): 7–12.

———. "'V'etnam' i 'Don Kikhot'" ["Vietnam" and "Don Quixote"]. In *Gara Garayev. Ocherklar* [Gara Garayev: Essays], edited by Gulnaz Abdullazade, Shahla Mahmudova and Gulzar Mahmudova, 38–56. Baku: Chinar Chap, 2003.

Adilova, Ayanda. "Nazim Khikmet v tvorchestve azerbaidzhanskikh kompozitorov" [Nazim Hikmet in the works of Azerbaijani composers]. Synopsis of PhD diss., Baku Music Academy, 2004.

———. *Puteshestvie k sebe: mir poeticheskikh substantsii Nazima Khikmeta v muzyke Frangiz Alizade* [Journey to herself: The substance of Nazim Hikmet's poetry as depicted in the music of Frangiz Alizade]. Baku: Adiloglu, 2003.

Agaeva, Suraia, ed. *Entsiklopediia azerbaidzhanskogo mugama* [The Encyclopedia of Azerbaijani mugham]. Baku: Sharg-Garb, 2012.

Akhmadova, Sevindzh. *Arshin Mal Alan pokoriaet Los-Andzheles* [The Cloth Peddler conquers Los-Angeles]. E-magazine of the American-Azerbaijani Promotion Fund. Accessed February 23, 2015. http://www.net-fax.org/index.php?article=news_851.

Akhundov, Fuad. "Shovkat Mammadova: Audacious Challenge: The First Azerbaijani Woman on Stage." *Azerbaijan International,* Winter 1997, 34–37.

Akhundova, Nigar. "Simfonicheskoe tvorchestvo Arifa Melikova: k probleme obnovleniia zhanra" [The symphonic works by Arif Malikov: On the problem of the innovative interpretation of the genre]. Synopsis of PhD diss., Baku Music Academy, 1995.

Akhundova, Nigar, and Aida Huseynova. "Arts: Composers: The Caucasus." In *Encyclopedia of Women and Islamic Cultures. Vol. 5: Practices, Interpretations and Representations,* 4–5. Leiden: Brill, 2007.

———. "Arts: Performers and Performing Groups: Azerbaijan." In *Encyclopedia of Women and Islamic Cultures Vol. 5: Practices, Interpretations and Representations,* 64–65. Leiden: Brill, 2007.

Alasgarli, Kamalya, ed. *Khayyam Mirzazade hagginda yazilar, fikirler, megaleler, dushunjalar* [Publications, thoughts, articles, and considerations on Khayyam Mirzazade]. 2 vols. Baku: Nurlan, 2011.

Albright, Daniel. *Modernism and Music: An Anthology of Sources.* Chicago: University of Chicago Press, 2004.

Alekperova, Nelli. *Arif Melikov: Stranitsy zhizni i tvorchestva* [Arif Malikov: Vignettes of his life and music]. Baku: Ishig, 1988.

Alieva, Narmina. "K voprosu ob elementakh mnogogolosiia v azerbaidzhanskoi narodnoi muzyke" [About polyphonic elements in Azerbaijani folk music]. In *Iskusstvo Azerbaidzhana* [The art of Azerbaijan]. Vol. 12: 54–66. Baku: Izdatel'stvo Akademii nauk Azerbaidzhanskoi SSR, 1968.

———. "K voprosu polifonicheskogo mnogogolosiia v azerbaidzhanskom mugame" [About the polyphonic category of multipart texture in Azerbaijani mugham]. In *Borbad i khudozhestvennye traditsii narodov Tsentral'noi i Perednei Azii: istoriia i sovremennost'* [Borbad and artistic traditions of the peoples of Central and Near Asia: History and modenity]. 347–49. Dushanbe: Donish, 1990.

Alieva, Nigar. *Bellissimo! Fidan and Khuraman.* Baku: Friends of Azerbaijani Culture Foundation, 2005.

———. "Passakaliia i fuga v tvorchestve Kara Karaeva: K probleme vzaimodeistviia klassicheskikh polifonicheskikh form s osnovopolagaiushchimi chertami azerbaidzhanskoi muzyki ustnoi traditsii" [Passacaglia and fugue in the music of Gara Garayev: On the problem of the relationship between classical polyphonic forms and the major principles of Azerbaijani music of the oral tradition]. Synopsis of PhD diss., Kyiv State Conservatory, 1989.

Ali-Sade, Frangis [Alizade, Frangiz]. Introduction to"*Mugam-Sajahy,*" 3. N.p.: Edition Sikorski, 1993.

Aliyeva, Farah. *Azerbaijan musigisinda uslub akhtarishlari* [Exploring Azerbaijani musical style]. Baku: Elm va Hayat, 1996.

———, ed. *XX asr Azerbaijan musigi madaniyyati tarikhinin gaynaghlari* [Sources on twentieth century-Azerbaijani music]. 3 vols. Baku: Nurlan, 2005–2006.

———, *XX asr Azerbaijan musigisi: tarikh va zamanla uz-uza* [Twentieth-century Azerbaijani music: Encountering the history and the epoch]. Baku: Elm, 2007.

———. *Musigi tariximizin sahifalari* [Vignettes of our music history]. Baku: Adiloghlu, 2003.

Alizade, Frangiz. "Muzyka nuzhdaetsia v krasote" [Music is in need of beauty], interview with Marina Kareva. *Muzykal'naia Akademiia*, no. 1 (2002): 190–93.

———. "Ot 'Leili i Medzhnun" k Tret'ei simfonii" [From "Leyli and Majnun" to the Third Symphony]. In *Gara Garayev. Ocherklar* [Gara Garayev: Essays], edited by Gulnaz Abdullazade, Shahla Mahmudova, and Gulzar Mahmudova, 92–112. Baku: Chinar Chap, 2003.

Allworth, Edward, ed. *Central Asia: 130 Years of Russian Dominance, a Historical Overview*. Durham, NC: Duke University Press, 1994.

Alstadt, Audrey L. *Azerbaijani Turks: Power and Identity under Russian Rule*. Stanford, CA: Hoover Institution Press, 1992.

Alstadt-Mirhadi, Audrey L. "Baku: Transformation of a Muslim Town." In *The City in Late Imperial Russia,* edited by Michael Hamm, 282–318. Bloomington: Indiana University Press, 1986.

Anar [pseud.]. "Dahi bastakarimiz" [Our great composer]. In *Uzeyir Hajibeyov Ensiklopediyasi* [The Encyclopedia of Uzeyir Hajibeyli], 10–16. Baku: Azerbaijan Nashriyyati, 1996.

———. "Svet Karaeva" [The Light of Garayev]. *Muzykal'naia Akademiia*, no. 1 (2002): 174–78.

Anderson, Benedict. *Imagined Communities: Reflections on the Origin and Spread of Nationalism*. London: Verso, 2006.

Appadurai, Arjun. *Modernity at Large: Cultural Dimensions of Globalization*. Minneapolis: University of Minnesota Press, 1996.

Applebaum, Anne. *Between East and West: Across the Borderlands of Europe*. New York: Pantheon, 1994.

Azerbaijan arkhivi: Azerbaijan Dovlat Konservatoriyasinin tarikhindan (1920–1957) [The archives of Azerbaijan: From the history of the Azerbaijan State Conservatory (1920–1957)], no. 2–3 (1985).

Babayev, Elkhan. *Ananavi musigimiz: mushahideler ve mulahizeler* [Our traditional music: Observations and considerations]. Baku: Elm, 2000.

———. *Azerbaijan mugham destgahlarinda ritmintonasiya problemlari* [Problems of rhythm and intonation in Azerbaijani mugham destgah]. Baku: Ergun, 1996.

———. *Shifahi ananali Azerbaijan musigisinda intonasiya problemlari* [Problems of intonation in the Azerbaijani music of oral tradition]. Baku: Elm, 1998.

———. "Vpolne v nashikh silakh" [Completely in our competence], interview with Aida Huseynova. In *Sansiz saninla* [Without you but still with you], edited by Hajar Babayeva, 217–24. Baku: Adiloghlu, 2006.

Badalbeyli, Afrasiyab. *Izahli monografik musigi lughati* [Comprehensive music dictionary]. Baku: Elm, 1969.

Badalbeyli, Farhad. "Altmishinjilarin nailiyyatlarini itirmak olmaz" [We should not forget the accomplishments of the 1960s], interview with Aida Huseynova. *Gobustan*, no. 1–2 (1998): 26–31.

———. "Vek nyneshnii i vek minuvshii" [The present and past century]. By Leyla Abdullaeva and Farah Alieva. *Muzykal'naia Akademiia*, no. 1 (2002): 230–32.

Baghirova, Sana. "Azerbaijani Mugham: Declared Masterpiece of Oral World Heritage by UNESCO." *Azerbaijan International,* Winter 2003, 25.

Baghirova, Sanubar. *Azerbaidzhanskii mugam. Stat'i. Issledovaniia. Doklady* [Azerbaijani mugham. Articles. Research papers. Presentations]. Baku: Elm, 2007.

———. "Etiudy o Gadzhibekove" [Essays about Hajibeyli]. *Muzykal'naia Akademiia,* no. 1 (2002): 203–6.

Bakst, James. *A History of Russian-Soviet Music.* New York: Dodd, Mead, 1966.

Barry, Ellen. "Eurovision Joy Deflects Cares for a While." *New York Times,* May 15, 2011.

Barski, Vladimir. "Faradzh Karaev: 'Genug' or 'not Genug.'" In *"Ex-Oriente . . . -II": Nine Composers from the Former USSR,* edited by Valeriia Tsenova, 173–83. Berlin: Verlag Emst Kuhn, 2003.

Bartok, Bela. "The Influence of Peasant Music on Modern Music." In *Modernism and Music: An Anthology of Sources,* edited by Daniel Albright, 244–48. Chicago: The University of Chicago Press, 2004.

Baum, Michael. *A Wider Europe: The Process and Politics of European Union Enlargement.* Lanham, MD: Rowman and Littlefield, 2000.

Bauman, Max Peter. "Folk Music Revival: Concepts between Regression and Emancipation." *World of Music* 38, no. 3 (1996): 71–86.

———. "The Local and the Global: Traditional Musical Instruments and Modernization." *World of Music* 42, no. 3 (2000): 121–44.

Bayramova, Alla. "Literatura v zhizni i tvorchestve Kara Karaeva" [Literature in the life and work of Gara Garayev]. *Muzykal'naia Akademiia,* no. 3 (2013): 96–101.

———. "Rol' muzeev v sbore, sokhranenii, izuchenii i propagande materialov muzykal'-noi kul'tury Azerbaidzhana" [The role of museums in collecting, preserving, studying, and promoting the sources of Azerbaijani musical culture]. PhD diss., Baku Music Academy, 2004.

Beibutova, Saida, and Aida Guseinova [Huseynova]. "Elmira Mirza Riza gizi Nazirova." In *Vydaiushchiesia deiateli fortepiannoi kul'tury Azerbaidzhana* [Prominent representatives of the piano culture of Azerbaijan], edited by Tarlan Seidov, 115–29. Baku: Ishig, 1988.

Beliaev, Victor. *Central Asian Music: Essays in the History of Music of the Peoples of the USSR.* Middletown, CT: Wesleyan University Press, 1975.

———. *Ocherki po istorii muzyki narodov SSSR* [Essays in the history of the music of the peoples of the USSR]. 2 vols. Moscow: Gosmuzgiz, 1962.

Bilinski, Yaroslav. "Education of the Non-Russian Peoples in the USSR, 1917–1967: An Essay." *Slavic Review* 28 (1968): 411–38.

Blair, Betty. "All Eyes on Aziza: Catching Up with Azerbaijan's Famous Jazz Artist." *Azerbaijan International,* Spring 2002, 24–27.

———. "Hajibeyov's Opera 'Koroghlu' (Son of a Blind Man)." *Azerbaijan International,* Autumn 2001, 59.

Blair, Betty, and Fuad Akhundov. *About Uzeyir Hajibeyov – A Conversation with Ramazan Khalilov.* Accessed February 23, 2015. http://www.hajibeyov.com/bio/bio_life /khalilov_ramazan/khalilov_ramazan_eng/khalilov_ramazan.html.

Blair, Betty, Fuad Akhundov, Shamil Fatullayev, Fakhreddin Miralayev, and Jala Garibova. "Architecture of the Oil Baron Period." *Azerbaijan International,* Winter 1998, 29–41.

Blum, Stephen. "Hearing the Music of the Middle East." In *The Garland Encyclopedia of World Music. Vol. 6: The Middle East,* edited by Virginia Danielson, Scott Marcus, and Dwight Reynolds, 3–13. New York: Routledge, 2002.

Blume, Friedrich. *Renaissance and Baroque Music: A Comprehensive Survey.* New York: W. W. Norton, 1967.

Bohlman, Philip. "The European Discovery of Music in the Islamic World and the 'Non-Western' in 19th-Century Music History." *Journal of Musicology* 5 (1987): 147–63.

——. *The Music of European Nationalism: Cultural Identity and Modern History.* Santa Barbara, CA: ABC-CLIO, 2004.

——. "World Music at the 'End of History.'" *Ethnomusicology* 46 (2002): 1–32.

——. *World Music: A Very Short Introduction.*Oxford: Oxford University Press, 2002.

Born, Georgina, and David Hesmondhalgh, eds. *Western Music and Its Others: Difference, Representation, and Appropriation in Music.* Berkeley: University of California Press, 2000.

Bowie, Andrew. "Music and the Rise of Aesthetics." In *The Cambridge History of Nineteenth-Century Music,* edited by Jim Samson. 29–54. Cambridge: Cambridge University Press, 2002.

Boyce, Mary. *Zoroastrians: Their Religious Beliefs and Practices.* New York: Routledge, 2001.

Braker, Hans. "The Muslim Revival in Russia." In *Russia Enters the Twentieth Century, 1894–1917,* edited by Erwin Oberlander, George Katkov, Nikolaus Poppe, and Georg Von Rauch, 182–98. New York: Schocken Books, 1971.

Brown, David. *Mikhail Glinka: A Biographical and Critical Study.* London: Oxford University Press, 1974.

Brown, Malcolm Hamrick, ed. *Russian and Soviet Music: Essays for Boris Schwarz.* Ann Arbor, MI: UMI Research Press, 1984.

Bukhanov, Viktor. "Iskusstvo obiazyvaet: rasskazyvaet Kara Karaev" [Art obliges: Gara Garayev talks]. *Molodezh' Azerbaidzhana,* December 18, 1963.

Bukofzer, Manfred F. *Music in the Baroque Era: From Monteverdi to Bach.* New York: W. W. Norton, 1947.

Burkholder, Peter J., Donald Jay Grout, and Claude V. Palisca. *A History of Western Music.* 8th ed. New York: Norton, 2010.

Calvocoressi, Michel Dimitri. *A Survey of Russian Music.* Harmondsworth: Penguin Books, 1944.

Carl, Robert. Review of *Ali-Zadeh. Oasis. Apsheron Quintet. Music for the Piano. Mugam Sayaghi* by Kronos String Qartet (*Nonesuch 79804-2*) *Fanfare* 28, May/June 2005, 77–78.

Chatterjee, Partha. *Nationalist Thought and the Colonial World: A Derivative Discourse.* Minneapollis: University of Minnesota Press, 1993.

Chelebiev, Faik. "Morfologiia dastgiakha" [The morphology of destgah]. Synopsis of PhD diss., Russian Institute of the Art History, 2009.

Cojean, Annick. "Rostro le flamboyant revient a Bakou" [Flamboyant Rostropovich returns to Baku]. *Le Monde,* May 7, 1997.

Cooke, Mervyn. "'The East in the West': Evocations of the Gamelan in Western Music." In *The Exotic in Western Music,* edited by Jonathan Bellman, 258–80. Boston: Northeastern University Press, 1998.

Cooper, Martin. *Russian Opera.* London: M. Parrish, 1951.

Dadashzade, Zumrud. "*Actis Testantibus:* po prochtenii novogo issledovaniia o Kara Karaeve" [*Actis Testantibus:* Upon reading a new work on Gara Garayev]. In *Gara Garayev. Ocherklar* [Gara Garayev: Essays], edited by Gulnaz Abdullazade, Shahla Mahmudova, and Gulzar Mahmudova, 255–73. Baku: Chinar Chap, 2003.

———. *Agshin Alizade.* Baku: Shur, 1992.

———. "Javanshir Guliyevin total musigi akhtarishlari" [Javanshir Guliyev in a quest for the total music]. In *Biz da bu dunyanin hissasiyik* [We are also a part of this world], 104–16. Baku: Nurlan, 2004.

———. "Musigida mavi semanin bir parchasi: Rahilya Hasanova" [Music depicting a piece of blue sky: Rahilya Hasanova]. In *Biz da bu dunyanin hissasiyik* [We are also a part of this world], 150–62. Baku: Nurlan, 2004.

———. *Simfoniyanin fezasi. 1970–80ci illar Azerbaijan simfoniyasi: esas temayuller* [The space of the symphony. The Azerbaijani symphony in the 1970s and 1980s: Major trends]. Baku: Elm, 1999.

Dahlhaus, Carl. *Between Romanticism and Modernism: Four Studies in the Music of the Late Nineteenth Century.* Berkeley: University of California Press, 1980.

Danilevich, Lev. *D.D. Shostakovich.* Moscow: Sovetskii Kompozitor, 1958.

Danilov, Daniil. *Fikret Amirov* [Fikrat Amirov]. Baku: Azgosizdat, 1965.

Deschenes, Bruno, ed. "The Music of "Others" in the Western World." Special issue, *World of Music* 47, no. 3 (2005).

Dilbazova, Minira. *Iz muzykal'nogo proshlogo Baku* [From Baku's musical past]. Baku: Ishig, 1985.

Djani-Zade, Tamila. "Mnogourovnevaia realizatsiia khudozhestvennogo kanona v ispolnitel'skoi praktike azerbaidzhanskikh mugamov" [Various levels of realization of the artistic canon in the performing practice of Azerbaijani mughams]. In *Traditsii muzykal'nykh kul'tur narodov Blizhnego, Srednego Vostoka i sovremennost'* [Traditions of the musical cultures of the peoples of the Near and Middle East in the modern age], edited by Dilbar Rashidova and Tokhtasin Gafurbekov, 106–12. Moscow: Sovetskii kompozitor, 1987.

———. "Music of Azerbaijan." In *Garland Encyclopedia of World Music. Vol. 6: The Middle East*, 921–32. New York: Routledge, 2001.

Djumaev, Alexander. "Musical Heritage and National Identity in Uzbekistan." *Ethnomusicology Forum* 14 (2005): 165–84.

———. "Power Structures, Power Policy, and Traditional Music in Soviet Central Asia." In "Musical Processes in Asia and Oceania." Special issue, *Yearbook for Traditional Music.* 25 (1993): 43–50.

Dolzhanskii, Aleksandr. "Iz nabliudenii nad stilem Shostakovicha" [From the observations over Shostakovich's style]. *Sovetskaia Muzyka*, no. 10 (1959): 95–102.

Dumas, Alexander. *Adventure in Caucasia.* Westport, CT: Greenwood Press, 1962.

During, Jean. *La musique traditionnelle de l'Azerbayjan et la science des muqams* [The traditional music of Azerbaijan and the study of mughams]. Baden-Baden: Bouxwiller, Koerner, 1988.

———. "Power, Authority, and Music in the Cultures of Inner Asia." *Ethnomusicology Forum* 14 (2005): 143–64.

———. "The Place of the Azerbaijani Mugham in Its Caucasian and Iranian Environment." In *Proceedings of the Second International Musicological Symposium 'Space of Mugham' (15–17 March 2011)*, 65–72. Baku: Sharg-Garb, 2011.

———. "Third Millennium Tehran: Music." *Iranian Studies* 38 (2005): 373–98.
———. "Recording Reviews: Two Essays on Recordings of Music from Azerbaijan." *Ethnomusicology* 44 (2000): 529–38.
———. "Hearing and Understanding in the Islamic Gnosis." *World of Music* 39 (1997): 127–37.
Editorial, *Bakinskii Rabochii,* May 6, 1997.
Efendieva, Imruz. *Azerbaidzhanskaia sovetskaia pesnia* [The Azerbaijani Soviet song]. Baku: Yazichi, 1981.
———. *Vasif Adigozalov.* Baku: Shur, 1999.
Efimenko, Sergei. "Faradzh Karaev. Zhizn'. Tvorchestvo. Idei" [Faraj Garayev. Life. Works. Ideas]. Master thesis, Moscow State Conservatory, 2002.
Eldarova, Emina. *Iskusstvo ashugov Azerbaidzhana* [The art of Azerbaijani ashigs]. Baku: Ishig, 1984.
———. "Nekotorye voprosy muzykal'nogo tvorchestva ashugov" [Some questions on the musical art of ashigs]. In *Azerbaidzhanskaia muzyka* [Music of Azerbaijan], edited by Jovdat Hajiyev, Daniil Danilov, Daniel' Zhitomirskii, Gara Garayev, Said Rustamov, and Nigar Usubova, 64–85. Moscow: Gosmuzgiz, 1961.
Emslie, Barry. *Wagner and the Centrality of Love.* Woodbridge: Boydell Press, 2010.
Ewing, Jack. "Singers from Azerbaijan Win Eurovision Contest." *New York Times,* May 16, 2011.
Fanning, David. *The Breath of the Symphonist: Shostakovich's Tenth.* London: Royal Musical Association, 1988.
Farkhadov, Rauf. "Fikret Amirov vo vremeni i prostranstve" [Fikrat Amirov in time and space] *Shargi,* no. 2 (2002): 68–70.
———. "Takaia korotkaia zhizn'" [Such a short life], *Kultura* portal. Accessed February 23, 2015. http://www.kultura.az/articles.php?item_id=20110622044803652&sec _id=16.
———. *Vagif Mustafazade.* Baku: Ishig, 1986.
Farkhadov, Rauf, and Fariza Babayeva. *Rafik Babaev: Ot temy k improvizu* [Rafig Babayev: From theme to improvisation]. Baku: Letterpress, 2010.
Farkhadov, Rauf, and Vladimir Tarnopolskii, "Napriazhenie Faradzha Karaeva/Besedy o tvorchestve Faradzha Karaeva" [The tension of Faraj Garayev: Conversation about Faraj Garayev's music], in *Muzykal'naia Zhizn',* no. 1 (2006): 38–40.
Fay, Laurel. *Shostakovich: A Life.* New York: Oxford University Press, 2000.
Fedosova, Eleonora. *Diatonicheskie lady v tvorchestve D. Shostakovicha* [Diatonic modes in the music of Shostakovich]. Moscow: Sovetskii Kompozitor, 1980.
Felzer, Oleg, and Alla Bretanitskaia. "Faradzh Karaev (eskiz portreta)" [Faraj Garayev: A sketch of the portrait]. In Vol. 5 of *Kompozitory soiuznykh respublik* [Composers from the Soviet republics], edited by Marina Nest'eva, 139–67. Moscow: Sovetskii Kompozitor, 1986.
Ferenc, Anna. "Music in the Socialist State." In *Soviet Music and Society under Lenin and Stalin,* edited by Neil Edmunds, 8–18. London: Routledge Curzon, 2004.
Fierman, William. "Language Vitality and Paths to Revival: Contrasting Cases of Azerbaijani and Kazakh." *International Journal of the Sociology of Language,* no. 198 (July 2009): 75–104.
Finkelstein, Sidney. *Composer and Nation: The Folk Heritage in Music.* New York: International Publishers, 1989.

Frolova-Walker, Marina. *Russian Music and Nationalism from Glinka to Stalin.* New Haven: Yale University Press, 2007.

Gabai, Iurii. "Monolog prodolzhaetsia" [The monologue continues]. *Sovetskaia Muzyka,* no. 10 (1986): 26–32.

Gadzhibekov, Uzeir [Hajibeyli, Uzeyir]. "Ob azerbaidzhanskoi tiurkskoi narodnoi muzyke" [About Azerbaijani Turkic folk music]. *Na Rubezhe Vostoka,* no. 3 (1929): 76–78.

———. "Muzykal'no-prosvetitel'nye zadachi v Azerbaidzhane" [The tasks of music education in Azerbaijan] *Iskusstvo,* no. 1 (1921): 10–11.

———. *O muzykal'nom iskusstve Azerbaidzhana* [About the musical art of Azerbaijan]. Baku: Azerneshr, 1966.

Gann, Kyle. "Master of Mugham." *Village Voice,* February 20, 2000.

Gellner, Ernest. *Nations and Nationalism.* Ithaca, NY: Cornell University Press, 2006.

Gevinson, Alan. *Within Our Gates: Ethnicity in American Feature Films, 1911–1960.* Berkeley: University of California Press, 1997.

Gillies, Malcolm, ed. *Bartók Remembered.* London: Faber, 1990.

Gliere, Reinhold. Letter from 29 June 1914. In Vol. 1 of *Reingol'd Moritsevich Gliere. Stat'i. Vospominaniia. Materialy* [Reinhold Moritsevich Gliere. Articles. Memoirs. Materials], edited by Valerian Bogdanov-Berezovsky, 376–77. Moscow: Muzyka, 1965.

———. "Muzyka azerbaidzhanskikh kompozitorov" [Music of Azerbaijani composers]. *Bakinskii Rabochii,* December 29, 1944.

———. "Narod – velikii uchitel'" [People are the best teachers]. In Vol. 1 of *Reingol'd Moritzevich Glier. Stat'i. Vospominaniia. Materialy* [Reinhold Moritsevich Gliere. Articles. Memoirs. Materials], edited by Valerian Bogdanov-Berezovsky, 293–99. Moscow: Muzyka, 1965.

Gokalp, Ziya. *Turkish Nationalism and Western Civilization: Selected Essays.* Westport, CT: Greenwood Press Publishers, 1981.

Grigor'ev, Lev, and Iakov Platek. "Besedy s masterami: Kara Karaev" [Conversations with the masters: Gara Garayev]. *Muzykal'naia Zhizn',* no. 6 (1974): 15–17.

Guliyev, Tofig. "Songs That Never Die." *Azerbaijan International,* Winter 1995, 74–75.

Guseinova, Aida [Huseynova, Aida]. "Frangiz Alizade: Sliianie mirov" [Frangiz Alizade: Merging worlds]. In *Frangiz Alizade: Triumfal'nye peresecheniia Vostoka i Zapada* [Frangiz Alizade: Triumphal crossings of the East and the West], edited by Khadid-zha Ordukhanova, 29–47. Baku: Sharg-Garb, 2009.

———. "K voprosu sravnitel'noi kharakteristiki avtografa i redaktsii Gliera opery Muslima Magomaeva *Nargiz*" [On the question of the comparative analysis of the original version and Gliere's version of the opera "Nargiz" by Muslim Magomaev]. Master's thesis, Azerbaijan State Conservatory, 1987.

———. *Muslim Magomaev. Opernoe tvorchestvo: Opyt muzykal'no-tekstologicheskogo analiza* [Muslim Magomayev. Operas: Musicological and textological study]. Baku: Azerbaijan Gadini, 1997.

Hajibeyov, Uzeyir [Hajibeyli, Uzeyir]. "Azerbaijan musigi heyatina bir nazar" [Glance at the musical life in Azerbaijan]. *Madaniyyat ve Injasanat,* no. 1 (1926): 27–30; no. 2–3 (1926): 23–26.

———. *Azerbaijan turklarinin musigisi hagginda* [About the music of Azerbaijani Turks]. Baki: Adiloglu, 2005.

———. *Principles of Azerbaijani Folk Music.* Baku: Yazichi, 1985.

Hasanova, Jamilya. *Azerbaijan musigisinin megamlari* [The modes of Azerbaijani music]. Baku: Elm va Tahsil, 2012.

Henry, James Dodds. *Baku: An Eventful History.* London: Archibald Constable, 1905.

Hilsman, Hoyt. "An Azerbaijani Operetta at the Dorothy Chandler," *Huffington Post,* September 9, 2013.

Hirsch, Francine. "Toward an Empire of Nations: Border-Making and the Formation of Soviet National Identities." *Russian Review* 59 (2000): 201–26.

Ho, Allan, and Dmitry Feofanov, eds. *Biographical Dictionary of Russian/Soviet Composers.* New York: Greenwood Press, 1989.

———. *Shostakovich Reconsidered.* London: Toccata Press, 1998.

Hobsbawm, Eric J. *Nations and Nationalism since 1780: Programme, Myth, Reality.* Cambridge: Cambridge University Press, 1990.

Holland, Bernard, "Four Unknown Works, Four Different Styles." *New York Times,* September 27, 1994.

Hroch, Miroslav. *Social Preconditions of National Revival in Europe.* Cambridge: Cambridge University Press, 1985.

Hunter, Mary. "The Alla Turca Style in the Late Eighteenth Century: Race and Gender in the Symphony and the Seraglio." In *The Exotic in Western Music,* edited by Jonathan Bellman, 43–73. Boston: Northeastern University Press, 1998.

Huseinova, Aida [Huseynova, Aida]. "Newsmakers: Agshin Alizade: New Ballet – Journey to the Caucasus." *Azerbaijan International,* Winter 2002, 12.

———. "Politically Correct Music: Stalin's Era and the Struggle of Azerbaijani Composers." *Azerbaijan International,* Summer 2006, 56–64.

———. "Shostakovich's Tenth: Azerbaijani Link – Elmira Nazirova." *Azerbaijan International,* Spring 2003, 54–59.

Huseynova, Aida. "Azerbaijani Mugam Opera: Challenge of the East." In *Identity, Culture, and Language Teaching,* edited by Pavel Sysoev, 60–67. Iowa City: University of Iowa: Center for Russian, East European and Eurasian Studies, 2002.

———. "Baku, Philharmonic, Shostakovich. . . ." *DSCH Journal,* no. 21 (2004): 52–53.

———. "Choral Music in West and Central Asia." In *The Cambridge Companion to Choral Music,* edited by Andre de Quadros, 169–76. Cambridge: Cambridge University Press, 2012.

———. "The Heart of the Tenth Symphony." *DSCH Journal,* no. 17 (2002): 38–40.

———. "In Memoriam: Elmira Nazirova." *DSCH Journal,* no. 41 (2014): 66.

———. "Mstislav Leopoldovich Rostropovich (1927–2007): A Tribute from Azerbaijan." *DSCH Shostakovich Journal,* no. 27 (2007): 71–72.

———. *Muslim Magomayev: Essays.* Baku: Chinar-Chap, 2003.

———. "Relating Shostakovich." *DSCH Journal,* no. 18 (2003): 39–40.

Huseynova, Lala. *Azerbaijan Bestekarlar Ittifagi: boyuk yolun tarikhi (1934–2009)* [The Composers Union of Azerbaijan: History of the Remarkable Journey (1934–2009)]. Baku: "E.L." NPS MMC, 2010.

Imanova, Ulviyya. "Klassitsizm XX veka i muzyka Kara Karaeva" [Twentieth-century classicism and the music of Gara Garayev]. Synopsis of PhD diss., Tashkent State Conservatory, 1990.

———. "Starinnye tantseval'nye zhanry i zhanry, blizkie k tantseval'nym, v muzyke Kara Karaeva" [Ancient dance and dance-like genres in the music of Gara Garayev].

In *Gara Garayev. Ocherklar* [Gara Garayev. Essays], edited by Gulnaz Abdullazade, Shahla Mahmudova, and Gulzar Mahmudova, 57–70. Baku: Chinar-Chap, 2003.

Islamzade, Arif. "Soviet's Pride, Azerbaijan's Hell." *Azerbaijan International*, Autumn 1994, 26–27, 30.

Ismayilov, Mammad Saleh. "Azerbaijan khalg megamlarinin gohumlug munasibetleri hagginda" [About the relationship among Azerbaijani folk modes]. *Uchenye Zapiski Azerbaidzhanskoi Gosudarstvennoi Konservatorii* [Research Papers of the Azerbaijan State Conservatory], no. 9 (1972): 5–43.

———. *Azerbaijan xalg musigisinin janrlari* [Genres of Azerbaijani folk music]. Baku: Ishig, 1984.

———. *Strukturnye osobennosti ladov azerbaidzhanskoi narodnoi muzyki* [Structural particularities of the modes of Azerbaijani folk music]. Baku: Azerbaijan State Conservatory, 1981.

Ismayilov, Murad. "State, Identity, and the Policy of Music: Eurovision and the Nation-Building in Azerbaijan." *Nationalities Papers* 40 (2012): 833–51.

Ismayilova, Gamar. *Muslim Magomayev*. Baku: Azerneshr, 1986.

Kafarova, Zemfira. *"Keroglu" Uzeira Gadzhibekova* ["Koroghlu" by Uzeyir Hajibeyli]. Baku: Yazichi, 1981.

Kaiser, Robert J. *The Geography of Nationalism in Russia and the USSR*. Princeton: Princeton University Press, 1994.

Karaev, Kara [Gara Garayev]. "Liubov' k trem Kavkazam" [Love for the three Caucasuses], interview with Ramil Khakimov. *Vecherniaia Ufa*, November 23, 1972.

———. "Neskol'ko myslei o tragicheskom v muzyke" [A few thoughts about the tragedy in music]. *Sovetskaia Muzyka*, no. 4 (1957): 62–65.

———. "Ob Uzeire Gadzhibekove" [About Uzeyir Hajibeyli]. In *Kara Karaev. Stat'i. Pis'ma. Vyskazyvaniia*, 10–12.

———. "Prazdnik muzykal'noi kul'tury" [The celebration of musical culture]. *Bakinskii Rabochii*, October 8, 1968.

———. "Tol'ko v rabote chelovek vyrazhaet aktivnoe otnoshenie k zhizni" [Only through work one can express an active attitude toward life]. By Liana Genina. *Sovetskaia Muzyka*, no. 2 (1978): 32–41.

———. "O D.D. Shostakoviche" [About D. D. Shostakovich]. In *Kara Karaev. Stat'i, Pis'ma, Vyskazyvaniia*, 13–18.

———. "Slovo ob uchitele" [A word about the teacher]. *Sovetskaia Muzyka*, no. 9 (1976): 12–14.

Karagicheva, Liudmila. *Kara Karaev* [Gara Garayev]. Moscow: Sovetskii Kompozitor, 1960.

———. *Kara Karaev. Lichnost'. Suzhdeniia ob iskusstve* [Gara Garayev. His personality. Thoughts about art]. Moscow: Kompozitor, 1994.

———, ed. *Kara Karaev. Stat'i. Pis'ma. Vyskazyvaniia* [Gara Garayev. Articles. Letters. Observations]. Moscow: Sovetskii Kompozitor, 1978.

———. "Mugamnaia opera Azerbaidzhana" [The mugham opera of Azerbaijan]. *Sovetskaia Muzyka*, no. 12 (1988): 86–93.

———. "Novye balety Karaevykh" [The new ballets of the Garayevs]. *Sovetskaia Muzyka*, no. 1 (1970): 33–39.

———. "Pishite kak mozhno bol'she prekrasnoi muzyki" [Write as much wonderful music as you can]. *Muzykal'naia Akademiia*, no. 4 (1997): 202–11.

Karimi, Siyavush. "A Place for Mugham: Azerbaijani Music Is Focus for New Conservatory." *Azerbaijan International*, Winter 2001, 60–61.

Karimov, Majnun. *Azerbaijan musigi aletleri* [Musical instruments of Azerbaijan]. Baku: Yeni Nasil, 2003.

Kartomi, Margaret J. "The Processes and Results of Musical Culture Contact: A Discussion of Terminology and Concepts." *Ethnomusicology* 25 (1981): 227–49.

Kartomi, Margaret J., and Stephen Blum, eds. *Music-Cultures in Contact: Convergences and Collisions.* Basel, Switzerland: Gordon and Breach Publishers, 1994.

Kasimova, Solmaz. *Opernoe tvorchestvo kompozitorov Sovetskogo Azerbaidzhana* [Operas of the composers in the Soviet Azerbaijan]. Baku: Azgosizdat, 1973.

Kasumov, Imran [Gasimov, Imran]. "Brigantina Kara Karaeva" [The brigantine of Gara Garayev]. In *Kara Karaev. Stat'i. Pis'ma. Vyskazyvaniia*, 97–105.

Kazimova, Lala. *Gazeli Fizuli v azerbaidzhanskoi muzyke* [Fuzuli's gazals in Azerbaijani music]. Baku: Azerbaijan, 1997.

Khalid, Adeeb. *The Politics of Muslim Cultural Reform: Jadidism in Central Asia.* Berkeley: University of California Press, 1998.

Khalig-zade, Fatah. "Mugham ve khettatlighin bazi elagelerine dair" [On the interrelationship of mugham and calligraphy]. In *Proceedings of the First International Musicological Symposium "Space of Mugham," 18–20 March, 2009*, 203–7. Baku: Sharg-Garb, 2009.

Klotyn, Arnold. "Voskhishchenie i razmyshleniia" [Admiration and considerations]. *Sovetskaia Muzyka*, no. 11 (1975): 24–36.

Korev, Iurii. "'Nargiz': Na general'noi repetitsii" ["Nargiz": At the dress rehearsal]. *Rabochaia Moskva*, April 11, 1938.

Korolev, Kirill, ed. *Russkii mir: geopoliticheskie zametki po russkoi istorii* [The Russian world: Geopolitical notes on Russian history]. Moscow: Eksmo; Saint Peterburg: Terra Fantastica, 2003.

Kozinn, Allan. "A Mix of Azerbaijan and the West." *New York Times*, February 8, 2000.

Kravetz, Nelly. "A New Insight into the Tenth Symphony of Dmitry Shostakovich." In *Shostakovich in Context,* edited by Rosamund Bartlett, 159–74. Oxford: Oxford University Press, 2000.

———. "Novyi vzgliad na Desiatuiu simfoniiu Shostakovicha" [New insight into the Tenth symphony of Dmitry Shostakovich]. In *D.D. Shostakovich. Sbornik statei k 90-letiiu so dnia rozhdeniia* [D. D. Shostakovich: A collection of articles on the 90th anniversary of his birth], edited by Liudmila Kovnatskaia, 228–35. St. Petersburg: Kompozitor, 1996.

———. "Revelations – the Tenth Symphony." DSCH *Journal*, no. 1 (1994): 24–25.

Krebs, Stanley. *Soviet Composers and the Development of Soviet Music.* New York: W. W. Norton, 1970.

Kuhn, Laura, ed. *Baker's Dictionary of Opera.* New York: Schirmer Books, 2000.

Lazarus, Neil. *Nationalism and Cultural Practice in the Postcolonial World.* Cambridge: Cambridge University Press, 1999.

Ledogorov, Igor. "'Shahsenem' Gliera" [Gliere's *Shahsenem*]. *Bakinskii Rabochii*, December 17, 1927.

Leeuw, Charles van der. *Azerbaijan: A Quest for Identity, a Short History.* New York: St. Martin's Press, 2000.

Lemercier-Quelquejay, Chantal. "Islam and Identity in Azerbaijan." *Central Asian Survey* 3, no. 2 (1984): 29–55.

Leonard, Richard. *A History of Russian Music.* New York: The Macmillan Company, 1957.

Levin, Theodore. *The Hundred Thousand Fools of God: Musical Travels in Central Asia (and Queens, New York).* Bloomington: Indiana University Press, 1996.

———. Liner notes to *Music of Central Asia. Vol. 6: Alim and Fargana Qasimov: Spiritual Music of Azerbaijan.* Washington, DC: Smithsonian Folkways Recordings, sfw40525, 2007, compact disc and DVD.

———. "Making Marxist-Leninist Music in Uzbekistan." In *Music and Marx: Ideas, Practice, Politics,* edited by Regula Burkchardt-Qureshi, 190–203. New York: Routledge, 2002.

———. "Music in Modern Uzbekistan: The Convergence of Marxist Aesthetics and Central Asian Tradition." *Asian Music* 12, no. 1 (1980): 149–58.

———. "The Reterritorialization of the Culture in the New Central Asian States: A Report from Uzbekistan." *Yearbook for Traditional Music* 25 (1993): 51–59.

Locke, Ralph P. "Reflections on Orientalism in Opera and Musical Theater." *Opera Quarterly* 10, no. 1 (1993): 49–64.

MacDonald, Ian. "Writing about Shostakovich: Dating the Tenth Symphony." *DSCH Journal,* no. 13 (2000): 10–14.

MacFadyen, David. *Estrada?! Grand Narratives and the Philosophy of the Russian Popular Song since Perestroika.* Montreal: McGill-Queen's University Press, 2002.

———. *Red Stars: Personality and the Soviet Popular Song, 1955–1991.* Montreal: McGill-Queen's University Press, 2001.

Mahmudova, Jeyran. *Azerbaijan bestekarlarinin mahnilarinda poeziya ila musiginin garshiligli elageleri* [Interrelations between poetry and music in the songs of Azerbaijani composers]. Synopsis of doctoral diss., Baku Music Academy, 2012.

Makhmudova, Gulzar. *Genezis i evoliutsiia ostinatnosti v azerbaidzhanskoi muzyke* [The genesis and evolution of ostinato in Azerbaijani music]. Baku: Nurlan, 2010.

Makhmudova, Shahla. *Tematizm azerbaidzhanskogo mugama* [The thematism of Azerbaijani mugham]. Baku: Shur, 1997.

Malikov, Arif. "Symphonic Music Built upon Legend and Imagination," interview with Aida Huseynova. *Azerbaijan International,* Spring 2005, 32–35.

Mamedova, Leyla. *Khorovaia kul'tura Azerbaidzhana* [Choral culture in Azerbaijan]. Baku: Adiloghlu, 2010.

Mamedova, Maya. "Arshin Mal Alan, ili kak Stalin prikazal Gollivud perepliunut'" [The Cloth Peddler, or how Stalin ordered to outdo Hollywood]. *Trud,* April 27, 2003.

Mamedova, Rena. *Muzykal'no-esteticheskie osobennosti azerbaidzhanskikh mugamov* [Musical and aesthetic characteristics of Azerbaijani mughams]. Baku: Znanie, 1987.

———. *Problemy funktsional'nosti v azerbaidzhanskom mugame* [The problems of functionality in Azerbaijani mugham]. Baku: Elm, 1989.

Mamedova, Shovkat [Mammadova, Shovkat]. "Slovo o moem druge i uchitele" [A word about my friend and teacher]. In Vol. 2 of *Reingol'd Moritsevich Glier. Stat'i. Vospominaniia. Materialy* [Reinhold Moritsevich Gliere. Articles. Memoirs. Materials], edited by Valerian Bogdanov-Berezovsky, 246–56. Moscow: Muzyka, 1966.

Mammadaliyeva, Turan. "Azerbaijan bestekarlarinin yaradijilighinda jaz harmoniyasi" [Jazz harmony in the works of Azerbaijani composers]. Synopsis of PhD diss., Baku Music Academy, 2007.

Mammadov, Tariyel. *Ashig sanati* [The art of ashigs]. Baku: Shur, 2002.

———. *Koroghlu: Ashig havalari* [Koroghlu: Ashig melodies]. Baku: Apostrof, 2010.

Martin, Terry. *The Affirmative Action Empire: Nations and Nationalism in the Soviet Union, 1923–1939*. Ithaca: Cornell University Press, 2001.

Martynov, Nikolai. "Pis'ma Shostakovicha. Stranitsy iz zapisnoi knizhki" [Letters of Shostakovich. Pages from a notebook]. In *D.D. Shostakovich. Sbornik statei k 90-letiiu so dnia rozhdeniia* [D. D. Shostakovich. A collection of articles on the 90th anniversary of his birth], edited by Liudmila Kovnatskaia, 276–305. St. Petersburg: Kompozitor, 1996.

Mazel, Leo. "Razdum'ia ob istoricheskom meste tvorchestva Shostakovicha" [Thoughts on the historical role of the Shostakovich's works]. In *D. Shostakovich. Stat'i i materialy* [D. Shostakovich. Articles and materials], edited by Grigory Shneerson, 56–72. Moscow: Sovetskii kompozitor, 1976.

———. *Simfonii Dmitriia Shostakovicha. Putevoditel'* [Symphonies of Dmitry Shostakovich. A Guide]. Moscow: Sovetskii Kompozitor, 1960.

———. "Vospominaniia i blagodarnost'" [Memoirs and gratitude]. In *Kara Karaev. Stat'i. Pis'ma. Vyskazyvaniia*, 81–83.

Mazo, Margarita, "The Present and the Unpredictable Past: Music and Musical Life of St. Petersburg and Moscow since the 1960s." *International Journal of Musicology* 5 (1996): 371–400.

McCalla, James. *Twentieth-Century Chamber Music*. New York: Routledge, 2003.

Mekhtieva, Nailya. "Opera R.M. Gliera 'Shahsenem': istoriia sozdaniia i nekotorye voprosy stilia" [Opera "Shahsenem" by R. M. Gliere: The history of its creation and some aspects of its style]. *Uchenye zapiski Azerbaidzhanskoi Gosudarstvennoi Konservatorii* [Research papers of the Azerbaijan State Conservatory], no. 3 (1966): 3–39.

Melikov, Arif [Malikov, Arif]. "Bessmertie" [Eternity]. In *Slovo ob Uzeire Gadzhibekove* [A word about Uzeyir Hajibeyli], edited by Akhmed Isazade, 130–32. Baku: Elm, 1985.

Meyer, Kshishtof. "Moi vstrechi s Karaevym" [My meetings with Garayev]. In *Kara Karaev: Stat'i. Pis'ma. Vyskazyvaniia*, 90–91.

———. *Shostakovich: Zhizn', tvorchestvo, vremia* [Shostakovich: Life, works, epoch]. Saint Petersburg: Kompozitor, 1998.

Mihaiu, Virgil. "A 1984 Panorama of Soviet Jazz." In *Russian Jazz: New Identity*, edited by Leo Feigin, 160–61. New York: Quarter Book Limited, 1985.

Minor, William. *Unzipped Souls: A Jazz Journey through the Soviet Union*. Philadelphia: Temple University Press, 1995.

Mirzazade, Khayyam. "Variations," interview with Anna Amrakhova. *Muzykal'naia Akademiia*, no. 1 (2002): 167–72.

Mirzoeva, Svetlana. "Gorzhus' tem, chto ia syn Vostoka" [I am a proud son of the East]. *Bakinskii Rabochii*, September 4, 1991.

Moisenko, Rena. *Realist Music: 25 Soviet Composers*. London: Meridian Books, 1949.

Naroditskaya, Inna. "Azerbaijani Mugham and Carpet: Cross-Cultural Mapping." *Ethnomusicology Forum* 14 (2005): 25–55.

——. *Song from the Land of Fire. Continuity and Change in Azerbaijanian Mugham.* New York: Routledge, 2003.

Nettl, Bruno. ed. "Persian Classical Music in Tehran: The Processes of Change." In *Eight Urban Musical Cultures: Tradition and Change,* 146–85. Chicago: University of Illinois Press, 1978.

——. "Some Aspects of the History of World Music in the Twentieth Century: Questions, Problems, Concepts." *Ethnomusicology* 22 (1978): 123–36.

——. *The Western Impact on World Music.* New York: Schirmer Books, 1985.

——. "Western Musical Values and the Character of Ethnomusicology." *World of Music* 26, no. 1 (1984): 29–43.

Nissman, David B. "The Origins and Development of the Literature of 'Longing' in Azerbaijan." *Journal of Turkish Studies* 8 (1984):199–207.

Norris, Christopher. "Socialist Realism." In Vol. 23 of *New Grove Dictionary of Music and Musicians,* edited by Stanley Krebs, 599–600.. London-New York: McMillan, 2001.

O'Brien, Matthew. "Uzeyir Hajibeyov [Uzeyir Hajibeyli] and His Role in the Development of Musical Life in Azerbaidzhan." In *Soviet Music and Society under Lenin and Stalin,* edited by Neil Edmunds, 209–27. London: Routledge Curzon, 2004.

Oldfield, Anna. *Azerbaijani Women Poet-Minstrels/Women Ashiqs from the Eighteenth Century to the Present.* Lewison, NY: Edwin Mellen Press, 2008.

Patow, Ulrike. *Frangis Ali-Sade: Leben und Schaffen der aserbaidschanisdhen Komponistin und Pianistin; eine Dokumentation* [Frangiz Alizade: The life and work of Azerbaijani composer and pianist: Documents]. Saarbrücken: Pfau, 2007.

Patterson, Jean. "Piecing Together History, String by String: The Reconstruction of Azerbaijan's Medieval Instruments." *Azerbaijan International,* Winter 1997, 28–31.

Prentice, William. "Sharga Gramofon galir" [The Gramophone goes East]. *Musigi Dunyasi,* no. 3–4 (2000): 196–97.

Prokofiev, Sergey. "Moi pervyi pedagog" [My first teacher]. In Vol. 1 of *Reingol'd Moritsevich Glier. Stat'i. Vospominaniia. Materialy.* [Reinhold Moritsevich Gliere. Articles. Memoirs. Materials], edited by Valerian Bogdanov-Berezovski, 53–55. Moscow: Muzyka, 1965.

Rahimova, Aytaj. *Azerbaijan musigisinda meykhana janri* [The genre of *meykhana* in Azerbaijani music]. Baku: Nurlan, 2002.

Rahimova, Nigar. "K probleme azerbaidzhanskoi ladovoi funktsional'nosti" [On the problem of functionality in Azerbaijani modes]. In *Proceedings of the Inter-Republican Research Conference "The National Music Culture: Problems and Perspectives,"* 42–44. Tbilisi: Tbilisi State Conservatory, 1988.

——. "K probleme vostochnoi funktsional'noi teorii lada (na primere arabskikh, persidskikh makamov i azerbaidzhanskikh mugamov)" [On the problem of Eastern functional modal theory (examples of Arab and Persian maqams and Azerbaijani mughams)]. In *Izvestiia Akademii Nauk Azerbaidzhanskoi ssr* [The News of the Academy of Sciences of Azerbaijan ssr], no. 1 (1987): 92–98.

Ritzel, Rebecca J. "Silk Road Ensemble Enlivens Ancient Opera." *Washington Post,* March 14, 2009.

Sabinina, Marina. *Shostakovich-simfonist: Dramaturgiia, estetika, stil'* [Shostakovich as symphonic composer: Dramaturgy, aesthetics, style]. Moscow: Muzyka, 1976.

Safaraliyeva, Kovkab. "Muzykal'noe obrazovanie v Azerbaidzhane" [Music education in Azerbaijan]. In *Azerbaidzhanskaia muzyka* [Music of Azerbaijan], edited by Jovdat Hajiyev, Daniil Danilov, Daniel Zhitomirskii, Kara Karaev, Said Rustamov, Nigar Usubova, and Emina Eldarova, 277–94. Moscow: Gosmuzgiz, 1961.

Safarova, Zemfira. *Azerbaijanin musiqi elmi (XIII–XX asrlar)* [Music studies in Azerbaijan (thirteen through twentieth centuries)]. Baku: Azerneshr, 2006.

———. *Muzykal'no-esteticheskie vzgliady Uzeira Gadzhibekova* [Musical and aesthetical views of Uzeyir Hajibeyli]. Moscow: Sovetskii Kompozitor, 1973.

———. "Shusha – khram nashei muzyki" [Shusha is a temple of our music]. *Muzykal'naia Akademiia*, no. 1 (2002): 207–11.

Said, Edward. *Orientalism*. New York: Vintage Books, 1994.

Saller, Rene Spenser. "Disciples of the Difficult Are Back." *Illinois Times,* May 19, 2005.

Samadoghlu, Vagif. "The Emergence of Jazz in Azerbaijan." *Azerbaijan International,* Winter 1997, 72–75.

Samson, Jim. "Nations and Nationalism." *The Cambridge History of Nineteenth-Century Music,* edited by Jim Samson, 568–600. Cambridge: Cambridge University Press, 2002.

Sawenko, Svetlana. "Zum Weiterwirken der Schostakowitsch ausgehenden Traditionen im Schaffen sowjetischer Gegenwartskomponisten" [About the impact of Shostakovich's traditions on the works of contemporary Soviet composers]. In Vol. 37 of *Sowietische Musik. Betrachtungen und Analysen* [Soviet music: Thoughts and analyses], 345–57. Berlin: Akademie der Kunste der DDR, 1984.

Schwartz, Boris. *Music and Musical Life in Soviet Russia, 1917–1970.* New York: W. W. Norton, 1972.

Scott, Derek. "Orientalism and Musical Style." In *Musical Style and Social Meaning,* 137–63. Farnham: Ashgate, 2010.

Seidov, Tarlan. *Azerbaidzhanskaia fortepiannaia kultura XX veka: pedagogika, ispolnitel'-stvo, kompozitorskoe tvorchestvo* [Twentieth-century Azerbaijani piano culture: Education, performance, composed works]. Baku: Azgosizdat, 2006.

Selimkhanov, Jahangir. "Proshlo desiat' let . . ." [Ten years have passed]. *Muzykal'naia Akademiia* no. 1 (2002): 153–57.

Seyidova, Saadat. "Muzyka v drevnikh obriadakh Azerbaidzhana: na materiale traurnykh pesnopenii" [Music in ancient Azerbaijani rituals: Songs of lament]. Synopsis of PhD diss., Tbilisi State Conservatory, 1981.

———. "Uzeyir Hajibeyov va dini musigi" [Uzeyir Hajibeyli and religious music]. *Musigi Dunyasi,* no. 3–4/5 (2000): 139–41.

Shahverdi, Kamil. "'Arshinnye' uspekhi ' . . . mal alan'a" [The impressive successes of 'The Cloth Peddler']. *Azerbaijan-IRS,* no. 4 (2002): 36–38.

Sharifova, Vazifa. "Tret'ia simfoniia Karaeva" [Garayev's Third Symphony]. In Vol. 2 of *Iz istorii russkoi i sovetskoi muzyki* [From the history of Russian and Soviet music], edited by Aleksei Kandinskii, 334–59. Moscow: Muzyka, 1976.

Sharifova-Alikhanova, Vazifa. *Fikret Amirov: Zhizn' i tvorchestvo* [Fikrat Amirov: His life and music]. Baku: Sada, 2005.

Shchedrin, Rodion. "Dzhaz vozvrashchaet muzyke to, chto ona nekogda poteriala" [Jazz returns to music what has once been lost]. *Sovetskaia Muzyka,* no. 8 (1984): 54–55.

———. "Nazidatel'nyi tvorcheskii put'" [Edifying creative path]. In *Kara Karaev. Stat'i. Pis'ma. Vyskazyvaniia,* 83–90.

Shostakovich, Dmitrii. "Neskol'ko slov o balete" [A few words about ballet]. *Za Sovet-skoe Iskusstvo,* April 4, 1961.

———."Otlichnaia kompozitorskaia shkola" [Excellent school of composers]. *Druzhba Narodov,* no. 11 (1957): 242–45.

———. "Rady vzletu azerbaidzhanskoi muzyki" [Happy to witness the flourishing of Azerbaijani music]. *Bakinskii Rabochii,* May 7, 1964.

Shushinskii, Firidun. *Narodnye pevtsy i muzykanty Azerbaidzhana* [Folk singers and musicians of Azerbaijan]. Moscow: Sovetskii Kompozitor, 1979.

Signell, Karl. "Mozart and the Mehter." *Turkish Music Quarterly* 1, no. 1 (1988): 9–15.

Sipos, Janos. *Azeri Folk Songs: At the Fountain-head of Music.* Budapest: Akademiai Kiado, 2004.

Slezkine, Yuri. "The USSR as a Communal Apartment, or How a Socialist State Promoted Ethnic Particularism." *Slavic Review* 53 (1994): 414–52.

Slobin, Mark. "Micromusics of the West: A Comparative Approach." *Ethnomusicology* 36 (1992): 1–88.

Starr, Frederick. *Red and Hot: The Fate of Jazz in the Soviet Union. 1917–1991.* New York: Limelight Editions, 1994.

Stites, Richard. "Russian Popular Music to 1953." In *Soviet Music and Society under Lenin and Stalin,* edited by Neil Edmunds, 19–32. London: Routledge Curzon, 2004.

Stokes, Martin, ed. *Ethnicity, Identity and Music: The Musical Construction of Place.* Oxford: Berg, 1994.

———. "Globalization and the Politics of World Music." In *The Cultural Study of Music: A Critical Introduction,* edited by Martin Clayton, Trevor Herbert, and Richard Middleton, 297–308. New York: Routledge, 2003.

———. "Turkish Rock and Pop Music." In *Garland Encyclopedia of World Music. Vol. 6: The Middle East,* edited by Virginia Danielson, Scott Marcus, and Dwight Reynolds, 247–53. New York: Routledge, 2001.

Strazhenkova, Irina. "My "uslyshali" Goiu" [We "have comprehended" Goya]. *Sovet-skaia Muzyka,* no. 10 (1972): 49–53.

Stupnikov, Igor. "The Legend of Love." In vol. 1 of *International Dictionary of Ballet,* edited by Martha Bremser and Lorraine Nicholas, 841. Detroit: St. James Press, 1993.

Sultanov, Rain, ed. *Jazz in Azerbaijan: Anthology.* Baku, 2004.

Sultanova, Razia. *From Shamanism to Sufism: Women, Islam and Culture in Central Asia.* London: I. B. Tauris, 2011.

Suni, Ronald. *Revenge of the Past: Nationalism, Revolution and the Collapse of the Soviet Union.* Stanford, CA: Stanford University Press, 1993.

Swietochowski, Tadeusz, and Brian Collins. *Historical Dictionary of Azerbaijan.* Lanham, MD: The Scarecrow Press, 1999.

Tagizade, Aida. *Akshin Alizade* [Agshin Alizade]. Baku: Ishig, 1986.

———. *Dzhevdet Gadzhiev* [Jovdat Hajiyev]. Baku: Ishig, 1979.

———. *Sultan Gadzhibekov: Zhizn' i tvorchestvo* [Soltan Hajibeyov: Life and music]. Baku: Yazichi, 1985.

Tairova, Farah. *Dmitrii Shostakovich i azerbaidzhanskaia muzykal'naia kul'tura* [Dmitry Shostakovich and Azerbaijani musical culture]. Baku: Nurlan, 2006.

Tahmasib, Mammad Huseyn. *Azerbaijan khalg dastanlari: orta asrlar* [Azerbaijan folk dastans: The Middle Ages]. Baku: Elm, 1972.

Taruskin, Richard. *Defining Russia Musically: Historical and Hermeneutical Essays.* Princeton: Princeton University Press, 1997.

———. "Entoiling the Falconet: Russian Musical Orientalism in Context." *Cambridge Opera Journal* 4, no. 3 (Nov. 1992): 253–80.

———. "Nationalism." In Vol. 17 of *The New Grove Dictionary of Music and Musicians,* edited by Stanley Sadie, 689–706. London: Macmillan, 2001.

Topping, Seymour. "Leningrad Ballet in Premiere; Announces Tour of U.S. in Fall." *New York Times,* March 23, 1961.

Toumani, Meline. "For the Love of Layla." *New York Times,* March 1, 2009.

Turino, Thomas. "Formulas and Improvisation in Participatory Music." In *Musical Improvisation: Art, Education and Society,* edited by Bruno Nettl, 103–16. Chicago: University of Illinois Press, 2009.

Vinogradov Viktor. *Mir muzyki Fikreta* [The world of Fikrat's music]. Baku: Yazichi, 1983.

———. *Uzeir Gadzhibekov i azerbaidzhanskaia muzyka* [Uzeyir Hajibeyli and Azerbaijani music]. Moscow: Sovetskii Kompozitor, 1938.

Vodarsky-Shiraeff, Alexandria. *Russian Composers and Musicians.* New York: Greenwood Press, 1940.

Volkov, Solomon, ed. *Testimony: The Memoirs of Dmitry Shostakovich.* New York: Limelight Editions, 1984.

Vysotskaia, Marianna. *Mezhdu logikoi i paradoksom: kompozitor Faradzh Karaev* [Between logic and paradox: composer Faraj Garayev]. Moscow: Moscow State Conservatory, 2012.

Walsh, Thomas. "Jazz Mugham." Unpublished manuscript, 2001. Microsoft Word file.

Wilson, Elizabeth. *Shostakovich: A Life Remembered.* London: Faber and Faber, 1994.

Yusifova, Adilya. *Dzhevdet Gadzhiev (1917–2002). Khronika zhizni. Stat'i. Vyskazyvaniia* [Jovdat Hajiyev (1917–2002). Life chronicle. Articles. Observations]. Baku: Tahsil, 2013.

Zeidman, Boris. "Glier i azerbaidzhanskaia muzykal'naia kul'tura" [Gliere and Azerbaijani musical culture]. In Vol. 2 of *Reingol'd Moritzevich Glier. Stat'i. Vospominaniia. Materialy.* [Reinhold Moritsevich Gliere. Articles. Memoirs. Materials], edited by Valerian Bogdanov-Berezovski, 216–36. Moscow: Muzyka, 1966.

Zemtsovsky, Izaly. "An Attempt at a Synthetic Paradigm." *Ethnomusicology* 41 (1997): 185–205.

———. *Fol'klor i kompozitor: teoreticheskie etiudy* [Folklore and the composer: Theoretical essays]. Leningrad: Sovetskii Kompozitor, 1978.

———. Liner notes for *Faik Chelebi, Tar: The Classical Muğam of Azerbaijan in Solo Instrumental Performance.* Silk Road House, SRH 003. 2013, compact disc.

———. "Musicological Memoirs on Marxism." In *Music and Marx: Ideas, Practice, Politics,* edited by Requla Burckhardt Qureshi, 167–89. New York: Routlege, 2002.

———. "On Reading Three Responses." In *Proceedings of the Conference "Folklore and Traditional Music in the Soviet Union and Eastern Europe," UCLA, May 16, 1994,* edited by James Porter, 42–44. Los Angeles: UCLA Ethnomusicology Publications, 1997.

Zemtsovsky, Izaly, and Alma Kunanbaeva. "Folklore and Communism." In *Proceedings of the Conference "Folklore and Traditional Music in the Soviet Union and Eastern Europe," UCLA, May 16, 1994,* edited by James Porter, 3–23. Los Angeles: UCLA Ethnomusicology Publications, 1997.

Ziyadli, Aydin. *Emotsional'no-vyrazitel'nye vozmozhnosti ladov azerbaidzhanskoi narodnoi muzyki* [The expressive capacities of the Azerbaijani folk modes]. Baku: Azerbaijan State Conservatory, 1989.

"Znachitel'noe iavlenie sovetskoi muzyki" [The significant event of Soviet music]. *Sovetskaia Muzyka,* no. 6 (1954): 119–34.

Zokhrabov, Ramiz. *Azerbaidzhanskie tesnify* [Azerbaijani tasnifs]. Moscow: Sovetskii kompozitor, 1983.

———. *Teoreticheskie problemy azerbaidzhanskogo mugama* [Theoretical problems of Azerbaijani mugham]. Baku: Shur, 1992

———. *Zarbi mughamlar* [Zarbi mughams]. Baku: Mars-Print, 2004.

———. Course packet for the "Principles of Azerbaijani Folk Music"class. Baku: Azerbaijan State Conservatory, 1985.

INDEX

Ledogorov, Igor, 94
Legend of Love (Malikov), 15, 45, 157–58, *159*, 160–61
Lemercier-Quelquejay, Chantal, 18
Levin, Theodore, 18–19, 237, 271
Lewis, John, 226
Leyli and Majnun (G. Garayev), 77, 83, 156
Leyli and Majnun (Hajibeyli), 1, 23, 67, 70, 77, 265–66, 269, 279n11, 291n6; compared to *Mughamsayaghi* (F. Alizade), 186; East-West synthesis, 31–33; and Islamic musical traditions, 57; and Italian opera, 89; *mughams* in, 262–63; "Night of Separation," 114–20, *115*, *116–19*; orchestral intermezzo, 120–21, *120*, *122–23*, 124; orchestration, 42; use of *zarbi-mugham*, 151. See also *Layla and Majnun*
linearism, 108, 145, 163, *163*; F. Alizade's music, 183–84; in Mirzazade's style, 173–74. *See also* melody and contour
Liubarskii, Iakov, 93
Lohmann, Francesca, 269
"Lullaby for Shusha" (Adigozalov), 246

Ma, Yo-Yo, 8, 26, 33, 237, 257; cello solo, 262, 264; and *mugham* tradition, 256, 258; on performance of *Layla and Majnun*, 267; on Silk Road Project, 255. See also *Layla and Majnun*
MacFadyen, David, 197
Madaniyyat (Culture) (TV), 254
Magomayev, Muslim, 16, 54, 69, *134*; cello repertoire, 89; "firsts," 132; influence on Amirov, 150–51; "mass" song, 197; *Shah Ismayil* (opera), 133, 135, *136*
Magomayev, Muslim, works of: "Azerbaijan," 215; Nargiz, 58; *Nargiz* (opera), 58–60, 93–94, 95–96, 135, 150; *Shah Ismayil* (opera), 32, 135–39, 150, 151, 286n13; other works, 54, 89, 135
Magomayev, Muslim (singer), 213, *214*, 215
Mahavishnu Orchestra, 226
Mahler, Gustav, 105–6
mahur (mode), 39
Mahur Hindi (*mugham*), 267
Maiden's Tower (Badalbeyli), 43, 60

Maiden's Tower (Garayev), 45
majlis (cultural gatherings), 22
Malikov, Arif, 15, 64, 284n40; as songwriter, 196–97; tragic spirit, 107
Malikov, Arif, works of: *Legend of Love* (ballet), 45, 157–58, *159*, 160–61; Second Symphony, 167; Sixth Symphony, 167
Mammadov, Ali Asgar, 266
Mammadov, Murtuza. *See* Bulbul
Mammadova, Aliya, 247
Mammadova, Shovkat, 34, *36*, 75, 92, 93, 95
Mansurov, Bahram, *80*, 249
Mansurov, Eldar, 248–50
maqam tradition, 13, 29, 219, 238, 244
Marana Films, 33–34, 280n15
Maria Callas Grand Prix, 3
marsiyya, 56, 57
Martin, Terry, 6
Martynov, Nikolai, 98
"mass" song, 197
Mazel, Leo, 145
Mekhtieva, Nailya, 94
melisma, use of, 151, 185, 204, 207, 227
melody and contour: *ashig* melody, 114, 165; melismas in melody, 227; in traditional music, 38, 137, 152, 227. *See also* folk music; linearism; modal theory; twelve-tone techniques; *and specific compositions*
Meyer, Kshishtof, 98
meykhana, 198, 199
Middle Eastern calligraphy, 268, 269
Middle Eastern court tradition, 41
Mighty Handful, 50, 89, 90, 91. *See also* Glinka, Mikhail; Russian Empire; Russian influences
Mihaiu, Virgil, 224
Miller, Marcus, 234
minimalism, 48, 191–92. *See also* avant-garde techniques
Minor, William, 225, 235
Mirzayev, Elmir, 239, 247
Mirzayev, Musa, 60, 284n40
Mirzazade, Khayyam, 91, 172–74, *173*, 218, 239, 284n40
modal system: associations in tone rows, 163, 164, *164*, 170, *170*, *171*; condensed in

Guliyev's *Seven Pieces with Interludes in Mugham Modes*, 191; diminished intervals, 136–37; features of, 109; fusion of systems, 127, *130–31*, 141; harmonization in *Leyli and Majnun* (Hajibeyli), 266; modal logic, 121; parallels with romanticism, 136–37. *See also* Azerbaijani sonata

modal theory, 20–22, *21*, 38–40. *See also* Azerbaijani music; *and specific modes*

modernization. *See* Westernization and modernization

Modern Jazz Quartet, 226

Moscow Philharmonic Society, 68

Mozart, Wolfgang Amadeus: C major Sonata, 124, *125*, 126–27; influence on Aziza, 233; quotation of, 192; Turkish influence, 114

Mravinsky, Evgeny, 105

Mugam-Sayagi (Kronos Quartet recording), *187–89*, *190*, 271. *See also* Mughamsayaghi

mugham: aesthetics, 132, 263; *aruz* poetic system, 16; contrasts in, 107–8; introduction to, 1, 5, 13–14, 20–23; notation of, 54–55, 150–51; parallels with baroque style, 111–13; performance format, 54; role in national musical identity, 13, 29–30, 66–67, 177–78, 242–44. *See also* Azerbaijani music; improvisation; jazz *mugham*; modal theory; *mugham* opera; *mugham* trio; national musical identity; Soviet era; symphonic *mugham*; *and specific* mughams

mugham opera, 23, 32, 96, 279n8; and baroque period, 111; break with norms of, 133; ideological attacks and, 56–57; precedents to, 30; proletarian culture's impact on, 50–51. See also *Leyli and Majnun* (Hajibeyli); opera

Mughamsayaghi (F. Alizade), 185, 186–91, *187–89*, *190*

"Mugham Sebastian Bach," 111–12

mugham trio, 22, 112–13, 166, 225. See also *kemancha*; *khanende*; *tar*

Mukhalif (mugham), 266

multiculturalism, 10, 258, 269

Musavat Party, 59, 74, 282n55

Mushvig, Mikayil, 51

music after Hajibeyli, 77–78

musical affect, 22, 113, 186, 194

musical cryptograms, 104–5, *105*, 107, 109–10

musical nationalism, 68; Azerbaijani Democratic Republic (ADR) era, 37–40; and cadre of national composers, 64; emergence of, 28–37; Soviet era, 40–41

musical pluralism, 10

musical quotation of composers, 192–93

musical theater, 34

musical training. *See* music education

Music and Culture of Azerbaijan (project), 213

Music Day, 77

music education, 23, 60–63, 66, 70, 75, 88, 241; effect of Soviet ideological goals, 62–63; establishment of conservatories, 17; music schools, 34–37; Russian influences on, 60–63, 88, 89, 102; in traditional forms and genres, 13, 68, 72–73, 81, 252–54; traditional instruments, 252. *See also* Azerbaijan State Conservatory; Baku Music Academy

Music for Piano (Alizade), 185

Muslumov, Mohlat, 62

Mustafazade, Vagif, 45, 217, 222, 227, 229–30, 232, 248; "Bayati Shiraz," 226, 227, 228; links with Babayev, 221, 224–27

Mustafa-Zadeh. *See* Mustafazade

Mutallimov, Tofig, 211

"My Country" (Zeynalli), 139–41, *140*, *141*, 142–43, 144, 231–32

"My Little Chicks" (Huseynli), *210*, 211

"My Spirited Horse" (Jahangirov), 272

naghara, 94, 168, 185, 272, 290n19. *See also* traditional instruments

Nagorno-Karabakh conflict, 19–20, 243, 245–46. *See also* Garabagh district

Nargiz (Magomayev), 93–94, *95–96*, 135

Narimanov, Nariman, 74–75, 283n19

AIDA HUSEYNOVA, a musicologist from Azerbaijan, is Adjunct Lecturer in Music at the Jacobs School of Music at Indiana University. She received her PhD from the Saint Petersburg State Conservatory, Russia. Since 2006, she has served as a research advisor and interpreter for the Silk Road Project under the artistic direction of world-renowned cellist Yo-Yo Ma. She also has been involved in a number of projects sponsored by the Aga Khan Music Initiative, including collaboration with the Kronos Quartet. She is author of four books on Azerbaijani music published in Azerbaijan, as well as author of the educational DVD *Music and Culture of Azerbaijan* and coauthor of the DVD *Music and Culture of Kyrgyzstan* both produced with the support of the Indiana University Inner Asian and Uralic National Resource Center. Her awards include a Fulbright Fellowship (2007–08) and a fellowship from the Junior Faculty Development Program (2001–02) sponsored by the US State Department.